Foreword by **Mike Parker Pearson**

A Field Guide to
the Megalithic Sites
of Britain and Ireland

The Old Stones

The Megalithic Portal
Edited by Andy Burnham

WATKINS
Sharing Wisdom Since 1893

Dedication

This book is dedicated to all Megalithic Portal contributors, especially those who have passed to the realms of the ancestors.

Tom Bullock (Tom_Bullock), who visited more than 1,200 stone circles to create his CD-ROM guide

Jack Morris-Eyton (JackME), who spent years developing his intriguing theory about shadow casting at megalithic sites (see page 184)

Holger Rix (Holger_Rix), who contributed around 4,500 images and over 6,300 site pages from all over Europe

The Old Stones
The Megalithic Portal
Edited by Andy Burnham

First published in the UK and USA in 2018 by
Watkins, an imprint of Watkins Media Limited
Unit 11, Shepperton House, 89–93 Shepperton Road
London N1 3DF
enquiries@watkinspublishing.com

Commissioning Editor: Fiona Robertson
Editor: Jackie Bates
Proofreader and Indexer: James Hodgson
Senior Designer: Francesca Corsini
Head of Design: Georgina Hewitt
Production: Uzma Taj
Map Design: Andy Burnham
Commissioned Artwork: Jay Kane

A CIP record for this book is available from the British Library.

ISBN: 978-1-78678-154-3

10 9 8 7

Typeset in ITC Lubalin Graph
Colour reproduction by XY Digital
Printed in China

www.watkinspublishing.com

Note: Site information is correct to the best of our knowledge at the time of going to press, but it is advisable to check access details before visiting. Inclusion in this guide does not imply a site has public access or is safe to visit.

Contents

Foreword

Mike Parker Pearson, Professor of British Later Prehistory at University College London

Megaliths are among the most enduring remains from our prehistoric past. Whether as single standing stones or impressive stone circles and tombs, they provide a glimpse into a vanished way of life that may seem beyond our comprehension. Yet, as Vicki Cummings points out so well in her introduction to this book, megalithic monuments represent the tip of the iceberg in terms of what has survived from thousands of years ago. Thanks to advances in archaeology, both technical and organizational, we are learning much about the people who built the megaliths. The remains that usually survive only below ground – the houses, portable material culture, non-megalithic monuments and environmental evidence – are becoming better understood. Thanks to analyses of chemical isotopes and ancient DNA, we are learning about the people themselves – who their ancestors were, where they came from and how mobile they were. With the application of so many new scientific methods, this is an exciting time to be an archaeologist.

Even as I write, new results from ancient DNA analysis are revealing that Britain's Neolithic inhabitants show little evidence of genetic mixing with the indigenous Mesolithic hunter-gatherers who lived in Britain before the arrival of agriculture. These Neolithic farmers, in turn, appear to have been substantially replaced by the Beaker people and their Bronze Age descendants; current evidence suggests that, by 1500BC, only 10 per cent of people's genes

derived from the previous Neolithic population of Britain. Isotope analyses also show that these prehistoric people were highly mobile in all periods from the Neolithic to the end of the early Bronze Age. Megaliths would have been some of the few human-constructed fixed points in their lives.

The growing evidence from genes and isotopes has taken many archaeologists by surprise. I am of a generation that was taught by our professors that prehistoric societies in Britain and Europe evolved largely independently without long-distance migrations. While the previous generation of archaeologists acknowledged that the domesticated animals and crops of the Neolithic originated in the Middle East, their view was that the migration theories of earlier writers such as Gordon Childe were simply wrong. Things have come full circle; the latest evidence seems to support many of the ideas put forward by Childe and his contemporaries.

Yet we must remember that genes are not (pre)history and that pots are not people. We can now think about changes in lifestyle and material culture alongside population changes, instead of having to use one as a proxy for the other. Despite apparent near-total population replacement by the Beaker people, the traditions of megalith building continued across Britain and Ireland even though the Beaker people's ancestors came from parts of Europe and Eurasia that either never had traditions of megalith building or had given them up centuries earlier.

This is not to say that megalith building did not change with the coming of the Beaker people. Although megalithic monuments are often hard to date, it appears that Beaker period and Bronze Age monuments were generally smaller than those of the Neolithic. The enormous workforces required for monuments such as Avebury, Stonehenge and Silbury Hill were either no longer persuadable or simply not required. The small stone circles, standing stones, stone rows and round barrows of the Bronze Age hint at a more decentralized social and political world. Mobilizing sufficient labour to move bluestones from Wales or to dress Stonehenge's stones was now a thing of the distant past. Although Stonehenge continued to be modified into the Bronze Age, its later stages consisted of minor rearrangements that can have required only a relatively small labour force.

This book is a wonderful guide to the many megaliths and related monuments of Britain's Neolithic and Bronze Age. The online Megalithic Portal has had a huge impact in making people aware of this rich prehistoric heritage, so it is great to see this guide to megalithic sites in book form. It will be especially valuable as a companion to visiting monuments on the ground. As more people visit such sites, so they come to better appreciate them. As we become more aware of their value, instances of thoughtless damage – as occurred at the Priddy Circles in Somerset, for example – should become rarer. We will also learn to ask new questions about the prehistoric people who erected these megaliths, and to further appreciate the value of the non-megalithic – the more ephemeral remains that lie below the ground.

Photo © Martyn Copcutt

The Langstone With its distinctive lightning-strike shape, this fine stone is a notable landmark on Langstone Moor.

Introduction

Andy Burnham, founder and Editor of the Megalithic Portal

This is the first book written by and for prehistoric site enthusiasts. It is a truly collaborative project – just like the Megalithic Portal website itself – that brings together photographs, site information, theories and expertise from the thousands of people that use and post on the site. Focusing on sites from the Neolithic and Bronze Age, this is the most comprehensive guide ever created to the best ancient places to visit in Britain and Ireland, offering an up-to-date look at the archaeology, including many extraordinary discoveries and theories that have been featured on the pages of the Megalithic Portal over the years, as well as a taster of the more mysterious side of things.

Just as the Portal is a collaborative effort, so no one person's ideas or theories are given more weight in this book. Instead, we celebrate the advances in archaeological practice, theory, dating and analysis that have taken place in the last 25 years. Geophysics, excavation and dating techniques have progressed in this time. There has also been an increased recognition of the importance of accepting non-academic viewpoints, whether from schoolchildren, community volunteers or some of the more leftfield theorists. Alternative ways of exploring and appreciating sites and wider landscapes – previously the realm of a radical fringe – have filtered into the mainstream. Landscape archaeology has in many cases accepted – if not wholeheartedly embraced – phenomenology and multi-sensory approaches, which anyone can try with an open mind and a bit of practice. Advances in technology offer new ways of experiencing sites, for example through augmented reality that merges GIS (geographical information system) landscape models with 3D reconstructions of structures.

Recently, I've been rereading early 1990s editions of *3rd Stone* magazine, styled "for the new antiquarian", the realm of ley hunters and earth mysteries researchers. Have we moved on in 25 years? Ideas of alignments between sites, of stone shapes matching the landscape, of the importance of colour, sound and experiencing sites in different frames of mind have filtered through to theoretical archaeology, to be discussed openly in papers and at conferences – even if they don't always get past the gatekeepers of archaeology books and magazines for consumption by the "general public".

About the Megalithic Portal

The Megalithic Portal is completely independent, with no outside funding save for what we can raise with a bit of advertising on the site, and now through royalties from this book, all of which are being ploughed back into the day-to-day running and further development of the website and our other projects. For the last 10 years we have run as a membership society, similar to any other archaeology society, except with an international reach and outlook. We hold meetings by phone conference and our society members hail from all over Europe, as well as

Photo © Golux

Ardlair recumbent stone circle Cows represent one of the biggest challenges faced by the megalith enthusiast!

North America, Australia, New Zealand, Japan and beyond.

One of the inspirations for the Megalithic Portal was my own experience, in the 1980s and early 1990s, of reading about sites in books or magazine articles with no accurate location details. Even now, articles and papers often don't give proper location information. I started compiling links to sites on the early web in 1996. People began to offer their own information and photos, and a collaborative project was born. The Megalithic Portal was formed in 2001 to continue this process. Much of the site's content has been created by a group of several hundred dedicated volunteers, but there is a huge range in involvement, from those sending in a couple of photos or sites, to people who have contributed more than 10,000 of these.

About this Book

This book is not just made up of my own favourite sites but has been compiled in a collaborative way, just like the Megalithic Portal itself. Contributions in the form of articles, which appear throughout the book, have come in from scores of writers, from archaeologists to alternative theorists to keen site visitors. Many of Britain and Ireland's top prehistorians have kindly contributed pieces about their research.

I have included opinions from a wide range of people who have original ways to approach ancient sites. While I don't personally go along with all of the ideas proposed, I feel it's important to at least give them an airing and let you, the reader, make up your own mind. Sometimes thinking about a problem in a new and creative way can lead to unexpected breakthroughs and we should not be closed minded to different ways of experiencing ancient sites.

The Megalithic Portal photo gallery contains images from several thousand different contributors. Each photo has a voting button allowing visitors to "like" a specific site. This anonymous voting data provided the basis of a longlist for sites to include in the book, from which a team of Megalithic Portal members selected the final list of sites to include for each region. With the voting data in mind, as well as their local knowledge, the team identified the very "best" sites and gave these a star ⭐ rating . The voting data also provided the basis for most of the Top 10 and 15 lists you will see throughout the book. After all this, we are confident this is the most comprehensive and democratically selected list of prehistoric sites that has ever been put in a book like this, grouped into regions for convenient visiting and browsing.

Site descriptions have been compiled from the available sources, including excavation reports and blogs from all over the various countries and regions. I must here send thanks to the various online national site databases: Canmore (Historic Environment Scotland), PastScape (Historic England), Coflein (Wales), the National Monuments Service Historic Environment Viewer (Republic of Ireland), the Northern Ireland Sites and Monuments Record, and the Manx Museum for their information and help, which has been invaluable. Some of the online entries are quite complex and hard to interpret so I hope our pithy summaries are helpful. Again, these entries have been checked and amended by Megalithic Portal members from all over the UK and Ireland. The vast majority of pictures in the book have been sent in by Megalithic Portal contributors. People have been so generous with their photos, taking time to look through their personal archives. Images have come from members as far afield as New Zealand and Japan. It has been tricky to keep track of exactly how many sites we've included – in the spirit of the "countless stones" of folklore, we kept getting different totals. However, I can confidently say we feature over 1,000 sites, with more than 600 with a full profile, plus some 400 "Nearby" listings, covering five countries and not forgetting the Isle of Man!

Each site listing includes an eight-figure Ordnance Survey map reference, and gives the OS paper map sheet the site is found on. For the UK the map sheets are: E – Explorer (orange); OL – Outdoor Leisure (yellow); L – Landranger (pink); and D for the Discoverer maps of Northern Ireland. In the Republic of Ireland, the D is for Discovery Map, whose numbering is shared with the North. For Sat Nav and GPS users we also give latitude and longitude locations for sites.

We have not given full directions to each site as we could fill up a book just with these! The Megalithic Portal (**www.megalithic.co.uk**) has a page for each of the entries in this book (directly linked from the ebooks), where you will find more information. You can search by site name or by map reference using the box at top left of any Megalithic Portal page. We also have a great app that allows you to search for sites by name or on a map. Each page links to various online map services and satellite images. Look on the web pages for the Nearby Sites list to find the more obscure sites that we couldn't fit in. You will also find visitor comments and source references at the bottom of each site page. If you know any sources of information we don't currently list or have any comments about sites featured in this book or on the website, please do submit them.

The Megalithic Portal includes a wide range of ancient sites, so I should mention some that we

SAFETY

Do not rely purely on modern technology for navigation; always carry a backup map and compass. Know your limits and take care around ancient monuments, which can be dangerous places with unseen holes, cliffs and other pitfalls. Take a torch with you and suitable rations if trekking long distances. Wear appropriate footwear and clothing.

haven't had space to cover in this book: Iron Age features, such as hill forts, brochs and souterrains; Palaeolithic and Mesolithic find spots and camps; early Christian crosses and other early medieval sites; holy wells and sacred springs; modern stone circles; natural features that may have been revered by or inspired prehistoric people.

As this is a "field guide" we have only included a very few (particularly interesting) sites where there is little or nothing to see on the ground. In fact there are many more lost sites that have been destroyed. The Raunds Area Project in Northamptonshire, for example, found more than 20 vanished mounds, barrows, avenues and causewayed enclosures in the Nene valley, near Wellingborough. We list the ones we know about on the website and welcome photos of the surrounding landscape – even if there are no prehistoric remains still to be seen. Visiting sites that are no longer there, imagining what they were like or how they were used, is true "hardcore" site visiting and for this we salute you!

For reasons of space we have had to limit ourselves to the UK, Isle of Man and Ireland. We haven't included sites on the Channel Islands, as these have more in common with the sites of France, and that's something for another day. We did originally look at including parts of continental Europe but felt it would be impossible

to do justice to the many thousands of megalithic sites in countries such as Germany, Denmark, France, Spain and Portugal, and in eastern Europe. There are also many ancient sites in the USA and the rest of the Americas. Not forgetting India, China and … why am I trying to list them all? The Portal features sites from 136 countries – including Liechtenstein, which I recently had to add so one of our contributors could post an entry.

How to Get Involved

We have tried to ensure the information in this book is as accurate as possible, but if you find any errors please do let us know so that we can update future editions. We would also love to hear from you on the website. At the Megalithic Portal we aim to be a sounding board for discussion, as well as a repository for accurate and up-to-date information on specific sites and monuments – and all of this requires constant input from our contributors. We strive to be fair to everyone and create an atmosphere where views can be challenged and disagreed with constructively and respectfully. We have, for example, a Sacred Sites and Megalithic Mysteries forum where we encourage discussion of all manner of experiences and theories relating to ancient sites. Just be respectful to others, even if you disagree with their ideas, and you'll be welcome.

Also on the site is a visit log feature, where you can keep a record of all the ancient sites you have visited, along with your comments and personal ratings as you go. This can be found on the right-hand side of each site entry, along with the link to submit photos of your own.

These days, electronic devices such as smartphones are available to all, and these have changed the way we interact with the outdoors,

CODE OF CONDUCT

Much damage is done accidentally by people who mean no harm. Think twice, and don't do anything which would cause degradation to the monument. For more details on visiting sites, see the Megalithic Portal Charter, linked at the bottom of any page on the website.

- Check access. Exclusions to the "right to roam" include private gardens and cultivated farmland (unless on footpaths or field margins).
- Get permission to visit sites on private land. This is usually granted if asked for politely – many landowners appreciate their sites as much as we do, but repeated unauthorized visits could lead to access being denied to all.
- Don't climb on the stones or on rock art.
- Don't try to remove lichen or dig near an ancient site.

- Don't use wax candles or nightlights inside tombs. You can get very effective LED candles that are much cleaner and safer.
- Don't light fires close to sites.
- Do not move, mark or alter the site in any way, even temporarily.
- Don't hide caches immediately in or around sites or use metal detectors.
- Any artefacts found should be reported to the local museum or via the Portable Antiquities Scheme (finds.org.uk).
- Do not fly drones around ancient sites without permission – for aerial photography try a kite or long pole instead.
- All in all, please be respectful, keep dogs under control and don't "hog" the monument for your own rituals/purposes if there are others around.

whether with augmented reality, audio guides, geocaching, Pokémon Go or simply being able to access information while on the move. Academic papers are increasingly put online and even traditional closed journals are getting in on the the act, offering free trial periods or codes to get through their paywalls. Many archaeology site databases are now available online. But better linking of information sources is still badly needed and that's something that we try to do at the Megalithic Portal. Official site databases could be better at curating links, and projects should plan for the long-term availability of their data. I have lost count of the number of projects that forget to renew their web addresses, while entire online archives disappear as researchers lose funding, move on or just go for a redesign. Keeping knowledge free and available amounts to the "archaeology of the internet". But to get off my soapbox, it's amazing that this unprecedented amount of information is available to everyone – it's there to be made use of. And don't forget traditional libraries, archives and just getting out there to do your own research.

This book is testament to the passion for prehistoric sites held by so many. Everyone can play a part in adding to our knowledge of ancient sites, and anyone can put time into researching, finding, photographing, monitoring and tidying them. I can only imagine what our stone-raising ancestors would have made of people all over the world communicating and rather obsessing over their efforts with seemingly magical writing devices, 5,000 years into the future! It's a strange but humbling thought.

For a free extra year's membership of the Megalithic Portal Society (two years for the price of one), go to: **www.megalithic.co.uk/double**

11

THE OLD STONES

12

Photogrammetry

Hugo Anderson-Whymark, Curator of Early Prehistory at National Museums Scotland

Photogrammetry is a technique almost as old as photography, but in recent years "structure-from-motion" (SfM) photogrammetry has become a popular tool in cultural heritage for the production of 3D models of artefacts, archaeological excavations and outstanding buildings and monuments. At its simplest level, the technique requires photographs taken on a camera (ideally a DSLR with a good lens), a computer (a high-end gaming computer for the best-quality models) and a piece of specialist software such as 3DF Zephyr, Agisoft Photoscan or Reality Capture. As the technique does not require expensive specialist equipment, structure-from-motion offers an extremely time- and cost-efficient means by which to record and portray complex architectural spaces. Moreover, as some of the software is available free of charge, anyone can now produce their own 3D models.

The production of a SfM photogrammetric model is a comparatively straightforward process, but the key to producing an accurate model lies in capturing good-quality photographs. It's also worth remembering that the resolution of the final model is dependent on the resolution of the image and the proximity at which it was taken (e.g. high-megapixel images taken close to an object will produce the most detailed models). The photographs need to be well lit, crisply focused and taken at regular intervals around the site or artefact, with a minimum of a 70 per cent overlap between each image. This is easily achieved for a regular building, but the complex architecture of Neolithic and Bronze Age monuments presents a particular challenge as many of the photographs need to be taken in narrow passages and dark, confined chambers. For the interior of the tombs and dark spaces, images can be taken with a fixed flash. A minimum of two overlapping images is required to generate a photogrammetric 3D model, but hundreds, sometimes thousands, of photographs are required to create detailed models of complex monuments.

Once you have taken your photographs they can be loaded into your image-based modelling software for processing. This typically involves masking areas of images to be excluded from the model (e.g. the sky, blurred areas, and people or animals that have crept into the shot) and aligning the images before calculating the 3D geometry, which may take hours or days depending on your computer's processing power. The next task is to accurately scale and orient the resulting model (these options are not always available in free or low-cost software, but can be achieved in open source software, such as Blender). The final part of the process is to render a surface texture, creating a photo-real representation of the monument.

Scans and models of many hundreds of prehistoric sites and artefacts have been uploaded to Sketchfab.com – search for models by Hamish Fenton, Hugo Anderson-Whymark and many others.

Imagining Prehistoric Landscapes

Vicki Cummings, Professor of Neolithic Archaeology at the University of Central Lancashire

As a prehistoric archaeologist I have visited many hundreds of sites over the years, covering the length and breadth of Britain and Ireland. Some sites are phenomenal and awe-inspiring while others are smaller and may seem elusive, the challenge of working out what is going on half the fun. The aim of this introduction is to give a little information to help you interpret what you are seeing – not only to tell you about the type of site you are looking at but also to place it in its wider context. In particular, I will highlight some of the interesting ways in which archaeologists are thinking about these sites, based on the latest research and excavation findings.

The first thing to bear in mind is that the landscapes in which these sites are set would have been radically different in the past. The hills and mountains would have been the same in prehistory, but virtually everything else would have been different. First, you need to remove all the modern boundaries that divide the British and Irish countryside into fields. While some hedgerows may date back hundreds, and more rarely, thousands of years, there is very little evidence of permanent land division in the Neolithic (the best example is Ceide Fields in Ireland). While Neolithic and early Bronze Age people were agriculturalists, they seem to have been predominantly mobile, moving around with their animals and growing crops in small and temporary garden plots. So, picture the scene without the fields and hedgerows. Next, there were many more trees than there are today.

At the start of the Neolithic (around 4000BC), most of Britain and Ireland was forested, including northern Scotland. People did clear woodland, but it often grew back – so you would have seen a patchwork of woods and small clearings.

Other things were different, too. Rivers and streams now follow carefully maintained routes but in prehistory they would have meandered and changed course from time to time. Six thousand years ago a lot more land would have been marshy and marginal – we have reclaimed hundreds of acres in Britain and Ireland via drainage systems. Flood plains, too, would have been inundated after heavy rain. In contrast, upland areas now covered by blanket bog would have been better quality land as much, although not all, bog formed later on in prehistory. You also need to imagine the detritus left behind from the last ice age. The ice sheets that covered most of Britain and Ireland deposited boulders and stones across the landscape. The vast majority of these have been cleared over the millennia, providing an excellent source of building material for houses, roads and walls. Back in the Neolithic, however, many landscapes would have been strewn with large and small stones. You would also have seen a wide variety of now-extinct animals, including aurochs (wild cows), wolves and bears. Other, more familiar species had not yet been introduced, including rabbits, hares and grey squirrels.

Against all this change it is still possible, however, to imagine prehistoric landscapes. In

most areas, sea levels would have been more or less the same as they are now. Our impressive mountain ranges would have dominated their surroundings just as they do today. While trees may have obscured some views out from sites, most species were deciduous at this time, so in the winter views would have opened up, just as in the summer trees would have enclosed sites with their canopies of leaves. The first challenge, then, for the megalithic visitor (after finding the site!) is an act of imagination – what might this site have looked like in its Neolithic landscape? Keep this in mind as we think about some of the specifics of the sites you might be looking at.

The Start and Spread of the Neolithic

People did not always build monuments. In Britain and Ireland, the practice started in the Neolithic, after about 4000BC. In the preceding period, the late Mesolithic, people were mobile hunter-gatherers. Their ritual lives appear to have been focused on their interactions with the natural world, in particular animals (Conneller 2004). They also seem to have had a special affinity with the sea and water. They did not bury their dead in graves or cemeteries but most likely disposed of them in other ways including excarnation (exposing the body to the elements and predators) or leaving them in watery places (Conneller 2006). It seems likely people venerated natural locations; monument construction was not part of their way of doing things.

With the onset of the Neolithic, however, monument building was practised much more widely. The Neolithic also saw people making and using pottery for the first time, keeping domesticated crops and animals, and making polished stone tools. This is often referred to as the Neolithic "package" and these were practices and technologies introduced into Britain and Ireland from continental Europe.

There is ongoing debate regarding quite how this happened. Some suggest that these new ideas were acquired by the native population, while others suggest it was a result of an incoming migrant population from Europe (Sheridan 2010; Thomas 2013; Whittle et al. 2011). It's likely to have been a combination of both, and to have varied from area to area (Cummings and Harris 2011). It is important to note that there are no precise analogues for the British or Irish Neolithic in mainland Europe. This means that while the ideas and knowledge of Neolithic practices definitely came from the mainland these things were applied in slightly new ways. Thus British pottery and monuments of the period do not have exact parallels on mainland Europe.

While we might not be able to fully understand how Neolithic things and practices became established in Britain and Ireland, we do now have a really precise chronology for the start of the Neolithic (Whittle et al. 2011). Neolithic practices were first introduced into southeast England around 4050BC and spread into south-central England around 3900BC. It was only around 3800BC that Neolithic practices were adopted more widely in Britain and it was perhaps another hundred years before people across the whole of Britain and Ireland seem to have adopted the Neolithic way of doing things. Even then, not all communities adopted all aspects of the Neolithic – not every community in Britain or Ireland seems to have been involved in monument construction, for example.

With all this in mind, let us now look at these monuments.

Pentre Ifan Balanced on slim uprights, the massive capstone seems almost to float in the air.

The Development of Monumentality

Like pottery and domesticated animals, the concept of monumentality had a European origin. There were communities on the mainland who were building monuments in the fifth millennium BC, long before people in either Britain or Ireland adopted a Neolithic way of life. Many of the monuments in this book are built of stone, and one European area in particular stands out as having an exceptional record of building with stone in the fifth millennium BC. This is Brittany, which has many surviving stone monuments. People there were erecting enormous standing stones (menhirs) and building various types of chambered tomb (Scarre 2011). People in other areas built monuments from earth and timber, including in the long-barrow tradition of northern Europe (known as the TRB – Trichterbecherkultur – or Funnel Beaker culture) and the earthen enclosures of the Cerny culture of northeast France (Midgley 2005). So monument building was a practice adopted from outside, and once again adopted in a distinctive, localized style. Monument construction in parts of both Britain and Ireland was very enthusiastic, with dense concentrations of monuments being built in western and northern Britain and the northern half of Ireland.

The very earliest monuments are in the southeast of England, where Neolithic practices were first adopted (from about 4050BC; Whittle et al. 2011). Coldrum (see page 126), one of the so-called Medway Megaliths, is a good example. From this point Neolithic practices spread both northward and westward – but this does not exclude the possibility that there were multiple points of contact between people on the Continent and people in Britain: monument building may have been introduced into Britain many times

from different areas. We do know that in some areas people used stone to create monumental structures but in other areas wood and earth were used. We also know that people constructed monuments in comparable ways, so while there may not have been a specific template there are broad similarities in both form and use. After the first monuments were built, those that came later often referenced earlier sites. The Stonehenge landscape is a good example of this, where Bronze Age round barrows cluster around older monuments.

The division of the Neolithic into early, middle and late works well for most areas because these time frames correspond with peaks in the construction of various types of monument: certain types of chambered tombs in the early Neolithic; passage graves in the middle Neolithic, especially in Ireland; and stone and timber circles, often in complexes, in the late Neolithic. However, partly because Neolithic practices were adopted over a 350-year period in different areas, and partly because people started doing things in more regionally specific ways after they became Neolithic, it is hard to provide clear boundaries, either in space or time, for these subdivisions. In some areas it is easiest just to use early and late Neolithic: this is particularly the case for northern Scotland. Nevertheless, this is a more satisfactory way of approaching the evidence than thinking about sites just by type. Quite clearly, Neolithic people were aware of broader trends across these islands and complex networks of exchange and contact were in place.

Early Neolithic Monuments

As noted above, the uptake of Neolithic practices occurred at different times in different parts of Britain and Ireland. In southeast and south-central England this took place between 4050 and 3900BC. Much of the rest of Britain and Ireland waited until around 3800BC, and northern Britain until around 3700BC to adopt the Neolithic package. The earliest forms of monument were fairly small-scale sites, often (but not always) associated with the burial of the dead. These are stone chambered tombs, found mainly in western and northern Britain and Ireland, and structures of earth and wood typically constructed in eastern Britain. There are also swathes of both islands where no monuments were built, indicating that monument construction was not required everywhere. It is clear to see that stone-built chambered tombs do not occur in eastern Britain, apart from in the very north of Scotland. It is harder to comment on the distribution of timber monuments, since they are only visible as cropmarks in fields and in many cases no trace of them would survive in the archaeological record. A little later on, some communities started building causewayed enclosures: these are earth and timber monuments on a much larger scale than chambered tombs. They are only found in parts of Britain (the south for the most part), with just a couple of examples in Ireland.

Chambered tombs (early Neolithic)

Stone-built chambered tombs are iconic monuments of the Neolithic period. Many, although by no means all, are early Neolithic in date. Most have some characteristics in common: they have a chamber or chambers for the deposition of human remains; they are set within substantial long cairns or mounds and they have a focal area at the front for people to gather. They are described by archaeologists according to their geographical location, so there are Cotswold-Severn monuments, Clyde cairns, stalled cairns (in northern Scotland – also

referred to as Orkney-Cromarty) and court cairns (in Ireland). Among the Cotswold-Severn group, well-known examples are Wayland's Smithy, Belas Knap and West Kennet (see pages 113, 82 and 109. The Clyde cairns are located in western Scotland and include sites such as Cairn Holy I and II (see pages 269–70). Clyde cairns are very similar to court cairns in Ireland, good examples of which include Audleystown, County Down (see page 400) and Creevykeel, County Sligo (see page 393). Stalled cairns (where the chamber is divided into compartments by slabs of stone, reminding early excavators of horse stalls) are found in northern Scotland, and, unusually, some are set in smaller round cairns. Later examples are larger and set in long cairns, such as Midhowe on the island of Rousay, Orkney.

These are great sites to visit in the field because you can often make out key architectural features. In most instances the cairn or mound survives more or less to its original height, although some cairns have been robbed for their stone. The chambers are frequently visible, and in some cases you can actually get inside them: West Kennet in Wiltshire (see page 109) and Blackhammer on Orkney are two excellent examples with accessible chambers. The chamber was the location for the deposition of human remains, sometimes fleshed, but in some cases already disarticulated or cremated.

I like to think about how people would have used these sites: how would they have placed the remains of their loved ones into these monuments (not always as straightforward as you might think – in some cases bones may have been curated or kept elsewhere for many years before being placed in the tomb, or sorted and re-sorted once they were in there), and where did they gather after the event? If you visit a number of sites in one area you may see similarities between them: they often share certain features.

In recent years archaeologists have written a lot about the setting of these monuments. This approach is known as phenomenology and it looks at how people might have engaged with and experienced the landscapes they lived in (see, for example, Tilley 1994 and Cummings 2009). The idea here is that people would not have just built their tombs randomly in the landscape – the selection of the site was significant and important. Tombs would have been positioned in relation to settlement, probably not immediately next to where their builders lived, but also not really far removed. Occasionally, chambered tombs are built over earlier occupation remains, including Mesolithic activity, as occurred at Hazleton North in Gloucestershire. However, when the remains of early Neolithic occupation are discovered, it tends to be in the valleys below chambered tombs, close to water for obvious reasons. So when you visit a chambered tomb you can straight away start to imagine where people lived: perhaps at this spot initially, and then later on, lower down in the valley, so that they would have looked up-slope to their burial monuments. They would also have had beliefs that influenced what they did and where. The placement of sites like chambered tombs suggests that beliefs may have involved natural places: rock outcrops, mountain tops, springs, rivers and so on. If you stand at the chambered tomb of the Giants' Graves on Arran (see page 264), there are views across to the mountain of Goat Fell as well as out to sea and to Holy Island. Indeed, when we look at the setting of early Neolithic chambered tombs in the landscape they are repeatedly located in relation to specific features, particularly water and mountains (Cummings 2009). It seems likely or at least possible that these places may have

been important in understandings of the world and the afterlife. So, when visiting a chambered tomb have a look around – what is visible from the site? As soon as you start visiting different types of site you will notice each type is set in a different kind of landscape that was potentially important to people in the Neolithic.

Dolmens

These sites are another form of early Neolithic monument, also built from stone but differing in some crucial ways from the chambered tombs discussed above. Like chambered tombs they have a stone chamber, but in dolmen monuments these are rather different. First, unlike chambered tombs, the capstones on dolmens are typically enormous, much larger than would have been needed in practical terms. The largest dolmen in Britain is Garn Turne in Pembrokeshire (see page 218), where the capstone is estimated to have weighed around 80 tonnes (88 tons). The largest dolmen of all, however, is in Ireland. The amazing monument at Browne's Hill in County Carlow (see page 375) has a phenomenal capstone, estimated to weigh over 100 tonnes (110 tons). This was the largest stone ever used in a monument in Britain or Ireland in prehistory. A capstone of this size was not required just as a "roof" for a chamber! The huge capstones are supported by upright stones, which do create a chamber area of sorts. Many of these uprights include a "portal": two upright stones with a central slab set at 90 degrees between them. This feature gives them their name – portal dolmens, or portal tombs in Ireland. Some of these monuments, such as Poulnabrone in County Clare (Lynch 2014) (see page 378) were definitely used for the burial of human remains. The dolmens of Cornwall, known locally as "quoits", could similarly have been used for burial. However, most dolmen

Photo © Ken Williams

Ballynahatty A burial chamber stands at the centre of the huge henge known as the Giant's Ring.

chambers have sizeable gaps between their stones, which would not have created a box-like chamber as with other chambered tombs. When excavated, many dolmens produce only a few scraps of bone suggesting that their primary role was not as places for the burial of the dead, but as statements in stone (Cummings and Richards forthcoming). Some archaeologists have argued that the gaps in the sides of the chambers of dolmens could have been infilled with dry-stone walling, which would then be concealed by the cairn or mound which they assume covered these monuments. But the crucial piece of evidence against this idea is that mounds or cairns are very rarely found around dolmens, and when they are they are only small – the size of a platform rather than a full-size cairn. Although it might be argued that the cairns have been robbed, it's worth asking why so many monuments with impressive capstones have lost their cairns, while other chambered tombs with lesser roofstones have not. It's a convincing argument that chambered tombs were just that – monuments designed for burial, encased in mounds or cairns – while dolmens were a different sort of monument, never completely covered by a cairn. Indeed, why bother lifting and using a stone that weighed 100 tonnes if it was just going to be covered up? These were monuments that were meant to be seen.

If dolmens were not (primarily) burial monuments the question is why were they built?

Archaeologists think these sites were intended to bring together communities that were otherwise quite dispersed to work together on a project, the end result of which would have been truly awe-inspiring. Dolmens were like the cathedrals of the Neolithic — they would have been amazing constructions with great importance in people's belief systems. Stone seems to have been particularly important in the Neolithic, so lifting up and displaying a big capstone as these dolmens did is likely to have been significant.

Dolmens are located in interesting parts of the landscape. If you have the chance to visit sites in different parts of the country, you will be able to identify regional differences in their settings. The dolmens of Cornwall, for example, are often located in quite prominent locations, so Chûn Quoit (see page 39) is positioned very close to the summit of the hill on which it sits. If you explore the dolmens of southeast Ireland, however, you will find that some of them are discreetly placed in the bottom of small stream valleys. One of my favourite sites in Ireland is the dolmen at Aghnacliff, County Longford. This spectacular monument is tucked away at the bottom of a steep-sided valley, meaning it would have been hard to find unless you knew exactly where it was. Dolmens look absolutely breathtaking from certain directions, but less so from others. I like to think about the approaches to these sites and how they are presented within their wider landscape. The access of lots of sites is controlled by the constraints of modern agriculture or infrastructure, but you can consider how the approach would change if you arrived from a different direction. Some sites, like Pentre Ifan in Pembrokeshire (see page 220), seem to incorporate natural features – outcrops displayed on the horizon, or a distinctive mountain in the distance.

Long barrows, cairns and timber mortuary structures

Timber mortuary structures are early Neolithic monuments constructed from wood and built to contain the remains of the dead. Essentially, they were large wooden boxes, often with half a single large timber post at either end, with the box sitting between the posts. At one end archaeologists often find the remains of a façade of posts, creating a forecourt area, as at Dorstone Hill in Herefordshire (see page 132). Interestingly, these timber structures were often burnt down once they had been used for burial. At Street House in Cleveland, for example, the wooden monument was set ablaze (Vyner 1984). The timbers very rarely survive in the archaeological record, with the occasional exceptional example such as Haddenham in Cambridgeshire where the timbers were preserved by the surrounding peat (Evans and Hodder 2006). In most instances the timbers have rotted (or been burnt) away leaving only impressions or carbonized remnants. These remains would rarely survive ploughing, except that these timber mortuary structures were often covered, and therefore preserved, underneath a long barrow or cairn. Long barrows and cairns survive fairly well into the present because they are often pretty sizeable – the long barrow covering Haddenham was 52m long and 16m (171ft and 52ft) wide. Timber mortuary structures are usually only found when long barrows or cairns are excavated – and only a very small number of such sites have seen modern excavation. It is therefore not possible to say whether all long barrows and cairns without stone chambers had wooden chambers instead. However, excavations of some sites such as South Street long barrow in Wiltshire produced no evidence for either a stone chamber or a wooden one, so it appears that some long barrows and cairns were just that – large piles of earth or stone with no chamber for the dead at all.

Causewayed enclosures

A very different type of early Neolithic monument is the causewayed enclosure. These are exactly as described – monuments that enclose an area of land. The enclosure was created by digging a series of ditches in a circuit. The ditches were not continuous, but had multiple gaps between them – the causeways, which allowed access and entry into the central enclosed area. Causewayed enclosures were sometimes made by digging just a single circuit of ditches, but in other examples, including the well-known Windmill Hill in Wiltshire (see page 104), there were three circuits of ditches. Alongside the ditches wooden palisades were also sometimes constructed – these would have been high, with closely set wooden posts creating screens and working in conjunction with the ditches. These are very different monuments from chambered tombs because they are much larger sites – Windmill Hill encloses 8.5ha (21 acres) of land. They would also have taken much more time and effort to build – it's estimated they took 10 times as long as to build a chambered tomb (Renfrew 1973). Not everyone in early Neolithic Britain built causewayed enclosures, however – they have a distinctly southern British distribution. This means that whatever the motivation was for building them, most early Neolithic communities did not require one. The latest research on these sites has shown that many of these monuments were built around 3650BC (Whittle et al. 2011), by which time a Neolithic way of life had been well-established.

When causewayed enclosures have been excavated, considerable quantities of material culture has been found in the ditches, including the remains of food and pottery, but also more special items such as polished stone axes. Some sites have also yielded large quantities of human remains, leading to suggestions that these might have been meeting places where communities came together for a wide range of activities, including trading, negotiating, feasting and dealing with the dead. At Crickley Hill in Gloucestershire archaeologists also found evidence of a violent attack – many arrowheads were found around the entrances and the palisade had been burnt down. This shows that in this instance the gathering at this site went badly wrong – good evidence that the early Neolithic was not a peaceful period. Some of the human remains recovered from this period also show evidence of violence (Schulting 2012).

Visiting these sites is interesting but can be challenging because it is rarely possible to clearly make out the circuits of ditches on the ground. If you plan to visit a causewayed enclosure it is worth planning ahead and taking a detailed plan of the site with you – you may well have to figure out precisely where the ditches were. But a visit to the site will enable you to appreciate the size and scale of these monuments. It is also worth noting that some sites were reused in the Iron Age, often as hill forts – such as Maiden Castle in Dorset (see page 85), and this makes a visit even more challenging, because the later activity has often obscured the earlier evidence.

Other early Neolithic sites

There are some other early Neolithic sites that will be mentioned here, many of which are well worth a visit. Of particular interest are the stone axe quarries (sometimes still called axe factories, but better described as stone axe extraction sites). The locations have been identified by petrology, so we know that these were places where Neolithic people went to get stone to make into beautiful polished stone axes (Clough and Cummins 1988). What is so extraordinary about some of these sites is how difficult they were to access. The best-known stone axe quarry is the Langdale Pikes in Cumbria (see page 175). Toward the summit of the Langdale Pikes are exposed pinnacles of rock and it was these outcrops which were quarried for stone. Large swathes of scree can still be seen, among which are the remnants of the quarrying process. Once the stone was quarried it was transported back down into the valley to be made into axes. Langdale stone is a beautiful blue-grey colour, and many tens of thousands of Langdale stone axes were made in the Neolithic (Bradley and Edmonds 1993). Remarkably, those axes are found the length and breadth of Britain, and in Ireland. They were clearly highly prized objects. Other stone axe quarries were in similarly exposed settings, including Penmaenmawr (Graig Lwyd) in north Wales and Tievebulliagh Mountain in Ireland. (Please remember if you are visiting these sites that they are scheduled ancient monuments and it is not acceptable to take any stone away.) The early Neolithic flint mines are equally important. These are found only in Sussex, for example at Black Patch, and are where people dug into the earth to follow seams of flint. It is interesting that flint occurs in considerable quantities on the surface, so there was no practical need to mine it. This practice seems to have been imported from the Continent with other aspects of the Neolithic package.

Another amazing early Neolithic site to mention is the Sweet Track (see page 76). This wooden trackway was constructed in 3806BC and was built across reed swamp to connect two areas of dry land in the Somerset Levels. Incredibly, the trackway survived into recent times by virtue of being waterlogged, and when it was excavated archaeologists found not only the wooden trackway but a series of deposits along its length, including pots filled with food and a beautiful and exotic jadeite axehead (Coles and Coles 1986). This axehead was not hafted, (so was presumably never intended to be "used" in any practical sense) and had been imported from Europe. In fact, the stone used to make the axehead was from the Italian Alps – a rare and exotic find in Britain. These objects, therefore, seem to have been ritual deposits, indicating that the trackway was both functional – in that it linked together parts of the landscape – and a monument of sorts, crossing an important and perhaps sacred landscape. While the original trackway is no longer in situ, you can still walk its route and see a replica of it.

Middle Neolithic Monuments

The early Neolithic can be characterized by an exuberance of monumental construction. People across many parts of Britain constructed sites from earth, stone and timber. In contrast, the middle Neolithic, which covers around 400 years, from around 3500–3400BC to the turn of the millennium, saw the creation of fewer monuments, although the existing sites were sometimes still in use. The middle Neolithic is characterized by the use of a new type of pottery, Peterborough ware, and also seems to have seen a decline in the growing of cereal crops and a general lack of permanent settlement. Across most of Britain, very few new monuments were built, with the exception of the rather intriguing earthen cursus monuments. In Ireland, on the other hand, along with the Western and Northern Isles, there was an intensification of monument construction, specifically a new type of chambered tomb, in the form of passage graves. These can be considered the pinnacle of megalithic construction, involving the investment of enormous periods of time and, for the first time, completely altering entire landscapes.

Passage graves (middle Neolithic chambered tombs)

These monuments are a form of chambered tomb, but there are some key elements that set them apart from early Neolithic examples. As their name suggests, they have a passage which leads to a chamber area. In the largest examples, such as Newgrange in Ireland (see page 381), the passage is long – 19m (62ft) long in the case of Newgrange. The chambers vary in shape, but many passage graves have a distinctive "cruciform" chamber with niches or recesses off the central area. Excellent examples of this feature are found in Orkney, for example at Maeshowe (see page 348), and in Ireland as at the Carrowkeel sites (see page 390). The passage and chamber are set within a round cairn or mound, and many of the Irish examples are also encircled by a kerb of stones. Some of the kerb stones are elaborately decorated with complex and intricate rock art; indeed, some stones in the interior of passage graves are also covered with art, including scratched lines and pecked designs (created through indirect percussion, where one stone is used like a chisel and another stone antler or bone tool is used as a hammer). The most spectacular passage grave rock art is found within the Brú na Bóinne complex in County Meath which includes the world-famous sites of Newgrange and Knowth (Hensey 2015) (see pages 381 and 383). The Brú na Bóinne sites also highlight another key feature of some passage graves: they are often found in complexes where multiple sites were constructed across a single landscape. The scale of this construction, for the first time, altered an entire landscape into a monumental complex – this idea only really takes hold in Britain after 3000BC, in the late Neolithic.

One of the most spectacular aspects of many of these sites is their hilltop location. This is most notable with the Loughcrew (see page 386) monuments, the Carrowkeel complex and some truly spectacular examples on the summits of mountains including Slieve Donard (see page 400) in the Mourne Mountains, located at 848m (2,782ft) above sea level. These hilltop locations mean the tombs were highly visible in the surrounding landscape, and also had views out over large tracts of land. It is interesting to compare these sites to other chambered tombs – passage graves are the only ones positioned on hilltops and mountain summits. It is hard to envisage these being anything other than sacred locations in Neolithic belief systems, with a particular connection between these monuments and the sky. This makes it even more interesting that many of these monuments are aligned on specific solar events. Both Newgrange and Maeshowe have their passages aligned on the movement of the midwinter sun – Newgrange the sunrise, and Maeshowe the sunset – marking the shortest day of the year. This must have been an important moment in the year, marking the point from which days start getting longer.

In recent years archaeologists have started to think about these sites not just in terms of formal deposition of the dead but also of creating very distinctive experiences for the living. I've talked about the amazing passage grave rock art, but passage graves also incorporate different coloured stones in their fabric. In some cases there is good evidence that stones in passage graves have come from further afield. At Newgrange, stones were brought from both the

Mourne Mountains to the north and the Wicklow Mountains to the south (Cooney 2000). Anyone visiting one of these sites, or perhaps even going into them, would see colourful, engraved and exotic stones, making them visually spectacular. In addition to this, archaeologists have discovered that passage graves also have distinctive acoustic properties. When people sing and make noise within these monuments such as banging a drum, it can create Helmholtz resonance – this is the effect produced when you blow over the top of a bottle (Watson and Keating 1999). The same effect within a passage grave, however, would have been very unsettling for people within it, possibly even inducing nausea or blurred vision. What on earth would people in the Neolithic, with no understanding of physics or acoustics, make of these effects? Almost certainly, I think, they would have attributed the phenomena to otherworldy beings such as the dead, spirits or malevolent forces. Alternatively, some sounds or resonances may have produced an uplifting or euphoric experience, equally inexplicable, of course, but with a very different impact.

I like to think of passage graves as places of transition, from the living to the dead, but also places where the living underwent altered states, perhaps as part of rituals developed for rites of passage. We might envisage younger members of the community entering the monument, engaging with the dead, participating in a range of otherworldly experiences, and emerging as adults (Moore 2016). When you visit these sites imagine all this as you look around. What would it be like to spend time within the chamber, surrounded by the dead, only to emerge into the light on midwinter morning, or the darkness of the longest night? People who have done it describe it like being reborn, so perhaps these were places for both life and death, the end of one

year and the start of another: places where our world connected with other worlds. This would make them incredibly powerful and significant sites in the landscape.

Cursus monuments

These curious monuments are not the most spectacular sites to visit because they have been subject to millennia of erosion. Many are barely visible on the ground, yet some were originally vast. Many, although not all, cursus monuments consist of a pair of banks and ditches running in parallel, and the largest example is 10km (6 miles) in length. The extraordinary Dorset Cursus (see page 87) is a pair of banks and ditches, essentially enclosing a strip of land. Incorporated into the monument are earlier sites, including long barrows and causewayed enclosures. Precisely what these cursus monuments were for remains unclear, because, when excavated, the ditches tend to be mostly devoid of any archaeological material. This suggests that perhaps they were ceremonial routeways through the landscape, designed to be walked along (Tilley 1994), or perhaps beside (Johnston 1999).

Rock art

It is extremely difficult to date rock art, because the material needed for the usual methods of dating (radiocarbon samples on carbonized remains or bone, or the presence of diagnostic types of pottery) is rarely found at these sites, and where it does occur it is difficult to demonstrate that it is contemporary with the rock art. Nevertheless, we know some rock art dates from the middle Neolithic as it is found inscribed on the passage tombs of Ireland, which can be securely dated. You might wonder if the art was perhaps added later on – and that could be the case in some instances – but much passage grave rock art could not have been done post-construction as it is found on stones that, judging by their position, must have been carved before the monument was built. So rock art was definitely being made in the middle Neolithic, and it seems likely that this carried on into the late Neolithic and early Bronze Age (Bradley 1997). It seems to have been a particularly enduring way of inscribing the landscape. British and Irish rock art is not figurative, in that it does not depict people or animals, unlike rock art elsewhere in Europe. Instead, it is abstract, with a series of lines, circles and indentations (cup-marks) placed carefully on slabs of rock, usually horizontal surfaces of outcrops, such as at Kilmichael Glassary or Baluachraig near Kilmartin (see pages 297 and 298), but also sometimes as part of other monuments. When visiting rock art sites you can soon identify which marks were made by people and which are natural/geological. The careful interplay between human-made and natural features is fascinating. It's worth visiting rock art in the rain to see how water changes the way you view these sites. If you are struggling to see the art on the panels, an oblique light across the rock face will help you pick out the engravings.

Late Neolithic Monuments

Passage grave complexes were the first to alter entire landscapes, but they were not constructed everywhere in Britain and Ireland. Indeed, there are only a small number of passage grave complexes, and all are found in Ireland (see above). However, the act of altering landscapes on this phenomenal scale was practised much more widely in the late Neolithic, and monumental complexes of this date are found widely throughout Britain and Ireland. These late Neolithic complexes incorporate monuments built from a variety of different materials including stone, timber and earth, and often all three together. Moreover, these monuments were often built and then further altered over substantial periods of time. Without excavation to help us unpick the chronology of these sites it is often difficult to work out what was built when, and because of the scale of these sites it is difficult for archaeologists to excavate them in their entirety. Essentially when visiting these places you should think of them as multi-phase sites, which would have been like construction sites for long periods of time, sometimes centuries!

Stone circles

One common form of late Neolithic monument is the stone circle. Many, although not all, are true circles with a number of unshaped stones set upright. Late Neolithic circles were sometimes enormous, such as the outer circle at Avebury in Wiltshire (see page 102), the Ring of Brodgar in Orkney (see page 344) and Stanton Drew in Somerset (see page 78). Stone circles sometimes have internal features, like the two smaller stone circles within the outer circle at Avebury, a central hearth feature at the Stones of Stenness, Orkney (see page 345) and even a small megalithic tomb set at the centre of Calanais I (see page 338) on the Isle of Lewis. Other stone circles have a "cove" – an arrangement of three or more stones set together (as at Arbor Low, see page 139), the function of which is unclear. Many stone circles have no visible internal features. Some stone circles were then themselves encircled by a ditch cut into the surrounding earth, and a bank made from the earth from the ditch. This component is called a henge, although not all henges had stone circles within them. It also appears that many henges are a little later in date, possibly early Bronze Age in many cases.

Photo © Martyn Copcutt

Down Tor circle and row The stones increase in size at the end of the row, as the circle is approached uphill.

Timber circles

Another common form of late Neolithic monument was the timber circle, and an associated variation of this, the palisade enclosure. These of course no longer survive above ground, so archaeologists are only able to identify them through fieldwork, as at Woodhenge in Wiltshire (see page 98), where the remains of multiple circuits of timbers were excavated, or through geophysics, as at Stanton Drew, where timber circles were found within the stone circle. Other examples are known from cropmarks. There are some truly monumental late Neolithic monuments made from timber. A really good example of this was discovered in the Walton Basin in Powys (see page 235), where the Hindwell palisade enclosure had a perimeter of 2.5km (nearly 1½ miles)! These would have been very impressive monuments when first built, and the timbers may even have been carved, decorated or hung with cloth. Some timber circles, like stone circles, were enclosed by the bank and ditch of a henge.

Complexes

These monuments made of stone, timber and earth are often found in isolation, but they were also built as complexes, where multiple types of site were built within a single landscape. Moreover, monuments were sometimes linked together through the construction of avenues, as at Avebury where the central stone circle was linked to other places in the landscape via the Beckhampton Avenue and the West Kennet Avenue (see page 107). At Stonehenge the stone circle is linked to the nearby River Avon by an avenue, and the river also connects Stonehenge and the nearby Durrington Walls (Parker Pearson 2015) (see page 98). Other famous late Neolithic complexes include the Brodgar-Stenness complex in Orkney and the Calanais stone circles on Lewis where nine stone circles are laid out across the landscape. One of the fascinating aspects of these complexes of circular monuments is that they themselves are set within circular landscapes that appear to echo the circular monument. A really nice example of this is the stone circle at Castlerigg, Cumbria (see page 177), where the monument is carefully positioned to be encircled by the Cumbrian fells. There are wide views out to the fells, which appear equidistant from the stone circle. It is an element that is repeated at other sites, such as the Stones of Stenness in Orkney, Avebury and Stonehenge.

Some of the most influential work in recent years has focused on the Stonehenge area, but this work has wider implications for understanding late Neolithic monuments throughout Britain. Mike Parker Pearson has suggested that stone represented the realm of the ancestors in the late Neolithic, and that as such, monuments built from stone were set aside from the world of the living. In contrast, monuments built from wood were designed to be used by the living for ceremonies and feasting (Parker Pearson and Ramilisonina 1998). This idea works very nicely for Stonehenge and Durrington Walls. At the latter the remains of houses where people lived have been found, along with piles of rubbish left over from feasting events. In contrast, at Stonehenge there is very little evidence for people living or feasting there,

the site instead being used for the deposition of the remains of the dead. Clearly, this particular complex involved an enormous amount of work and seems to have involved people coming together from a wider area at particular times of year to celebrate and construct the monuments. It has been convincingly demonstrated that people came together here at midwinter, which as we saw above was already being referenced at passage graves in the middle Neolithic. By the late Neolithic, the celebration of the shortest day of the year seems to have been more widespread (Parker Pearson 2015).

Because these monumental complexes altered entire landscapes they can be hard to fully appreciate as a visitor. If you are able to walk aspects of a site it is worth doing so in order to gain a sense of the size and scale of these places. Visit armed with a detailed plan and, if there is one, a sequence of construction, which will help you understand what was built first and which components were added later on. Have a look at the wider effect of the landscape from the centre of the monument if you can, and consider the different types of stone used to construct stone circles in particular, as research has shown that stones often came from different parts of the landscape (Richards 2013).

Houses

Also dating to the late Neolithic are the remarkable stone houses found in Orkney. The best-known example is the village at Skara Brae (see page 349) on the beach at Skaill Bay, famously uncovered by a storm. These dwellings are remarkably well preserved and include stone furniture. There are other known examples, such as at Barnhouse (see page 345), close to the stone circle at the Stones of Stenness (Richards 2005), and more examples have been coming to light in recent years (Richards and Jones 2015). One of the most amazing finds in Orkney recently has been at the Ness of Brodgar (Card 2015) (see page 346). Located in amongst other late Neolithic sites, including the Stones of Stenness and the Ring of Brodgar, the Ness has yielded the remains of a number of very large buildings. These can be best understood as ceremonial houses, monumental in size and clearly designed for special use involving congregating and feasting. This site demonstrates the importance of houses in late Neolithic society, when they were clearly more than simply places to live. Instead, at the Ness of Brodgar they seem to have been material expressions of wider communities, recreated in massive, monumental form.

Early Bronze Age Monuments

From the middle of the third millennium BC metalwork began being made in Britain and Ireland. While the period is known as the Bronze Age, copper and gold artefacts are also found along with bronze. In addition to this, new types of pottery were produced, including beakers. All of this seems to be indicative of new (or revitalized) connections with communities in Europe, along with the actual movement of people into Britain and Ireland at this time. However, many of the late Neolithic monumental complexes discussed above continued to be used and altered. In this sense there was considerable continuity with the late Neolithic, but as well as these existing places people also started to design new forms of monument. The early Bronze Age can be characterized by the sheer number of different types of monument being constructed. We also begin to see the emergence of regionally distinctive ways of building monumental architecture. Some monument types are found

throughout Britain. These include round cairns or barrows, which were built widely and in large numbers in the landscape. There are variations on the basic mound, including bell barrows, saucer barrows and disc barrows, but the general principle is the same: a small upstanding circular monument (Woodward 2000). Most are associated with a burial or burials, sometimes in a grave cut but also in stone or wooden boxes (cists or coffins). Superficially they may appear to be fairly small, simple constructions but, when excavated, archaeologists have found that they are often complex, multiphase monuments which saw the addition of multiple layers and burials, often over extended periods of time. They frequently cluster in groups (or cemeteries, as they were once known) around pre-existing sites – there are many barrow clusters around both Stonehenge and Avebury, for example. They were also built in parts of the landscape where there were no known monuments, in both low-lying locations and hilltops. (It is worth noting that while many nowadays are found in hilltop settings this is partly an issue of preservation, as many low-lying examples have been ploughed away.)

People also continued to build henge monuments, possibly on a smaller scale than during the late Neolithic. Henges are enclosed areas surrounded by a bank and ditch. In all but one example the ditch is internal and the bank external. The anomalous site is Stonehenge, from where the name derives, which has an internal bank and external ditch. The recent excavation of some henges in northern Scotland has shown that they were definitely constructed in the early Bronze Age (Bradley 2011). As well as henges, people also built stone rows and it seems likely that many single standing stones were erected during this period. These sites are difficult to date as this form of monument seems to have endured from the early Neolithic right through the Bronze Age. Moreover, their function is often obscure – perhaps they marked out key points in the landscape or were used for navigation.

In Scotland a new type of stone circle was constructed in this period, mostly in what is now Aberdeenshire. These are known as recumbent stone circles because the ring of stones also contains one large stone set on its side (the recumbent), flanked by two upright stones. These are wonderful monuments, often set in stunning locations – Tomnaverie, for example (see page 317), has wide views out over distant mountains (Bradley 2005). These circles frequently feature different types of stone in the same monument, so it is always worth looking at the geological composition of these sites when you visit. Another localized Scottish building tradition in the early Bronze Age were the Highland Clava cairns (see page 325). These monuments seem to have been constructed in relation to both the sun and the moon and suggest an increased interest in celestial bodies at this time (Bradley 2000). In Ireland monumental forms were different again during this period. Of particular note are wedge tombs, so named because the cairn which surrounds the chamber is wedge-shaped. Over 500 of these were constructed and their orientation to the west and southwest again suggests an interest in the setting sun.

One of the most important things to remember when thinking about these early Bronze Age monuments is that they were constructed in landscapes that were already filled with earlier monumental forms. By the early Bronze Age people had been building monuments for 1,500 years and it seems clear that in many instances they drew on the significance of earlier places.

When visiting a site of this period it is worthwhile investigating what other monuments are found nearby – is the early Bronze Age site located so that it is visible from the earlier site? Is the site carefully positioned so that it makes reference to other sites? And how is a site presented within the local landscape? It seems that many of these places were designed to be seen from afar, in a world increasingly altered by people.

Concluding Thoughts

This introduction has been a whistle-stop guide to a range of monuments found in Britain and Ireland dating from the Neolithic and Bronze Age. A great deal more can be said about all monument types in terms of what has been found when archaeologists have explored them through survey or excavation. However, I hope that you will get a sense of how much can be gained from trying to understand the sites on the ground. It may be a challenge to find the site in the first place – negotiating landowners, barbed wire fences, feisty cows and swollen streams – but that's half the fun! And once you're there, trying to figure out what was going on at a site and looking at its wider location in the landscape is very rewarding. Like many people, I much prefer visiting quieter sites to the big, famous ones such as Stonehenge and Avebury, but ironically one's experience at the latter is probably closer to what it was like when they were built – these were monuments designed for large gatherings of people. It is also fair to say that some sites can appear almost magical in certain weather conditions, be that a beautiful sunny day, a mysteriously misty one or in the blanketing snow. The people who built and used them may well have considered them as special or sacred, and perhaps magical, too. And it's impossible to know precisely when these sites were in use; it may have been in daylight, but equally it may have been at night, and it can be as interesting visiting these sites by moonlight as it is in the day. It is not hard to imagine how these were powerful and religious places, in many instances set aside from the worlds of the living.

Further Reading

If you would like an overview of the Neolithic period in Britain and Ireland you might like to read my book *The Neolithic of Britain and Ireland*, published by Routledge in 2017. I have put references in the text to enable you to follow up specifics on individual site types and ideas, with those references listed below.

References

Bradley, R. 1997. *Rock Art and the Prehistory of Atlantic Europe*. London: Routledge.

Bradley, R. 2000. *The Good Stones: A New Investigation of the Clava Cairns*. Edinburgh: Society of Antiquaries of Scotland.

Bradley, R. 2005. *The Moon and the Bonfire: An Investigation of Three Stone Circles in North-east Scotland*. Edinburgh: Society of Antiquaries of Scotland.

Bradley, R. 2011. *Stages and Screens: An Investigation of Four Henges in Northern and North-eastern Scotland*. Edinburgh: Society of Antiquaries of Scotland.

Bradley, R. and Edmonds, M. 1993. *Interpreting the Axe Trade: Production and Exchange in Neolithic Britain*. Cambridge: Cambridge University Press.

Card, N. 2015. *The Ness of Brodgar*. Kirkwall: Ness of Brodgar Trust.

Clough, T. and Cummins, W. (eds) 1988. *Stone Axe Studies: Volume Two*. London: Council for British Archaeology.

Coles, B. and Coles, J. 1986. *From Sweet Track to Glastonbury*. London: Thames and Hudson.

Conneller, C. 2004. "Becoming Deer: Corporeal Transformations at Star Carr". *Archaeological Dialogues* 11, 37–56.

Conneller, C. 2006. "Death". In C. Conneller and G. Warren (eds), *Mesolithic Britain and Ireland: New Approaches*, 139–64. Stroud: Tempus.

Cummings, V. 2009. *A View from the West: The Neolithic of the Irish Sea Zone*. Oxford: Oxbow.

Cummings, V. and Harris, O. 2011. "Animals, People and Places: The Continuity of Hunting and Gathering Practices across the Mesolithic–Neolithic Transition in Britain". *European Journal of Archaeology* 14:3, 361–82.

Cummings, V. and Richards, C. Forthcoming. *A Wondrous Display: Rethinking Early Neolithic Megaliths in Northern Europe*. Oxford: Windgather.

Evans, C. and Hodder, I. 2006. *A Woodland Archaeology: Neolithic Sites at Haddenham: the Haddenham Project Volume 1*. Cambridge: McDonald Institute for Archaeological Research.

Hensey, R. 2015. *First Light: The Origins of Newgrange*. Oxford: Oxbow.

Johnston, R. 1999. "An Empty Path? Processions, Memories and the Dorset Cursus". In A. Barclay and J. Harding (eds), *Pathways and Ceremonies: The Cursus Monuments of Britain and Ireland*, 39–48. Oxford: Oxbow.

Lynch, A. 2014. *Poulnabrone: An Early Neolithic Portal Tomb in Ireland*. Dublin: Wordwell.

Midgley, M. 2005. *The Monumental Cemeteries of Prehistoric Europe*. Stroud: Tempus.

Moore, S. 2016. "Movement and Thresholds: Architecture and Landscape at the

Carrowkeel-Keshcorran Passage Tomb Complex, Co. Sligo, Ireland". In J. Leary and T. Kador (eds), *Moving on in Neolithic Studies: Understanding Mobile Lives*, 45–66. Oxford: Oxbow.

Parker Pearson, M. 2015. *Stonehenge: Making Sense of a Prehistoric Mystery*. York: CBA.

Parker Pearson, M. and Ramilisonina 1998. "Stonehenge for the Ancestors: The Stones Pass on the Message". *Antiquity* 72, 308–26.

Renfrew, C. 1973. "Monuments, Mobilisation and Social Organisation in Neolithic Wessex". In C. Renfrew (ed.), *The Explanation of Culture Change*, 539–58. Pittsburgh: University of Pittsburgh Press.

Richards, C. 2005. *Dwelling Among the Monuments: The Neolithic Village of Barnhouse, Maeshowe Passage Grave and Surrounding Monuments at Stenness, Orkney*. Cambridge: McDonald Institute for Archaeological Research.

Richards, C. (ed.) 2013. *Building the Great Stone Circles of the North*. Oxford: Windgather.

Richards, C. and Jones, R. (eds) 2015. *The Development of Neolithic House Societies in Orkney*. Oxford: Oxbow.

Scarre, C. 2011. *Landscapes of Neolithic Brittany*. Oxford: Oxford University Press.

Schulting, R. 2012. "Skeletal Evidence for Interpersonal Violence: Beyond Mortuary Monuments in Southern Britain". In R. Schulting and L. Fibiger (eds), *Sticks, Stones and Broken Bones*, 223–48. Oxford: Oxford University Press.

Sheridan, A. 2010. "The Neolithization of Britain and Ireland: The 'Big Picture'". In B. Finlayson and G. Warren (eds), *Landscapes in Transition*, 89–105. Oxford: Oxbow.

Thomas, J. 2013. *The Birth of Neolithic Britain: An Interpretive Account*. Oxford: Oxford University Press.

Tilley, C. 1994. *A Phenomenology of Landscape*. Oxford: Berg.

Vyner, B. 1984. "The Excavation of a Neolithic Cairn at Street House, Loftus, Cleveland". *Proceedings of the Prehistoric Society* 50, 151–95.

Watson, A. and Keating, D. 1999. "Architecture and Sound: An Acoustic Analysis of Megalithic Monuments in Prehistoric Britain". *Antiquity* 73, 325–36.

Whittle, A., Healy, F. and Bayliss, A. 2011. *Gathering Time: Dating the Early Neolithic Enclosures of Southern Britain and Ireland*. Oxford: Oxbow.

Woodward, A. 2000. *British Barrows: A Matter of Life and Death*. Stroud: Tempus.

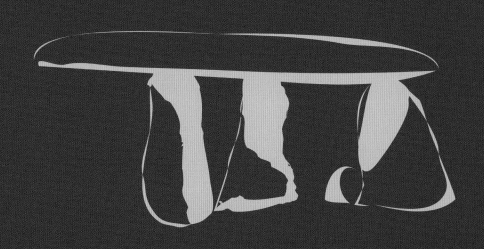

WEST OF ENGLAND

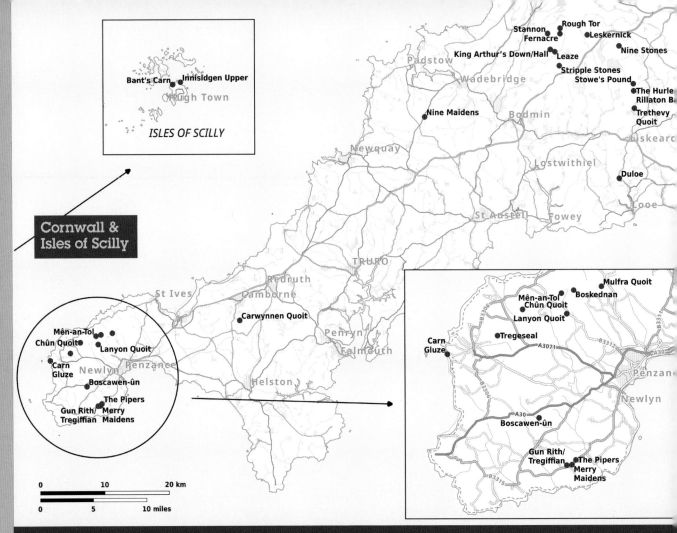

**Cornwall &
Isles of Scilly**

ISLES OF SCILLY

Bant's Carn   Innisidgen Upper
High Town

Padstow
Wadebridge
Newquay
Bodmin
Nine Maidens
St Austell
Lostwithiel
Fowey
Looe
Liskeard
Duloe

Stannon   Rough Tor
Fernacre   Leskernick
King Arthur's Down/Hall   Nine Stones
Leaze
Stripple Stones
Stowe's Pound
The Hurlers
Rillaton B.
Trethevy Quoit

TRURO
Redruth
Camborne
Carwynnen Quoit
St Ives
Penryn
Falmouth
Helston

Mên-an-Tol
Chûn Quoit
Lanyon Quoit
Carn Gluze
Newlyn   Penzance
Boscawen-ûn
The Pipers
Gun Rith/   Merry
Tregiffian   Maidens

Mulfra Quoit
Boskednan
Mên-an-Tol
Chûn Quoit
Lanyon Quoit
Tregeseal
Carn Gluze
Penzance
Newlyn
Boscawen-ûn
Gun Rith/
Tregiffian   The Pipers
Merry
Maidens

BANT'S CARN

Burial Chamber | Nearest Village: **Hugh Town**
Map: **SV 9099 1230** | Sheets: **E101 L203** | Lat: **49.9308N** | Long: **6.30747W**

Photo © Paul Blades

A very impressive 10m (33ft) entrance grave (one of some 80 such structures concentrated in Scilly) in a fine hilltop setting above Halangy Down prehistoric settlement. The site now overlooks the sea but in prehistoric times this would have been a valley landscape. A platform with kerbing surrounds a mound containing the stone chamber, which is taller than most entrance graves (up to 1.5m/5ft) and roofed with four huge capstones, the largest 2.5m (8ft) in length. The site was excavated at the turn of the 20th century and little was found, apart from some pottery and four piles of cremated human bones.

Nearby | At SV 9098 1237, 70m (230ft) NNW, is **Halangy Down** prehistoric settlement, dating back to the Bronze Age and overlaid with Iron Age remains. Between Halangy Down and Bant's Carn, and on the hill to the northeast, the earthworks of prehistoric field systems can be traced.

INNISIDGEN UPPER   Alt Name: **The Giant's Grave**

Burial Chamber | Nearest Village: **Hugh Town**
Map: **SV 9218 1265** | Sheets: **E101 L203** | Lat: **49.93456N** | Long: **6.29121W**

A well-preserved Scillonian entrance grave in what is now a breathtaking setting overlooking Crow Sound (sea levels were lower when the site was built), with the earthen banks of a prehistoric field system visible on the nearby hillside. The substantial mound, 9m × 8m (29ft × 26ft) and rising to 1.8m (6ft), is surrounded by the remains of a platform and a kerb of large stones. The inner chamber has five capstones.

Nearby | At SV 9211 1272, 100m (328ft) WNW of Innisidgen Upper, is another entrance grave: **Innisidgen Lower**. Its mound takes in natural rocky features and a kerb survives in places, as well as two capstones.

Photo © Paul Blades

"It truly is a wonderful place. The wind blows through the trees creating an eerie hush, only broken by the sound of waves lapping the shore." Tony (Enkidu41)

MERRY MAIDENS
Alt Names: Rosemodress Circle, Boleigh Circle, Dans Maen
Stone Circle | Nearest Village: **St Buryan/Trewoofe**
Map: **SW 4327 2450** | Sheets: **E102 L203** | Lat: **50.06507N** | Long: **5.58875W**

Photo © CazzyJane

Seen from the gate at the bottom of their field, the Merry Maidens look really splendid up on the skyline. All the stones in this elegant 24m (78ft) circle are around 1.2m (4ft) high and evenly spaced, apart from a large gap to the east that suggests a possible solar alignment. This is one of several 19-stone rings on the Lands End peninsula, although it seems the 19th stone was inserted in a second gap during the 19th century. There are lots of large stones in the hedge surrounding the circle, and in the next field, but it is hard to say if any are connected to the site, or perhaps to a second circle that was recorded by antiquarian William Borlase in the 18th century and apparently destroyed in the 19th century. As at many stone circles, a legend tells of careless girls turned to stone when, dancing past midnight at a wedding one Saturday night, they inadvertently broke the Sabbath (the Cornish name Dans Maen means "stone dance"). It's said the musicians who had been playing for them ran off as the St Buryan clock began to strike 12, but only got a little way before meeting the same fate as the dancers. This is one of Cornwall's best-known sites and easy to access (it's just off the B3315, where there is a convenient bus stop) and may be busy – try to get there early in the morning in summer.

GUN RITH
Alt Name: The Fiddler
Standing Stone | Nearest Village: **St Buryan**
Map: **SW 4294 2447** | Sheets: **E102 L203** | Lat: **50.06466N** | Long: **5.59333W**

The fiddler from the Merry Maidens' ill-fated party is to be found in a hedge in a field close to Tregiffian burial chamber. The stone has fallen several times in recent years; in 2003 it was restored in its former position but with its base set in concrete. William Copeland Borlase (the great-great-grandson of William Borlase) excavated here in 1871 and found a sandstone pebble, flattened on one side, which he conjectured had been used as a whetstone.

Photo © CazzyJane

TREGIFFIAN   Alt Name: **Cruk Tregyffian**
Chambered Tomb | Nearest Village: **St Buryan/Trewoofe**
Map: **SW 4304 2443** | Sheets: **E102 L203** | Lat: **50.06434N** | Long: **5.59191W**

Although on the mainland, this is a Scillonian type entrance grave, with a walled and roofed passage leading into a formerly circular mound (the northwest part of the mound was destroyed by the building of the road). Excavations have unearthed ashes and bone fragments. Four large capstones can be seen, and one of the portal slabs (a concrete replica – the original is in the Royal Cornwall Museum in Truro) is strikingly decorated with 25 deep cup-marks. From here, it is possible to see over to the Merry Maidens and also to Gun Rith.

THE PIPERS
Standing Stones | Nearest Village: **St Buryan/Trewoofe**
Map: **SW 4351 2479** | Sheets: **E102 L203** | Lat: **50.064778N** | Long: **5.58559W**

Photo © Paul Blades

In legend, the Pipers are two unfortunate musicians who were petrified as they fled the Merry Maidens' Sabbath-breaking dance. The tallest of Cornwall's remaining standing stones, the pair are in neighbouring fields more than 90m (295ft) apart. The southwest stone is 4.6m (15ft) tall; the northeast stone, which leans at quite an angle, is 4.1m (13ft 5in).

CARN GLUZE   Alt Name: **Ballowall Barrow**   ⭐
Chambered Tomb | Nearest Village: **St Just**
Map: **SW 3552 3125** | Sheets: **E102 L203** | Lat: **50.12225N** | Long: **5.70148W**

Hidden for many years beneath mine waste, Carn Gluze was excavated in the late 19th century by William Copeland Borlase, apparently drawn here by miners' tales of mysterious lights and dancing fairies. This is an unusual multiphase site, perhaps originally an entrance grave that was later incorporated into a much larger and more complex structure, and further complicated by the inauthentic 19th-century restoration. Inside the barrow, within two concentric rings of walls, Borlase found five stone cists, some containing Bronze Age pottery and cremations. With imagination, the dramatic appearance of the original site can be visualized, its huge mound in a spectacular cliff-edge location.

Photo Adam Stanford © Aerial-Cam Ltd

BOSCAWEN-ÛN
Alt Name: **Nine Maidens**

Stone Circle | Nearest Village: **St Buryan** | Map: **SW 4122 2736**

Sheets: **E102 L203** | Lat: **50.08985N** | Long: **5.61927W**

Set in its own hedged enclosure amid the gorse and bracken, the secluded stone circle of Boscawen-ûn evokes a feeling of tranquillity in many visitors. It is famous for surrounding a central pillar that leans at a dramatic angle, giving the site something of the appearance of a sundial. Excavation in the 1860s found that this 2.5m (8ft) stone had been deliberately set up at an angle. As at some other sites in the

Photo © Nick Le Boutillier

region (such as Tregeseal, see opposite), there are 19 stones in the circle; it has been theorized that this number may reference the 18.6-year cycle of the moon's wanderings across the sky. The stones at Boscawen-ûn are all granite except for one of quartz, which Aubrey Burl suggested may have been used as a back-sight in observing the May Day sunrise. The stones of the circle vary in

height but are all positioned with smoother sides facing inward, and are evenly spaced except for a larger gap in the west, which is too small for a missing stone and may indicate a solar alignment (there is a similar feature at the nearby Merry Maidens circle, see page 36).

In 1986 Ian McNeil Cooke discovered carvings of two axes in the northeast face of the central pillar. Tom Goskar, who recently used photogrammetry to create a 3D model of the carvings, believes the axes might actually represent a pair of feet, as seen on the anthropomorphic stones of Brittany and Guernsey. He also discovered a pair of circular features similar to those identified as breasts on some Breton monuments, and suggests this might indicate the reuse of a Breton-style decorated stone at Boscawen-ûn.

Nearby | At SW 4148 2763, in a field 374m (1,227ft) northwest of the circle, is the 2.6m (8½ft) **Boscawen-ûn Field** standing stone, with the **Boscawen-ûn Hedge** stone at SW 4173 2772, 265m (870ft) further east, in the hedge lining the signed track to Boscawenoon Farm.

> "I should keep this a secret! The best time to visit Boscawen-ûn is on a quiet May evening when bluebells are still carpeting the circle. Something to hang on to while we endure the bleak days of winter." Angie Lake

TREGESEAL   Alt Names: **Dancing Stones, Nine Maidens**
Stone Circle | Nearest Village: **St Just**
Map: **SW 3866 3237** | Sheets: **E102 L203** | Lat: **50.1337N** | Long: **5.65841W**

A heavily restored circle in an atmospheric setting on the edge of moorland climbing to Carn Kenidjack, which here is a very distinctive feature on the skyline. There were once two or even three circles at Tregeseal lying next to each other on an east–west alignment, of which this 19-stone circle would have been the easternmost. Little trace remains of the other circles: the western or possibly central circle was cleared for agriculture in 1961, and sightings of cropmarks are the only indication

Photo © Paul Blades

of the third circle. Land management is controversial, as at some other Penwith sites (see page 41), as grazing cattle have loosened and dislodged stones and can discourage visitors. This circle is sometimes known as the Dancing Stones, referring to the common legend of maidens petrified when they broke the Sabbath.

Nearby | At SW 3901 3262, some 430m (1,410ft) ENE of the circle, are the **Kenidjack Common** holed stones. There are five stones here, one of them fallen and broken, with another stone to the northwest of the group. Follow the path from Tregeseal E stone circle, keeping to the lower path at each junction. The path passes a couple of tumuli, one of which is said to have a cist within it, the other the possible remains of a stone chamber.

CHÛN QUOIT   ★
Portal Dolmen | Nearest Village: **Madron**
Map: **SW 4022 3396** | Sheets: **E102 L203** | Lat: **50.14865N** | Long: **5.63771W**

Photo © Cazzy-Jane

A perfectly preserved and charming portal dolmen with a somewhat mushroom-like appearance, its round, domed capstone (with a cup-mark on top) extending over an enclosed chamber. High on Chûn Downs, within 300m (985ft) of Chûn Castle Iron Age hill fort, the site offers spectacular views down to the sea. In 2013 the Chûn Downs area was re-registered as common land following a campaign by Save Penwith Moors (see page 41).

MÊN-AN-TOL   Alt Name: **Crick Stone**
Holed Stone | Nearest Village: **Madron**
Map: **SW 4265 3494** | Sheets: **E102 L203** | Lat: **50.15851N** | Long: **5.60443W**

Photo © Nick Le Boutillier

Famously picturesque. The Cornish name means "stone with the hole", and the hole may be natural. As well as the uprights, there are six fallen stones here, some buried. The westernmost stone has been moved into line with the others at some point since 1815. William Borlase's 1749 plan suggests the stones formed part of an arc, perhaps of a circle, although it's unclear whether the holed stone was part of this or another structure. Being passed or crawling through the hole was once held to cure childhood rickets and tuberculosis, as well as aiding fertility, rheumatism or spinal problems in adults. There are also stories of a fairy guardian with the power to heal the sick. Recent changes in land management here have been very controversial (see opposite).

    Nearby | At SW 4269 3530, 362m (1,187ft) north of Mên-an-Tol, is the 2m (6½ft) **Mên Scryfa** ("inscribed stone"), which may date to the Bronze Age but was carved in the 5th–8th century AD with RIALOBRANI CUNOVALI FILI – "Royal Raven Son of the Glorious Prince". Over 1m (3ft 3in) of its length may be buried. At SW 4268 3592, 620m (less than ½ mile) north of Mên Scryfa, is the **Carn Galver round barrow**. At SW 4273 3600, incorporating one of the main tors of **Carn Galver**, are linear arrangements of large stones thought to be a Neolithic enclosure.

BOSKEDNAN   Alt Name: **Nine Maidens**
Stone Circle | Nearest Village: **Madron**
Map: **SW 4342 3513** | Sheets: **E102 L203** | Lat: **50.16055N** | Long: **5.5938W**

Photo © Jim Champion

The Boskednan stones stand on wild moorland, with the distinctive mound of Carn Galver a dominating feature on the horizon to the northwest and the Ding Dong mine a dramatic sight to the south. Boggy trackways lead here from Boskednan Farm and from Mên-an-Tol. The circle was restored a few years ago and there are now 11 stones, three of which are fallen, but there were once at least 19 – perhaps 22 or 23 – stones here, positioned with their smoothest sides facing inward. The stones average about 1.2m (4ft) in height apart from two taller ones in the northwest that would both have reached about 2m (6½ft) – one of which is now broken. SSE of the circle are the remains of a round cairn, a rocky mound around 10m (33ft) in diameter and 1.2m (4ft) high.

Nearby | At SW 4327 3531, 234m (768ft) northwest of Boskednan stone circle, and just off one of the footpaths coming from the direction of Mên-an-Tol and Mên Scryfa, is **Boskednan northern** kerbed cairn. This is one of several cairns in the area, with part of its retaining circle still visible.

MULFRA QUOIT
Portal Dolmen | Nearest Village: **Mulfra**
Map: **SW 4518 3536** | Sheets: **E102 L203** | Lat: **50.16337N** | Long: **5.56936W**

This portal dolmen is not as well preserved as Chûn Quoit but its impressive hilltop setting, with views down to the coast and St Michael's Mount, make it well worth the climb. Having lost one of its four supporting uprights, the capstone has slipped from the top of the monument and now leans against the chamber walls. Nearby are traces of a round barrow about 12m (39ft) across.

Nearby | At SW 4688 3802, up on the moors 3.2km (2 miles) northeast of Mulfra Quoit, is **Zennor Quoit**, which was nearly dismantled in 1861 to build a cow shed (the posts can still be seen). Its capstone has slipped and now leans on other stones. Unusually for a quoit, it has an impressive façade that forms an antechamber. Most easily approached via Higher Kerrowe and Mill Downs.

Fighting Moorland Enclosure in Penwith
Ian McNeil Cooke, Co-ordinator, Save Penwith Moors 2008–2018

Save Penwith Moors (SPM) was set up in July 2008 by six local residents concerned about government plans to enclose – for the first time ever – large areas of heathland in the Land's End peninsula with barbed-wire fencing, gates and cattle grids. This stockproofing of previously unfettered moorland – the iconic heartland of West Penwith – took place under "conservation grazing" agreements intended to benefit plants and wildlife.

As we feared would happen, cattle-rubbing at Tregeseal circle destabilized stones a dozen times over several years. The cattle also failed to trample down the bracken as intended. At Mên-an-Tol, cattle churned up an unsightly mess of deep mud and dung. There was public uproar after SPM complaints, but the cattle are still there. Carnyorth Common, where cattle continue to graze, is almost totally a Scheduled Ancient Monument with remnants of numerous prehistoric field systems and settlements.

As well as publicizing what was going on, SPM has forced a number of gates and cattle grids to be removed as well as preventing enclosure of several areas of heathland. Our campaign to re-register areas of formerly open-access moor as common land has resulted in the protection of nearly 500ha (1,236 acres) of moorland. These include areas with important archaeological sites, such as Chûn Downs, containing Chûn Quoit and Chûn Castle, as well as Carnyorth Common, site of Tregeseal circle and other features. We continue to campaign for the removal of stockproofing at Carn Galva, Mên-an-Tol, Lanyon Quoit and parts of Watch Croft. Find out more at: www.savepenwithmoors.com

41

LANYON QUOIT Portal Dolmen

Nearest Village: **Madron** | Map: **SW 4298 3369**
Sheets: **E102 L203** | Lat: **50.14743N** | Long: **5.59898W**

Photo © CazzyJane

A capstone on three uprights makes for an iconic if somewhat inauthentic structure, sited conveniently close to the road. Antiquarian drawings show that it used to be possible to ride a horse beneath the capstone, but the stones collapsed during a storm in 1815 and were re-erected in 1824 at a reduced height, with three uprights instead of four. Large stones at the southern end of a mutilated barrow may indicate cists or other structures.

Nearby | At SW 4281 3437, 700m (½ mile) NNW of Lanyon Quoit, is **Bosiliack** Bronze Age settlement. At least 12 hut circles were found here.

CARWYNNEN QUOIT Alt Names: **The Giant's Quoit, Pendarves Quoit,**

Devil's Frying Pan, Giant's Frying Pan | **Portal Dolmen** | Nearest Village: **Troon**
Map: **SW 6501 3721** | Sheets: **E104 L203** | Lat: **50.18818N** | Long: **5.29335W**

Photo © Paul Blades

Reduced to rubble by an earth tremor in 1967, Carwynnen Quoit was excavated and restored to its former glory in 2014 by the late Pip Richards and the Sustainable Trust. It is now an impressive sight, the huge capstone balanced on three uprights. Finds from the excavation included flint arrowheads and a greenstone pestle.

NINE MAIDENS

Stone Row | Nearest Village: **St Columb Major**
Map: **SW 9366 6759** | Sheets: **E106 L200** | Lat: **50.47117N** | Long: **4.90967W**

The Nine Maidens stand in an evenly spaced row in a field beside the busy A39, southwest of Wadebridge. The nine stones are of unworked local grey slate veined with quartz, some stones are only stumps while the tallest is 2m (6½ft). A further stone known as the Fiddler stands on a ridge to the northeast 678m (2,224ft) along the same alignment. Richard Carew, in his *Survey of Cornwall* (1602), noted that the stones were then known as the Sisters. The fields and hedges around here are littered with large stones, and there could once have been many more in this row.

Strange Experiences at Ancient Sites

Rune, Admin on the Megalithic Portal

In contemporary western society, people who report experiencing anything at all unusual at ancient sites or elsewhere are often derided, although other cultures have greater respect for "otherworldly" experiences. Much depends on your approach to a site. If you barge in looking for photo opportunities, you aren't likely to have much in the way of spiritual experiences. However, if you deliberately shift your consciousness by approaching a site as a sacred space, asking permission to enter and abiding by the answer, you are more likely to experience something special. Your intuition and perception will be heightened while your rational brain will be quieted, which is essential for any out-of-the-ordinary experience. Feeling ready for something unusual to happen doesn't guarantee that it will, but if it does then you are more likely to experience it fully. Be respectful. According to several accounts, a certain site in Ireland will deter disrespectful visitors by making them slip, trip or fall.

When you walk into a stone circle, you may notice an immediate change in ambience. This might manifest as a feeling of pure peace or perhaps as a change in temperature. Maybe the wind that had seemed biting now loses its chill, although the stones are too low to provide physical shelter. Some people have found that each site seems to have a boundary or boundaries around it, which manifest as three rings or bands. At the Ring of Brodgar, for example, you can feel a change in atmosphere at each band (at the top of the ditch, at the bottom of the ditch and at the top of the inner bank).

You can dowse for the bands or simply try experiencing them.

One experience that really stands out for me took place at Duloe, an absolutely enchanting stone circle, with its blocks of white quartzite. I was suffering from a fair bit of pain in my hips as I walked or rather hobbled into the circle. I was near the centre, just taking in the atmosphere, when I heard three short sounds, one after the other. I have no idea what they were – certainly not traffic noise, nor any sound I could place. Immediately after, the pain disappeared and I was overjoyed to be able to walk normally and really enjoy my time in the circle.

If a place gives you the creeps, or you feel that it is "evil", heed your instincts and go home. You are in the wrong frame of mind to connect with the site.

People report many different sensations from touching standing stones, ranging from pleasant tingles to electric shocks. They might identify warm spots, bands of different sensations, or even a pulse or a heartbeat in the stone. Some have been literally thrown off their feet through contact with a megalith, while others have experienced a flood of insight and knowledge akin to a sudden information download. Some people develop a real affinity with a site and are drawn to return to it again and again over the years. Of course, just because one person has had an experience, does not guarantee that anyone else can replicate it.

As a start, try leaning against a stone supporting yourself with just your head (be careful) or a hand. What happens?

ROUGH TOR

Megalithic Complex | Nearest Village: **Camelford**
Map: **SX 1449 8080** | Sheets: **E109 L200** | Lat: **50.59736N** | Long: **4.62257W**

On the summit of Rough Tor is a Neolithic tor enclosure built between two outcrops, with two lines of stone walling visible on the west and hut circles inside the enclosure. Rough Tor is a distinctive landmark within a complex prehistoric landscape, with the Bronze Age hut circles, enclosures and field systems to the northwest and on its southern slopes. Cairns and other burial monuments are scattered across the moorland and the stone circles of Fernacre, Stannon and Louden are close by, with Fernacre only 200m (656ft) away.

Photo © Paul Blades

ROUGH TOR LONG CAIRN

At SX 1430 8172, on the northern slopes of Rough Tor, is this huge stone cairn, 500m (1,640ft) long and 5–8m (16–26ft) wide, apparently aligned with the summit of the tor. Excavation showed that the structure is made up of two retaining walls of larger stones, infilled with rubble. Other stones buttress the walls. Alongside the cairn there is evidence of a stone "pavement". It was found the turf had been stripped from the site before the cairn was built, perhaps as a form of ritual cleansing of the land.

Nearby | At SX 1492 8131, 742m (just under ½ mile) ESE, is **Showery Tor** ring cairn, at the summit. A large, well-defined ring of stones surrounds a beautifully (and naturally) balanced pile of slabs.

The Rough Tor Triangle: A Theory

Roy Goutté, author, amateur archaeologist and founding member of TimeSeekers

Nestling neatly in the shadow of Rough Tor on Bodmin is the stone circle of Fernacre. Just 2km (under 1¼ miles) to the west is Stannon circle, and 800m (½ mile) to the southeast of Stannon is the third in this triangle of large Cornish circles – Louden. All three were probably built in the late Neolithic, although a lack of accurate dating evidence in some Cornish circles is a problem. Within their settings they all feature a single, large, triangular upright made of granite. It is these iconic Cornish tri-stones and their possible meaning and connection to Rough Tor that I would like to concentrate on. The three circles have so much in common, and are so close together, that it doesn't take much to figure out that they are likely to be contemporaneous, and possibly erected by the same people.

All are big by Cornish standards, made up of a large number of small stones. Stannon has around 70 in an irregular ring of straight sections, but originally there may have been 80 or more. Fernacre also has a large number of stones in its setting; Louden has fewer at 52, confirmed by our TimeSeekers volunteer clearance group in 2015. All three circles have been labelled as "ceremonial" in certain quarters, but I visualize ceremonial circles as displaying magnificent uprights in their settings, with a true look of grandeur. But that is not the case here. It almost seems that the builders used any size stone they could get their hands on. This suggests to me that each circle was a part of a larger design.

What is the meaning of the large tri-stones in these three settings? It was only when I was photographing the tri-stone of Louden circle with Rough Tor in the background, that their similarity in shape dawned on me. To my amazement, I witnessed the same at Stannon, and this made me wonder if the builders had replicated Rough Tor as best they could with a single tri-stone in their ring settings.

So, we have three large, irregular, similarly sized stone circles with similarly sized stones, all with a prominent tri-stone and all in close proximity. It would be easy to suggest that if the people of their time revered Rough Tor, then the tri-stones may have been chosen and placed in the circles as a focus of ceremonies.

Where the tri-stones are positioned within each circle could also tell a speculative but interesting tale. Remarkably, the tri-stone of the circle to the east (Fernacre) is positioned due east in the setting, and the tri-stone of the circle to the west (Stannon) is positioned due west in the setting. To complete the set, the tri-stone of Louden, the southernmost circle, is due south in its setting. Why would all three circles have their individual tri-stones on the side of the triangle they themselves form in the landscape? Draw a direct line between those three circles and note that they form a scalene triangle (no equal sides) which "by chance" (?) just happens to be a mirror image of Rough Tor! So, is this, then, the intention of the designers, rather than the building of individual circles? Are the circles demarcation points where boundaries joined and possibly ceremonies took place – or is that just speculation on my part? On a map it can be seen that most signs of prehistoric activity in the area – cairns, hut circles and field systems – lie within this triangle formed by the three stone circles.

Lines drawn between the three circles create a triangle that seems to mirror Rough Tor exactly

The tri-stone of Louden circle, with Rough Tor visible behind

Photos © Roy Goutté

FERNACRE

Stone Circle | Nearest Village: **St Breward**
Map: **SX 1447 7998** | Sheets: **E109 L200** | Lat: **50.58999N** | Long: **4.62245W**

Fernacre stands on desolate, boggy moorland, with Rough Tor rising dramatically up to the north, Brown Willy to the east and Garrow Tor to the south. It is a very large circle, in keeping with others in the region, of *c.* 70 stones, 39 of which still stand. The circle is somewhat flattened, around 46 × 44m (151 × 144ft). The granite stones are sunk into the peat and would have been more impressive when first erected. Access is much easier since the building of a private track from Middle Moor Cross to Fernacre Farm. The circle is just north of the track, due south of Rough Tor peak. Park at the sign and walk to the circle.

Photo © Andy Burnham

> "Close to the circle the road seems to veer off. Rather than walk around, I decided to walk directly to the stones across the moor. This turned out to be a bad idea. The moor suddenly felt like a magic carpet and gave way under my feet leaving me waist deep in a bog. Quite a scary experience!" Lee Price

STANNON

Stone Circle | Nearest Village: **St Breward**
Map: **SX 1257 8002** | Sheets: **E109 L200** | Lat: **50.58974N** | Long: **4.64928W**

On a sloping site on open moorland, just south of Stannon china clay works (now a landscaped reservoir) and visible from the track, Stannon is a large (41.5m/136ft diameter), unevenly spaced circle with 77 remaining stones of local granite. Of these, 47 still stand. The stones are unusually small, none more than 1m (3ft 3in) in height, and in some parts of the circle are placed very close together. As with most circles on this part of Bodmin, the largest stone is triangular in shape.

Nearby | At SX 1321 7950, on the track that runs southwest from Fernacre and 823m (½ mile) ESE of Stannon circle, is **Louden** stone circle. Thanks to clearance by the TimeSeekers group, about 40 stones are visible of the 52 they found. Five are still standing, including the large tri-stone.

Photo © CazzyJane

KING ARTHUR'S HALL
Rectangular Stone Enclosure | Nearest Village: **St Breward**
Map: **SX 1297 7764** | Sheets: **E109 L200** | Lat: **50.56849N** | Long: **4.64244W**

Photo © Cazzy Jane

Many prehistoric sites are associated locally with King Arthur, but this must be the most unusual. This mysterious and unique enclosure resembles a rectangular henge, its banks surrounding a marshy interior. There's an internal kerb of 56 visible stones, some taller than the bank and looking like chairs, giving the site its name. Clearance work revealed a retaining wall and a granite paved area, and suggested there might have originally been around 140 uprights. Various suggestions for the site's purpose include use as a mortuary enclosure, or as a reservoir.

KING ARTHUR'S DOWNS   Alt Names: **Emblance Down NW, Leaze NW**
Stone Circles | Nearest Village: **St Breward**
Map: **SX 1347 7751** | Sheets: **E109 L200** | Lat: **50.56748N** | Long: **4.63532W**

Follow the track eastward from King Arthur's Hall for about 500m (1,640ft) to find the remains of two adjacent, and very ruinous, circles. King Arthur's Downs NW (so called, although it is actually on Emblance Downs) is in better condition, about 23m (75ft) in diameter, with eight stones remaining of which six are still standing, including two triangular-shaped stones. Two more fallen, perhaps displaced stones are to be found in the centre of the circle. There may have been 15 stones in the circle originally. It's pretty wet here and the stones are often surrounded by large pools of water. The circle is sometimes described as "recently discovered" but was mentioned as early as 1860.

Just a few metres ESE, King Arthur's Downs SE (at SX 1349 7750) is a similar size but even more badly damaged. Four stones remain standing, while four others have fallen. Those closest to the wall are the most obvious.

LEAZE
Stone Circle | Nearest Village: **St Breward**
Map: **SX 1367 7729** | Sheets: **E109 L200** | Lat: **50.56557N** Long: **4.63239W**

47

Photo © Nick Le Boutillier

Some 300m (985ft) southeast from the King Arthur's Downs circles is a ruinous stone circle on private land. The site is bisected by a wall and 10 of the original 28 stones are still standing, with six fallen. The small stones (average height of 1.1m/3½ft) are strikingly regular and pillar-like.

STRIPPLE STONES

Stone Circle & Henge | Nearest Village: **Blisland**
Map: **SX 1435 7521** | Sheets: **E109 L200** | Lat: **50.5471N** | Long: **4.62176W**

Photo © Paul Blades

On private land on the southeast flank of Hawk's Tor are the remains of an interesting circle and henge that in 2015 was partially restored with the help of Roy Goutté. A field boundary wall that ran through the site was removed, a buried fallen stone was exposed and three stones were re-erected, bringing the total number of stones standing to seven out of the 16 that survive from the original 28. The 44.8m (147ft) stone circle is set within a 68.3m (224ft) henge that has a 4.6m (15ft) gap, possibly an entrance, at the WSW. It has been speculated that the 3.7m (12ft) fallen stone within the circle was used as a backsight from which an observer, guided by three semi-circular bulges on the edges of the henge, would have viewed the major northern moonrise at the NNE, the equinoctial sunrise at the east, and May Day sunset at the WNW.

Nearby | At SX 1311 7501, 1.3km (just over ½ mile) west, are the **Trippet Stones**. Of an original 26 or 28, eight still stand in the 33m (108ft) circle, with five fallen. The stones are bigger than is usual in Cornwall, with the tallest 1.6m (5ft 3in). The name "Trippet" may refer to the delicate footwork of a dancer, indicating that here too merrymakers were turned to stone for breaking the Sabbath.

LESKERNICK

Megalithic Complex | Nearest Village: **Altarnun**
Map: **SX 1871 7980** | Sheets: **E109 L201** | Lat: **50.58971N** | Long: **4.56252W**

There's plenty to see at Leskernick, on the saddle of land between Leskernick Hill and Beacon Hill. This beautiful setting on the eastern edge of Bodmin Moor is home to two stone circles, a long stone row and a large cairn, as well as settlements with numerous hut circles and enclosures on Leskernick Hill itself, which is enclosed by the region's highest and most iconic hills.

LESKERNICK 1 (SE)

This 30m (98ft) circle (at SX 1882 7964) was discovered in 1973. Its 20 remaining stones, which include a triangular one to the west, are mostly over 1.2m (4ft) long and are all fallen. There are stumps of seven further stones. The volunteer group led by Roy Goutté has uncovered buried stones, including the broken remains of a central stone and a possible cist.

Photo © Martyn Copcutt

LESKERNICK 2 (NW)

First recorded in 1983 by Peter Herring, and cleared in 2016 by the TimeSeekers volunteers, the 21m (70ft) circle 368m (1,207ft) northwest of Leskernick I (at SX 1858 7992) has 23 stones. Some of the stones uncovered during the clearance were so deeply buried they had to be covered up again so as not to be a hazard for walkers and animals. It has been suggested that the stones, which are noticeably smaller than in the southeast circle (only four stones are more than 1.2m/4ft here) may have been erected to draw attention to the large, almost central "whale-backed" stone, which may or may not have once stood erect itself.

Photo © Martyn Copcutt

LESKERNICK STONE ROW

Another recently cleared site, the row of 56 stones runs west–east from close to a cairn situated between the two Leskernick stone circles (at SX 1870 7986). The row has been recorded as 317m (1,040ft) in length, with 0.2m (8in) tall stones spaced at 4.5m (15ft) intervals. There's a stone setting or terminal at the western end, and the row appears to point directly at Brown Willy, Cornwall's highest hill, looking splendid on the horizon. During clearance work it was suggested that there are in fact two rows here, on slightly different alignments, with the tinners' gully (a relic of mining activity) dividing them. Stones 19 and 20 (counting from the west) are a twinned pair, and at the eastern end of the row, Roy Goutté's group discovered a possible cist.

LESKERNICK HILL SETTLEMENT

The remains of many huts and enclosures, as well as cairns and cists, survive on the southern flank of Leskernick Hill (around SX 1835 8000). In the late 1990s a project by University College London studied the area in detail, one of the first to apply cognitive archaeological ideas to a prehistoric landscape, in addition to traditional excavation and survey. The site was recently used in an experiment in multisensory archaeology and augmented reality, in which Stuart Eve created a GIS (geographic information system) model of the hill augmented with reconstructions of Bronze Age houses sized to fit the remains on the ground. Viewing the site on a screen with houses in position gave participants a new perspective on the settlement, which according to the report really "brought the landscape to life".

Nearby | At SX 2025 8073, about 1.6km (1 mile) ENE of the Leskernick circles, is **Westmoorgate** stone circle, north of the farm of the same name. Identified by Peter Herring in 2004, it has seven remaining stones in the southeastern arc. All are fallen but the line of the arc is obvious.

> "The views from the top of Leskernick Hill are unbelievable. This is a special place with the most wonderful, mainly Bronze Age settlement on the hill itself." Roy Goutté

NINE STONES

Stone Circle | Nearest Village: **Altarnun**
Map: **SX 2361 7814** | Sheets: **E109 L201** | Lat: **50.57629N** | Long: **4.49258W**

Photo © CazzyJane

Charming and unusually small (just 15m/49ft) for the area, the circle was restored in 1889. It's out on the open moor and livestock damage is a problem here, cows using the stones for scratching posts. The nine stones are granite; the central stone is probably a parish boundary stone, but could be original to the circle and moved to its present position. There may have been another stone in the large gap to the north.

Nearby | Just over 1km (0.6 miles) west of the Nine Stones, on a saddle to the west of Fox Tor, is **East Moor** stone row. Around 550m (1,800ft) long, it runs NNE to SSW (from SX 2237 7785 to SX 2257 7822), the stones mostly fallen. A large blocking stone stands some distance beyond the final stone at the southwest end.

THE HURLERS

Megalithic Complex | Nearest Village: **Minions**
Map: **SX 2583 7140** | Sheets: **E109 L201** | Lat: **50.5164N** | Long: **4.4581W**

Of this unusual group of circles William Camden wrote in 1587: "The neighbouring inhabitants term them Hurlers, as being by devout and godly error persuaded that they had been men sometime transformed into stones, for profaning the Lord's Day with hurling the ball." The three circles of shaped granite stones lie very close together on a northeast–southwest line, their smooth faces positioned inward. The recent Reading the Hurlers project discovered a large fallen stone that it's speculated may once have marked the start of a processional avenue to the Hurlers.

Photo © Thomas Marchhart

> "Heavy mists rolling in make for an otherworldly experience. Unnerving to watch the stone circles dart in and out of the fog." Merry Gordon

NORTHERN CIRCLE

A 34.7m (114ft) circle, with 15 stones remaining. Excavation has revealed the holes for 10 more stones, which are indicated by markers. In 2013 the Mapping the Sun project uncovered what was described as a "quartz causeway", an area of paving between this and the central circle, which had last been viewed during excavation in the 1930s.

CENTRAL CIRCLE

This is the largest of the circles, measuring 42 × 40.5m (137ft × 133ft). There are 14 stones standing and 14 markers to indicate where others stood. The stones in the central circle were hammered smooth, with chips from this activity found spread across the interior of the circle. The axis of this and the northern circle aligns northeast with Rillaton Barrow (see below).

Photo © CazzyJane

SOUTHERN CIRCLE

This is the smallest circle, at 32m (105ft) across, with nine stones remaining, of which seven are fallen. Its axis aligns with a cairn to the southwest.

THE PIPERS

This fine pair, petrified for playing music rather than sport, can be found 97.5m (320ft) WSW of the central circle (at SX 2571 7135), 2.1m (7ft) apart. One is 1.7m (5ft 5in) tall, the other 1.4m (4ft 9in).

RILLATON BARROW

Chambered Cairn | Nearest Village: **Minions**
Map: **SX 2602 7191** | Sheets: **E109 L201** | Lat: **50.52104N** | Long: **4.45567W**

At 35m (115ft) in diameter and 3m (10ft) high, this is the largest round barrow on Bodmin Moor, and the only one left of the four originally found here. It was in the cist here (rebuilt *c.* 1900) that the spectacular Rillaton gold cup was found in 1837, still intact thanks to having been protected within a ceramic vessel. (There's a legend that the priceless cup disappeared for some years,

Photo © PJ Photography

eventually re-emerging in George V's private collection, having been used for a time to store his collar studs! It is now in the British Museum.) The remains of a skeleton were also found, as well as other grave goods including an urn, a bronze knife and some glass beads. The entrance to the chamber is halfway up the eastern side of the mound (it has been suggested that this wasn't the primary burial) and the capstone can be clearly seen resting on the side slabs.

STOWE'S POUND

Prehistoric Settlement | Nearest Village: **Minions**
Map: **SX 2578 7247** | Sheets: **E109 L201** | Lat: **50.526N** | Long: **4.45931W**

There are two enclosures at Stowe's Pound, the southern, higher enclosure intersecting with a larger enclosure on lower ground to the north. The smaller, southern enclosure is said to have been used in medieval times as an animal pound, hence the name. This enclosure is bounded by a wall that links natural rock formations on the summit; this wall rises in height to 4.5m (14ft 7in), and can be as much as 4m (13ft) wide. Within the enclosure are some flat, turf-covered areas but few signs of occupation. The wall around the larger enclosure is lower, up to 1.5m (5ft) high, and there are up to 14 entrances. Around 110 hut circles have been identified within this northern enclosure, as well as 19 platforms cut into the ground.

Photo © Paul Blades

Nearby | At SX 2554 7055, just off the main road 800m (½ mile) southwest of Minions, is the **Longstone**, otherwise known as Long Tom. A cross has been carved on the head of this 2.8m (9ft) stone.

> "What a fantastic stone Long Tom is: slender and covered in some beautiful lichens."
> Martyn Copcutt

Under the Supermarket

Andy Burnham, founder and Editor of the Megalithic Portal

The remains of a prehistoric causewayed enclosure, now known as the Truro Eastern District Centre Neolithic Enclosure, were discovered in 2012 during building work on a future shopping and housing development. Initial findings suggest an early Neolithic date, with later activity including the deposition of late Neolithic grooved ware in pits. The finds included a stunning piece of Neolithic art, a slate disc carved with a chequerboard pattern on one side and lozenges with arrowhead decoration on the other.

This site was the first Neolithic causewayed enclosure to be found west of the Dorset–Devon border. There's nothing to see on the ground, as the site is now beneath a Waitrose supermarket. The slate disc is kept at the Royal Cornwall Museum in Truro.

TRETHEVY QUOIT
Alt Name: **Giant's House**

Portal Dolmen | Nearest Village: **St Cleer**

Map: **SX 2593 6881** | Sheets: **E109 L201** | Lat: **50.49316N** | Long: **4.45549W**

The impressive bulk and spectacular profile of this 2.8m (9ft) portal tomb make it one of Cornwall's best-known sites. Five massive uprights (one fallen inward) on a mound are topped by a huge capstone that has slipped from position and now leans at a dramatic angle. Interestingly, there is a small hole in the eastern corner of the capstone; it's speculated this might have been used for observing the heavens. One of the uprights protrudes, perhaps to create an antechamber at the front of the monument alongside another stone that has since been lost. "Trethevy" is Cornish for "place of the graves". John Norden recorded it in 1584: "a little howse raysed of mightie stones, standing on a little hill within a fielde".

Photo © Nick Le Boutillier

DULOE

Stone Circle | Nearest Village: **Duloe**

Map: **SX 2358 5831** | Sheets: **E107 L201** | Lat: **50.39812N** | Long: **4.48364W**

Cornwall's smallest stone circle, a lovely oval ring of eight large stones (the tallest 2.6m/8½ft), all of white quartz. One of the stones is fallen and broken. A Bronze Age urn with a horseshoe handle containing human bones was found here in the 19th century. A geophysical survey undertaken in 2013 and 2016 by the Southeast Kernow Archaeology Survey revealed several features within the circle strongly suggesting the existence of a cist. If confirmed, while cists have been found within stone circles in other parts of the country (notably Cumbria), this would be the first example in Cornwall. A previously unrecorded outer ditch was also discovered as well as small circular anomalies that may be evidence for cremations.

Photo © Jim Wearne

> "The most wonderful place, all white quartz – exquisite."
> Hamish

53

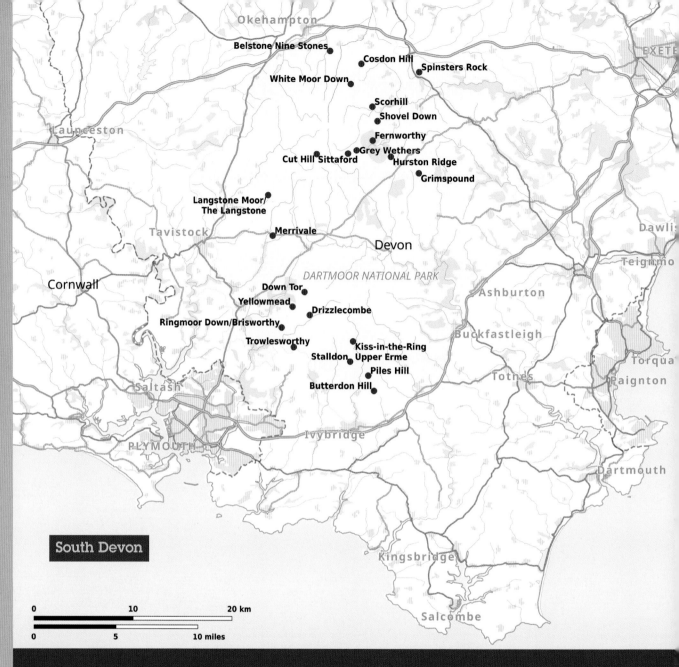

South Devon

| 0 | 10 | 20 km |
| 0 | 5 | 10 miles |

BUTTERDON HILL

Stone Row | Nearest Village: **Harford**
Map: **SX 6562 5962** | Sheets: **OL28 L202** | Lat: **50.421025N** | Long: **3.892994W**

This stone row some 2km (1¼ miles) long runs roughly north–south and links Piles Hill with Butterdon Hill, where it passes close to a large cairn. A path tracks the route of the row, mostly keeping to its western side. As is usual with the longer rows, the stones are in general relatively small – and many are well buried in undergrowth. Some of the larger stones were added as late as the 1800s.

PILES HILL
Stone Rows | Nearest Village: **Harford**
Map: **SX 6588 6111** | Sheets: **OL28 L202** | Lat: **50.43448N** | Long: **3.88987W**

An avenue of stones (large ones for Dartmoor), running for almost 1km (0.6 miles) east–west over the ridge of Piles Hill. Great fun can be had tracing the line of the stones, which are now mostly fallen and buried with just their tops showing or visible as a bump in the ground.

Nearby | At SX 6605 6085, 310m (1,017ft) east of Piles Hill runs the **Glasscombe Corner** row, which is a double row in part. At the northeast end is a damaged cairn circle, with no stones left standing.

STALLDON   Alt Names: **Stalldown, The Cornwood Maidens**
Stone Row | Nearest Village: **Cornwood**
Map: **SX 6323 6248** | Sheets: **OL28 L202** | Lat: **50.44617N** | Long: **3.92766W**

Photo © Martyn Copcutt

A truly impressive stone row containing 119 identified stones that follow a sinuously curving path over Stalldon Barrow hill for 859m (just over ½ mile). The stones are large for a Dartmoor row, with most over 1m (3ft 3in) and the tallest 2.3m (7ft 5in) high. The four biggest stones – the Cornwood maidens – can be seen for miles, appearing in the distance like walkers striding over the hilltop. The row was partly restored in the late 19th century; at the southern ends the slabs still lie on the ground. Apart from the circular cairn beside the row near the top of the hill, there are several other cairns to be seen, a couple still with their central cists.

There are superb views from the hilltop cairn circle, and the row is all the more spectacular at sunset.

Nearby | At SX 6366 6228, some 470m (1,541ft) ESE of Stalldon Row and up on the top of Stalldown Barrow, is the large **Hillson's House** cairn, which has been used over the years as a shelter.

> **"Wild moorland stretches off to the north, while to the south, way below, is a patchwork of fields and then the beautiful blue sea. Plymouth Sound, with its ships, can be seen to the southwest."** Martyn Copcutt

UPPER ERME

Stone Row | Nearest Village: **Cornwood** | Map: **SX 6352 6447**
Sheets: **OL28 L202** | Lat: **50.46413N** | Long: **3.9243W**

This is the longest ancient stone row in Britain, and possibly the world. At 3,386m (just over 2 miles), it stretches from Kiss-in-the-Ring stone circle up to a cairn near the top of Green Hill, crossing the river twice. Thanks to its remote location, about 1,000 stones have survived, which is likely to be around half the original number. As with most Dartmoor stone rows, the stones are rather small (about 0.5m/1½ft above the modern turf), and it can be hard to see them in summer when the vegetation is at its most exuberant. A path and darker grass by the stones show the direction of the alignment. The site is very exposed and the moor is almost featureless out here: avoid in bad weather.

Photo © Graeme Field

KISS-IN-THE-RING   Alt Names: **Upper Erme Stone Circle, Stall Moor**

Stone Circle | Nearest Village: **Cornwood**
Map: **SX 6351 6444** | Sheets: **OL28 L202** | Lat: **50.46386N** | Long: **3.92443W**

At the southern end of Upper Erme stone row, Kiss-in-the-Ring stone circle is a long desolate walk from anywhere. It's well worth the effort, though. The tallest stone in this 16–17m (52ft 6in–56ft) circle is 1.5m (5ft 3in) high and most are less than 1m (3ft 2in) tall. There are 26 stones, but, as at all the best circles, it's hard to count them and you may come up with a different result! The stones are unevenly spaced, with more on the western side, but none is thought to be missing. There's a low barrow in the centre. The views south over the Erme valley are lovely, and the four large stones (the Cornwood Maidens) at the northern end of Stalldon row can clearly be seen, as can the Upper Erme row.

Photo © Martyn Copcutt

TROWLESWORTHY
Megalithic Complex | Nearest Village: **Shaugh Prior**
Map: **SX 5765 6398** | Sheets: **OL28 L202** | Lat: **50.4576N** | Long: **4.00744W**

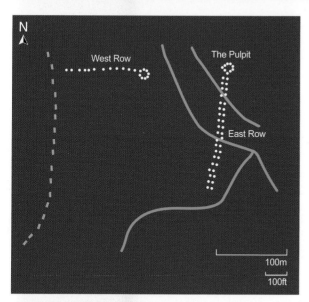

N

West Row

The Pulpit

East Row

100m
100ft

Photo © Martyn Copcutt

On the lower slopes of Trowlesworthy Tor, above the boggy land around the Blacka Brook, are a number of rows and cairns. To the north of the features described below, the remains of a large settlement can be seen, with several big enclosures walled with large slabs, and hut circles (remains on higher ground are in the best condition).

TROWLESWORTHY EAST ROW

The eastern of the two rows is a splendid double avenue that winds its way diagonally across the hillside for 127m (416ft) from SX 5762 6383. Most of the original stones still remain, and are generally larger than is typical for Dartmoor avenues. A couple of leats cut through the avenue, the higher one now dry and largely filled in, but the lower still very wide, which makes following the line of the stones quite tricky.

THE PULPIT

This 6.7m (22ft) circle stands at the northern end of the double row (at SX 5765 6398), all eight stones still upright. The tallest stone is positioned where the avenue joins the circle.

TROWLESWORTHY WEST ROW

The western, single row runs 82m (269ft) downhill from its cairn and circle (at SX 5755 6398). There are 44 stones remaining out of perhaps 50 originals. The row curves toward the south before terminating at a 1.3m (4ft 2in) high triangular block. Unusually, some of the stones are set across the line of the row, rather than along it. The earthwork visible a few metres from the southern end of the row has been confused with a barrow but is actually a pillow mound, created to farm rabbits and not prehistoric. At its eastern end is a 7m (23ft) round cairn, surrounded by a ring of stones.

BRISWORTHY

Stone Circle | Nearest Village: **Shaugh Prior**
Map: **SX 5646 6549** | Sheets: **OL28 L202** | Lat: **50.47161N** | Long: **4.0241W**

Photo © Martyn Copcutt

An attractive restored 24.7m (81ft) circle, with 24 stones surviving of an original 42. The stones increase in height from the south to the north, with the tallest being 1.1m (3ft 8in) high, and the flat sides of the stones face inward. A bank is visible around the northeastern quadrant of the circle and LIDAR imagery has shown this to extend around almost the entire circle. Visitors to the site have commented on various features that make this circle an unusual one, such as the broad stones, the bank and the hillside position.

RINGMOOR DOWN

Megalithic Complex | Nearest Village: **Shaugh Prior**
Map: **SX 5640 6580** | Sheets: **OL28 L202** | Lat: **50.47438N** | Long: **4.02506W**

On the open moor of Ringmoor Down, to the north of Brisworthy, an impressive collection of ancient sites are to be found. These include Ringmoor Down circle and row, and several cairns and settlements.

RINGMOOR DOWN CAIRN CIRCLE

At SX 5633 6581, 345m (1,132ft) uphill northwest of Brisworthy stone circle, is the inauthentically restored Ringmoor Down cairn circle. Some of its 11 stones are not original (it's said to have had five). Despite their diminutive height (1m/3ft 3in or less), the position of the circle in its tremendous setting at the top of the moor means it's visible against the skyline. There is a cairn in the centre of the circle.

RINGMOOR STONE ROW

The stone row was apparently also subject to an ill-advised restoration in 1909 and as a result little is known as to its original length or format. It's currently 369m (1,210ft) long, heading north from the circle, in some places a single row and sometimes a double. None of the southern stones was standing prior to the restoration, all having been affected by medieval ploughing.

CAIRNS

The remains of several cairns are nearby, the most impressive of which is Ringmoor Down Cairn 2, a 5m (16ft) cairn found at SX 5659 6576, 264m (866ft) east of Ringmoor Down circle. It has an intact rectangular cist and the large coverstone is still partly in place.

Photo © Martyn Copcutt

DRIZZLECOMBE

Megalithic Complex | Nearest Village: **Sheepstor**
Map: **SX 5921 6702** | Sheets: **OL28 L202** | Lat: **50.48603N** | Long: **3.98595W**

Wild ponies may be your only companions at this fantastically varied complex, acclaimed by some as the best on Dartmoor. The site includes three long stone rows and over 20 cairns, dramatically sited on moorland rising to Higher Hartor Tor. Each of the rows leads up to a cairn and, at the other end, down to a terminal pillar. Row 1 is a single row at either end but a double row for almost a third of its 150m (492ft) length. At SX 5899 6694, some 100m (328ft) northwest of Row 1's terminal stone, is Stone 4. This is possibly a terminal stone for a fourth row that was never built, although it is only 1m (3ft 3in) tall, so may have been part of another structure, possibly a stone circle. On higher ground, the remains of Bronze Age enclosures and hut circles can be found. The picture (below right) shows Row 1 with its terminal stone. In the distance the terminal stones of the other two rows are visible.

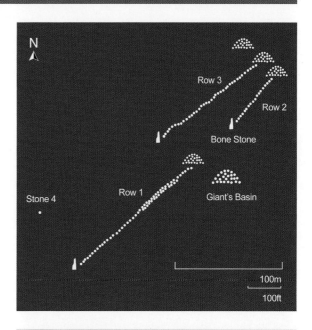

GIANT'S BASIN

At SX 5920 6695, to the southeast of Rows 2 and 3, is the Giant's Basin, a massive, damaged cairn measuring 22m (71ft) across and 3m (10ft) high. It has been reduced from its original height by 1m (3ft 3in) or more. Several smaller cairns can be found around the perimeter and in the surrounding area.

BONE STONE

The characterful stone closing Row 2 is named the Bone Stone for its unusual shape. At 4.3m (14ft), this is the tallest standing stone on Dartmoor – and some say by far the finest in the west of England! The carvings on the northeastern face, resembling Chinese characters, were apparently put there by students in the 1950s.

Photo © Paul Blades

59

YELLOWMEAD

Stone Circles | Nearest Village: **Sheepstor**
Map: **SX 5748 6784** | Sheets: **OL28 L202** | Lat: **50.49298N** | Long: **4.01063W**

Photo © Sandy Gerrard

Restored in 1921, these four concentric circles of stones of varying size occupy a tremendous moorland location with views up to Sheepstor, Peek Hill and Sharpitor. The innermost circle, which is formed of the largest stones, set close together, once enclosed a cairn that now is barely visible. A double stone row heads in a southwest direction from the circles, and it is possible that outliers on the western side were once part of further rows. A short distance uphill to the northeast from these circles is the remains of a small cairn, with a surrounding ring of stones. From parking near the building known as the Scout Hut, it is a very boggy 20-minute walk to the circles.

DOWN TOR   Alt Name: **Hingston Hill**

Cairn Circle & Stone Row | Nearest Village: **Sheepstor**
Map: **SX 5868 6927** | Sheets: **OL28 L202** | Lat: **50.50612N** | Long: **3.99427W**

This stone row 349m (1,145ft) long undulates with the contours of the land, rising at both ends from a central low point. The drama of the uphill approach to the stone circle is enhanced by an increase in the size of the stones as the row leads up to an impressive 2.7m (9ft) terminal pillar just before the circle. Cairns lie west of this stone. The circle itself, composed of small stones (about 0.5m/1½ft in height), encloses a ruined cairn. A compass is useful for the 2km (1¼ mile) walk east from the car park at the northeast end of Burrator Reservoir.

> "My new favourite site. Simply amazing!"
> Jeff Demetrescu

Photo © Martyn Copcutt

The Stone Rows of Dartmoor

Sandy Gerrard, archaeologist and author of the English Heritage Book of Dartmoor

It is currently thought there are around 295 surviving prehistoric stone rows in Britain, with at least a further 30 known from documentary sources but now completely destroyed. The densest concentration of rows is on Dartmoor, where about 86 have been identified, the shortest (currently thought to be Merrivale's Row 4, see page 63) measuring a mere 2.97m (9ft 9in), while the longest, Upper Erme (see page 56), extends for 3,386m (just over 2 miles).

Stone rows are notoriously difficult to date. Radiocarbon-dating of a stone in the row at Cut Hill indicates that it had perhaps been erected and toppled some time before 2360BC. This date is consistent with field evidence elsewhere on the moor demonstrating that the rows at Assycombe, Hook Lake, Hurston Ridge, Leeden Tor, Yar Tor and at least one of the rows at Shovel Down are all earlier than middle Bronze Age fields and enclosures that partly overlie them.

The form of these rows varies considerably and their identification is often complicated by their similarity to field boundaries, natural outcrops or lines of stones raised in historic times. Some include only three stones, while others are formed by hundreds. Some are exclusively large uprights, others a mixture of stone sizes, and still others very small stones that barely protrude through the turf. All the long rows (more than 200m/650ft long) are sinuous in form and even some of the shorter rows are far from straight. The spacing of stones varies considerably, though this may sometimes be a result of later damage, and there is no dominant orientation or altitude.

The purpose of stone rows remains enigmatic. Many, as at Merrivale, are directly associated with funerary monuments, which implies they may have been the focus for ritual activity. The evidence suggests that the rows are earlier than the terminal cairns; the upper end of Merrivale's Row 3, for example, is incorporated into a later cairn. The fact that so many cairns are not in perfect alignment with the rows may also indicate that they are not precisely contemporary with each other and were generally built in two stages.

Recent work has indicated that many rows were carefully positioned to provide particular definable visual links with the landscape. Various features in the surrounding hillsides may have been significant to the builders of Conies Down row, for example. If you walk south down the row, the five distinct tors visible on the horizon to the southwest are hidden one by one, with Great Mis Tor only disappearing as the end of the row is reached. Observations about the rows' placement in the landscape, as well as their positioning in relation to contemporary routes (as at Lakehead Hill), may provide vital clues to their purpose.

If we accept that the reason why so many stone rows have survived on Dartmoor is because of the difficult terrain here, then we must also conclude that there were originally thousands throughout Britain and we are left with just a tiny fraction. Certainly the rows of smaller stones would not have survived in areas that were more intensively farmed.

Find out more about stone rows at:
stonerows.wordpress.com

MERRIVALE   Alt Names: **The Plague Market, The Potato Market**
Megalithic Complex | Nearest Village: **Princetown**
Map: **SX 5548 7477** | Sheets: **OL28 L191** | Lat: **50.55477N** | Long: **4.0415W**

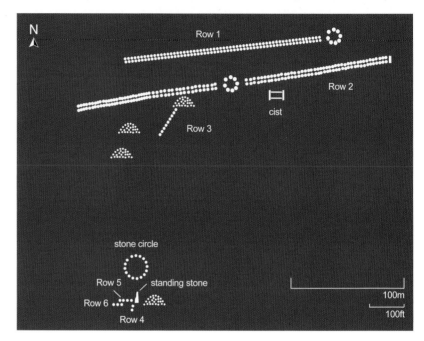

In a stunning setting above the River Walkham, Merrivale lives up to its name ("pleasant valley"), and, for Dartmoor, is pretty accessible. This complex prehistoric landscape, includes multiple stone rows, a stone circle, a large standing stone, many burial cairns and cists, and a prehistoric settlement. It's also known as the Plague Market, this name deriving from the story that provisions were left here for the people of Tavistock when the town was isolated during an outbreak of plague in 1625. If you park by the B3357 and walk up, you'll pass through part of the Bronze Age settlement (there are more huts on the other side of the road). There are around 36 huts altogether, and the settlement is thought to have been in use for some 1,500 years. There is also evidence of medieval and post-medieval activity here, such as a large, flat apple-crusher stone, used in cider-making.

ROWS 1, 2 AND 3

Photo © Angie Lake

Rows 1 and 2, the two double stone rows, march roughly east to west across the moor and are almost parallel, about 25m (82ft) apart. A 19th-century leat (artificial stream) separates them. Row 1 is now 183m (600ft) long and probably once extended further to the west. There is a blocking stone at its eastern end, as well as the remains of a kerbed cairn. Row 2 is a fine 263.5m (863ft) double row, with blocking stones at both ends; the large, triangular one to the east is particularly impressive. There is a kerbed cairn at its centre, built on top of the row. A fine cist (pictured, left) lies just south of Row 2, close to a single stone row (Row 3) that ends in a small cairn. The terminal slab of the row is set within the south side of the cairn, indicating that the row predates the cairn. This row extends for at least 60m (196ft).

Photo © Jim W

STONE CIRCLE

At SX 5535 7463, south of Row 3, is a stone circle with 11 stones no more than 0.5m (1½ft) tall.

STANDING STONE

At SX 5536 7459, 42m (137ft) SSE of the circle, is a tall, slender stone, 3m (10ft) high. About 10m (33ft) to the east is a fallen slab, 2m (6½ft) in length, which may have been a companion, although there is no evidence it originally stood. Erected in 1895, it fell over not long after.

ROWS 4, 5 AND 6

These are all short rows close to the standing stone. The stones are generally quite small and therefore it can be hard to figure out exactly what's going on. Row 4 is south of the standing stone and runs northeast–southwest. There are four small stones. Row 5 is west of the standing stone and in line with it, running east–west, so the standing stone appears at the eastern end of the row. There are six stones of various sizes in a 7m (23ft) alignment. Row 6 is south of Row 5 and runs east–west, heading further west than Row 5.

Photo © CazzyJane

LANGSTONE MOOR
Stone Circle | Nearest Village: **Peter Tavy**
Map: **SX 5563 7822** | Sheets: **OL28 L191** | Lat: **50.58581N** | Long: **4.04072W**

Photo © Martyn Copcutt

Splendidly situated high above the Walkham valley, this circle would once have been an imposing sight on the skyline, but most of the stones were destroyed when they were used for target practice during World War II. The circle is still worth visiting for the views in all directions (including, to the south, to Merrivale). It is in the Merrivale live firing range, so check range opening times beforehand.

THE LANGSTONE
Standing Stone | Nearest Village: **Peter Tavy**
Map: **SX 5502 7874** | Sheets: **OL28 L191** | Lat: **50.59033N** | Long: **4.04953W**

Photo © Martyn Copcutt

Peppered with bullet holes during target practice in World War II, this stone has a distinctive lightning-strike shape. It is in the Merrivale live firing range, so check range opening times beforehand. Beware of attempting a direct route from here to the Langstone Moor circle, as a nasty mire lies in between.

Nearby | At SX 5424 7867, 780m (just under ½ mile) west of the Langstone, on top of **White Tor**, is a fortified enclosure with cairns, huts and other structures dating back to the Neolithic.

GRIMSPOUND ★
Prehistoric Settlement | Nearest Village: **Widecombe-in-the-Moor**
Map: **SX 7007 8090** | Sheets: **OL28 L191** | Lat: **50.6133N** | Long: **3.8378W**

Viewed from Hookney Tor or Hameldown, Grimspound is an impressive sight on the moor, enclosed by a wall that averages 3m (10ft) in width. This is an accessible and fascinating Bronze Age settlement with 24 hut circles within the walls, and at least nine more outside, to the southeast. In the southeast there's a dramatic entrance, with a 2m (6½ft) wide paved passage running between walls that at this point are over 2m (6½ft) high. Excavation here in 1894 unearthed hearths, benches, pottery, cooking stones and other items that evoke the day-to-day experience of domestic life several millennia ago. It's been suggested that the name Grimspound relates, as with other sites (such as Grim's Dyke), to the

Photo © CazzyJane

god Woden, but it seems this place name was recorded for the first time in 1797. Some of the reconstruction that took place here in the 1890s is now thought to be inauthentic.

Nearby | At SX 6898 8082, around 1km (0.6 miles) west of Grimspound, **Challacombe** is an unusual triple stone row, badly damaged at its northern end by tin-mining activity in Chaw Gully. The row has been restored and now stretches for some 160m (528ft). The three rows draw closer together at the southern, uphill end, where there is a large blocking stone. In local legend, Chaw Gully is a dangerous place inhabited by malevolent spirits, where rumours of buried gold have led many greedy treasure hunters to their doom.

HURSTON RIDGE ★

Stone Rows | Nearest Village: **Postbridge**
Map: **SX 6726 8244** | Sheets: **OL28 L191** | Lat: **50.62714N** | Long: **3.8775W**

A rarity for Dartmoor, as this double row is likely to be complete and undamaged, with all 99 stones in 49 pairs (plus one blocking stone) still in place. It's set in a great location with wonderful views north and east. The rows run from a ruined cairn (where the Hurston Ridge urn was found in 1900) down the ridge for about 150m (492ft) NNE. The end stone of the east row is almost 2m (6½ft) tall, and can be seen for miles around. Many of the pairs are opposing slabs and pillars. A Bronze Age enclosure wall cuts through the avenue about two-thirds of the way down.

Photo © Martyn Copcutt

"A middle Bronze Age enclosure was built across the row, presumably after it was abandoned. The large recumbent stones form part of the enclosure boundary. Note that these are bigger than the stones used to build the row."
Sandy Gerrard

GREY WETHERS

Stone Circles | Nearest Village: **Postbridge**
Map: **SX 6387 8313** | Sheets: **OL28 L191** | Lat: **50.63192N** | Long: **3.9262W**

Photo © Christopher Bickerton

Climb Sittaford Tor for tremendous views of these two beautiful circles, and look out for skylarks. The circles were restored by Rev Sabine Baring-Gould (who wrote "Onward Christian Soldiers") in 1909, following excavation toward the end of the 19th century, when a layer of charcoal was discovered to cover the original ground surface. Both circles, one positioned almost due north of the other, are about 33m (108ft) in diameter, and would have consisted of 30 stones; today the southern circle has 29 stones, the northern one 20 stones. You can park at Fernworthy Reservoir and walk through the forest, taking in Fernworthy stone circle before turning left on to moorland to find the Grey Wethers. It's a long, often wet walk that offers great rewards.

> **"One of the more common legends (told to me by my father) about Grey Wethers is that the stones were once sold to a drunk farmer as a well-behaved flock of sheep!"**
> Matt Impey

FERNWORTHY Alt Name: **Froggymead**

Megalithic Complex | Nearest Town: **Chagford**
Map: **SX 6548 8410** | Sheets: **OL28 L191** | Lat: **50.64101N** | Long: **3.9038W**

At Fernworthy you'll find a stone circle and several stone rows with terminal cairns. The setting in a modern plantation clearing is atmospheric but can be very wet and boggy, justifying the site's alternative name of Froggymead.

FERNWORTHY STONE CIRCLE

Photographs from before the trees were planted show that Fernworthy, like the Grey Wethers, once stood in an open landscape. There are 29 stones in the 19m (62ft) circle (slightly flattened in the north), 26 of which are standing. The largest is about 1.2m (4ft) high. As at Grey Wethers, excavation found charcoal all over the interior of the circle. Several cairns surround the circle, including one some 73m (240ft) to its east, visible as a low mound and originally surrounded by a stone circle, of which only three stones remain. Excavated in 1898, it contained a central pit packed with stones and a bronze spearhead or knife, a flint knife, a button, and a Beaker-type food vessel.

STONE ROWS AND CAIRNS

A double row of charmingly petite stones starts 140m (460ft) north of the circle, extending for 101m (331ft) and ending at a cairn (at SX 6554 8433) with a cist and a large stone. Much of the row has been destroyed by tree planting. South of the stone circle are two badly damaged double rows. The southwest row is the better preserved, with a cairn toward the northern end (at SX 6547 8410). The small stones of the southeast row are hard to see among the tree stumps. There's a terminal cairn at its northern end (at SX 6549 8409).

Nearby | At SX 6690 8400, on the edge of the Fernworthy Reservoir, is **Metherall** prehistoric settlement, where hut circles and enclosure walls can be seen. Four of the eight huts are now usually underwater but can be seen when the reservoir level falls during prolonged dry weather.

SITTAFORD

Stone Circle | Nearest Village: **Postbridge**
Map: **SX 6301 8281** | Sheets: **OL28 L191** | Lat: **50.62884N** | Long: **3.93823W**

The first stone circle to be found on the high moor in more than 100 years, Sittaford was discovered by Alan Endacott in 2007. It's about 300m (985ft) SW of Sittaford Tor, north of the reave which runs along the summit ridge. Follow this wall, and look out for the standing stone built into it; probably originally an outlier for the circle. There are 30 fallen stones in a 30m (98ft) circle. Be aware that it's always extremely wet and boggy up here, even after weeks of fine weather.

Photo © CazzyJane

CUT HILL

Stone Row | Nearest Village: **Postbridge**
Map: **SX 5992 8275** | Sheets: **OL28 L202** | Lat: **50.62757N** | Long: **3.98187W**

Photo © Guy Wareham

It is hard to get to this fallen stone row, discovered in 2004 by Tom Greeves on Cut Hill, one of the highest and most isolated parts of Dartmoor. Nine fallen stones have been found, some exposed by peat cutting and others still buried. Carbon-dating of peat suggests that at least one of the stones had fallen (or been placed flat) by 3350–3100BC, an earlier date than had previously been suggested for stone rows. The regular placement of the fallen stones, which Greeves compared to railway sleepers, may indicate that they were placed that way, even if at some point they had been standing (as is indicated by packing stones found at the end of at least one stone). Be prepared for a walk of about two hours, whichever direction you approach from.

The Cist on Whitehorse Hill

Andy Burnham, founder and Editor of the Megalithic Portal

Thanks to its remote moorland location, it was not until the 1990s that the Bronze Age stone cist on Whitehorse Hill was discovered, undisturbed by human activity. Erosion had partially exposed the site to the elements and the contents of the chamber were not expected to have survived, but the results of excavation in 2011 were astounding.

Archaeologists found the cremated remains of a young adult, thought to be a woman interred some time around 1730–1600BC, the cremation wrapped in the pelt of a brown bear and secured with a copper pin. More than 200 beads were found, some of non-local clay and amber, as well as a braided woven band or bracelet of cow hair studded with tin beads (the earliest examples of tin objects found on Dartmoor), a textile fragment with delicate leather fringing – possibly a belt, and unique in Europe – and a woven basket. Usually this sort of organic material has long since rotted away, so the finds (preserved by the peat in which the cist was buried) are quite remarkable. Two pairs of labrets or ear studs are the only ones to have been found in the southwest, the earliest evidence of woodturning in the UK.

The finds offer insights into Bronze Age life, from the existence of trading networks that brought amber beads to Dartmoor, to personal adornment styles to the range of crafting techniques practised. Replicas of some of the finds can be seen at the National Park Visitor Centre in Postbridge.

SHOVEL DOWN

Megalithic Complex | Nearest Town: **Chagford**
Map: **SX 6595 8599** | Sheets: **OL28 L191** | Lat: **50.65811N** | Long: **3.89784W**

Less than 1.6km (1 mile) from Scorhill stone circle (see page 71), the Shovel Down complex includes a stone circle, a four-ringed cairn circle, various rows, both double and single, a very large standing stone, several cairns and the remains of a prehistoric settlement. You can park at Batworthy Corner, right up on the moor, and then it's a short walk along a fairly well-defined trackway to the first of the sites.

FOURFOLD CIRCLE

At the upper, southern end of Row 2 (at SX 6595 8603) four concentric rings of stone slabs surround a central pit, probably a robbed cist. Originally set in a *c.* 9m (30ft) mound, most of the stones have been taken for wall building, enabling the construction of the cairn to be seen. Although enticingly named, the structure is rather smaller and much less impressive than the Yellowmead fourfold (see page 60).

STONE CIRCLE

Unusually positioned on a slope, and perhaps the oldest of the monuments at Shovel Down, the badly damaged stone circle (at SX 6582 8620) lies to the west of the northerly end of Row 3. Three standing flat-topped slabs remain of this 18m (59ft) circle, along with three fallen stones which were probably part of the circle.

STONE ROWS

There are six stone rows, five of them double rows, and some in a ruinous state. At the top end of Row 2 is a large pair of fallen stones, one of which has parish markers cut into it. Running up the hillside to the south, where it terminates at a cairn, Row 4 is the most complete of the

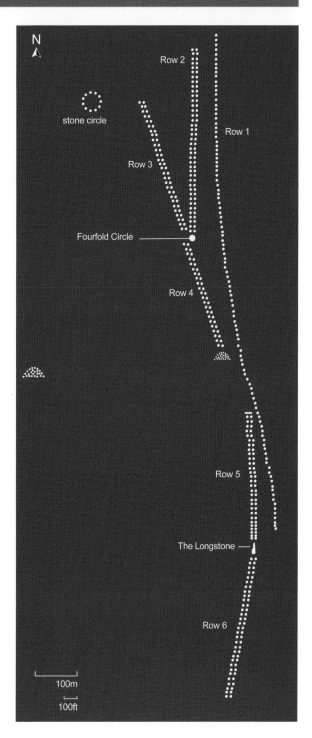

Photo © CazzyJane

alignments and about 120m (393ft) long, with nicely paired stones.

Although there's not much left of it, Row 6 originally ran south of the Longstone for 170m (557ft) to the surviving stone of the Three Boys. South of here, another alignment (of which nothing now remains) ran toward Fernworthy. Leaning so far as to be almost fallen, the Three Boys stone faces across the southern end of Row 6.

West of the rows, circles, cairns and standing stones are the remains of a settlement. The remains of four or five huts can be seen, with associated field systems and boundary walls, some of which are made from massive edge-set slabs.

THE LONGSTONE

This splendidly enormous standing stone, set in a slight dip in the landscape (at SX 6603 8568), is over 3m (10ft) tall. It possibly once formed a blocking stone at the end of Row 5, as it is set square on to the rows. Parish boundary markings have been carved into three of its faces.

> "The Longstone is said to revolve slowly at sunrise, so as to warm each of its faces." Martyn Copcutt

Nearby | At SX 6653 8633), around 670m (almost ½ mile) east of Shovel Down, is the **Kestor** settlement, where the hillside is covered with hut circles, field systems and boundary walls. Some of this walling, made of massive edge-set slabs, is still in use to mark boundaries today. Reused in the Iron Age and the medieval period, the site includes major Bronze Age remains, as well as evidence of settlement dating back to the Neolithic and even earlier.

At SX 6639 8685, just short of 1km (0.6 miles) northeast of Shovel Down, the **Round Pound** settlement is an impressively massive construction, around which the local road curves. A huge external wall, up to 4m (13ft) wide and 2m (6½ft) high, encloses a pound including a large hut circle with paved entrance, stone sill and steps still visible. Outside the pound, to the north, is a walled lane also made of massive slabs. The site was reused during the Iron Age.

Photo © CazzyJane

SCORHILL

Stone Circle | Nearest Town: **Chagford**

Map: **SX 6545 8739** | Sheets: **OL28 L191** | Lat: **50.67058N** | Long: **3.90542W**

A dramatic setting, especially magnificent in low sun, makes this 27m (89ft) circle (its name pronounced "Scorral") a very worthwhile visit. Approached from the north, the stones resemble a large congregation of people on the slopes of the moor. Of an original 65–70 stones, 34 remain, of which 25 still stand. Two cart tracks pass through the circle, which some feel adds to the sense of drama. The stones are unevenly spaced, with the tallest, at 2.5m (8ft), in the northwest. A huge fallen stone, 1.8m (6ft) long and 1.5m (5ft) wide, lies at the SSW. The Bradford leat partly encircles the circle and can be a challenge to cross. To the southwest the leat has been repaired using several large stones taken from the circle. It's a short walk from Batworthy Corner, over the clapper bridge, or a small parking area is available at Scorhill Farm.

Photo © Angie Lake

WHITE MOOR DOWN   Alt Name: **Little Hound Tor**

Stone Circle | Nearest Village: **South Zeal**

Map: **SX 6328 8961** | Sheets: **OL28 L191** | Lat: **50.69002N** | Long: **3.93693W**

Photo © Cazzy Jane

A truly lovely stone circle, reconstructed in 1896, in a desolate but spectacular setting between Little Hound Tor and Hound Tor. You'll need a map, and it's a tough 4km (2.5 mile) mostly uphill walk, which can be dangerously boggy in wet weather. However, those who make the effort on a fair day are rewarded by an impressive site, with fantastic views. There are 18 stones remaining of a probable 19, one of which is fallen, arranged with their smoother sides inward in a 20m (66ft) diameter circle. The White Moor Stone stands 150m (492ft) to the southeast; 1.7m (5½ft) in height, it's a parish boundary stone, but may be much older and is possibly associated with the circle. Between this stone and the circle are the remains of a cairn.

> **"In wet weather, the extensive mire just to the northeast of the circle threatens to engulf the walker who strays from the high ground to the west. Beware!"** Martyn Copcutt

COSDON HILL

Stone Rows | Nearest Village: **South Zeal**
Map: **SX 6434 9159** | Sheets: **OL28 L191** | Lat: **50.70807N** | Long: **3.92266W**

On the eastern side of Cosdon Hill are the splendid remains of a cairn and triple stone row. The 8m (26ft) cairn at the higher, western end of the rows is damaged, but the remains of a double cist, including a capstone, are clearly visible. From here the three parallel rows, about 1.5m (5ft) apart, stretch away for at least 140m (449ft), curving slightly to the north as they descend the hill. As usual, the larger stones are nearer the cairn. Each row has a large blocking slab at its western end. The upper parts of the rows are in a good state, but lower down are ruinous. Partway down a track has been driven through the rows, but even here stones remain standing between the sections of the track.

Photo © Martyn Copcutt

> "Rather a long uphill trek to get there or you could go the longer way around from South Zeal and take in White Moor circle, too. This way isn't so steep but can be very wet and boggy." CazzyJane

Nearby | The five **Cosdon Hill summit cairns** more or less follow the ridge of the hill in a north–south alignment (running SX 636 914 to SX 637 917). The southernmost is massive, with modern alterations rising up to 3m (10ft) high and 25m (82ft) in diameter. There are two ring cairns, a round cairn containing a cist, and an impressive kerbed cairn containing two or three concentric rings of stones.

SPINSTERS' ROCK

Burial Chamber | Nearest Village: **Drewsteignton**
Map: **SX 7010 9079** | Sheets: **OL28 L191** | Lat: **50.70219N** | Long: **3.84085W**

Photo © Graeme Field

A dolmen (rare for Dartmoor) with a huge capstone weighing some 16 tonnes (17.6 tons), delicately balanced on three uprights. In 1862 the tomb collapsed and was reconstructed, but not exactly as originally. It's said that the fallen stones were one day re-erected (before breakfast!) by three spinsters (in the sense of spinners of wool) – hence the name. The 18th-century antiquarian William Chapple suggested the name derived from the Celtic *lle yspiennwr rhongoa*, "open star-gazing place". He and others reported seeing many stone rows and circles in the area, which have since vanished.

BELSTONE NINE STONES
Alt Name: **Seventeen Brothers**

Cairn Circle | Nearest Village: **Belstone**

Map: **SX 6123 9284** | Sheets: **OL28 L191** | Lat: **50.71857N** | Long: **3.96715W**

A neat little circle on the moors below Belstone Tor. It is almost certainly the remains of a round cairn, and traces of the burial chamber can be seen within the circle. The Nine Stones are one of the more easily reached of Dartmoor's sites, as the circle is only a 1km (0.6 mile) walk from the church in Belstone village, mostly along a trackway.

CHALLACOMBE LONGSTONE

Standing Stone | Nearest Village: **Challacombe**

Map: **SS 7051 4307** | Sheets: **OL9 L180** | Lat: **51.17216N** | Long: **3.85364W**

Photo © Martyn Copcutt

Exmoor's standing stones are usually small in comparison to Dartmoor's, and often broken, but this fine, elegant slab of slate (the tallest standing stone on Exmoor) is almost 3m (10ft) tall and still intact, despite measuring just 0.15–0.2m (6–8in) across. From here several barrows are visible on the horizon. A very boggy 3km (2 mile) walk from the nearest road.

CHERITON RIDGE

Ring Cairn | Nearest Village: **Cheriton**

Map: **SS 7456 4478** | Sheets: **OL9 L180** | Lat: **51.18843N** | Long: **3.79634W**

An unusually extensive cairn survival for Exmoor, set in a saddle on Cheriton Ridge. A standing stone is set within a ring cairn composed of stone rubble and the remnants of an inner retaining wall. Much of the construction material has been scattered over the ground, and the cairn has also been damaged by vehicle tracks.

Nearby | At SS 7492 4432, 583m (1,913ft) to the southeast on Cheriton Ridge, is a **minilithic setting** that may have incorporated a triple row. Four stones still stand, all under 0.3m (1ft) tall. There are also various other minilithic settings in the area, the stones small and hard to find.

Photo © Martyn Copcutt

North Devon,
Somerset &
Gloucestershire

PORLOCK COMMON

Stone Circle | Nearest Village: **Porlock**
Map: **SS 8451 4467** | Sheets: **OL9 L181** | Lat: **51.18955N** | Long: **3.65399W**

A 24m (79ft) circle, originally of 21 stones, with seven still standing of the 14 that remain. All are local sandstone. The fallen stones lie close to their original positions. The circle was disturbed during World War II, when the area was used for military training. The largest stone, a fallen one to the SSE, is about 2m (6½ft) in length.

"There is a nearby associated 'avenue' 70m (230ft) to the east: tiny little stones in two parallel rows." *Martyn Copcutt*

Photo © Martyn Copcutt

The Miniliths of Exmoor

Martyn Copcutt, Chair of the Megalithic Portal Society and lifelong stones enthusiast

Geologically, Exmoor consists not of granite but of the softer Devonian sandstone, shale and slate. No granite megaliths are therefore to be seen, but that does not mean that ancient people did not create monuments here. Although much of the Exmoor National Park has been heavily farmed, the upland wilds still contain a wealth of relics from prehistoric times, including many ridge-top cairns and barrow cemeteries that can make for an interesting skyline.

Perhaps the most intriguing of the ancient remains are the many enigmatic settings of small stones (often less than 0.3m/1ft), termed "minilithic" by Aubrey Burl. A recent survey identified 57 such monuments, which appear to be unique to Exmoor, and more are likely to be discovered as more people start looking for them. The stones are grouped in varying geometrical patterns, including quincunxes (quadrilateral arrangements with a central stone) and what appear to be random forms. Unlike other stone monuments, the minilithic settings would have required the labour of only one person over a short time to erect them. Sites can be very hard to find, as the stones are often well hidden among heather and grass. Although this type of monument was recognized by 17th-century antiquarians, the miniliths have been little studied and not much is known about them. It is only recently that detailed research into miniliths has been undertaken, with several studies made in collaboration with the Exmoor National Park authority, including by the universities of Leicester and Southampton.

Given the small size and relative fragility of the stones, the survival of these unprotected settings is remarkable. Sadly, many of the stones are now broken or missing, and the remaining minilithic sites are endangered by people riding and driving over the moor, as well as by bracken cutting. At Beckham Hill, for example, three of the original nine stones (set in three rows of three) were recorded as fallen in 1965; when I visited I found only eight stones, with just three of them still standing.

Find out more about Exmoor's miniliths at: www.exmoorher.co.uk

EAST PINFORD

Stone Alignment | Nearest Village: **Simonsbath**
Map: **SS 7965 4272** | Sheets: **OL9 L180** | Lat: **51.17101N** Long: **3.72285W**

In a wild Exmoor setting, on the west-facing slope of a hill above a stream, this is a six-stone rectangle, or two rows of three stones. The rows are 4m (13ft) apart and the stones rise no higher than 0.8m (2½ft), with all of them still standing.

Photo © Martyn Copcutt

WITHYPOOL

Stone Circle | Nearest Village: **Withypool**
Map: **SS 8383 3431** | Sheets: **OL9 L181** | Lat: **51.09629N** | Long: **3.66037W**

A little-known circle with very small stones (most under 0.5m/1½ft) in an attractive moorland setting with great views. Around 36m (118ft) in diameter, it was first described in 1906, when 37 stones out of a possible original total of 100 were still in place. There are currently around 30, some fallen.

    Nearby | At SS 8761 3431, 3.8km (under 2½ miles) east, are the **Wambarrows**, three damaged Bronze Age bowl barrows on top of Winsford Hill. The westernmost is the largest, 27m (88ft) in diameter, but less well defined and more overgrown than the others. Easy access for Exmoor, and superb views.

TROUT HILL

Stone Setting (Quincunx) | Nearest Village: **Simonsbath**
Map: **SS 7940 4322** | Sheets: **OL9 L180** | Lat: **51.17546N** | Long: **3.72659W**

There are various stone settings on Trout Hill, including this possible quincunx of which only four stones remain, one of which is fallen. The three standing are 0.5–0.8m (1ft 6in–2½ft) in height, with the stones about 7m (22ft) apart.

Photo © Martyn Copcutt

SWEET TRACK

Ancient Trackway | Nearest Village: **Westhay**
Map: **ST 4240 4080** | Sheets: **E141 L182** | Lat: **51.16353N** | Long: **2.82512W**

Amazing engineering dating to 3806/3807BC, this elevated footpath ran for *c.* 2km (1.2 miles) across the swampy Somerset Levels. Ash, oak and lime trees were cut and transported to the site, crossed poles were driven into heavier poles underwater and pegged together, and an oak platform was laid on top. Some of the oak trees were 400 years old. The track was only in use for 10 years or so, probably due to rising water levels; this waterlogging protected it from decomposition. It was discovered by peat worker Ray Sweet in 1970. Wooden artefacts found by the track included yew pins, arrow shafts, paddles, parts of bows, and a dish. Other finds included flint arrows, pottery and two fine axes, one of flint and one of jadeite (from the Italian Alps). Some of these items could have been lost but the sheer volume of finds suggests many were deliberately left, perhaps as offerings. Sections of the track are on display in the British Museum, while much has been conserved in situ at Shapwick Heath Nature Reserve, where visitors can view replica sections along the original route. Associated with the Sweet Track is the even earlier (by about 30 years) Post Track, which followed more or less the same path and was probably dismantled when the Sweet Track was built.

PRIDDY CIRCLES

Henge-type Structures | Nearest Village: **Priddy**
Map: **ST 5400 5280** | Sheets: **E141 L182** | Lat: **51.27248N** | Long: **2.66079W**

Considered the most important Neolithic site in Somerset but hard to see at ground level, the Priddy Circles include four 200m (655ft) earthwork enclosures arranged in a line roughly SSW–NNE. The first three are quite close together, while the northernmost circle is separated from the others by a gap of 350m (1,150ft), which appears to be deliberate. A Roman road runs through this gap. The circles have an external rather than an internal ditch, with internal banks that seem to have been revetted by wooden posts. These features have led to much speculation about whether they are henges or not; possibly they are a type of enclosure that predates henges and may have had a different function. It's considered likely that the western third of the northernmost circle was never enclosed. In 2011, the southernmost circle was damaged.

Photo © J.J. Evendon

Nearby | **Priddy Nine Barrows** is a group of nine Bronze Age round barrows on North Hill (at ST 5392 5149), seven more or less in a row, with a further two 137m (450ft) to the north. Some 560m (1,837m) to the north, the **Ashen Hill Barrows** (at ST 5390 5205) is a further group of eight barrows arranged along a ridge.

DEVIL'S BED AND BOLSTER

Chambered Tomb | Nearest Village: **Rode**
Map: **ST 8149 5333** | Sheets: **E143 L183** | Lat: **51.27881N** | Long: **2.26676W**

A long barrow with a very disturbed, almost levelled 35m (114ft) mound. Wide ditches once ran along either side of the mound but are no longer visible on the surface. At the eastern end of the mound are a number of large stones, both upright and fallen, which may have formed parts of a central passage and side chambers. Legend holds that past attempts to move or disturb the stones have always been foiled by bad weather.

Photo © Martyn Copcutt

> "Take the footpath opposite the pub to reach a field. Follow the field boundary right, then go through a gap between fields. Keep left. Go through the next gap and follow the boundary left. The tomb is in the field corner." Paul Beastie Baker

STONEY LITTLETON   Alt Names: **Bath Tumulus, Wellow Tumulus**

Long Barrow | Nearest Village: **Wellow**

Map: **ST 7350 5720** | Sheets: **E142 L172** | Lat: **51.31328N** | Long: **2.38159W**

Photo © Jeff Demetrescu

This Cotswold-Severn long barrow is surely one of the loveliest and most atmospheric in the southwest. The setting is beautiful, surrounded by wide valleys and with low hills in every direction. The impressive trapezoidal mound, running northwest–southeast, is about 30m (98ft) long, 12.5m (41ft) wide at its widest point and 2m (6½ft) high (it's believed to have originally been much higher). It's surrounded by a restored drystone wall, and the entrance, to the southeast, is at the back of a recessed forecourt, flanked by drystone walling. The left hand "door jamb" is decorated with a striking 0.3m (1ft) ammonite cast, and more fossils are to be found on the inner walls. Inside, there's a 13m (43ft) gallery with three pairs of side chambers. The barrow was constructed using material from a now infilled ditch on each side. In 1816, an excavation uncovered human bones within the chamber. The walk up from the car park is straightforward, but can be muddy.

> **"A torch is a must as it is a crawl to the end of the barrow. Wonderfully atmospheric."**
> Scott Whitehouse

STANTON DREW   Alt Name: **The Weddings**

Megalithic Complex | Nearest Village: **Stanton Drew**

Map: **ST 6000 6330** | Sheets: **E155 L172** | Lat: **51.36734N** | Long: **2.57596W**

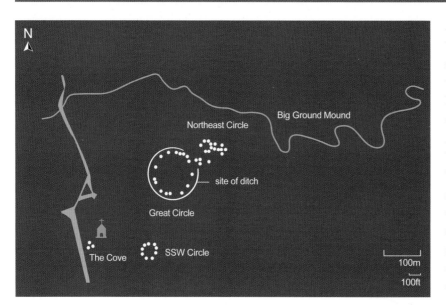

A large, complex site with various monuments scattered around the tiny village of Stanton Drew. The circles were described by John Aubrey in 1664 and by William Stukeley in 1776. The remains of three stone circles and two avenues can be found, as well as the standing stones known as the Cove (a group of three) and Hautville's Quoit.

A recent geophysical survey by English Heritage revealed that what we see today is only part of an elaborate prehistoric complex. The site's other name, the Weddings, comes from the traditional story of guests dancing into the Sabbath and being turned to stone. As at many such sites, it's said to be impossible to count the stones!

GREAT CIRCLE

At 113m (370ft) in diameter, this is the second-largest stone circle in Britain (after Avebury). In 1998 geophysical investigation revealed the startling news that the Great Circle contains nine concentric

Photo © Nicky Dancer

circles of closely spaced pits that perhaps once held huge wooden posts, as at Woodhenge (see page 98) or the Sanctuary (see page 112). It was also discovered that the stone circle is sited within a 135m (443ft) enclosure, ringed by a ditch 7m (23ft) wide. Up to 26 stones remain in the circle of a possible 30 originals. The henge ditch has a large gap or entrance on the northeast, and an avenue of which five standing stones remain leading from this for some 88m (288ft) in the direction of the River Chew. There's a legend that one of the stones will violently repel anyone who pushes it hard enough.

It's speculated that the gap in the henge would have framed Big Ground Mound, a flat-topped hill north of the river, beyond the floodplain. Recent geophysical analysis by the Bath and Camerton Archaeological Society (BACAS) has shown this to be a natural outcrop, however it's still possible that it may have played a part in the overall ritual landscape. Flooding was common here before Chew Valley Lake was built, and Big Ground would have been surrounded on three sides by water that stretched to the edge of the northeast circle.

NORTHEAST CIRCLE

Just under 100m (328ft) east of the Great Circle is an irregular 30m (98ft) circle of eight large stones. Four pits, each one aligned with an opposing pair in the outer ring, were found at the centre of the circle. It's been speculated that these could have once held uprights or been ritual pits of some sort. A second ruined avenue heads east toward the floodplain of the River Chew and would have joined with the line of the avenue leading from the Great Circle.

SSW CIRCLE

Some distance to the SSW, on higher ground and in a separate field, this ruinous 43m (145ft) circle has between nine and 12 fallen stones. It occupies a plateau with views north across the other circles to the river, and west to the Cove.

THE COVE

The three massive stones of the Cove, forming a rectangle with an open side to the southeast, are handily located in the garden of the Druid's Arms pub. A line drawn through the centres of the Northeast Circle and Great Circle extends to this monument. The church and farm now interfere with any sightlines with the SSW Circle, and the Great Circle is on lower ground so may never have been visible from here. The "back" slab (4.4m/14ft 4 in) has

Photo © Martyn Copcutt

fallen, but the other two (3.1m/10ft and 1.4m/4ft 5in) remain upright. The stones here are of different rock from the circle stones, suggesting a different origin and possibly an earlier date. In folklore, the two upright Cove stones are the bride and groom, with the fallen stone the drunken parson.

Nearby | At ST 6017 6381, less than 500m (1,640ft) NNE across the River Chew from the Northeast Circle, is **Hautville's Quoit**, a large fallen stone that's assumed to once have stood, possibly as part of a chambered tomb. This stone lies on a line running through the centres of the Great Circle and the SSW Circle. Stukeley recorded it as being 4m (13ft) but it has since been broken and is now about 2.2m (7ft). The stone is said to be named for Sir John Hautville, a 13th-century knight who was supposed to have hurled it into its current position.

HETTY PEGLER'S TUMP   Alt Names: **Uley Long Barrow, Uley Tumulus**   ★
Chambered Tomb | Nearest Village: **Uley**
Map: **SO 7896 0003** | Sheets: **E168 L162** | Lat: **51.69861N** | Long: **2.30583W**

This Cotswold-Severn-type transepted gallery grave has two chambers on each side of its passage plus an end chamber. The entrance is in a forecourt on the east and the mound rises to 3m (10ft). Human and animal bones, as well as Neolithic pottery, were found

> "When I was a child you had to get the key from a house in the village. My dad unlocked the little door and in we crawled. The smoke from the last visitor's candle was still hanging in the air. Unforgettable." Jackie Bates

here during excavations in the mid-19th century. It's named after Hester Pegler, who appears to have owned the land on which it stands in the 17th century.

Nearby | At SO 7940 0132, 1.4km (under 1 mile) NNE of Hetty Pegler's Tump, **Nympsfield** long barrow is another chambered long barrow or transepted gallery grave of the Cotswold-Severn type, with a pair of side chambers and an end chamber. Excavations in 1862, 1937 and 1974 uncovered skeletons (perhaps from as many as 20–30 individuals).

THE LONG STONE (MINCHINHAMPTON)

Standing Stone | Nearest Village: **Minchinhampton**
Map: **ST 8835 9992** | Sheets: **E168 L162** | Lat: **51.69788N** | Long: **2.16997W**

Photo © D.L. Upton

A lovely 2.3m (7ft 5in) stone with several holes that offer lots of opportunities for fun photos as people put their hands through, as well as added healing properties if the folklore is to be believed. It's been speculated that this, as well as another stone in the nearby field wall, are the remains of a burial chamber.

Nearby | At ST 8823 9899, just under 1km (0.6 miles) SSW of the Long Stone, in the Gatcombe Park estate that is home to Princess Anne, is the **Tingle Stone**, probably the remains of another chambered long barrow. It's on private land so stick to the footpath (which doesn't reach the stone) or wait for the horse trials.

The Rev N. Thornbury removed the three **Avening** burial chambers c.1806 from either Avening Court or Norn's Tump long barrows and set them up in the garden of his rectory at Avening (at ST 8789 9837). The "porthole"-style entrance is unusual for Britain. Permission from the landowner is needed to visit them, but two can be seen (just about) to the east of the main road north of Avening.

> "Folklore has it the stone wanders around the field when church bells strike 12 – AND that it is haunted by a former owner of Gatcombe Park on a horse!" 4clydesdale7

HORESTONE (RODBOROUGH)

Standing Stone | Nearest Village: **Rodborough**
Map: **SO 8577 0241** | Sheets: **E168 L162** | Lat: **51.72023N** | Long: **2.20739W**

Photo © 4clydesdale7

Rediscovered in a back garden in 2001, thus settling years of controversy over whether this stone, last recorded in 1636, still existed. There is a medieval boundary stone about 250m (820ft) away, which has been mistaken for the stone in the past, but the true Horestone is 1.8m (6ft) tall and made of the same holey freestone as so many other local standing stones. Further details of this stone and its neighbour can be found by searching the Megalithic Portal for the Horestone (Rodborough) and the Horestone (Sullivan) respectively.

LONG STONE (STAUNTON)

Standing Stone | Nearest Village: **Staunton**
Map: **SO 5593 1206** | Sheets: **OL14 L162** | Lat: **51.80543N** | Long: **2.64056W**

Standing beside the A4136, this characterful 2.5m (8ft) stone is of deeply scored and weathered sandstone. Local tradition states that it will bleed if pricked with a pin at midnight.

Nearby | Ochre mining at **Clearwell Caves** (at SO 5770 0822), on the western edge of the Forest of Dean, may date back 7,000 years, with stone tools from 4,500 years ago discovered here. Clearwell ochre contains high levels of iron, giving it an unusually strong colour pigment, and it is still mined here today.

Photo © Christopher Bickerton

BELAS KNAP

Long Barrow | Nearest Village: **Winchcombe**
Map: **SP 0209 2545** | Sheets: **OL45 L163** | Lat: **51.92756N** | Long: **1.97101W**

Photo by Adam Stanford © AerialCam Ltd

A fine long barrow (pictured opposite), its current impressive appearance shaped by restoration in 1928–30. The 55m (180ft) mound runs north–south and was once larger, now rising to 4m (13ft) high and stretching to 20m (66ft). Unlike other local barrows, there's no entrance or central passage; instead, at the northern end, there's a "false entrance", with two standing stones and a lintel, between the curved horns of the forecourt. The four chambers, two on the east, one at the southern end and one on the west, each have individual entrances. Excavation uncovered the remains of 37 people in the four chambers and under the false entrance. Romano-British pottery was also found, showing that it was accessible in that era.

> "Belas Knap is part of an ancient landscape that includes Cleeve Common, and the barrow is intervisible with the upper slopes of the common to the west. It's worth taking a whole day to explore the area, as there are Bronze Age dykes and an Iron Age camp – oh and the stunning views …" Dr Olaf

WINTERBOURNE NINE STONES
Alt Names: **Devil's Nine Stones,**
Nine Ladies, Lady Williams and Her Dog | **Stone Circle** | Nearest Village: **Winterbourne Abbas**
Map: **SY 6108 9043** | Sheets: **OL15 L194** | Lat: **50.71219N** | Long: **2.5526W**

Photo © Steve Simmons

First recorded by John Aubrey in the 17th century and hardly changed since, this little circle (8m/26ft) is unusually located in a valley bottom. It is unexpectedly atmospheric, despite the proximity of the A35. The stones, of varying size, are evenly spaced, with a larger gap to the north. Aubrey described another circle (no longer there) about 800m (½ mile) west of here. The fallen 2m (6½ft) Broad Stone lies semi-buried beside the road about a mile to the west. Access from the A35 has been blocked, but at the time of writing, parking is possible across the field to the east, at the site of the old Little Chef (pending redevelopment). A gate here gives on to a path to the stones.

Nearby | On Long Barrow Hill (at SY 5717 9115), **Long Bredy** bank barrow is, at 195m (640ft), the second longest in Britain (after the one at Maiden Castle, see page 85). Ditches run in parallel along either long side. The barrow can be seen in both directions from the A35; look for the V-shaped notch. There are various other sites close by, including what may be cursus to the northeast, and other barrows.

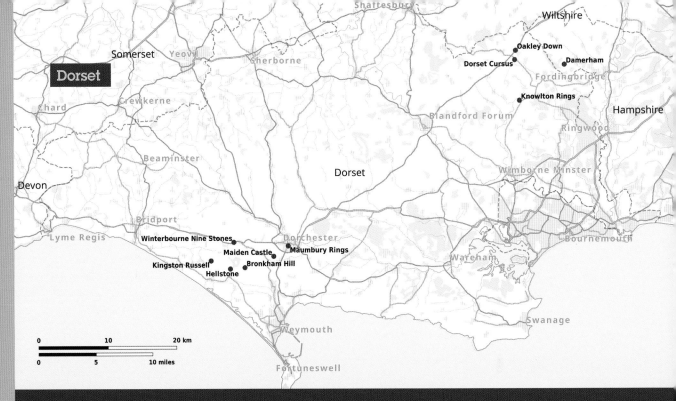

KINGSTON RUSSELL

Stone Circle | Nearest Village: **Abbotsbury**
Map: **SY 5779 8783** | Sheets: **OL15 L194** | Lat: **50.68858N** | Long: **2.59889W**

Photo © Jim Champion

On a chalk ridge above the Bride valley, with views south and west to the sea, this irregular 30m (98ft) circle of fallen sarsen and conglomerate stones is not far from the Grey Mare and Her Colts. There are 18 stones, one of which was still standing in 1815. Two similar stones lie close to a nearby fence. Some of the stones are partially buried and so may be larger than they appear.

Nearby | At SY 5839 8706, just short of 1km (0.6 miles) southeast of Kingston Russell circle, **Grey Mare and Her Colts** is a well-preserved long barrow with a 24m (78ft) mound. At the southeast end are four impressive sarsens, three of which are still standing. A fifth, possibly the capstone, lies at the southwest end of the row. The remains of a collapsed chamber lie behind the sarsens.

> "Parking is only possible on verges of minor roads a mile or two away. Resist the temptation to drive down the farm-access tracks as you may get into trouble!"
> Jim Champion

HELLSTONE

Long Barrow | Nearest Village: **Portesham**
Map: **SY 6058 8670** | Sheets: **OL15 L194** | Lat: **50.67861N** | Long: **2.55928W**

A much-damaged and inaccurately restored but very dramatic-looking long barrow. The mound is at least 24m (78ft) long, up to 12m (40ft) wide and 1.5m (5ft) high near the chamber, but further southeast it is much disturbed and barely 0.6m (2ft) high. The chamber was rebuilt in 1866 and nine stones, up to 1.7m (5ft 7in) tall, now support the huge 3 × 2.4m (10 × 8ft) capstone.

BRONKHAM HILL

Barrow Cemetery | Nearest Village: **Portesham**
Map: **SY 6267 8688** | Sheets: **OL15 L194** | Lat: **50.68037N** | Long: **2.52972W**

Photo © Jim Champion

A group of round barrows stretching northwest-southeast for about a mile along the Ridgeway. The group includes four bell barrows and a double bowl barrow.

Nearby | There are various other barrow cemeteries to be explored in the area. The **Hardy Monument** barrows (at SY 6130 8760), 1.5km (just under 1 mile) WNW of Bronkham Hill, have spectacular views.

MAIDEN CASTLE

Causewayed Enclosure & Bank Barrow | Nearest Village: **Winterborne Monkton**
Map: **SY 6690 8846** | Sheets: **OL15 L194** | Lat: **50.69483N** | Long: **2.46999W**

The dramatic Iron Age hill fort is the most impressive element of the site, but this hilltop has been the focus of occupation for more than 6,000 years. A Neolithic causewayed enclosure, one of the largest in England (approximately 8ha/20 acres), is buried under the embankments of the early phase hill fort, which probably followed its outline. When the enclosure went out of use, a 550m (1,805ft) bank barrow was built across its western side, flanked by ditches. The barrow is still visible, just about. In the early Iron Age, a single rampart was built on top of the earlier enclosure, and later the fort was extended to enclose more than double the original area. The entrances became more complex, extra ramparts were added and the inner rampart was heightened. Maiden Castle was featured in the first-ever English-language archaeology TV show, broadcast by the BBC in 1937. A downloadable audio tour is available from English Heritage.

MAUMBURY RINGS

Henge | Nearest Town: **Dorchester**
Map: **SY 6901 8992** | Sheets: **OL15 L194** | Lat: **50.70808N** | Long: **2.44024W**

Photo © Robert Hurworth

Surrounded by new development, this late Neolithic henge, more than 100m (328ft) in diameter, was used as an amphitheatre by the Romans and as an artillery fort during the Civil War. Excavations in the early 20th century revealed a wide ditch inside the circular bank, with a series of shafts (possibly around 45) up to 11m (36ft) deep. Eight were found to contain red-deer skulls and human and animal bone fragments, as well as carved chalk objects (including the famous phallus). The shafts may have been deliberately backfilled. The entrance is to the northeast. A stone that once stood to the west of the entrance is said to have been discovered and reburied in the 19th century, its location now unknown.

Nearby | In the car park under the Dorchester Waitrose, the position of some post-holes from a huge timber circle are marked on the ground. Discovered during development, the circle is estimated to have been some 380m (1,245ft) in diameter, requiring the trunks of 600 mature oaks. It was radiocarbon-dated to around 2100BC. Also in Dorchester is the **Flagstones** enclosure, partly sited under the grounds of Max Gate, Thomas Hardy's old house. It is a 100m (328ft) interrupted ditch enclosure (similar to a causewayed enclosure), formed by a ring of pits. Human remains were found, including an infant and a baby in the pits, and a young man in a central barrow. Carbon-dating puts this burial about 1,000 years later than the enclosure, which dates to around 2486–2886BC.

KNOWLTON RINGS

Henge-type Structures | Nearest Village: **Gussage All Saints**
Map: **SU 0238 1028** | Sheets: **E118 L195** | Lat: **50.89199N** | Long: **1.96753W**

There are four henges or henge-type earthworks at Knowlton. The best-known and best-preserved is the Church Circle, which contains the ruins of a Norman church. To the east, is the Great Barrow, the largest round barrow in Dorset. Other barrows and ring ditches are scattered in the surrounding area. The Northern, Southern and Church Circles are generally accepted as henges, while the status of the fourth earthwork, known as the Old Churchyard, probably predates the medieval period. A large stone, ploughed out of the Southern Circle in the 1970s, features four concentric pecked rings. If this is indeed prehistoric rock art, it is highly unusual for the region.

Nearby | Some 5km (3 miles) southwest of Knowlton Rings, on private land with no access, **High Lea Farm** was until 2008 the focus of Bournemouth University's Knowlton Prehistoric Landscape Project. There's an early Bronze Age cemetery of round and oval barrows, most of which are now visible only as cropmarks.

OAKLEY DOWN

Barrow Cemetery | Nearest Village: **Sixpenny Handley**
Map: **SU 0182 1731** | Sheets: **E118 L184** | Lat: **50.95521N** | Long: **1.97546W**

Photo © Hamish Fenton

A fine cemetery containing over 30 round barrows of various types, some of which are clearly visible from the A354 south of Woodyates. The Roman road, Ackling Dyke, passes through the cemetery, over two of the disc barrows.

Nearby | The excavation into **Wor barrow** (at SU 0124 1729), 579m (1,900ft) west of Oakley Down barrows, by General Pitt Rivers in 1893–4, is considered to be the earliest investigation of a long barrow to modern scientific standards. In one of the first examples of experimental archaeology, Pitt Rivers then studied the re-silting of the ditches over the following years, and decided this wasn't a reliable method for dating earthworks. Six male skeletons were found inside the original mortuary chamber, but the site is best known for a secondary burial that was placed in the ditch after construction. The body had been preserved for 30–130 years before burial, making it the earliest known "mummy" in Britain. A flint arrowhead between the ribs gave insight into the probable cause of death.

DORSET CURSUS

Cursus | Nearest Village: **Sixpenny Handley**
Map: **SU 0175 1600** | Sheets: **E118 L184** | Lat: **50.94343N** | Long: **1.97717W**

Probably Britain's largest Neolithic site, the Cursus runs for 10km (6 miles) northeast–southwest across the chalk downland of Cranborne Chase. Originally a pair of parallel banks about 90m (295ft) apart, it is now mainly visible as cropmarks, although some earthworks are still present, including two associated long barrows and the remains of banks in Salisbury Plantation on Oakley Down, and on the northeast-facing slope of Bottlebrush Down. It's been estimated that the Cursus took around half a million hours to construct, and may have been built in two phases, with the 5.6km (3½ mile) southwest section completed first. It's well worth visiting, despite lack of visible remains. There is no public right of way along the whole of the Cursus but the area is criss-crossed with paths and lanes.

Dr Martin Green has excavated two shafts here, one (**Fir Tree Field, Down Farm**) giving dates from the Mesolithic to Beaker period. The second (**Monkton-up-Wimborne complex**) comprises a large circular pit surrounded by a circle of 14 pits, apparently used episodically for feasting. Special deposits found in the shaft fill include a pecked sandstone ball and a decorated chalk block.

Nearby | At **Wyke Down** (SU 0060 1530) are two henges (one found in 1995), 40m (131ft) apart.

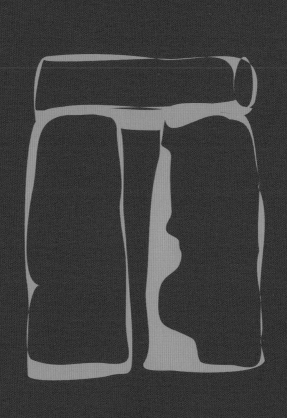

SOUTH OF ENGLAND

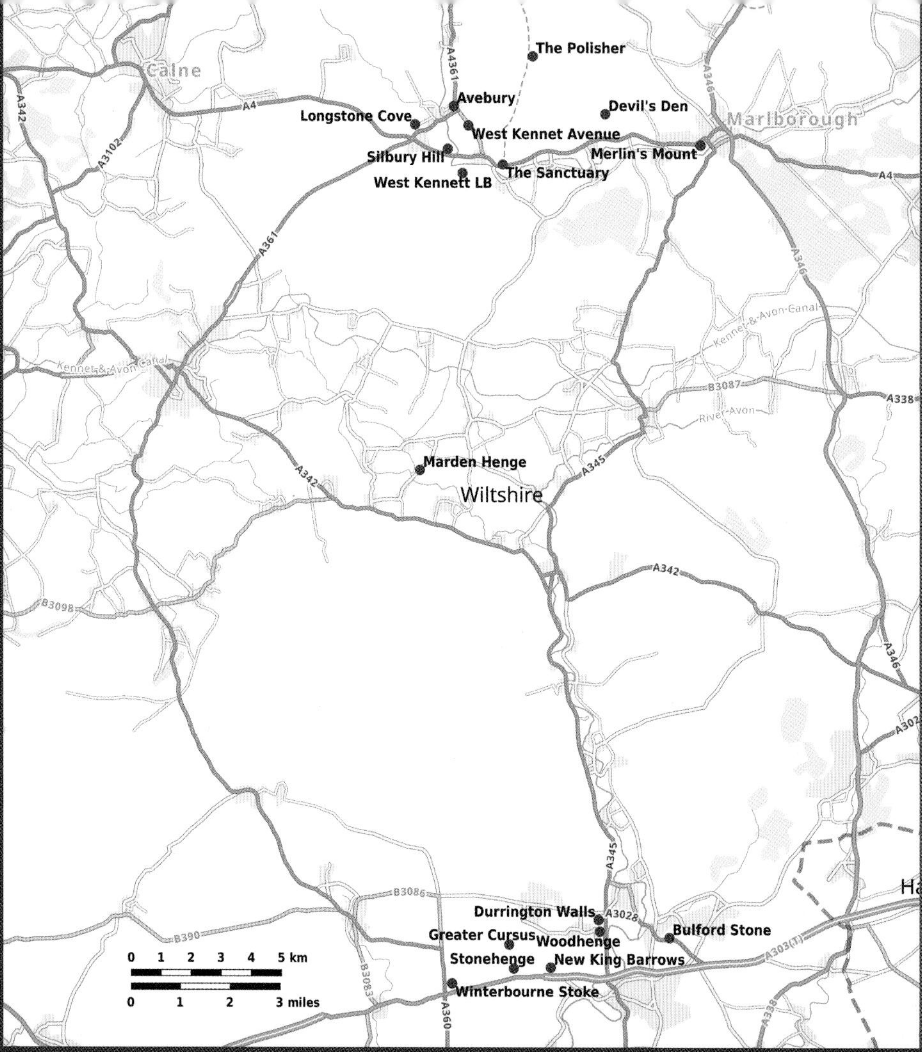
The Polisher
Calne
Avebury
Longstone Cove
Devil's Den
Marlborough
West Kennet Avenue
Silbury Hill
Merlin's Mount
West Kennett LB
The Sanctuary
Kennet & Avon Canal
River Avon
Marden Henge
Wiltshire
Durrington Walls
Greater Cursus
Woodhenge
Bulford Stone
Stonehenge
New King Barrows
Winterbourne Stoke
0 1 2 3 4 5 km
0 1 2 3 miles
A4
A342
A3102
A361
A4361
A346
A345
A338
A3087
B3087
B3098
B390
B3086
B3083
A360
A3028
A303(T)
A302

Wiltshire

Top 15 Stone Circles in England

1. **Stonehenge (Wiltshire)** p.91
2. **Avebury (Wiltshire)** p.102
3. **Castlerigg (Cumbria)** p.177
4. **Arbor Low (Derbyshire)** p.139
5. **Nine Ladies (Derbyshire)** p.139
6. **Stanton Drew (Somerset)** p.78
7. **Nine Stones Close (Derbyshire)** p.138
8. **Rollright Stones (Oxfordshire)** p.117
9. **Long Meg and Her Daughters (Cumbria)** p.183
10. **Mitchell's Fold (Shropshire)** p.133
11. **The Hurlers (Cornwall)** p.50
12. **Boscawen-ûn (Cornwall)** p.38
13. **Swinside (Cumbria)** p.174
14. **Doll Tor (Derbyshire)** p.138
15. **Merry Maidens (Cornwall)** p.36

STONEHENGE

Stone Circle | Nearest Town: **Amesbury**
Map: **SU 1222 4219** | Sheets: **E130 L184** | Lat: **51.17881N** | Long: **1.82656W**

Barney Harris

Photo © Richard Cassidy

The world's most famous and iconic stone circle, Stonehenge has all the facilities required to entertain over 1.3 million visitors every year, including a café, a shop, and a museum with nearly 300 ancient artefacts and an exhibition exploring the stones, the people and the wider archaeological landscape, as well as reconstructed Neolithic houses. There is full disabled access to the stone circle by shuttle bus and tarmac paths, and you also have the option of walking to the circle past the Greater Cursus and numerous barrows. Don't go expecting to have the stones to yourself, but, despite the crowds and the fencing, the spectacular arrangement of uprights and lintels remain hugely impressive.

BEGINNINGS (3000–2620BC): THE DITCH AND THE BANK

Approaching Stonehenge, visitors first pass through one of its earliest features: the ditch and bank. Roughly circular and running for around 320m (1,050ft), the ditch encloses a space of just over 9ha (2.2 acres) – an area slightly larger than a modern rugby field – and its construction involved the removal of around 1,200m³ (42,377ft³) of solid chalk, weighing an astonishing 3,250 tonnes (3,582 tons). As the ditch was dug, the resulting chalk spoil was piled up to create a 6m (20ft) wide bank on the inside of the ditch, which stood around 2m (6½ft) high. The banks of henge monuments are usually positioned outside the ditches, so this inverted arrangement at Stonehenge is unusual. Two gaps – one to the south, the other to the northeast – were left in the ditch and bank, presumably to facilitate access to the enclosure within. Radiocarbon dates obtained from material at the bottom of the ditch indicate that it was completed by around 2950BC.

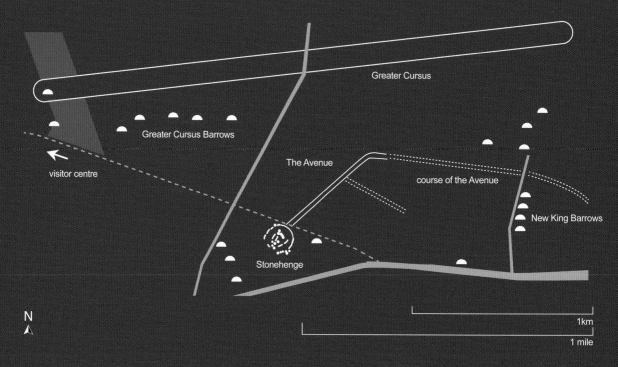

The ditch was dug using pick axes fashioned from red-deer antlers, known as antler picks. When William Hawley excavated roughly half the ditch in the 1920s he recovered scores of worn-down antler picks from the ditch floor, along with other offerings – including at least one cow bone, now known to have already been 100 years old by the time it was left in the ditch. Hawley also noted that the ditch had the appearance of a series of conjoined pits, or segments. He reasoned that each segment could have been dug by a different group or "work gang". Recent experiments have shown that two individuals can shift around 0.5m³ (17.6ft³) of chalk per hour using just antler picks and baskets. The ditch at Stonehenge would have therefore taken 10 people around a month to complete, though more people could easily have been involved.

AUBREY HOLES AND WOODEN STRUCTURES

Around the same time as they were digging the ditch, the builders of Stonehenge also dug a circle of 56 oval holes, known as the "Aubrey Holes" after John Aubrey, the first person to record them. The Aubrey Holes ran around the inside of the enclosure ditch and their location is shown today by concrete markers. Upon excavation, they were found to contain cremated human remains. Crushed chalk rubble was also recovered from the bottom of the holes, evidence that they probably once contained heavy "bluestone" pillars (bluestone is a catch-all term used to describe a variety of mostly igneous rocks deriving from Wales). Around the same time various timber structures – of unknown form and purpose – were installed in and around the enclosure and its entrances.

CHANGE OF FOCUS (2620–2480BC): SARSEN CIRCLE, TRILITHON HORSESHOE AND DOUBLE BLUESTONE CIRCLE

Some 400–500 years after the ditch was dug, as many as 15 enormous sarsen slabs were transported to Stonehenge, sculpted into regular blocks using hard, rounded "hammerstones" and built into the trilithon horseshoe, a towering, open-ended arrangement of five free-standing trilithons located at the centre of the site. Unlike the Stonehenge bluestones, which derive from a variety of quarries in the Preseli mountains of West Wales, sarsen is a hard sandstone that occurs just north of Stonehenge and in isolated patches across southern England. Today, two concentric circles of holes (known as the Q and R holes) and broken bluestone pillars surround what remains of the sarsen horseshoe. These are probably the remains of a double bluestone circle built around the same time, but since dismantled. The sarsen circle – a now partially ruined 30m (98ft) diameter ring of 30 sarsen uprights supporting 30 lintels – encircled both the sarsen horseshoe and bluestones settings. Strikingly, many of these sarsens were connected using mortice and tenons, a jointing method associated with woodworking.

ALTAR STONE, HEEL STONE, SLAUGHTER STONE AND STATION STONES

Photo © Jecfish Ping

Four sarsen Station Stones (of which only two now remain) were positioned just inside the enclosure so that they marked the corners of a near-perfect rectangle that enclosed all the central stone settings. The Slaughter Stone, now fallen, originally stood alongside another two stones in the middle of the northeastern enclosure entrance to create a short façade. The Heel Stone, the heaviest stone at Stonehenge, weighing nearly 30 tonnes (33 tons), was also erected, about 25m (82ft) outside the northeast entrance. Recent research suggests the Heel Stone, Slaughter Stone and the two remaining Station Stones were probably brought from the same location as most of the other sarsen stones (see page 94). The Altar Stone (one of the only non-local sandstones present at Stonehenge – it likely came from the eastern Senni Beds around Abergavenny or the Brecon Beacons) was given pride of place at the centre of the monument, just in front of the Great Trilithon.

In the 500 years that followed this intensive episode of construction, the bluestones were rearranged multiple times and a 2.5km (1.5 mile) long avenue was carved into the chalk, connecting Stonehenge to the former site of Bluestonehenge (see page 94) and the River Avon.

GREATER CURSUS AND THE GREATER CURSUS BARROWS

Some 700m (½ mile) north of the stone circle is the Greater Cursus, a Neolithic earthwork enclosure

Photo © Hamish Fenton

100–150m (328–492ft) wide that runs roughly east–west for 2.7km (1¾ miles), the ditch and banks still visible. The western end, with its two round barrows, can be viewed on the walk to or from the stone circle to the visitor centre. South of the Greater Cursus and running in parallel is a line of fine Bronze Age round barrows, built around 1,000 years after the cursus. Some of the barrows have names – the Monarch of the Plains, or Amesbury 55, for instance, which is a large bell barrow, 2.8m (9ft) high and 58m (190ft) across. There's also a twin bell barrow, Amesbury 44, with two closely spaced (or "confluent") barrow mounds surrounded by a single ditch.

CURRENT THEORIES ABOUT STONEHENGE

It is now known that Stonehenge began life as Britain's earliest and largest cremation cemetery. All but eight of the excavated Aubrey Holes contained cremated human remains and as many as 150–240 individuals were buried at Stonehenge in the third millennium BC. It was not until around 400 years after the first bluestones were brought to Stonehenge that its architecture began to reflect an increased concern with celestial bodies, a change that has led some to label Stonehenge an observatory. Certainly, these later stone settings emphasized an important axis running through the middle of Stonehenge; at its northeastern end the Heel Stone "hides" the rising midsummer sunrise, while the uprights of the Great Trilithon frame the midwinter setting sun to the southwest. Archaeoastronomers have confirmed that a second alignment – with the major summer and winter full moons – was created by the long sides of the rectangle delineated by the Station Stones.

More recent thinking has highlighted Stonehenge's importance as part of a wider network of prehistoric monuments scattered around the local landscape. The association between stone and death at Stonehenge is mirrored at another nearby monument that is also connected to the River Avon by its own avenue: Durrington Walls (see page 98). Rather than stones, this enormous henge contained a giant timber circle with its entrance aligned to the midwinter sunrise and midsummer sunset, the exact opposite of Stonehenge. Excavations here by the Stonehenge Riverside Project also revealed the presence of a sizeable Neolithic village that later became a giant feasting site. Durrington Walls was thus a place for the living and Stonehenge a place for the dead; people congregated around the timber circles of Durrington Walls to feast and celebrate life before proceeding down the river to Stonehenge to remember the dead among the stones.

The vast amount of labour required to build Stonehenge (over 30 million hours at the last count) has led some to conclude it is evidence for the existence of a prehistoric hierarchy or ancient elite. Certainly, it is difficult to understand why a single group of people would spend so long building something like Stonehenge, but more recent evidence points to the possibility that this effort may have in fact been shared across many groups from around Britain. Isotopic analysis of pig and cow bones from the Stonehenge area has revealed that animals were brought to Wiltshire from many parts of Britain. Far from being the product of a centrally controlled chiefdom, Stonehenge could have emerged out of the joint efforts of many smaller groups coming together for the common good. See page 222 for the Waun Mawn standing stones supposedly transported to become part of Stonehenge.

A core drilled from one of the sarsen stones in 1958 was recently rediscovered and its precise chemical composition compared to sarsen sampled from 20 sites throughout southern England. The best match is to sarsen stones found in West Woods 25km (15½ miles) to the north of Stonehenge. Related work using a portable x-ray fluorescence spectrometer (pXRF) has confirmed that 50 of the 52 remaining sarsens share a close chemical makeup, implying the majority of Stonehenge sarsens came from West Woods. This is close to the traditionally accepted source on the Marlborough Downs and supports previous suggestions that the sarsen stones were all erected at the same time. More research is needed but this is a fantastic discovery that will result in books on Stonehenge having to be rewritten (again!).

Nearby | At SU 1420 4137, c.2km (1¼ miles) ESE of Stonehenge, **Bluestonehenge** is a previously unknown monument found in 2009 beside the River Avon, at the beginning of the ceremonial avenue that led all the way to Stonehenge. The monument probably comprised 26 bluestone pillars in a circle, but all that remains today is stone-holes – so there's nothing to see on the ground.

Top 10 Pieces of Music Inspired by Prehistory

Andy Burnham, founder and Editor of the Megalithic Portal

1. "Tumulus" by Drombeg, from the album *Earthworks* (2016): piano, electronics and field recordings expertly mixed by Thom Brooks, who is based in Co. Kerry, Ireland.

2. "Nine Stones Close" by Nick Jonah Davis, from the album *Of Time and Tides* (2011): this ace fingerpicking guitarist is from Nottingham, so not a million miles from the Derbyshire site.

3. *Symphony No. 9* by Ralph Vaughan Williams: the second movement alludes to Tess's arrest at Stonehenge in Thomas Hardy's *Tess of the D'Urbervilles*. It was composed in 1956–7 and first performed under the baton of Sir Malcolm Sargent in 1958 only four months before Vaughan Williams' death.

4. "Stanton Drew" by folk band Titus (2011): a song about the legend of the fiddlers playing past midnight into the Sabbath and everyone being turned to stone! While I was previewing this the next song that came up was *The Wedding at Stanton Drew* by Bully Wee Band, another folk tune about exactly the same legend. It does involve fiddles, after all, so you can see the attraction for folk musicians.

5. "The Imagined Sound of Sun on Stone" by Sally Beamish (2000): a piece for saxophone and chamber orchestra. Sally describes visualizing the beam of light that enters Maeshowe as like a stylus playing the sound out of the stone.

6. "King of Boys" by Steve Martin & Edie Brickell, from the album *Love Has Come for You* (2013). Steve the comedian, on banjo, and Edie the singer-songwriter, both from Texas, teamed up to make this album. This track about the prehistoric gold cape found in Mold, North Wales (now in the British Museum) was written as lighthearted challenge from Steve to stretch Edie's songwriting skills.

7. "A Circle inside a Circle" by James Holden, from the album *The Inheritors* (2013): with a cover clearly inspired by the rock art of Northumberland, you could call this folk-techo with a nod to Steve Reich. One for those who like their electronic music a bit organic and unprocessed, When alternative music blog *The Quietus* calls an album an "exhausting, complex and disorientating listen", you know you're in for something wild.

8. "Woodhenge" by Mike Oldfield, from the album *Platinum* (1979): ambient music with gentle marimba rhythms, the B side to the vinyl single release of the *Blue Peter* theme.

9. "The Ring of Brodgar" by Dawn & Dusk Entwined, from the album *A L'aube des Jours Anciens* (2011): fitting the stormy weather typically experienced at this Orkney site, this is slow, moodily orchestrated rock with doom-laden drumming from the French outfit who disbanded in 2012.

10. "Doggerland" by Ian Anderson, from the album *Homo Erraticus* (2014): one for the deep prehistorians as Doggerland would have been well and truly flooded under the North Sea by the time the first standing stone was erected. Ian also wrote and performed the song "Dun Ringill" with Jethro Tull, from the album Stormwatch (1979) about an Iron Age "broch-like structure" (to be completely accurate – as we at the Megalithic Portal try hard to be). The lyrics also mention waiting in stone circles.

Stonehenge: Model of a Geocentric Universe?

Jon Morris, author of *Stonehenge: Solving the Neolithic Universe*

When the sun leaves the north for the winter, the land becomes cold. For the people who built Stonehenge, knowledge of solar movement may have been seen as fundamental to their very existence. It could even be that the site acted as both a depository of knowledge and as the setting for a spectacular public educational display.

The concept of a geocentric universe appears to have been embodied in the layout of Stonehenge, if its various elements are taken to signify a circular Earth (the sarsens), a circular heavens (the inner and outer henge banks and the Aubrey Holes), the points of the sun's movement (the Station Stones) and the polar axis (the Heel Stone, the Slaughter Stone and the Avenue). This layout appears to have been adjusted to make it more precise, with some of the Avenue's stones removed around the time the sarsen ring was built, while the Heel Stone and the Slaughter Stone were retained. These two remaining, or possibly repositioned, stones are in the correct positions to represent the polar axis relative to the true cardinal directions. When the horizon is even slightly elevated (as at Stonehenge) and without magnets, only tracing a line to the Pole Star enables an exact cardinal layout. Aligning a tree pole with the Pole Star (Thuban), and dropping a plumb bob to the centre of the stone circle, would have given a precise setting to true north when the shadow from the pole aligned with the plumb bob at midday. Is it possible that Stonehenge was built to provide a working model of the sun's movements? One stone pair (Stones 53 and 54) have a socket that could have held a tree pole pointed at the Pole Star. A second pole, with a ball suspended from the end, could then have been rotated around it, and mirrors placed to focus sunlight onto the ball as shown in the diagram below. (Crude mirrors could have been fashioned from tin that has since degraded.) If the device enabled the ball to be rotated, raised and lowered according to the seasonal position of the sun, it could have been used to create a ball of light to simulate the sun, demonstrating its movement in an apparently geocentric universe to a crowd gathered in the Avenue.

The outer bluestone circle exists in just the right place to provide solid support points for mirrors to be tilted for each season. Other stones are positioned in locations needed for a geocentric device. Stonehenge's entire plan layout can thus be shown to function as an idealized geocentric description of the universe. To prove that this works and show that the ideas are new, I applied for a UK patent for the idea (GB2486636), which was granted in April 2018.

Morris, J. 2013. *Stonehenge: Solving the Neolithic Universe*. North Charleston: CreateSpace

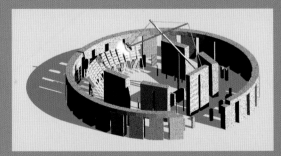

Possible set-up of mirrors, pole and ball to demonstrate the movements of the sun

Stonehenge and the Neolithic Cosmos

N.D. Wiseman, who researches the UK Neolithic from the United States

While Stonehenge had for generations been researched in isolation, the past two decades have seen the monument emerge as a centrally located, culturally fluid metaphor for a sun-based belief system we scarcely imagined could have existed.

During its history, Stonehenge steadily evolved as functions changed, and though certain beliefs transferred through the 2,000-year life of the monument, new ones were introduced. The monument went from being a moon-ruled, regional cemetery to embodying a precise definition of the cosmos itself, with the fabled stone setting positioned at the centre of the universe – not only as a symbolic omphalos, but physically, across the known world.

As a final statement of the Neolithic era, Stonehenge unified all the diverse concepts of previous generations. The ever-moving minuet of sun, moon, Earth and those who dwell there now existed in a harmonic environment that referenced life, death and renewal.

The sun was the father of life, the stone circle was his earth-wife, the cup-shaped trilithon horseshoe was her womb. At summer solstice, the Heel Stone created a phallic shadow deeply piercing the horseshoe, while the Altar Stone was where that shadow fell. In December, stone 16, with its bulging midriff, was a mother heavy with child looking southwest, bidding her husband farewell. The harbinger of life's eternal cycle, she will deliver her bounty at vernal equinox, nine months after the father's solstice visit.

These and many other ideas are detailed in the following book, written for the curious layperson: Wiseman, N.D. 2015. *Stonehenge and the Neolithic Cosmos*. Cape Cod: The Vinland Press

WINTERBOURNE STOKE

Barrow Cemetery | Nearest Village: **Winterbourne Stoke**
Map: **SU 1017 4171** | Sheets: **E130 L184** | Lat: **51.17453N** | Long: **1.8559W**

The Winterbourne Stoke barrow cemetery features examples of pretty much every kind of barrow, from a Neolithic long barrow (with multiple burials) through the various Bronze Age types. The long barrow is next to the Winterbourne Stoke roundabout – you can see it from the road – and there are also pond, ditch and bell barrows. Eleven of a total of around 27 barrows are aligned with the earlier long barrow. Five of the round barrows here are very early, dating from about 2100BC, and contained inhumations (burials) rather than cremations. The King Barrow is one of the best known, 51m (167ft) across and 3m (10ft) high, excavated by Sir Richard Colt Hoare in 1812. He gave it the name (it's also known as Barrow 16 and Winterbourne Stoke 5) due to the fancy grave goods that were found there, including a bronze awl with a bone handle, two bronze daggers and sherds of pottery from Brittany, as well as an elm tree-trunk coffin. Some of the finds from Colt Hoare's many excavations here can be seen at Salisbury Museum.

NEW KING BARROWS

Barrow Cemetery | Nearest Town: **Amesbury**
Map: **SU 1345 4222** | Sheets: **E130 L184** | Lat: **51.17905N** | Long: **1.80896W**　　Barney Harris

Known simply as the Seven Barrows in the 1600s, the New King Barrows gained their modern name when John Aubrey likened the way they were positioned beside one another to the arrangement of royal graves at Westminster Abbey. This north–south alignment of round barrows lies within a wooded area on King Barrow Ridge, just over 1km (0.6 miles) east of Stonehenge. The barrows are visible as circular mounds, covered with grass and trees and ranging 2–4m (6ft 7in–13ft) in height and 20–40m (66ft–131ft) in diameter. They were likely built during the earlier Bronze Age (c.2000–1500BC), a period when people started to become less nomadic and began farming and grazing the land more intensively. They built scores of other round barrows, often in groups or lines, within which they buried their dead with grave goods such as bronze axes, flint tools and gold items. Today, well over 900 such barrows exist within just the military training area on Salisbury Plain.

The barrows were excavated in the late 20th century after they were damaged by uprooted trees. These limited excavations revealed that they were made mostly of soil and stacked turves (layers of grass), with a thick layer (or "capping") of white chalk rubble cast over the top. In some cases the chalk had been dug out of a circular ditch that surrounded the mound. Analysis of the turves showed that humans had managed the grazing of the land for around 30 years before they were built.

WOODHENGE

Henge | Nearest Town: **Durrington**
Map: **SU 1505 4338** | Sheets: **E130 L184** | Lat: **51.18941N** | Long: **1.78602W**　　Barney Harris

Woodhenge was an arrangement of six concentric, oval rings of timber posts (the positions of which are marked today by concrete bollards), surrounded by a circular ditch and bank measuring 85m (279ft) across. It is situated around 200m (656ft) to the south of Durrington Walls (see below), close to the River Avon, and was built at around 2300BC. A gap in the ditch and bank at Woodhenge to the northeast looks directly toward Durrington Walls, hinting at some kind of relationship between the two. The third ring from the outside contained the largest timber posts, some of which measured around 1m (3ft 3in) in diameter. There are convincing parallels between Woodhenge and Stonehenge: for example, the longest axis of the oval timber settings at Woodhenge shares the same orientation as the principal axis as Stonehenge (midsummer sunrise–midwinter sunset).

DURRINGTON WALLS

Henge | Nearest Village: **Durrington**
Map: **SU 1501 4375** | Sheets: **E130 L184** | Lat: **51.19277N** | Long: **1.78658W**　　Barney Harris

Dating to around 2600BC, Durrington Walls is one of Britain's largest henge monuments. The roughly circular ditch and bank, parts of which are still visible today, follow the contours of a natural combe (small valley) down to the River Avon. They enclose an area of some 17ha (42 acres), a space equivalent to 24 modern football fields. The bank, made entirely of chalk rubble, originally stood around 4m (13ft) tall and reached a maximum width of 30m (98ft). Its construction entailed the removal of around 70,000m³ (2.47 million ft³) of solid chalk bedrock, weighing well over 150,000 tonnes (165,346 tons). There are at least two, possibly three, short gaps in the earthworks, thought to have been entrances to the site. The southeastern entrance has been investigated most thoroughly and in 2005 it was discovered to have been linked to the River Avon by a *c.*20m (66ft) wide, flint nodule-cobbled avenue, the only one of its kind in the UK. The remains of two timber circles, contemporaneous with the earthworks, have also been located. The best-preserved of these, known as the Southern Circle, comprised six concentric rings of large timber posts and measured just under 40m (131ft) in diameter. The width of some of the Southern Circle's post-holes showed that the timbers used to construct the circle could be enormous, in some cases measuring over 1m (3ft 3in) in diameter.

There are numerous architectural features at Durrington Walls that link it to Stonehenge. For example, the avenue from the River Avon to Durrington Walls was aligned on the midsummer sunset, whereas at Stonehenge the approach from the avenue is directed toward the midwinter sunset. The diameters of the inner four timber circles within the Southern Circle at Durrington Walls also roughly match those of the innermost four bluestone and sarsen stone settings at Stonehenge.

In 2019, a series of massive geophysical anomalies was identified just south of Durrington Walls henge monument during a survey by the Stonehenge Hidden Landscapes Project. These large pits appear to trace out a 2km (1¼ mile) circle centred on the henge. Several pits have already been excavated and confirmed as natural solution hollows, though others may yet prove to be deliberate constructions. If confirmed, the site would rank as one of the biggest prehistoric monuments in Europe.

BULFORD STONE   Alt Name: **Tor Stone**

Standing Stone | Nearest Village: **Bulford**
Map: **SU 1736 4318** | Sheets: **E130 L184** | Lat: **51.18755N** | Long: **1.75297W**

The Bulford Stone is a sarsen stone, 2.8m (9ft) long, lying in a 30m (98ft) diameter ring ditch. Excavation revealed the hole the stone originally stood in, and also the pit it probably came from in the first place, suggesting that sarsens were perhaps as common on Salisbury Plain as they were on the Marlborough Downs. An almost-central burial contained a small food vessel and the cremated remains of one adult along with selected unburnt bones from a second adult. Grave goods included bone spatulae, a wild boar's tusk and a miniature "megalith" carved from limestone, as well as rock crystal which may have come from South Wales – or possibly the Alps. A second food vessel cremation was added later.

Photo © Paul Blades

Feasting and Monument Building

Barney Harris, PhD candidate at the Institute of Archaeology, University College London

Feasting remains a widespread phenomenon across cultures. As well as reaffirming existing social bonds or forming new ones, the act of feasting has been – and still is – used to mobilize labour for the creation or renovation of buildings and monuments. As recently as 2006, ethnographers on the Sumatran island of Sumba recorded large-scale feasting during stone-pulling ceremonies, where boulders weighing in excess of 10 tonnes (11 tons) were transported using simple ropes and wooden sledges. Could feasting have formed an important part of megalithic and earthwork monument building in Neolithic Britain?

The later Neolithic site of Durrington Walls, Wiltshire (see page 98) is one of the few contexts where feasting is apparent in the archaeological record. In 2005, archaeologists discovered the remains of houses at the site, which lies just 2.8km (1¾ miles) northeast of Stonehenge. These buildings formed part of a late Neolithic village – one of the largest in northwestern Europe at the time – that predated the construction of the henge at Durrington Walls. As well as the remains of their houses, the inhabitants left behind vast quantities of pig and cow bone, pottery and flint tools. Radiocarbon-dating has shown that this activity occurred around the same time that Stonehenge was built, leading some to suggest that this was where the builders of Stonehenge once lived and feasted.

Certainly, analyses of the animal bones at Durrington Walls have indicated that the site was used to host enormous, lavish feasts, attracting visitors from across Britain – events that may have provided the numbers of people needed to shift the enormous stones of Stonehenge. Guests apparently brought their own cattle to the event, as chemicals within the bones showed much of the meat eaten was not raised locally. It is likely these animals were transported while still alive – both for practical reasons and because bones from all parts of the body were present, rather than just those from meaty joints.

Patterns of burning on the pig bones revealed that comparatively wasteful methods of cooking, such as barbecuing, were favoured, and the presence of large dumps of bones with no rodent gnawing marks indicated the leftovers were probably buried soon after eating had ceased. Analysis of fatty residues preserved on the inside of pottery fragments indicate cow's milk, cheeses or butters may also have been consumed. The pigs' teeth were found to be relatively small and unworn, providing further evidence for extravagance, as it demonstrated that many were slaughtered before reaching full maturity. The teeth also revealed that many pigs were slaughtered during the autumn/midwinter period, indicating this may have been an important time of year for feasting – a fact which further emphasizes links to Stonehenge, whose architecture is aligned toward the midwinter solstice setting sun.

If the evidence from Durrington Walls is anything to go by, places such as Stonehenge were constructed willingly by a well-fed set of honoured guests, rather than by an oppressed gang of labourers.

MARDEN HENGE Alt Name: **Hatfield Earthworks**

Henge | Nearest Village: **Marden**

Map: **SU 0908 5820** | Sheets: **E130 L173** | Lat: **51.32283N** | Long: **1.87108W**

Barney Harris

Enclosing an area of some 14ha (35 acres), Marden Henge ranks as one of Britain's "mega-henges", alongside Durrington Walls, Dorchester and Avebury. It is situated roughly halfway between the great monumental complexes at Stonehenge and Avebury. Dating to around 2400BC, the enormous enclosure bank and ditch are more irregular than that at Durrington Walls, comprising a series of straight sections rather than smooth arcs. Two entrances into the enclosure exist: one to the southeast and one to the north, where excavations in 1969 located the skeleton of a young woman along with pottery, antler picks and flint tools. A gravel-covered avenue links the southeastern entrance to the River Avon. In 2010, not far from this entrance, archaeologists located the remains of a single Neolithic building. The purpose of the structure is puzzling, but the remains of a large central hearth led the excavators to suggest it may have functioned as a sweat lodge.

Cat's Brain: A House for the Living?

Andy Burnham, founder and Editor of the Megalithic Portal, with thanks to Jim Leary

In summer 2017, Dr Jim Leary and a team from the University of Reading excavated a long barrow site a few kilometres east of Marden Henge known as Cat's Brain. It's been accepted for decades that Neolithic long barrows are burial monuments; however, many don't contain much in the way of human remains, and none at all were found at Cat's Brain. Instead of a tomb, the dig revealed evidence of a huge timber hall, 20 × 10m (66 × 33ft) across at the front, with giant posts and horizontal beams as foundations. The slots for these were particularly deep across the front, suggesting a frontage designed to impress. So a substantial gathering place, or, as Jim Leary suggests, possibly a ceremonial house, storehouse for sacred artefacts, dwelling place of the ancestors (complete with bones) – or, indeed, all these things. But one that looked more like a "house of the living" than of the dead, and imbued with great power and community identity.

During construction, two decorated chalk blocks were deliberately deposited in a post-hole. They have carved lines and hollows – and there is no doubt these were made deliberately. This is similar to the art found in Sussex flint mines such as Harrow Hill (see page 124) and on plaques discovered at various sites (see page 52). This form of graffiti-like art is coming to seem more significant the more that's found of it, and suggests the act of building a monument, or mining chalk, or stone for axes had an importance beyond the mere practical.

Frequently timber "houses" like these were in use for only two or three generations (the lifetime or memory of one individual perhaps?) before being deliberately burned down or abandoned. At Cat's Brain, deep ditches were dug either side, suggesting that quarried chalk was piled over the crumbling building, transforming it into the permanent memorial we know as an earthen long barrow.

AVEBURY

Stone Circle | Nearest Village: **Avebury**

Map: **SU 1026 6996** | Sheets: **E157 L173** | Lat: **51.42855N** | Long: **1.85381W**

Joshua Pollard

Photo © Richard Hayman

Writing in the 17th century, John Aubrey said that Avebury "does as much exceed in greatness the so renowned Stonehenge, as a cathedral doeth a parish church". Many visitors will agree. While Avebury does not have the architectural sophistication of Stonehenge, nor its sublime grandeur, it stands as one of the most impressive prehistoric monuments in Europe. Like Stonehenge, this is a complex monument built in a series of stages over perhaps a millennium, from the early–mid third to the early second millennium BC. The henge encloses a low ridge to the east of the Winterbourne stream, overlooked by low hills on most sides. Its structure is best conceived as a series of nested spaces, the "deepest" and perhaps most sacred of these being defined by the central settings within the Inner Circles. Outwardly it is defined by a massive earthwork, 420m (1,378ft) in diameter. Set inside the bank and ditch is the Outer Circle (the largest stone circle in the world), itself enclosing two Inner Circles (Northern and Southern) with substantial megalithic settings at their centres (the Cove and former Obelisk). Several additional megaliths are scattered along the low ridge running north–south through the henge.

There have been various campaigns of excavation, the most notable being in 1865 by A.C. Smith and W. Cunnington, from 1908–22 by Harold St George Gray, and 1937–9 by Alexander Keiller. The latter were on an ambitious scale, and tied to a programme of restoration, which included the raising of fallen and buried stones and marking of others long taken away, and the removal of several buildings inside the circles. Keiller's work effectively created the Avebury we see today.

BANK AND DITCH

Typical of many henges, the earthwork enclosure is formed of an external bank and internal ditch, broken by four entrances through which modern roads now run. This is known to be of two-stage construction, though it remains uncertain when the initial earthwork was created (estimates would place it somewhere between 3000 and 2600BC). The bank and ditch we see today date to the 26th century BC. A true sense of the original scale of the earthwork can only be appreciated when it is realized that the bank has settled and slumped and the ditch half-filled with silt. Gray's excavations showed the ditch against the southern entrance to be 10m (33ft) deep, reaching the top of the water table. The builders would have used antler picks and perhaps wooden digging sticks to cut through the chalk.

OUTER CIRCLE

The Outer Circle follows the inner edge of the ditch, and on present evidence looks to have been created soon after this was dug. Comprising an estimated 98 stones, each standing 2–4m (6ft 7in–13ft) high, it represents one of the largest single exercises in megalith building in Neolithic Europe. The stones are graded, with the largest and most geometric blocks set at the entrances. As with all the Avebury megaliths, the stones are unshaped and likely chosen for their size, natural shape and perhaps connections to particular parts of the landscape.

INNER CIRCLES

The Southern and Northern Inner Circles are set along the natural ridge enclosed by the henge, and being on higher ground afford better views of the surrounding landscape than other spaces within the monument. Though much smaller than the outer circle, they are still colossal at around 100m (328ft) in diameter, and make use of particularly large sarsen blocks.

103

OBELISK, Z-FEATURE AND COVE

Contained within the Inner Circles and so set in the "deepest" space in the monument are further megalithic settings: the Obelisk and what is known as the Z-feature in the Southern Inner Circle; and the Cove in the Northern. They are notable for the size of their stones, and in being square elements within a monument otherwise made up of circles. The western stone of the Cove is now known to be deeply set in the ground, and to comprise a block of c.100 tonnes (110 tons) – by weight perhaps the largest megalith in Britain. While long-since destroyed, according to antiquarian records, the Obelisk was around 7m (23ft) long. Recent geophysical survey shows the Obelisk to have been enclosed by a square arrangement of megaliths c.30m (98ft) across, with stones much larger than those re-erected by Keiller on the restored western side. There is tantalizing evidence that the whole was constructed around the site of a much earlier Neolithic house, and that this relatively modest wooden structure provided the focus for unfolding monumentalization that would ultimately lead to the Avebury we see today. The Inner Circles and their internal settings may be among the earliest elements of the site.

The henge is often assumed to have been a centre of gathering and worship. Curiously, little in the way of later Neolithic artefacts have been found during excavation. Either the monument was kept "clean" or it was visited by only a few: in this sense being a reserved sacred space within the landscape. By the early Bronze Age deposits of human bone were being placed in the henge ditch, suggesting a deep connection to ancestral rites and worship.

Nearby | At SU 0867 7144, some 2km (1¼ miles) WNW of Avebury, the early Neolithic enclosure on **Windmill Hill** is among the largest sites of its kind, its scale reflecting its importance and the level of participation in its construction and use. It may even be regarded as the precursor to the Avebury henge. The enclosure is made up of a series of three concentric circuits of ditches, the

Photo © Jim Champion

outer 360m (1,181ft) across, enclosing 8.5ha (21 acres). As is characteristic of so-called causewayed enclosures, the ditches are interrupted by numerous causeways rather than being continuous. The enclosure was constructed in stages during the 37th century BC. Excavations during the 1920s, 1950s and 1980s discovered rich collections of animal bone and artefacts, much of it carefully deposited in the ditches. Human remains were also present. While the primary focus of the site was gathering and feasting, it looks as though Windmill Hill was also a place of settlement, of mortuary and ancestor rituals, and many other activities that made up the diversity of early Neolithic life.

Development of the Avebury Landscape

Joshua Pollard, Reader in Archaeology at the University of Southampton

The Avebury monuments cluster around the headwaters of the upper Kennet valley in north Wiltshire, close to the northern edge of the Wessex chalk uplands. Much of the archaeological fame of this region resides in its spectacular late Neolithic monuments. The Avebury henge (see page 102), its megalithic avenues (see page 107), Silbury Hill (see page 108) and the West Kennet palisaded enclosures (see page 110) are among the largest megalithic, earthen and wooden constructions found in the Neolithic of Atlantic Europe.

While monument building here reached its apogee in the centuries around 2500BC, the origins of this remarkable ceremonial complex, and the pre-eminent status of this landscape, must be sought in developments during the earlier Neolithic. On present evidence, the first farming communities in the region look to have been established close to 4000BC. By the 37th century BC they were well established, and the wider Avebury landscape – taking in the chalk downlands to the south, west and east – relatively well populated. Key monuments such as the Windmill Hill enclosure (see opposite) and the West Kennet long barrow (see page 109) – one of 30 or so long barrows in the wider landscape – belong to this time. Both stone-chambered and earthen/chalk-mounded examples are present; the latter more common in the western half of the region. Many were tombs of sorts, others, such as South Street, near Avebury Trusloe, had no funerary function. By virtue of its scale and the wealth of material found in its ditches, particularly animal bone, the enclosure on Windmill Hill was a major, extra-regional focus for gatherings and feasting events, establishing a tradition of collective ceremonial activity that was to continue and grow.

During the first half of the third millennium BC, both settlement and monument building were more focused on the valley floor around the Winterbourne and head of the River Kennet. At the heart of the area is the Avebury henge, which seems to have the longest history of construction and use of the region's ceremonial sites. Its stone circles and avenues make use of the local sarsen stone: a silcrete rock that was originally widely distributed across the Avebury landscape.

By 2500BC the pace of monument building had markedly increased. This repeats a picture found across Wessex, and could mark a response to the ideological challenge posed by the introduction of the new ways of life and beliefs of Continental Beaker groups. The numbers of Beaker newcomers are likely to have been small to begin with, but their impact would prove profound and lasting. Building ever-larger monuments like Silbury Hill may have been a way of reinforcing existing belief systems and ancestrally sanctioned authority in the face of these new world views. Over the space of a few generations many of the elements of the Avebury henge, Silbury Hill, the Sanctuary (page 112) and the West Kennet palisaded enclosures were created. Separate sites were integrated into a single ceremonial complex through the creation of linking avenues connecting Avebury with the Sanctuary and the Longstones); while the Sanctuary, West Kennet palisades and Silbury Hill are visually linked and connected to a degree by the River Kennet. This may have served to structure landscape-scale as opposed to site-specific ceremonial activity, and, by tying together places with history, enforced a particular narrative of the landscape and its occupation. The process would have involved participation from far and wide, and stretched resources to the limit. It likely culminated with the building of the colossal mound of Silbury Hill.

Communities were still being drawn into the region during the early Bronze Age (2200–1500BC), as testified by the 300 or so round barrows that cover a variety of burials, and by the ongoing deposition of human remains within Avebury henge. Much of this remarkable history of ceremonial activity remains visible in the landscape, even though ploughing, stone breaking and decay have taken their toll. Avebury preserves a distinct sense of place and a connection to an intriguing past. Archaeological fieldwork is ongoing, with new geophysical surveys across the landscape, and a programme underway to investigate prehistoric settlements. The Living with Monuments project has highlighted the scale of settlement within the region, showing this was by no means a reserved "ritual" landscape. A connection existed between monument building and routine living, and certain locations with long histories of Neolithic settlement, such as on Overton Hill and at Avebury itself, were later monumentalized.

Unique Transfigurative Rock Art?

Terence Meaden, archaeologist and former Professor of Physics at Dalhousie University, Canada

My contention is that there is a master carving at Avebury Cove in which, with a changing viewpoint of a single carved surface, transfiguration takes place between (a) a fine human face sculpted in profile facing the winter solstice sunset, and (b) a hare seen in spring boxing mode when this same rock surface is viewed perpendicularly. The pecked carving is subtle, being highly refined. The head of the hare becomes the eye of the human when viewed edgewise. The back of the hare is the cheek of the human face.

Sunlight direction is optimal for viewing this rock art in the morning after 11 am, when the deep carving around the human eye can be seen to be particularly impressive and skilfully executed. This may be the only sculpture in the world in the prehistory and history of art that exhibits this extraordinary duality.

See page 363 for reference.

Photos © Terence Meaden

The dual hare/face-profile sculpture on one of the stones at Avebury Cove

LONGSTONE COVE
Alt Names: **Adam and Eve Stones,**
Beckhampton Avenue | **Standing Stones** | Nearest Village: **Avebury**
Map: **SU 0891 6931** | Sheets: **E157 L173** | Lat: **51.42273N** | Long: **1.87324W**

Joshua Pollard

Photo © Jim Champion

Known colloquially as Adam and Eve, the Longstones mark the end of Avebury's second megalithic avenue: the Beckhampton Avenue. Confirmed through excavation in 1999, the Beckhampton Avenue was very similar in form, date and surely function to the better preserved West Kennet Avenue. Eve is the one remaining visible stone of the Beckhampton Avenue. Adam is the remaining side stone of a box-like setting of large stones analogous to the Avebury Cove. This setting may both mark and memorialize the site of an earlier earthwork enclosure, which was briefly used, then deliberately levelled, during the late Neolithic.

WEST KENNET AVENUE
Stone Rows | Nearest Village: **Avebury**
Map: **SU 1069 6928** | Sheets: **E157 L173** | Lat: **51.42243N** | Long: **1.84764W**

Joshua Pollard

The West Kennet Avenue runs for 2.4km (1½ miles) from the southern entrance of the Avebury henge to the Sanctuary (see page 112) on Overton Hill. Until the 17th century much of its course remained quite visible, but, as with Avebury, stone removal, burial and breaking eradicated much. Its northern

third was excavated and restored by Alexander Keiller in 1934–5, and this is the best section to visit. For most of its course the Avenue comprises paired standing sarsen stones set 15m (49ft) apart, the pairs being spaced at 20–30m (66–98ft) intervals. There are indications that in its mid-section, as it approaches the dry valley around the hamlet of West Kennet, the form of the

Photo © Ben Cremin

Avenue changes to a single row of stones, potentially incorporating a short gap. It may have been created in stages. There are hints of a low turf bank contained within the lines of stones along at least part of its length. The best estimates for the date of the Avenue are within the range 2500–2200BC – it was certainly present by the time burials with Chalcolithic/early Bronze Age beakers were placed against some of the stones. Traces of axe polishing can be seen on two of the stones (19b and 32a).

Curiously, but with seemingly deliberate intent, at either end the Avenue fails to align properly with the monuments it "connects". Its northern end is offset to the southern entrance of the henge, while at the Sanctuary it runs askew to the axis of the timber circles, and entry into that monument was blocked by a large stone. Perhaps it was never intended for human procession, but acted as a spirit pathway.

Nearby | At SU 1098 6931, 290m (950ft) east of West Kennet Avenue and on the valley floor south of Avebury, **Falkner's Circle** is named for the Mr Falkner who first recognized it, in 1840. He saw one standing stone, two prostrate, and nine "hollow places" where stones had stood, forming a circle c.40m (131ft) in diameter. Only the standing stone now remains, partially buried in an old hedge line. Excavations in 2002 identified stone-holes and stone destruction pits relating to some of the missing megaliths. Unlike at the Sanctuary (see page 112), there was no timber phase to this monument. Had the one standing stone not survived, it is unlikely the circle would have been recognized. This raises the possibility of other, now fully cleared, small stone circles existing undetected within the landscape. A possible long barrow, now plough-flattened, lies to the north.

SILBURY HILL

Prehistoric Mound | Nearest Village: **Avebury**
Map: **SU 1001 6853** | Sheets: **E157 L173** | Lat: **51.4157N** | Long: **1.85744W**   Joshua Pollard

Silbury Hill is a remarkable monument, whose simple external geometry conceals a complex sequence of construction. It occupies a low-lying position among a number of springs that feed into the River Kennet. During the Neolithic, when the water table was likely higher, it may even have marked the source of that river. In its finished form it is the largest prehistoric mound in Europe, being 130m (427ft) in diameter and 40m (131ft) high. Through recent investigations we know its construction spans the 25th and 24th centuries BC, placing it at the end of the late Neolithic. Despite the mound's resemblance to a giant

Photo © Mike Bodman

barrow, there is no indication that it ever covered a burial. The monument seems to have developed almost organically, starting as a small, low gravel mound, which was subsequently enlarged and contained within a henge-like earthwork. This was then enveloped within progressively larger mounds. Much of the body of the mound comes from chalk quarried from a substantial encircling ditch. On the west side is a tank-like extension to the ditch whose function remains unknown. Whatever the precise purpose of Silbury, its connection to the source of the Kennet seems explicit. Silbury continued to exert an influence on later developments in the landscape. The Roman road from Mildenhall (Cunetio) to Bath (Aquae Sulis), passes the mound, and a large Romano-British settlement and shrine complex developed in its shadow. The summit of the mound looks to have been fortified during the late Saxon period.

WEST KENNET LONG BARROW ★

Long Barrow | Nearest Village: **Avebury**
Map: **SU 1050 6774** | Sheets: **E157 L173** | Lat: **51.40858N** | Long: **1.85042W**   Joshua Pollard

Photo © Travellight

To walk into the West Kennet long barrow is to enter a built space more than 5,500 years old. The barrow was constructed during the mid-37th century BC, around the same time as the Windmill Hill enclosure (see page 104). At 100m (328ft) long it is, along with the nearby East Kennet long barrow, one of the largest monuments of its kind. It is certainly exceptional in terms of the size and accessibility of its sarsen stone chambers. Other Cotswold-Severn barrows were constructed with very constricted passages and chambers. West Kennet looks to be a space in which gatherings and ceremonies would have taken place alongside burial.

The chamber area extends 12m (39ft) into the mound. Excavations in the 19th century by John Thurnam and then in 1955–6 by Richard Atkinson and Stuart Piggott uncovered the remains of around 36 individuals within the chambers, with adults and infants of both sexes buried here. The bodies had been allowed to decay, and the skeletal remains reordered, with certain elements (notably skulls and long bones) removed for use in ceremonies elsewhere. There was some variation in the kinds of people buried in each of the five chambers: adult males and a child in the west; male and female adults exclusively in the northeast; a majority of children in the southeast; and people of mixed age and sex in the southwest and northwest. The main phase of burial may have lasted only 30 years. After a hiatus, the chambers were deliberately infilled with deposits of pottery, worked flint, animal and further human bone, this activity taking place over 1,500 years. Large stones were used to block entry into the barrow during the middle or late Neolithic, creating today's impressive façade.

Nearby | Around SU 110 682, 678m (2,224ft) ENE of West Kennet long barrow, on the River Kennet valley floor, are two late Neolithic **palisaded enclosures**. Although nothing is now visible on the ground, they were both substantial timber-walled enclosures, with massive trimmed oak posts within deep palisade trenches. The eastern (Enclosure 1) straddles the River Kennet and encloses within its two circuits an area of 4ha (10 acres); Enclosure 2 lies immediately to the west, and south of the river, and encloses 5ha (13.5 acres). Within Enclosure 2 are smaller circular monuments, and two other circular structures lie to the south, connected to it by radial palisade lines. When the enclosures were investigated in 1987–92, large quantities of animal bone and grooved ware were discovered, hinting at feasting here. The date is uncertain, with radiocarbon dates from charcoal suggesting they were created in the late 4th millennium BC, while those from animal bone imply contemporaneity with Silbury Hill (dating to between the 25th and 24th century BC, see page 108).

At SU 1163 6684, 1.4km (almost 1 mile) ESE of West Kennet long barrow, is the **East Kennet** long barrow. There is no public access, but you can see it from the byway to the south of the village. Covered in trees, it's longer than West Kennet, at 105m (344ft) and up to 6.5m (21ft) high. It has never been excavated but is assumed to contain a chamber or chambers.

THE POLISHER ★

Axe Polisher | Nearest Village: **Avebury**
Map: **SU 1283 7150** | Sheets: **E157 L173** | Lat: **51.44234N** | Long: **1.81679W**

Above Avebury on sarsen-littered Fyfield Down (the stones are known as Grey Wethers for their resemblance to sheep) is a wonderful thing: a stone used to polish stone axes. It may or may not have begun life as a standing stone. The markings are a rare survival in the UK – although another example can be seen in the West Kennet Avenue – and looking at the grooves and smoothed bowl-shaped area created by sharpening and polishing axes, it's possible to feel a direct connection with the people who once used the stone.

Photo © Scott Whitehouse

Archaeoacoustics

Steve Marshall, author of *Exploring Avebury: The Essential Guide*

How did prehistoric people perceive sound? Many megalithic structures have strange and interesting acoustic properties, so were these deliberately engineered? The study of prehistoric sound is an exciting and relatively new field of archaeology that is making some fascinating discoveries around the world.

Rupert Till, of Huddersfield University, has studied the acoustics of decorated Paleolithic caves, and ancient structures such as the Hal Saflieni Hypogeum on Malta. Some of Till's work was conducted in the USA using a full-size concrete replica of Stonehenge to explore acoustic effects of the monument as it was when newly built. The acoustics of other megalithic sites around Britain have been investigated by Aaron Watson, Paul Devereux and others; Simon Wyatt has replicated the musical instruments of prehistory, such as Neolithic clay drums and swan bone flutes.

My own work is centred on Avebury. The sarsen standing stones of Avebury's monuments are extremely reflective to sound, producing clear and impressive echoes. How would these have been interpreted by Neolithic people? Perhaps echoes were regarded as the voices of ancestral spirits?

Only one stone survives of Avebury's Beckhampton Cove, once a rectilinear setting of four great sarsen stone slabs. On building a full-size model from sheets of chipboard, it was found that sound made inside the cove was reflected out by two splayed side stones. To a listener outside of the structure, the source of the sound could be heard but not seen, giving the impression that one of the end stones was "speaking". Was the cove perhaps used as an oracle?

The West Kennet long barrow, also near Avebury, has extraordinary acoustic properties. Its inner chambers of sarsen stone produce musical resonances that can alter and enhance the male speaking voice. It also has an infrasonic resonance of below 10 Hz that is too low to be heard but can be felt, producing strong impressions of an unseen "presence". My experiments have shown that by deliberately exciting the barrow's infrasonic resonance, altered states of consciousness can potentially be produced. Could this effect have been exploited in prehistory, perhaps in rites of initiation?

Whirling a bull roarer just outside the entrance makes West Kennet resonate with infrasound: those inside the barrow feel its immediate effects. I have used the bull roarer in the same way at other passage graves, including Newgrange, Fourknocks, Maeshowe and Barclodiad-y-gawres, and the Dolmens of Antiquera in Spain. No prehistoric wooden bull roarers have been found in Britain – they would anyway have quickly rotted in the damp climate. However, I have shown that knapped flint "knives" will also function as bull roarers, producing sound when attached to a string and whirled. Many thousands of these objects, showing no signs of use as knives, have been found at prehistoric sites around Britain and Ireland.

Marshall, S. 2016. *Exploring Avebury: The Essential Guide*. Stroud: The History Press

www.exploringavebury.com

THE SANCTUARY

Stone Circle | Nearest Village: **East Kennet**
Map: **SU 1183 6802** | Sheets: **E157 L173** | Lat: **51.41112N** | Long: **1.8313W**

Photo by Adam Stanford © Aerial-Cam Ltd

Set on the southern spur of Overton Hill, today the Sanctuary's presence is marked by a series of concrete markers. Until the early 18th century, the site survived as a concentric stone circle, made up of two rings of sarsen stone, around 40m (131ft) in diameter. It was connected to the Avebury henge via the West Kennet Avenue (see page 107). The Sanctuary was located and excavated by Maud Cunnington in 1930. In addition to the stone-holes of the two rings, she found post-holes belonging to a multi-ring timber structure. Grooved ware pottery shows this to be late Neolithic, and it shares similarities with the Southern Circle at Durrington Walls and Woodhenge (see page 98) though on a more diminutive scale. Although arguments have been made for this being a special-purpose building, the timber rings were likely free-standing and perhaps joined by lintels. While not used as a dwelling, the timber settings are perhaps best thought of as a shrine that draws upon the idea of a large hall or house. The stone circles seem to have replaced the timber rings.

The building of the timber and stone monuments came after a lengthy history of activity on this part of Overton Hill, which goes back to the early Neolithic. From the Sanctuary many of the region's key monuments can be seen, including the West Kennet long barrow, Silbury Hill and the site of the West Kennet palisaded enclosures.

Nearby | At SU 1196 6816, to the immediate east and northeast of the Sanctuary, are the well-preserved early Bronze Age round barrows known as the **Seven Barrows**. They were all dug into during the 19th century, revealing both cremation and inhumation burials. In the southernmost was a rich burial in a tree-trunk coffin with a bronze dagger, axe and pin.

MERLIN'S MOUNT   Alt Name: **Marlborough Mound**

Prehistoric Mound | Nearest Town: **Marlborough**
Map: **SU 1836 6865** | Sheets: **E157 L173** | Lat: **51.41657N** | Long: **1.73737W**

Permission is needed to visit this mound in the grounds of Marlborough College. It's had quite a life, being used as the motte of Marlborough Castle and the centrepiece of a 17th-century garden. There was debate for a long time as to whether it might be older than the Norman Conquest – perhaps even as old as the mound at Silbury. Recent archaeological investigation has shown this to be the case, dating it to the Neolithic (2400BC). As with its larger sibling, no one knows why it was built, but it's interesting to note that it sits in a similarly low-lying area to Silbury Hill, close to rivers and springs. Jim Leary's Round Mounds project has been busy investigating other mottes and garden mounds, making other intriguing discoveries such as the Iron Age date of the Shipsea mound in East Yorkshire.

DEVIL'S DEN

Burial Chamber | Nearest Village: **Fyfield**
Map: **SU 1521 6965** | Sheets: **E157 L173** | Lat: **51.42565N** | Long: **1.78262W**

Photo © Jim Champion

This burial chamber was reconstructed in 1921, when the remains of the mound, about 70m (230ft) long, could still be seen. Now all that's left are the two uprights and capstone, and two fallen stones. The chamber was at the southeastern end of the barrow, which was aligned southeast–northwest. It's a fine example of a classic dolmen, the fat capstone at a slight angle and one of the uprights leaning quite dramatically. There are cup-marks on the top of the capstone.

WAYLAND'S SMITHY ★

Long Barrow | Nearest Village: **Compton Beauchamp**
Map: **SU 2809 8539** | Sheets: **E157 L174** | Lat: **51.56669N** | Long: **1.59613W**

One of Britain's most famous prehistoric monuments, Wayland's Smithy is a reconstructed long barrow, just off the Ridgeway and not far from the Uffington White Horse. In the 1960s excavations demonstrated two phases of construction here: first, there was an earthen mound aligned north–south, containing a wooden mortuary enclosure, which held the remains of at least 14 people; this was later covered by a trapezoidal chalk mound, with a façade of large sarsens to the south and a passage leading to a central chamber and two side chambers. The site looked very different in the 19th century, with

Photo © Steve Simmons

the chambers exposed – if you see an old photograph of the site, or the model constructed by Alfred Lewis in 1860, you might be surprised. The story goes that if you leave your horse here overnight with a coin for payment, Wayland, the legendary master blacksmith, will shoe it for you.

Nearby | The National Trail known as the **Ridgeway** runs for 140km (87 miles) from Overton Hill near Avebury to the Ivinghoe Beacon near Ivinghoe, following the chalk escarpment that bisects southern England. Various ancient monuments lie along its course, including Wayland's Smithy, Uffington Castle hill fort and the Uffington White Horse. Although it's claimed to be, in part at least, the oldest continuously used road in Europe, with some of the route dating back at least 5,000 years, the section near Uffington Castle is unlikely to have been in use in later prehistory as it cuts across the ditches of a Bronze Age field system and a Romano-British farmstead. See page 148 for similar doubts concerning the authenticity of the Icknield Way as a long-distance prehistoric route.

WILTSHIRE | OXFORDSHIRE

113

Top 10 Prehistoric Sites in England with Sea Views

DORCHESTER CURSUS

Cursus | Nearest Village: **Dorchester-on-Thames**
Map: **SU 5685 9595** | Sheets: **E170 L164** | Lat: **51.65946N** | Long: **1.17953W**

There's a lot of archaeology at Dorchester-on-Thames, from Neolithic earthworks to Iron Age settlements. Gravel extraction and the construction of the bypass have damaged much of the Dorchester Neolithic cursus and what remains is visible as cropmarks. Originally, two parallel banks and ditches about 60m (197ft) apart ran broadly in parallel for at least 1.6km (1 mile) northwest–southeast. Recent work by Oxford Archaeology has shown that the Dorchester Cursus extended further to the north than previously realized.

DEVIL'S QUOITS ★

Stone Circle & Henge | Nearest Village: **Stanton Harcourt**
Map: **SP 4112 0476** | Sheets: **E180 L164** | Lat: **51.74004N** | Long: **1.40588W**

Photo © Hamish Fenton

An interesting monument and a triumph of the art of reconstruction, although the setting, close to a noisy landfill site and recycling centre, is not ideal. In the 17th century John Aubrey mentions three stones remaining here, one of which was taken by a farmer around 1680 to make a bridge (and later returned to the circle). The site was extensively damaged by gravel extraction, and also by the construction of an airfield during World War II, when the henge's original external bank was levelled for the construction of the runway. By 1940, only one stone remained, with some others buried near their former positions while the airfield was in use. Excavations in 1940, 1972, 1973 and 1988 provided a complete plan of the 79m (259ft) circle, with its stone-holes, and the position of a central setting of posts. The henge, with a ditch diameter of 120m (394ft) and entrances to the ESE and WNW, is late Neolithic; the date of the circle is less clear. Between 2002 and 2008 both circle and henge were fully restored and now once again 36 gravel conglomerate stones stand within the henge, bright and fresh-looking and almost golden in colour.

> **"A fine place in the sunshine on a cold day, the gulls wheeling above us and a glimpse at what a newly built circle might have looked like."** Jackie Bates

HOAR STONE (ENSTONE)   Alt Name: **The Old Soldier**
Chambered Tomb | Nearest Village: **Enstone**
Map: **SP 3779 2375** | Sheets: **E191 L164** | Lat: **51.911N** | Long: **1.45204W**

Discreetly sited in a copse beside the road, this is a very ruinous but impressively atmospheric tomb. Green with moss, there are only three stones remaining, one nearly 2.7m (9ft) tall, the others 1.5m and 0.9m (5ft and 3ft) respectively. In 1925 there were six stones and a mound, but there's no sign of the mound or the three missing stones now. At Midsummer's Eve, it is said, the largest stone goes down to the village to drink, or alternatively to the brook at Woodford. Another story relates that the stones are an old man, his horse and his dog, all turned to stone; and still another has it that a ghost has been seen walking from the tomb north toward the village.

> "During bright mornings in winter and early spring, when the sun is still low in the sky, the light gets in under the holly trees to illuminate the stones quite nicely."
> Hamish Fenton

Nearby | At SP 3593 2208, 2.5km (1½ miles) WSW of the Hoar Stone, is the **Thor Stone** at Taston, a hefty 2.1m (7ft) stone that leans dramatically into a garden wall in the centre of the village. One story goes that it was a thunderbolt thrown by Thor himself. The village is named for the stone – in 1278 it was called "Thorstan". The village cross nearby is said to have been placed there to counteract the negative emanations from the standing stone.

At SP 3392 2354, 4km (just under 2½ miles) west of the Hoar Stone, is the **Hawk Stone**, a wonderfully wrinkled stone an impressive 2.4m (8ft) tall, in a field west of the road between Chalford Green and Dean. Local legend suggests it might once have been part of a circle, or perhaps a burial chamber, but there's no evidence to support the idea. Elsie Corbett, in her *History of Spelsbury* (1962), records a colourful story that the cleft at the top of the stone was made by the chains of the witches who were tied to it and burnt.

LYNEHAM
Long Barrow | Nearest Village: **Ascott-under-Wychwood**
Map: **SP 2975 2107** | Sheets: **E191 L164** | Lat: **51.88740N** | Long: **1.56915W**

A rather hummocky and disturbed mound, but it does have a nice, chunky 1.8m (6ft) standing stone at the northern end, which may have been part of a false entrance. The mound is 32m (105ft) long and up to 1.75m (5ft 8in) high at the northeast end, where it's 19m (62ft) wide; in the southwest it becomes almost flat and is much narrower. In 1894, two chambers were excavated on the southeast side of the mound, and at least one was found to contain charcoal, bone fragments and pottery. Two Anglo-Saxon burials had been cut into the top of the mound.

Photo © Hamish Fenton

ROLLRIGHT STONES Alt Names: **The King's Men, Rollendrith**
Megalithic Complex | Nearest Village: **Long Compton**
Map: **SP 2958 3087** | Sheets: **E191 L151** | Lat: **51.97555N** | Long: **1.57080W**

The three Rollright sites are linked in folklore through the famous tale, first mentioned in brief in William Camden's *Britannia* (1586), of the would-be king of England who was turned to stone by a witch, along with his knights and foot soldiers, when seven strides failed to reveal to him the village of Long Compton in the valley below. In 2015, the media seized on the discovery of a female skeleton, buried below an Anglo-Saxon ritual spoon (patera), as proof of the existence of Long Compton's witch – although "Rita" (as she was dubbed) actually lived some three millennia after the raising of the circle. The find gives an insight into the continuation of ceremonial activity at the site into the historic era. The Rollright Stones have a strong draw for modern Pagans and ceremonies are held here to mark the various seasonal festivals.

KING'S MEN
These interestingly weathered, oolitic limestone stones are positioned in a 33m (108ft) ring, with their smoother sides facing inward. The stones (pictured on page 119) provide a habitat for colonies of rare lichen, with patches up to 850 years old. Comparisons of antiquarian drawings and lichen analysis reveal that many of the stones have been moved and re-erected over the centuries. It is thought they originally formed an almost continuous wall of some 80 uprights, built around 2500BC. The stones are thought to be of local origin, taken from the surface of the earth rather than quarried.

As at many sites, it is said to be impossible to count the King's Men. These are certainly active stones: there were tales of the King's Men returning to life, linking hands and dancing at midnight,

and they were also said to go down to a well at Little Rollright to drink – as did the petrified king himself at the sound of the church clock striking 12. The King's Men have for centuries been a focus of interest for antiquarians and others; their earliest-known visual depiction is on a late 1580s tapestry map, one of several that were commissioned by Ralph Sheldon.

KING STONE
Perhaps as many as 1,000 years separate the building of the circle from the raising of the King Stone, now found across the road from the circle, at SP 2962 3095. This 2.5m (8ft) standing stone may well have been a marker for a Bronze Age cemetery, as a round cairn (about 17m/56ft across) and a very small barrow have been discovered close by, both containing cremations, and with evidence of upright wooden post markers. The stone's odd shape was caused by

Photo © Richard L. Dixon

the historic practice of chipping off pieces as good-luck charms and amulets against the Devil, and it was protected (along with the other Rollright sites) by the first Schedule of Ancient Monuments in 1882. The King Stone was known in local legend as the meeting place of Long Compton's witches, and was also said to mark one of the entrances to the fairy halls under the circle.

WHISPERING KNIGHTS

At SP 2993 3084, 357m (1,171ft) east of the stone circle, this portal dolmen predates the King's Men by some 1,000–1,500 years. Five slabs remain, never covered by an earth mound. A piece of jawbone

Photo © Emmanuel Weber

found in the 1920s is the only evidence of burial here. Legend tells how the knights were turned to stone as they plotted against the king (or prayed, as another version goes). There are also tales of farmers trying to make use of the slabs, without success: one used the capstone as a mill dam, but every night the uncooperative stone returned to its rightful place. It is said that women used to question the Knights, pressing an ear against a stone to receive their oracular wisdom.

LAMBOURN SEVEN BARROWS ★

Barrow Cemetery | Nearest Village: **Lambourn**
Map: **SU 3289 8288** | Sheets: **E170 L174** | Lat: **51.54198N** | Long: **1.52901W**

Some 42 barrows have been identified in the Lambourn valley, with a group of 10 (the "Seven" Barrows) running in two parallel northwest–southeast rows close to the road and clearly visible. The barrows in the Lambourn valley are mostly bowl barrows, but there are some disc and saucer barrows, and a long barrow, too (see below). Some were found to hold intact burials, some cremations. Grave goods included various flint arrows and a small, highly polished, rectangular jet pendant, perforated with a hole that was very smoothed, showing it had been worn. (Circular jet buttons with perforations showing wear have also been found in several barrows near Rudston in Yorkshire.)

Nearby | At SU 3232 8338, 836m (½ mile) northwest of the Seven Barrows, **Lambourn long barrow** is one of the oldest examples of a long barrow in Britain, although not one of the most impressive. The mound is about 70 × 18m (230 × 59ft), with half of it covered in trees. The pile of stones at the eastern end is the remains of a rough cist or chamber, excavated in 1964 and found to contain a crouched burial and later internment.

Photo by Adam Stanford © Aerial-Cam Ltd

MONT DE LA VILLE   Alt Name: **The Druids' Temple**
Passage Grave | Nearest Town: **Henley-on-Thames**
Map: **SU 7796 8140** | Sheets: **E171 L175** | Lat: **51.52614N** | Long: **0.87763W**

Now a folly in the grounds of a private estate near Henley, set about with flowerbeds and floodlighting, this unusual site is a passage grave that once stood on Mount de la Ville, St Helier, Jersey. Marshall Conway, Governor of Jersey, was encouraged by Horace Walpole to dismantle the site in 1788 and ship it to London, from where it travelled by barge up the Thames to Conway's Berkshire residence. It is unlikely that the structure has been authentically recreated, but it is in good condition. Permission is required to visit, but you can get a very good view from the Bing Maps bird's-eye feature.

HOLDEN'S FIRS
Barrow Cemetery | Nearest Village: **Mortimer**
Map: **SU 6436 6506** | Sheets: **E159 L175** | Lat: **51.38095N** | Long: **1.0766W**

A barrow cemetery with seven barrows (and traces of an eighth), all mutilated to some degree, including two large bell barrows with ditches, a third, badly damaged bowl barrow, a disc barrow and, southeast of the main area of the cemetery, another bowl barrow between the houses. In 2017 concerns were raised about damage caused by people riding quad bikes over the barrows.

Photo © Cezary Namirski

KINGSMEAD QUARRY
Prehistoric Settlement | Nearest Village: **Horton**
Map: **TQ 0170 7520** | Sheets: **E160 L176** | Lat: **51.46664N** | Long: **0.53731W**

Although there is nothing to see on the ground, this site has a complex and fascinating history, with evidence of human activity stretching back 12,000 years to the end of the last Ice Age. Four early Neolithic houses were found here, dating to around 3700BC; it's extremely rare to find houses of this period, when people were first beginning to live in permanent settlements. The houses were all rectangular, with two built from wooden posts, and the others from upright oak planks set into foundation trenches. The largest measured 15 × 7m (49 × 23ft). Also discovered here was the grave of a woman, about 40 years old, with extremely rich grave goods, including a garment fastened with amber buttons, a lignite-bead bracelet and a necklace of folded sheet gold, lignite and amber beads. The grave dates from the Copper Age, about 2400 BC. Male burials with gold possessions are known from this date, but she's the earliest-known woman buried with this kind of treasure. In early 2018, pre-quarrying archaeology discovered a causewayed enclosure nearby.

WHITELEAF BARROWS

Long Barrow & Round Barrows | Nearest Town: **Princes Risborough**
Map: **SP 8222 0398** | Sheets: **E181 L165** | Lat: **51.72851N** | Long: **0.81094W**

There are three prehistoric barrows on the hill above Princes Risborough, with views over the Vale of Aylesbury and the Chiltern Hills. To the southeast of the Whiteleaf Cross hill figure (dating from at least 1738) is a long barrow, which was re-excavated and restored in the early 21st century; a little further to the north along the hilltop are two badly damaged Bronze Age round barrows.

THERFIELD HEATH FIVE HILLS

Barrow Cemetery | Nearest Town: **Royston**
Map: **TL 3410 4025** | Sheets: **E209 L154** | Lat: **52.04443N** | Long: **0.04607W**

The Therfield Heath barrow cemetery is now on a golf course but there is free access to the heath, just watch out for flying balls. It's one of the finest collections of barrows in eastern England, all five around 20m (66ft) across and over 2m (6½ft) in height.

Nearby | At TL 3415 4017, still on the golf course and under 100m (328ft) southeast of Therfield Heath barrow cemetery, is **Therfield Heath** long barrow, the only known

Photo © Peter Herring

example in Hertfordshire. It was excavated in 1855 and again in 1935. Several inhumations and two cists containing cremations were found. The mound is 38m (125ft) long and 26m (85ft) wide at the eastern end, narrowing to 15.5m (51ft). The higher, eastern end reaches 2.2m (7ft).

KING HENRY'S MOUND

Likely Prehistoric Barrow | Nearest Town: **Richmond-upon-Thames**
Map: **TQ 1860 7315** | Sheets: **E161 L176** | Lat: **51.44493N** | Long: **0.29482W**

According to the on-site information board, this large, much-modified artificial mound is a Neolithic barrow. It's at the highest point of Richmond Park, looking down over the Thames and east along an avenue of trees to the distant dome of St Paul's Cathedral. The view is protected, preventing developers from building anything that would block it.

HORSELL COMMON
Round Barrows | Nearest Town: **Woking**
Map: **TQ 0161 5977** | Sheets: **E160 L186** | Lat: **51.32796N** | Long: **0.54302W**

Horsell Common is where the Martians landed in H.G. Wells' *War of the Worlds*. You might not find any evidence of alien invasion but there are a number of large, saucer-shaped objects. At TQ 0161 5977, the bell barrow known as Horsell Common E is considered one of Surrey's finest examples. Close to the road and the car park, it has a central mound 20m (66ft) in diameter and about 1m (3ft 3in) high, surrounded by a berm (flat platform), which is contained by a circular ditch. Beyond that, an outer bank survives to the north and east.

Photo © Andy Burnham

At TQ 0140 5980, some 212m (695ft) west of Horsell Common E, is Horsell Common W, where there are two further barrows: a large, ditched bowl barrow (pictured), about 30m (98ft) across and 1.5m (5ft) high; and a disc barrow, which is much harder to see.

Nearby | At TQ 0790 5915 (sheets: E145 L187), 6.3km (4 miles) east of Horsell Common E in a heathland setting, is **Cockcrow Hill**, a large bell barrow some 42m (138ft) in diameter and 3.3m (11ft) high. The mound is covered in trees, and has been eroded by footpaths in places, but is still in fairly good condition. A cremation burial was found during excavation in 1911. The barrow is very close to the junction of the M25 with the A3, but on pleasant heathland and worth a visit. Park at Ockham Common car park.

MICHELDEVER WOOD
Round Barrows | Nearest Village: **Micheldever**
Map: **SU 5277 3721** | Sheets: **OL32 L185** | Lat: **51.13174N** | Long: **1.24722W**

There's an archaeological trail through Micheldever Woods that takes in a number of barrows and an Iron Age "banjo" enclosure. The bowl barrow is damaged on its northern side by quarrying for flints or clay, but is still some 25m (82ft) across and 2m (6½ft) high. The woods are stunning in spring when the bluebells are out.

SETLEY PLAIN
Round Barrows | Nearest Village: **Brockenhurst**
Map: **SU 2962 0002** | Sheets: **OL22 L196** | Lat: **50.79898N** | Long: **1.58107W**

On Setley Plain in the New Forest are three impressive disc barrows, all of them damaged by antiquarian investigation in the 18th century, when evidence of buried cremations was recorded. The ditch and outer bank of the northwestern barrow are interrupted by the bank of one of the others.

DAMERHAM

Barrow Complex | Nearest Village: **Damerham**
Map: **SU 0884 1534** | Sheets: **OL22 L184** | Lat: **50.93743N** | Long: **1.87556W**

At Damerham, a huge ceremonial complex has recently been discovered, dating back to the Neolithic and of unusual importance and size (covering some 200ha/494 acres). Cropmarks identified during a routine aerial survey revealed the first henge-type structures to be found in Hampshire, plus two big long barrows, the larger of which extends to 70m (230ft). The henges showed signs of post-holes, suggesting rings of timber uprights. Other monuments found included an unusual U-shaped enclosure with post-holes dating to the Bronze Age, as well as 26 round barrows and large quantities of pot sherds and flint tools and debris. One henge was found to be cut through a natural sink-hole filled with brightly coloured orange soil, which contrasted dramatically with the whiteness of the chalk. Dr Helen Wickstead, who led the excavation, suggests these colours would have played a part in the design. See page 84 for position on map, but there is little to see on the ground now.

LONG STONE (MOTTISTONE)

Standing Stone | Nearest Village: **Mottistone**
Map: **SZ 4071 8422** | Sheets: **OL29 L196** | Lat: **50.65624N** | Long: **1.42545W**

Despite the name there are actually two stones here, one fallen. The Long Stone itself is around 4m (14ft) tall, while its prostrate companion is about 2.4m (8ft). It's thought they are all that remains of a long-destroyed long barrow. The site has fine views over the downs to the sea.

Nearby | At SZ 4062 8469, 478m (1,568ft) NNW of the Long Stone, is **Mottistone Down** (or

Photo © Laurence Baker

123

Harboro Down) barrow cemetery, finely positioned on a ridge of the downs beside the Tennyson Trail. There are five bowl barrows up here, one very badly damaged. They're generally large and up to 3m (10ft) high.

CISSBURY RING

Hill Fort & Flint Mines | Nearest Village: **Findon**
Map: **TQ 1391 0803** | Sheets: **OL10 L198** | Lat: **50.86057N** | Long: **0.38286W**

Photo © fostersice

Dating from around 250BC, Cissbury Ring is the largest Iron Age hill fort in Sussex and the second largest in England, covering some 24ha (60 acres). Partially enclosed within its ramparts are Neolithic flint mines; when the mine shafts were excavated in the 1870s, three of the 13 investigated were found to contain rock art and carved chalk blocks. Further prehistoric art was found in another shaft excavated in the 1950s, suggesting once again that there was more going on here than the simple extraction of a raw material (see page 151). The site's name probably comes from 16th-century attempts to associate the fort with the Saxon chief Cissa.

Nearby | At TQ 0815 1000 (sheets: OL10 L197), 6km (3¾ miles) WNW of Cissbury Ring, **Harrow Hill** is another hill fort or enclosure built on earlier flint mines. It's on private land but access is sometimes arranged for Heritage Open Days. The earliest mines, at the top of the hill, were probably open-cast quarries, with the shafts leading down into galleries a later development. Despite considerable plough damage, 245 pits have been counted. Excavations in the 1920s uncovered a number of chalk blocks and surfaces with crosshatching and filled triangles – art of the type seen at Cissbury and Grime's Graves (see page 150). This suggests that prehistoric flint mines were monuments in their own right, perhaps with their own rituals that revered the underworld as a mirror image of the megaliths reaching to the sky.

WHITEHAWK CAMP

Causewayed Enclosure | Nearest City: **Brighton**
Map: **TQ 3303 0477** | Sheets: **OL11 L198** | Lat: **50.82719N** | Long: **0.11252W**

One of Britain's earliest Neolithic monuments, the earthworks at Whitehawk date from *c.* 3500BC. There are at least five concentric interrupted ring ditches or causewayed enclosures on the hill. Not much of the site, which covers about 6ha (14 acres), has been excavated, but burials have been found in the infill of the ditches, as well as pottery, flint tools and a large amount of animal bone, suggesting feasting took place here. The site has suffered somewhat from the construction of the racecourse, but is still quite well preserved in places.

BELLE TOUT

Prehistoric Enclosure | Nearest Town: **Eastbourne**
Map Ref: **TV 5610 9570** | Sheets: **OL25 L199** | Lat: **50.73996N** | Long: **0.21093E**

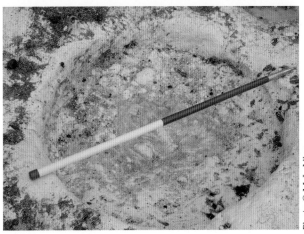

Photo © M.J. Allen

Coastal erosion is eating away at these earthwork enclosures at a rate of about 0.5m (1½ft) a year. Originally there were at least three here, but now only two remain, the largest of which is more than 1.2km (¾ mile) long and encloses more than 20ha (49 acres). Comprising an earth bank with a continuous ditch made from linked pits, it may have originally taken in the entire headland – and could well have been the largest enclosure in the country. The site has been investigated by Bournemouth University, raising as many questions as answers. The larger enclosure, known as A, may have been a stock corral dating to the Iron Age, but the finds from the interior are almost entirely struck flint, which suggests a Neolithic to middle Bronze Age date. The inner enclosures (including the now vanished Enclosure B) are assumed to be an enclosed Beaker settlement. Alternatively, the enclosures may have had a more ritualistic purpose, perhaps focused around a remarkable chalk-cut shaft exposed in 1971 by cliff erosion in Enclosure B. Just 1.7m (5½ft) wide, it was found to run down 43m (141ft) from the top of the cliff, with evidence of foot holes and tool marks. The bottom was waterlogged so the feature may have been a well, but has parallels with a Bronze Age ritual shaft at Wilsford, south of Stonehenge. The shaft has now been washed away, but remarkably in 2016 the very bottom – visible as a circular depression on the foreshore (pictured above) – was located by CITiZAN coastal archaeology volunteers, and excavated with the assistance of M.J. Allen. A coffee shop near the top of the cliff has a display about the site.

BOURNE HILL   Alt Name: **Willingdon Hill**

Round Barrows | Nearest Town: **Eastbourne**
Map Ref: **TQ 5770 0096** | Sheets: **OL25 L199** | Lat: **50.78676N** | Long: **0.23585E**

Up on Willingdon Hill, as well as fine views, you'll find a pair of bowl barrows, one of which was reused as a windmill tump between the 16th and 19th centuries, until the last mill was destroyed in a storm in 1817. The northeastern barrow is about 15m (49ft) across and 0.4m (1ft 3in) high, while the southwestern one is some 25m (82ft) across and 1.2m (4ft) high, with a flat top and a central hollow. A track climbs the eastern side of the mound. An almost circular flint knife was found nearby.

> **"This tumulus near Beachy Head is unusual because it has a flat top. If you want to show the curvature of the Earth, this is the place to do it."** Jon Morris

COLDRUM

Chambered Tomb | Nearest Village: **Trottiscliffe**
Map: **TQ 6544 6072** | Sheets: **E148 L178/L188** | Lat: **51.32152N** | Long: **0.37285E**

Photo © pxl.store

Signposted from Trottiscliffe (pronounced "Trosely"!), this is the best preserved of the Medway Megaliths. Named for the now demolished farm of the same name, Coldrum is an impressive site, with four large sarsens forming an exposed chamber overlooking the Medway valley. It's aligned east–west, and the mound, about 20m (66ft) in length, may have been surrounded by a kerb of smaller sarsens. A number of excavations have taken place here, one resulting in the discovery of the bones of some 22 people. The Medway Megaliths are generally considered among the earliest prehistoric monuments in Britain – Coldrum dates to around 4000BC, and the bones found there are some of the earliest remains of Neolithic people ever found. Some may have been interred elsewhere before being brought to the tomb.

THE CHESTNUTS

Chambered Tomb or Long Barrow | Nearest Village: **Addington**
Map: **TQ 6526 5917** | Sheets: **E148 L178/L188** | Lat: **51.30765N** | Long: **0.36955E**

Chestnuts is a partially reconstructed long barrow, standing on private land. Little remains of the 20m (66ft) mound; at its eastern end, 12 large sarsens form the chamber and façade. The capstone has been displaced. When the chamber was excavated in the 1950s, the cremated remains of at least nine people were found, as well as Neolithic pottery. A large number of Mesolithic flints have been found in the area, some beneath the tomb. The site is very close to the motorway but still peaceful and atmospheric.

Nearby | At TQ 6533 5910, 99m (325ft) southeast of the Chestnuts, is **Addington** long barrow, with a road built right through the middle of it. It's on private land, so permission is needed to access the site. About 25 stones remain, but it's a bit of a jumble and not that clear what's going on. It's thought the original mound could have been 70m (230ft) long, with the chamber at the northeastern end, which has mostly collapsed due to excavation in the mid-19th century.

> **"If you can't arrange access to the Addington long barrow, the top of the stones can be seen from the road that passes through it."** Martyn Copcutt

KIT'S COTY

Chambered Tomb or Long Barrow | Nearest Village: **Aylesford**
Map: **TQ 7452 6084** | Sheets: **E148 L178/L188** | Lat: **51.31989N** | Long: **0.50309E**

Photo © Valery Egorov

One of the best-known burial chambers in Britain, Kit's Coty is another of the Medway Megaliths. Although tightly fenced in with iron railings on the instructions of General Pitt Rivers (this was one of the first Scheduled Ancient Monuments), it's quite impressive, with the tallest stone 2.4m (8ft) tall and looking very much like a classic dolmen, with three uprights and a capstone, giving little sense of how it looked when first built. Some of the 80m (262ft) long mound remains, although this is clearest in aerial photographs, and the kerb stones are long gone. The chamber has been open since at least the late 16th century. The site is a popular place to celebrate the solstices, and the Kit's Coty Morris dance the sun up at the stones every May Day.

> "Early prints show a large stone marking the west end: this was called the General's Tombstone and was blown up in 1867, allegedly because it made ploughing difficult."
> Vicky Tuckman

UPPER WHITE HORSE STONE

Possible Chambered Tomb | Nearest Village: **Aylesford**
Map: **TQ 7535 6032** | Sheets: **E148 L178/L188** | Lat: **51.31496N** | Long: **0.51473E**

The Upper White Horse Stone is believed to be all that remains of a chambered tomb, although there is little or no evidence to support this. This large sarsen, 3 × 1.5m (10 × 5ft), gets its name from its alleged resemblance to a horse, or a horse's head. Another large upright, the Lower White Horse Stone, is said to have once stood about 300m (984ft) to the west, but was destroyed in 1823. The area around the stone was excavated as part of the works for the Channel Tunnel Rail Link, revealing evidence of late Bronze Age/early Iron Age settlement, and a very rare Neolithic longhouse. Sadly, the stone frequently suffers from vandalism.

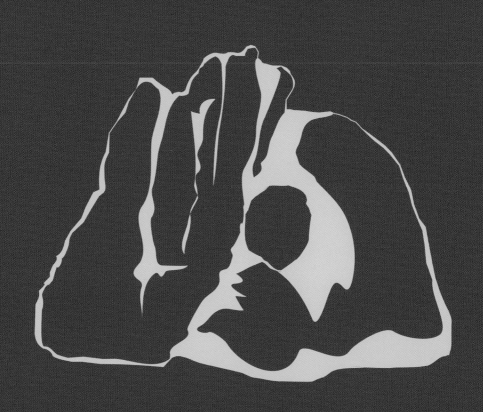

MIDLANDS & EAST OF ENGLAND

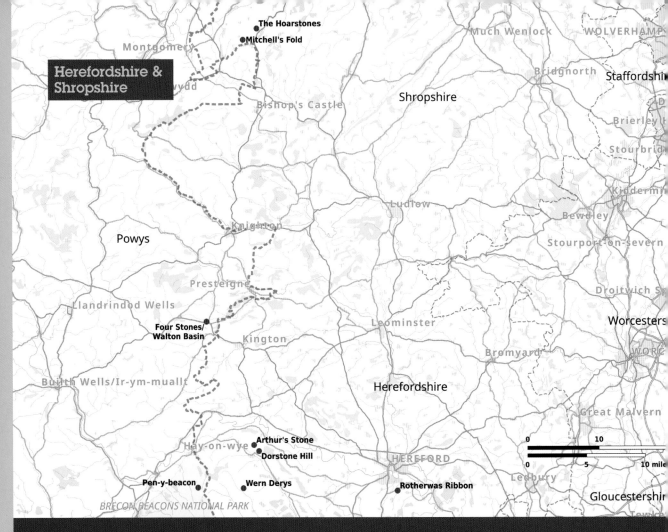

Herefordshire & Shropshire

The Hoarstones
Mitchell's Fold
Montgomery
Bridgnorth
Staffordshi
Shropshire
Brierley H
Bishop's Castle
Stourbri
Ludlow
Kidderm
Bewdley
Knighton
Stourport-on-severn
Powys
Presteigne
Droitwich S
Llandrindod Wells
Leominster
Worcesters
Four Stones/
Walton Basin
Kington
Bromyard
WOR
Builth Wells/Ir-ym-muallt
Herefordshire
Great Malvern
Arthur's Stone
Hay-on-wye
Dorstone Hill
HEREFORD
Pen-y-beacon
Wern Derys
Rotherwas Ribbon
Ledbury
Gloucestershir
BRECON BEACONS NATIONAL PARK

0   10
0   5   10 mile

Top 15 Timber & Earthen Sites in England

WERN DERYS
Standing Stone | Nearest Village: **Dorstone**
Map: **SO 3036 3726** | Sheets: **OL13 L161** | Lat: **52.02935N** | Long: **3.01647W**

Photo © Peter Nash

At 2.3m (7ft 9in), Wern Derys is Herefordshire's tallest standing stone. It was re-erected after falling in the 1980s.

> "There is a legend that a great general is buried here, and that a farmer once dug round the stone and hitched 12 horses to it to try to uproot it." Jonathan Sant

ARTHUR'S STONE
⭐
Chambered Tomb | Nearest Village: **Dorstone**
Map: **SO 3189 4313** | Sheets: **E201 OL13 L161** | Lat: **52.08231N** | Long: **2.99537W**

On the upper slopes of Merbach Hill, looking over to the Black Mountains, are the very impressive remains of this Cotswold-Severn chambered tomb. Five of the nine uprights (up to 1.1m/3ft 7in high) support a massive capstone (now split) and you can see the remnants of an entrance passage with a right-angled turn, running 5m (16ft) east–west and then south for some 3m (10ft). It's long been associated with King Arthur, either as the battlefield where he fought and slew a giant, or as the final resting place of the

Photo by Adam Stanford © Aerial-Cam Ltd

legendary king himself. The forecourt faces south to the Skirrid, known locally as the "Holy Mountain", on the horizon – it's difficult to know whether this is intentional. Current excavations show the site to be part of a much larger ceremonial landscape of monuments, and future excavations should reveal more information. It's easy to access, as you can park right next to the site.

> "To the south is a slab bearing small man-made cup-marks; legend tells these were made by Arthur's elbows as he prayed, or by a giant's as he fell." Andy Burnham

Nearby | At SO 3260 4230, just over 1km (0.6 miles) southeast of Arthur's Stone, is **Dorstone Hill**, which has also been the subject of recent excavations, see page 132.

Dorstone Hill: A Unique Configuration of Monuments

Andy Burnham, founder and Editor of the Megalithic Portal

During fieldwalking in the 1960s, 4,000 flints and other finds were picked up on Dorstone Hill, including arrowheads and fragments of polished flint or stone axes. Consisting of a huge bank that cut off a spur of the hilltop, the site was presumed to be a Neolithic promontory enclosure. Excavations in 2012, led by Professor Julian Thomas, uncovered three long mounds, aligned end-to-end.

The central mound was composed of burnt clay and timber, sealed within a layer of turf and supported by a timber palisade. A later cairn of stones was built over the lot.

The eastern mound had a long timber chamber between two huge post-holes. The timber chamber held bones. A series of stone chambers holding cremated remains were built into the side of the mound. Surrounding this was a shallow, horseshoe-shaped ditch.

The most extraordinary discovery was that the mounds had been built over the remains of one or more early Neolithic buildings (dating to 3900–3800BC). Post-holes and stake-holes were found beneath the central mound, and burnt structural timbers were identified in several locations. The evidence of the intensity of the fire suggests the buildings were deliberately burned, and indeed this was confirmed by excavations in 2014, with the discovery of the remains of house walls and a roof support inside the turf mound.

The western mound was trapezoidal in shape and included small loops of drystone walling. The 2015 dig revealed a post-hole structure of around 30 × 17m (98 × 56ft), including rows of holes that probably held the load-bearing posts of a timber building. The eastern wall of the building intersected with a series of stone-holes marking the façade of the stone-clad long mound, indicating this monument had been constructed on the same footprint as the earlier building.

It is unusual enough to find a series of long mounds end-to-end, and so many different types of stone and timber architecture in one place, but most remarkable is the way in which the fabric of the timber houses was incorporated into the stone building – which suggested that the barrows commemorate not only past generations but also the idea of a "house" as a social and physical entity (see page 101).

Another important find was 300 pieces of rock crystal, which doesn't occur naturally in the area and must have been brought to the site by human activity. The crystals seem to have been knapped into blades on site before, during and after the mound construction.

The 2017 excavations confirmed that the structure at SO 3271 4216 – previously thought to be an Iron Age promontory enclosure – is actually a fourth long mound, surrounded by a causewayed enclosure (probably a meeting place). There is no other site with this configuration of monuments. Both types are rare – to find them together is amazing. Consider also the deliberate burning of a giant timber longhouse – it must have been a spectacular event – to be memorialized and passed down through the generations.

Thomas, J., et al. 2015. *An Interim Report on Excavations at Dorstone Hill, Herefordshire, 2011–2014*.

ROTHERWAS RIBBON

Alt Name: Rotherwas Serpent

Ceremonial Trackway | Nearest Village: **Dinedor**
Map: **SO 5205 3690** | Sheets: **E189 L149** | Lat: **52.02842N** | Long: **2.7003W**

A fascinating site, although there is now little to see on the ground. An undulating ribbon-like feature of cracked stones, following a natural river bed, creating a three-dimensional, sculpted monument. There is a difference of opinion as to whether the stones were deliberately fire-cracked or whether the ribbon is a natural feature with the stones cracked by frost. The structure is not flat, so not intended to be walked on. It is thought to date to around 2000BC, and has been "preserved" beneath the new road, a decision that caused a great deal of anger and debate at the time.

Photo © Alun Salt

MITCHELL'S FOLD

Stone Circle | Nearest Village: **Chirbury**
Map: **SO 3042 9837** | Sheets: **E216 L137** | Lat: **52.57867N** | Long: **3.02824W**

Photo © Tim Prevett

Set between Corndon Hill and Stapeley Hill, Mitchell's Fold has great views across toward Wales. There are 15 stones remaining of perhaps 30 in a partially flattened 30 × 27m (98 × 89ft) circle, the tallest reaching just under 2m (6½ft). There's also a central stone, but it's hidden beneath the turf. The stones are dolerite, and probably come from Stapeley Hill, to the northwest.

An unusual legend is associated with Mitchell's Fold. During a famine, the local people survived on the milk of a fairy cow. She could produce endless milk, as long as no one tried to fill more than one bucket. Hearing this, a witch milked her into a riddle (sieve), continuing until the cow departed in protest at this ill treatment. The witch was turned to stone for her spite and the other stones were set up around her in a circle to pen her in. Another story tells of a local farmer who blew up some of the stones and used the pieces to line a pond, but afterwards was said to prosper no more.

Nearby | At SO 3080 9880, 573m (1,880ft) northeast of Mitchell's Fold, is the **Cow Stone** or Dead Cow, the name deriving from its resemblance to a reclining cow and clearly linked to the legend of Mitchell's Fold. The boulder is made of dolerite, like the stones of Mitchell's Fold and the Hoarstones (see page 134). At SO 3050 9500, around 3.5km (2 miles) to the south of Mitchell's Fold, is **Cwm Mawr** axe factory. There is not much to see on the ground but this is an interesting site as axes made from picrite, the distinctive stone quarried here, have been found throughout Britain, from the Welsh borders to as far away as Devon and Cornwall and the north of England.

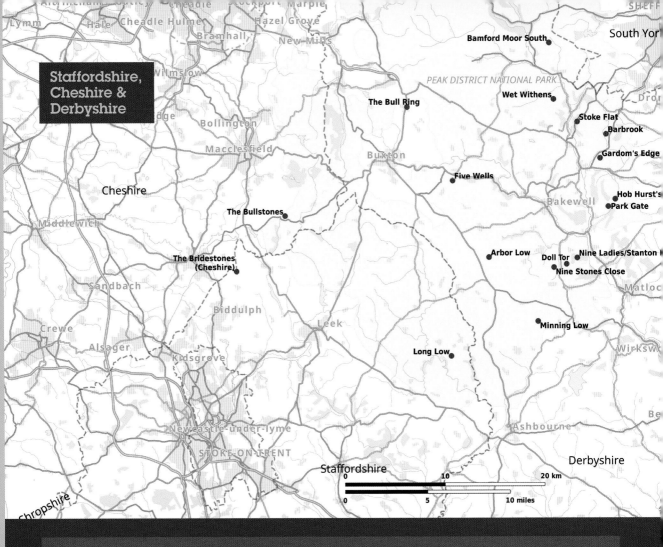

Staffordshire, Cheshire & Derbyshire

SHEFF

Bamford Moor South

South Yor

PEAK DISTRICT NATIONAL PARK

Wet Withens

Dro

The Bull Ring

Stoke Flat
Barbrook

Gardom's Edge

Buxton

Five Wells

Bakewell

Hob Hurst's
Park Gate

The Bullstones

Cheshire

Middlewich

The Bridestones
(Cheshire)

Arbor Low

Doll Tor   Nine Ladies/Stanton
Nine Stones Close

Matloc

Sandbach

Biddulph

Leek

Minning Low

Wirksw

Crewe

Alsager

Kidsgrove

Long Low

Ashbourne

Be

Newcastle-under-lyme

STOKE-ON-TRENT

Staffordshire

Derbyshire

Shropshire

| 0 | | 10 | | 20 km |
| 0 | | 5 | | 10 miles |

134

THE HOARSTONES Alt Name: **Black Marsh**

Stone Circle | Nearest Village: **Shelve** | Map: **SO 3241 9990**
Sheets: **E216 L137** | Lat: **52.59267N** | Long: **2.99934W**

On marshy ground south of the hamlet of Hemford is the Hoarstones stone circle with 37 dolerite stones (of an original 38), plus a central stone. The low stones are often obscured by grass

Photo © Tim Prevett

"The holes were apparently drilled by miners and filled with gunpowder to provide homemade pyrotechnics during wedding celebrations."
Barry Teague

and can be tricky to find. To approach via rights of way, take the track leading off the A488 just to the southwest of the crossroads of the A488 with the minor road heading to Shelve. Go through a gate and up to a stile, following the path across the fields and keeping an eye out for the circle on the right at the bottom of the field.

DEVIL'S RING AND FINGER

Holed Stone | Nearest Village: **Mucklestone**
Map: **SJ 7073 3779** | Sheets: **E243 L127** | Lat: **52.93663N** | Long: **2.43698W**

Photo © Richard L. Dixon

Believed to be part of a long-vanished chambered tomb, these two stones are on private land (seek permission) by the field boundary not far to the northeast of the footpath to Norton in Hales. Both stones lean dramatically and the Ring is holed, while weathering has created charismatic vertical grooves in the Finger.

LONG LOW

Long Barrow | Nearest Village: **Ilam**
Map: **SK 1220 5390** | Sheets: **OL24L119** | Lat: **53.08218N** | Long: **1.81932W**

Long Low is an unusual site, with a 160m (525ft) long mound with dry-stone walling linking two bowl barrows (one 27m/89ft across, the other 16m/55m). The northeast barrow contained a stone cist that held 13 crouched burials, and cremations were found in the bank and barrow.

Nearby | There are five other barrows and cairns within 1km (0.6 miles) in various directions.

Photo © Christopher Bickerton

"This is very reminiscent of the Broadmayne bank barrow in Dorset." Tim Prevett

THE BRIDESTONES (CHESHIRE)

Chambered Tomb | Nearest Village: **Timbersbrook**
Map: **SJ 9061 6218** | Sheets: **E268 L118** | Lat: **53.15668N** | Long: **2.14177W**

Photo © Richard L. Dixon

A once magnificent monument on the Cheshire/Staffordshire border, with fantastic views across the Cheshire Plain. The cairn was denuded to construct the turnpike in the 1760s, and other stones went to build the nearby farm and house. There is a story that an engineer employed on the Manchester Ship Canal demonstrated the art of detonation on one of the biggest stones; it was later cemented back in place. Although still an atmospheric site, it requires imagination to grasp how remarkable the original tomb was. Sources describe an enormous chambered tomb with a horned cairn and a paved forecourt of a Clyde cairn or court tomb type, as found in Scotland, Ireland and the Isle of Man, with no other examples found in mainland England. Dividing the main chamber was a stone with a 0.5m (1½ft) hole, about big enough to crawl through. (A similar holed stone is at the Devil's Ring and Finger, see page 135.) Two more chambers are supposed to have been located some 50m (164ft) away, but no traces remain.

THE BULLSTONES   Alt Name: **Bullstrang**

Stone Circle | Nearest Village: **Wincle** | Map: **SJ 9557 6761**
Sheets: **E268 L118** | Lat: **53.20554N** | Long: **2.06778W**

Photo © Christopher Bickerton

The Bullstones has a splendid setting on Brown Hill. This site has been classed as a barrow, yet it may be more aptly described as a stone circle. An 8.5 × 7.9m (28 × 26ft) circle of boulders surrounds a 1.1m (3ft 7in) stone with a bowl-shaped depression in its flat top. A burial, of a child along with an urn, cremated remains, a flint arrowhead and a flint knife, was found here in the 1870s. The circle's entrance was to the north, with a short row of stones leading to it. Two further rows of stones are reported to have curved to the circle from the start of the avenue.

Nearby | Just over 2km (1¼ miles) WSW of the Bullstones are the five **Bosley Minn** standing stones. Three are believed to be prehistoric (the ones that lean), and two more recent. The stone to the south (1, at SJ 9388 6585) leans dramatically and has spent some of its life as a gatepost, shown by the hinge settings on its north face. About 370 (1,214ft) NNE of this are another pair considered genuine (4 and 5, also known as Wincle Minn standing stones, at SJ 9400 6620), with the other two stones (2 and 3) in between.

Looking to the Land of the Ancestors

Vicky Tuckman (Morgan), former Editor of the Megalithic Portal

Cheshire is not known for its prehistoric monuments. Aside from an array of damaged Bronze Age barrows and a few destroyed stone circles, there are two main sites of interest.

The first is the Bridestones, located at 250m (820ft) above sea level on the crest of a pass, overlooking the Cheshire Plain. Neolithic chambered tombs with crescent-shaped forecourts like this are usually found in the Clyde region of Scotland (where they are known as Clyde cairns); Cairn Holy (see page 269) is one well-known example.

They are generally considered to be an early form of chambered tomb, and are believed to have been first built in Ireland. Research has shown that some Clyde cairns faced east and south – but those with crescent-shaped forecourts, such as the Bridestones, always pointed west, toward Ireland.

The second unusual site is the Bullstones, lying just over 7km (4.3 miles) to the northeast. Consisting of a large central standing stone surrounded by an ellipse of rounded cobbles on a small platform, the Bullstones resembles the Bronze Age centre-stone circles of southwest Scotland, the best example being Glenquicken (see page 269), which also has a central standing stone surrounded by a ring of low water-worn stones and an interior of tightly laid cobbles. Glenquicken lies within a landscape containing a number of Clyde cairns with their semi-circular forecourts.

So why did the prehistoric inhabitants of Cheshire choose this location for the Bridestones and the Bullstones, so dissimilar to anything else in the surrounding area? Could it be more than just coincidence that they seem to have borrowed from designs usually found in the area around the Irish Sea? The hills on which these sites were constructed would be visible for miles to anyone crossing the Cheshire Plain eastward. Did their builders deliberately site them to look west, toward the setting sun and perhaps to the lands from which their ancestors came?

MINNING LOW   Alt Name: **Roystone Cairn**

Round Cairn | Nearest Village: **Parwich**

Map: **SK 2093 5728** | Sheets: **OL24 L119** | Lat: **53.11229N** | Long: **1.68877W**

There are fantastic views from this site at the top of Minninglow Hill. At 44 × 34m (144 × 112ft), Minning Low is the Peak District's largest cairn and, despite being damaged, is an impressive monument that's visible for miles around. It's an interesting multiphase site, which was initially a single-chambered tomb with a limestone cairn, later covered by a four-chambered long cairn and then finally incorporated into a huge circular mound. Roman coins and pottery were found here during excavation in the 19th century.

NINE STONES CLOSE   Alt Name: **The Grey Ladies**

Stone Circle | Nearest Village: **Birchover**
Map: **SK 2253 6256** | Sheets: **OL24 L119** | Lat: **53.15969N** | Long: **1.6645W**

Photo © Alun Salt

Although only four stones (with a possible fifth in the field wall) remain of seven or more in a 13.7m (45ft) ring, this is a splendid circle in an elegant setting in a field beside a fine oak tree, with views southwest up to Robin Hood's Stride. Aubrey Burl points out that, viewed from the circle, the major southern moon appears to set between the two "ears" of this outcrop, an alignment that may have determined the siting of the circle. These are the tallest standing stones in Derbyshire, ranging from 1.2m (4ft) to 2.1m (7ft), the tallest stone having been measured at an even more impressive 3.5m (11½ft) before its re-erection in 1936. Legend has it that these Grey Ladies (the other name for the stones) dance when the clock strikes 12 (be that night or day).

Nearby | At SK 225 624, some 160m (525ft) SSW, is **Robin Hood's Stride**, a natural outcrop of weather-carved rock that makes an impressive landmark across the fields from Nine Stones Close. Legend tells that Robin Hood used to leap from rock to rock here. On the southeastern corner, behind the "chimney", is rock art: a well-defined circular groove surrounding a central dished area.

DOLL TOR

Stone Circle | Nearest Village: **Birchover**
Map: **SK 2383 6287** | Sheets: **OL24 L119** | Lat: **53.16245N** | Long: **1.64503W**

Photo © Richard L. Dixon

This is an enchanting little circle in a woodland setting with views across the valley. None of the stones in the 6 × 4.5m (19 × 15ft) circle rises above 1m (3ft 3in). It is possible that the stones are the remaining kerb of a long-gone mound. A cairn adjoins the circle to the northeast.

Nearby | At SK 2355 6215, 775m (just under ½ mile) SSW of Doll Tor, at **Rowtor Rocks**, is a massive gritstone outcrop marked by prehistoric cup-and-ring marks as well as the seats, nooks and steps thought to have been carved in the 17th century by Thomas Eyre of Rowtor Hall. There are five examples of rock art, at the outcrop's western end, with the best preserved adorning a boulder below the carved "armchair". A few metres to the west is a cup with a partial ring and trailing tail.

NINE LADIES — Alt Name: Stanton Moor II

Stone Circle | Nearest Village: **Birchover**
Map: **SK 2491 6349** | Sheets: **OL24 L119** | Lat: **53.16794N** | Long: **1.62883W**

One of the most accessible and charming of Derbyshire's many circles (and consequently vulnerable to damage from the high level of visitor numbers), the Nine Ladies are set among birch and oak on Stanton Moor. The stones, of millstone grit and all less than 1m (3ft 3in) tall, stand in a circle about 11m (36ft) in diameter, embedded in a grassy rubble bank. There was originally a cairn in the centre of the circle. A tenth stone, buried and invisible for many years, was discovered during the dry summer of 1976. The circle has been the focus of anti-quarrying campaigns on Stanton Moor (which is home to a variety of other sites) since the early 21st century, with environmentalists camping here in treehouses and tepees for almost nine years until proposals for sandstone quarrying on the moor were rejected in 2008. About 40m (130ft) WSW of the circle, there is a standing stone known as the King's Stone.

Nearby | There are many other stone circles, cairns and rock outcrops within 1km (0.6 mile) on Stanton Moor. Some to look for: **Stanton Moor Cairn T24** (at SK 2480 6333); **Stanton Moor 1** embanked stone circle – one to find in winter as it gets very overgrown (at SK 2494 6367); **Stanton Moor 3** or T56 ring cairn (at SK 2480 6326); **Stanton Moor T55** round cairn (at SK 2482 6313); **Stanton Moor 4** or T43 embanked stone circle, completely covered in heather (at SK 2470 6290).

ARBOR LOW

Henge & Stone Circle | Nearest Village: **Middleton**
Map: **SK 1603 6355** | Sheets: **OL24 L119** | Lat: **53.16882N** | Long: **1.76166W**

Photo © Guy Stephenson

> "When Thomas Bateman excavated the site in 1848, the main burial cist reputedly fell through his tunnel roof while he was digging, to be relocated in his own garden at Lomberdale Hall! Returned in 1938, it is still visible today, resembling a capstone on the top of the mound."
> Vicky Tuckman

Set on a ridge high on Middleton Common, Arbor Low is a fascinating ritual centre that deserves more than to be simply known as the "Stonehenge of the North". The bank of the massive 90m (295ft) henge still rises to over 2m (6½ft), with entrances at the northwest and SSE. Inside the henge, the circle stands on a platform and contains 50 stones of local limestone (some are broken fragments of the same stone), all but one of which is fallen – or were deliberately set as recumbents. Seven smaller blocks form a "cove" in the centre of the circle, where skeletal remains were found. The stones range from 1.6m to 2.1m (5ft 3in to 6ft 10in) in height (or length), except for those at the entrances which would have been taller, between 2.6m and 2.9m (8ft 6in to 9½ft). The stones were added after the construction of the henge, probably by 2000BC. Later, part of the outer bank was altered to make room for a round barrow. Another barrow nearby, Gib Hill, which is visible from Arbor Low, was probably the original focus of the site.

Nearby | At SK 1582 6332, some 300m (984ft) WSW of Arbor Low is **Gib Hill** long barrow. This impressive artificial hill might look like a round barrow, but it's actually a Neolithic long barrow with a later round barrow constructed on top. The long barrow probably predates Arbor Low by several hundred years.

FIVE WELLS
Chambered Tomb | Nearest Village: **Taddington**
Map: **SK 1238 7104** | Sheets: **OL24 L119** | Lat: **53.23628N** | Long: **1.81588W**

> "Some difficulty finding this from Taddington road. Best to head off the obvious trackway up between the two hills and climb up the hill to the right."
> CatrinM

This may be the highest megalithic tomb in Britain, high on Taddington Moor. The site has been denuded over the centuries by wall builders and damaged by excavation, but it's still an atmospheric place with two back-to-back chambers visible, each with its own passage. The eastern chamber is in the better condition (both are missing their capstones).

Photo © Roy Kennie

THE BULL RING
Henge | Nearest Village: **Dove Holes**
Map: **SK 0785 7824** | Sheets: **OL24 L119** | Lat: **53.30105N** | Long: **1.88367W**

For a long time, this henge was sadly neglected, but recent efforts have improved matters and made the monument a focus for the local community. Unlike at Arbor Low, there are no stones; according to an 18th-century source, however, there was originally a stone setting in the enclosure, with one stone remaining in 1789. Originally rising to perhaps 2m (6½ft) high, the bank is now about 1.1m (3ft 7in) high and up to 9.8m (32ft) wide, while the ditch is 12.2m (40ft) wide and 0.6m

Photo © Hamish Fenton

(2ft) deep. There are causewayed entrances at the north and south. The site has been damaged by quarrying and the interior was probably ploughed during medieval times. The Megalithic Portal held a very successful live event at the Bull Ring in 2011 and videos of the talks are available online (search for Bull Ring henge on YouTube).

PARK GATE

Stone Circle | Nearest Village: **Beeley**
Map: **SK 2805 6851** | Sheets: **OL24 L119** | Lat: **53.21291N** | Long: **1.58143W**

On marshy ground in Beeley Warren, this embanked 12m (39ft) circle has 10 surviving stones. Only one of them reaches 1m (3ft 3in) so the circle can be hard to spot when the grass is high. The bank is easiest to see to the west and southwest. A lovely spot to watch the sunset, with a clear view west.

Photo © Steve Fedun

HOB HURST'S HOUSE

Round Barrow | Nearest Village: **Beeley**
Map: **SK 2874 6923** | Sheets: **OL24 L119** | Lat: **53.21935N** | Long: **1.57103W**

Within 1km (0.6 mile) of Park Gate, on the wild moorland above Harland Edge, is this unusual squarish barrow, in legend the home of the sprite Hob. The rectangular mound, 8 × 7.5m (26 × 25ft) and just under 1m (3ft 3in) in height, is surrounded by a rectangular ditch and bank. A packhorse track has damaged the northern side of the bank, and the ditch may have been created when stones were taken to build walls. A central rectangular group of five stones may originally have contained 13. Excavation in 1853 discovered a grave or cist containing scorched human bones and some lead ore.

> "Much more impressive than I had expected, and it's beside a major pathway across the moor."
> Roger K. Read

GARDOM'S EDGE

Megalithic Complex | Nearest Village: **Baslow**

Map: **SK 2725 7322** | Sheets: **OL24 L119** | Lat: **53.25533N** | Long: **1.59297W**

This millstone grit ridge is an important ancient landscape, with roundhouses, enclosures, cairns and important rock art all within a few hundred metres of this curiously shaped standing stone. The unusual triangular shape of Gardom's Edge stone, with one face strikingly flat and tilted, and its apparently deliberate sundial-like angle (packing stones around the base indicate it was carefully set in position) has led to much speculation as to its purpose (see below). Excavation of the area in 1998 and 1999 revealed varying levels of occupation from the Mesolithic to the Iron Age, including three hut sites, and a large enclosure that dated to the late second millennium BC.

Photo © Roy Kennie

A Phenomenology of Shadow

Daniel Brown, astronomy lecturer at Nottingham Trent University

The use of shadow casting in monuments of this period is rare in Britain and Ireland, but examples include Newgrange and some Clava cairns in the northeast of Scotland. These seem to be linked to burial sites using the symbolism of a cyclical light-and-shadow display to represent eternity. Given the proximity of a Neolithic enclosure, the Gardom's Edge monolith could be another such example. Usually, standing stones are upright, and either tall, slender pillars or wide, thin diamonds; however, at Gardom's Edge, the stone appears to have been deliberately set at an angle. The stone seems to have been chosen for its smooth, flat and sloping side, with the other sides being vertical.

If we factor in changes in the Earth's tilt to the ecliptic plane over four millennia, it seems that the slanted side of the stone at Gardom's Edge would have been in shadow all day for half the year, but illuminated morning and evening during the summer months. Around the summer solstice, however, this slanted side of the stone would have been illuminated all day; this loss of shadow perhaps giving symbolic meaning to the location during the changing seasons and making the stone an ideal marker for a social arena for seasonal gatherings.

It appears that the shadow phenomena could have been used to empower the stone, which would have revealed its meaning during the time of the summer solstice. This insight could only have been gained through prolonged time spent at the site, watching and remaining within the phenomenon.

BARBROOK

Megalithic Complex | Nearest Village: **Baslow**
Map: **SK 2780 7580** | Sheets: **OL24 L119** | Lat: **53.27845N** | Long: **1.58454W**

Photo © Richard L. Dixon

On Ramsley Moor is a fascinating prehistoric landscape that includes an embanked stone circle, as well as some 80 cairns (mostly clearance cairns but probably including burial sites, too) and a possible cup-marked stone at SK 2764 7560. It's a beautiful setting with sweeping views over Big Moor.

BARBROOK 1

There are great views from Barbrook 1 (at SK 2785 7558), one of the Peak District's best-preserved stone circles, set in a dip on a raised plateau. There are 12 stones still standing in a 14.5 × 12.5m (48 × 41ft) ring, enclosed by a 19 × 17m (62 × 56ft) rubble bank.

BARBROOK 2

The most impressive of the sites is perhaps Barbrook 2 (pictured), at SK 2780 7580, a stone circle that has been restored following vandalism in the late 1980s and now appears as it would have done c.2000BC. It's not marked on the map but can be found around 225m (738ft) NNW of Barbrook I (which is marked). Nine of an original 10 stones are set in a low, 3.5m (11½ft) wide dry-stone wall in a 14.5 × 13.5m (48 × 44ft) circle, which encloses a small cairn.

BARBROOK 3

At SK 2833 7728, some 1.6km (1 mile) NNE of Barbrook 2, is Barbrook 3 (or Owler Bar) stone circle. Around 26 × 23.5m (85 × 77ft) in diameter, it is one of the largest circles in the Peak District, but the stones are tiny and it's almost comically tricky to see. The grass and peat conceal more or less everything and it's nearly impossible to photograph. However, it's a lovely walk if you're up on the moor visiting the other sites.

143

STOKE FLAT   Alt Name: **Froggatt Edge**

Stone Circle | Nearest Village: **Grindleford**

Map: **SK 2496 7679** | Sheets: **OL24 L119** | Lat: **53.28749N** | Long: **1.62705W**

Photo © Steve Fedun

A ruinous embanked stone circle overlooking the Derwent valley. The bank, which is 2m (6½ft) wide and 15.5m (51ft) in diameter, has two entrances directly opposite each other at the NNW and SSE. Interestingly, traces of walling in the northern entrance indicate it may have been deliberately blocked at some point. Four stones (of a possible 16) remain set in the bank, and the entrances are also lined with uprights, three in the northern entrance and four in the southern. The stones are generally small, about 0.5m (1½ft) tall, but one of the entrance stones rises to over 1m (3ft 3in).

> **"As with other Derbyshire sites, this one is best viewed before the bracken starts to grow too tall …"** Steve Fedun

WET WITHENS   Alt Names: **Eyam Moor I, Wet Withers**

Stone Circle | Nearest Village: **Grindleford**

Map: **SK 2255 7900** | Sheets: **OL24 L119** | Lat: **53.30747N** | Long: **1.66305W**

On Eyam Moor is the largest embanked circle in Derbyshire. Wet Withens (also known as Wet Withers) has an impressive bank up to 3m (10ft) wide, enclosing an area around 31 × 29.5m (101 × 96ft) in diameter. There are 10 or 11 millstone grit stones visible (out of a possible 16–18), of which seven are still standing, up to 0.7m (2ft 3in) in height. The tallest is chair-shaped, with three possible cup-marks on the back. There's a small cairn inside the circle.

Nearby | Just 10m (33ft) north of Wet Withens is **Eyam Moor barrow**, a large cairn, 27.5 × 17.5m (90 × 57ft) in diameter and just over 1m (3ft 3in) in height. It could once have been a long barrow, or possibly two or more funerary cairns. The cairn makes a good landmark to navigate by when heather covers the small stones of Wet Withens.

There are two smaller stone circles around 650m (less than ½ mile) to the east of Wet Withens. **Eyam Moor 2** (at SK 2316 7894) is a rather overgrown embanked stone circle, while **Eyam Moor 3**, a little further on (at SK 2323 7881), with no bank, has six stones, four of which are upright. Between Wet Withens and Eyam Moor 2 and 3 – on a slight ridge – is a prehistoric cairnfield of about 90 cairns. There are also traces of linear clearance banks, showing the area was split into little agricultural plots. Platforms for two prehistoric houses have been identified, and there are probably others. All this looks to be an area of intense agriculture and settlement in the Bronze Age right among these monuments.

BAMFORD MOOR SOUTH
Stone Circle | Nearest Town: **Hathersage**
Map: **SK 2211 8453** | Sheets: **OL1 L110** | Lat: **53.35719N** | Long: **1.66926W**

It may not be easy to find this small embanked circle among the heather but the effort is well worth it. The circle is just 8 × 7m (26 × 23ft), with six stones set in the bank plus two others visible, all about 0.5m (1½ft) tall. A slight slope makes the circle more visible from the south and west.

Nearby | At SK 2201 8467, 172m (564ft) to the northwest, is the **Old Woman Stone**, which was deliberately knocked over in the early 1900s, presumably by the landowners to stop it being used as a way-marker.

Photo © Richard L. Dixon

CRESWELL CRAGS ★
Rock Art & Caves | Nearest Village: **Creswell**
Map: **SK 5320 7410** | Sheets: **E270 L120** | Lat: **53.26124N** | Long: **1.20392W**

Creswell Crags are a group of small caves along both sides of a gorge on the border between Derbyshire and Nottinghamshire. The caves provided shelter for Neanderthal and anatomically modern humans between 130,000 and 10,000 years ago. Archaeological finds include flint and bone tools, as well as carvings, showing that Ice Age hunters visited the site to hunt reindeer and horses. Palaeolithic cave art was discovered in Church Hole, one of the Creswell caves, in 2003. These engravings are one of only two examples of Ice Age art in Britain, the other being an inscribed reindeer in Cat Hole Cave on the Gower peninsula in South Wales (see page 208). They include images of ibex, bison, ibis and deer, dating to around 13,000 years ago. Further carvings and bas-reliefs have been discovered since 2003, although this is controversial in some quarters. Natural light on sunny mornings gives perfect conditions for seeing the carvings; in some cases artificial light makes them harder or even impossible to see. The gorge is wheelchair accessible and has a very informative museum, from where you can take a guided tour to see the caves (see the Creswell Crags website for details).

Top 10 Sites of Prehistoric Industry

THE HUMBER STONE
Alt Names: **Hoston, Hell Stone, Holy Stone**
Standing Stone | Nearest Village: **Hamilton**
Map: **SK 6240 0730** | Sheets: **E233 L140** | Lat: **52.65983N** | Long: **1.07887W**

This stone, said to have once been around 2.7m (9ft) tall, would have been a majestic sight when upright (as it was until at least 1750). It's fallen now and mostly buried in an incongruous position, near a roundabout on the outskirts of Leicester. It's one of few standing stones in Leicestershire, and may have arrived here via glacial action. The Humber Stone is linked with several local legends, including one from the 1980s, when a boy and his grandmother were said to be haunted by the

Photo © Sam Tatt

"Humberstone ghost", a devilish entity with a goat's head. The stone was also believed to have cursed two farmers who tried to damage it, one whose haystack burst into flames, and the other who broke off a segment to plough around it and thereafter (as is so often the case) never prospered.

SEVEN HILLS
Barrow Cemetery | Nearest Town: **Ipswich**
Map: **TM 2245 4115** | Sheets: **E197 L169** | Lat: **52.02546N** | Long: **1.2418E**

Seven Hills in Suffolk is a fine example of a barrow cemetery. There are 12 or 13 barrows, mostly bowl barrows, 15–30m (49–98ft) in diameter. The site is likely to have been in use for hundreds of years.

INGATESTONE
Possible Standing Stones | Nearest Village: **Ingatestone**
Map: **TQ 6511 9959** | Sheets: **E175 L167** | Lat: **51.67082N** | Long: **0.38629E**

Photo © Martyn Copcutt

An unusual site offering a fascinating bit of urban prehistory. Essex is not known for its megaliths, but there are three large sarsens in the village, perhaps part of a single stone moved here via glacial action. Two of the stones can be seen at the entrance to Fryerning Road from the High Street, while the third was discovered in 1905 in the wall of the church of St Edmund and St Mary and is now in the churchyard.

Nearby | There are more mysterious stones on the other side of Essex, 26km (16 miles) northeast of Ingatestone, in a small village called **Alphamstone** right on the border with Suffolk. Here, surrounding the church of St Barnabas (TL 8787 3548) are seven sarsen stones that could perhaps have once been part of a stone circle.

Icknield Way: Ancient Track or Medieval Fantasy?

Keith Fitzpatrick-Matthews, Heritage Access Officer, North Hertfordshire Museum, Hitchin

The idea of long-distance trackways with histories that stretch thousands of years into the past is a temptingly romantic one. There's plenty of evidence for the development of permanent routes from the Neolithic period onward, but how far did these trackways extend? Archaeologists once believed that monuments were concentrated in upland areas, making it likely that these were linked by "ridgeways" following the chalk and limestone hills. However, as more prehistoric settlements were found in low-lying areas, this idea was brought into question. The notion of prehistoric ridgeway routes requires rigorous interrogation.

According to the Icknield Way Association, the track is "the oldest road in England", consisting of "prehistoric trackways, old when the Romans came". In this view, it was in use by the Neolithic period (after 4000BC), but perhaps originated even before then, running from East Anglia to the Thames valley. And here the uncertainty begins: does it start at Thetford, at Lowestoft or at Holme-next-the-Sea? And does it end at Wallingford, Marlborough or even Weymouth?

In the Middle Ages, it was regarded as one of the "four Royal Roads", first mentioned by Henry of Huntingdon in the 1120s. He says the first "is from east to west and is called Ichenild". This is the earliest appearance of the name outside 13th-century copies of earlier charters, which mention a track called Icknield in a 65km (40 mile) stretch from Wiltshire to Buckinghamshire – not the traditional location of the route – and we cannot be sure the name was found in the originals. Another problem is that the idea of "four Royal Roads" originates in Geoffrey of Monmouth's work of fiction-as-history, *Gesta Brittonum* (*The History of the Kings of Britain*), attributed to prehistoric King Belinus.

Sarah Harrison's research, published in the *Archaeological Journal* in 2003, is still largely ignored. She examined the archaeological evidence for a track on the traditional route along its entire length and found none, except in one short stretch. She found archaeological evidence only at Letchworth Garden City in Hertfordshire, and at Dunstable in Bedfordshire. Here, the route originates at the end of the Iron Age, when formal roads were already being constructed across southern England.

Even worse, she discovered that 18th-century antiquarians filled in the "missing" sections when they began tracing the route on the ground. This is the origin of the Upper and Lower Icknield Ways in Buckinghamshire: nothing more than farm tracks. Medieval tracks, such as Ashwell Street in south Cambridgeshire and northern Hertfordshire, were incorporated into the system. While the antiquarians' ideas convinced early prehistorians, the "fact" of Icknield Way was built on medieval storytelling.

If this seems negative, that's because Icknield Way is such a wrongly conceived concept. The history goes back almost 900 years, which is nowhere near as long as the claimed date of the route. We can sometimes learn more by examining wrong ideas than by just following generally accepted "truths".

Must Farm: An Extraordinary Fenland Survival

Jackie Bates, a writer with an enthusiasm for megalithic sites

Quarrying had already destroyed part of the late Bronze Age settlement at Must Farm (at TL 2370 9760 near Whittlesey), when excavations began there in 2010, ahead of further quarrying. By 2015 the site was making national news. An astonishing range of finds – including roundhouses, boats, fish traps, textiles, jewellery, weapons and pots still full of food – were found at this extraordinary site, built on oak piles driven into the bed of the River Nene in the Cambridgeshire fens. It seems that at some point between 1000 and 800BC, shortly after the site's construction, fire broke out and swiftly took hold, leading to the sudden collapse of the whole settlement into the water, ensuring exceptional levels of preservation. The site has been described as one of the most significant of its kind ever found in Britain, and its nickname of the "Fenland Pompeii" refers to both the swiftness of the fire damage and the plethora of finds.

As the roundhouses were plunged into water still containing all the necessities for late Bronze Age life, Must Farm has allowed archaeologists to extend their understanding of many different aspects of domestic living in this era, from where various activities took place within the home, to how clothes were made, to details of construction, crafts and farming. The site has produced the largest collections in Britain of Bronze Age beads, textiles, wooden items, domestic metalwork (from sickles, hammers and razors to knives and axes), as well as complete sets of jars, bowls and cups – all the pots were unbroken. There's nothing to see at the site, but many of the artefacts found here can be explored in Peterborough Museum.

FLAG FEN

Prehistoric Settlement & Archaeology Park | Nearest City: **Peterborough**

Map: **TL 2270 9890** | Sheets: **E235 L142** | Lat: **52.57408N** | Long: **0.19084W**

Famously discovered by accident when Francis Pryor tripped over a protruding Bronze Age timber on the way back to the pub in 1982, the impressive Flag Fen site includes a remarkable 1km (0.6 mile) wooden causeway preserved in the wetland. Excavations in the 1980s revealed that the causeway (dating to 1365–967BC) was constructed across a waterlogged low-lying area, with over 60,000 posts arranged in five 5m (16ft) wide rows, and a timber platform. The site features reconstructions, including an Iron Age roundhouse, and some of the causeway posts are on display. Only about 10 per cent of the site has been investigated, and the sheer number of finds, including ritually damaged weapons (broken daggers, with the halves placed on top of each other), jewellery and white beach pebbles (transported here from afar), suggests that the site may have been a ceremonial centre where items were deliberately placed in the water. Modern drainage of the Fens, the development of Peterborough and climate change are all putting the wetlands at risk, and excavation and preservation are ongoing.

GRIME'S GRAVES

Neolithic Flint Mine | Nearest Village: **Weeting**

Map: **TL 8175 8978** | Sheets: **E229 L144** | Lat: **52.47587N** | Long: **0.67394E**

Photo © Skyscan

The name of Grime's Graves has an Anglo Saxon origin, referring to the god Grim (Woden). The heathland here is pockmarked by more than 400 prehistoric mine shafts, creating a strange lunar-like landscape. From around 3000BC to the Bronze Age these shafts, up to 13m (43ft) deep, were dug into the chalk with antler picks in order to retrieve flint, with horizontal galleries running up to 15m/49ft from the deeper shafts. Only a handful of Neolithic flint mines have been discovered in Britain; this is the most impressive and the only one open to the public.

Why the flint was mined here is the subject of debate; it has been pointed out that flint was available on the surface and that the act of retrieving it may have had a ritual purpose. Others suggest that the pits were necessary to access bands of floorstone flint (not found on the surface), which is both aesthetically pleasing (glossy black) and also flakes easily, making it suitable for toolmaking. Ritual activity is indicated by many objects found at Grime's Graves, such as ornate grooved ware pots, chalk carvings (including of phalluses, cups and balls; see opposite) and a carefully symmetrical arrangement of a Cornish greenstone axe and a bird skull between two antler picks.

There is public access to Pit 1, which requires descent by a vertical 9m (30ft) ladder (no children under 10), from where the galleries can be viewed but not entered. The 12m (39ft) shaft known as Greenwell's Pit has recently opened for guided tours, with ladder access and a winch and harness for safety.

> **"The risk of collapse must have been considerable as, of course, were the rewards."**
> Sandy Gerrard

Chalk Artefacts

Anne Teather, freelance archaeologist and researcher into the European Neolithic

It is believed chalk artefacts were probably made as replicas of artefacts that existed in other materials – chalk axes, for example, are not functionally useful! Some artefact forms do have evidence of use, but chalk as a material was almost certainly seen as a symbolic medium for making "things that looked like other things" in the Neolithic. A range of chalk artefacts, such as chalk balls, occur at many Neolithic sites on the chalklands. They haven't been assessed like some other artefacts so it's difficult to be certain of numbers, but it is likely that they were more common than we think. Dr Gillian Varndell completed the first modern analysis of chalk artefacts as part of the Grime's Graves excavation. She noted perforated artefacts and small, slightly dished artefacts she called "working surfaces". These may have been used to scrape chalk in small quantities to use as pigment and/or body paint. The excavation of the village at Durrington Walls yielded new types of chalk artefact, such as polishers (perhaps used to apply chalk as a body decoration in the Neolithic) and chalk beads. These have no evidence of suspension, but we know they were made in any case.

There is also increasing evidence of marks made in monuments, and flint mines, that are similar to rock art but are made in chalk – in other words, chalk art. They were noted from the early excavations of flint mines at Cissbury, Grime's Graves, Church Hill and Harrow Hill, but also in the ditch at Flagstones, Dorset and the Maumbury Rings shafts. Inscribing spaces in this way is similar to carving into stone at other monuments and should be seen as an extension of this cultural behaviour. The art in flint mines seemed to be located at the base of some, but not all, shafts, and at the end of galleries.

The most famous prehistoric chalk artefacts are the three Folkton drums, currently on display at the British Museum. Associated with the burial of a child, they were found in a barrow in East Yorkshire by Canon Greenwell in the late 19th century. Each is of a different size and although there is no radiocarbon date, their decoration is suggestive of late Neolithic or early Bronze Age art. They were thought to be unique until the discovery of another, undecorated, chalk drum in a Neolithic pit at Lavant, West Sussex in the 1990s, indicating such artefacts are unusual, but not unique. There are a few other extremely unusual chalk artefacts, such as the chalk figurine from Maiden Castle (also currently on display at the British Museum); the Grime's Graves Goddess, which is thought to be a fake, and numerous chalk phallic forms that range from quite small ones such as that from the Thickthorn Down long barrow, Dorset, and the Windmill Hill causewayed enclosure, Wiltshire, to the truly enormous chalk phallus from the Maumbury Rings (on display at Dorset County Museum).

One of the Folkton chalk drums

SEAHENGE Alt Name: **Holme-next-the-Sea I**
Timber Circle | Nearest Village: **Holme-next-the-Sea**
Map: **TF 7112 4526** | Sheets: **E250 L132** | Lat: **52.97683N** | Long: **0.54687E**

This is where, in 1998, coastal erosion exposed a remarkable Bronze Age timber circle comprising 55 oak posts and a central inverted oak stump in the intertidal zone near Holme-next-the-Sea, Norfolk (see below). The 1999 excavation of the remains was controversial, but leaving the circle in place would have resulted in its destruction. There's nothing to see at the site now; visit the museum in King's Lynn to see a reconstruction, as well as some of the original timbers.

Photo © Duncan Stirk

Nearby | Seahenge wasn't the only timber circle found at Holme-next-the-Sea. Early in the 21st century the timbers of **Holme II** were also spotted (approximately at TF 712 453). Some timbers that still remained in 2013 were dated by dendrochronology to 2049BC, as at Seahenge, so it seems this monument was part of the same complex. Erosion is likely to reveal (and destroy) further sites in the area – in 2003–8 some 41 features from various periods were recorded on Holme Beach.

Insights from a Bronze Age Timber Circle
Andy Burnham, founder and Editor of the Megalithic Portal

The name Seahenge itself is a misnomer, the site being neither a henge, nor originally in the sea – the area was more likely waterlogged saltmarsh at the time of construction.

Radiocarbon-dating has put the site to between 2310 and 1740BC, and dendrochronology dates the felling of the inverted stump to the spring of 2049BC. Axe marks from around 50 different axes indicate group organization, and also that these axes were more common than previously thought, the date being just after bronze was first smelted in Britain.

Some of the timbers can now be viewed at Lynn Museum, having taken almost a decade to dry out. The conservation process, conducted by archaeologists at Portsmouth's Mary Rose Trust, involved immersion in wax and freeze-drying. Archaeologists have concluded that Seahenge must have been some sort of ceremonial site, possibly used for excarnation, with bodies of the dead exposed to birds, animals and the elements to hasten decomposition and the trip to the afterlife. Two of the earliest timbers to be sited have an approximate northeast alignment to the midwinter sunset and midsummer sunrise, so it's possible the posts functioned as some sort of calendar or festival marker. It's also been theorized that the tree stump could commemorate the death of a significant tree, the fact that it had been turned upside down perhaps relating to the concept of the underworld. Could it even be that large post-holes found elsewhere held upturned trees in much the same way?

SALTHOUSE HEATH

Barrow Cemetery | Nearest Village: **Salthouse**
Map: **TG 0797 4241** | Sheets: **E250 L133** | Lat: **52.93877N** | Long: **1.09342E**

Salthouse Heath is home to Norfolk's largest barrow cemetery, with over 30 mounds dispersed over an area of the heath around 1.6 × 1.2km (1 × ¾ mile), with cropmarks on the arable land surrounding the heath suggesting it was originally even larger. The bigger mounds include Three Farthing Hill, Three Halfpenny Hill and Gallow Hill (at TG 0797 4241), which is the largest example at 2m (6½ft) high and 27m (88ft) across. The site appears to have been in use for over 2,000 years.

BULLY HILLS

Barrow Cemetery | Nearest Village: **Tathwell**
Map: **TF 3312 8272** | Sheets: **E282 L122** | Lat: **53.32466N** | Long: **0.00278W**

There are seven bowl barrows here, best viewed from the road at TF 326 829. All are substantial earthworks, about 3m (10ft) high, 12–26m (39–85ft) across, and aligned southwest–northeast. Having suffered antiquarian excavation, the largest barrow, third from the south, is only 2m (6½ft) high, with a hollow in the centre. No ditches are visible but it's assumed that all these Lincolnshire barrows have them, as others in the area do.

Nearby | At TF 2945 8225, 3.7km (2¼ miles) west of Bully Hills, is **Tathwell** long barrow, visible from the A153. Trees and bushes grow on the barrow and rabbit activity has exposed the underlying chalk structure.

GRIM'S MOUND

Round Barrow | Nearest Village: **Burgh on Bain**
Map: **TF 2325 8693** | Sheets: **E282 L122** | Lat: **53.36487N** | Long: **0.14924W**

This grass-covered round barrow, 2.6m (8½ft) high in places and 18m (59ft) across, swells appealingly on the horizon. There are remarkable views in all directions from the top of the mound, especially on a clear day.

Nearby | At TF 2129 8497, 2.8km (1¾ miles) WSW of Grim's Mound, is **Burgh on Bain**, which looks like a round barrow but is actually a Neolithic long barrow. It's 27m (88ft) long and 2.2m (7ft 2in) high at the western end, reducing to 1.5m (5ft).

At TF 2145 8406, 3.4km (just over 2 miles) southwest of Grim's Mound, is **Burgh Top**, where there are three round barrows, two badly reduced by ploughing, and the third with a decommissioned Royal Observer Corps (ROC) bunker from the Cold War era built into it. It's right beside the road.

Photo © John F. Holl

153

NORTH OF ENGLAND

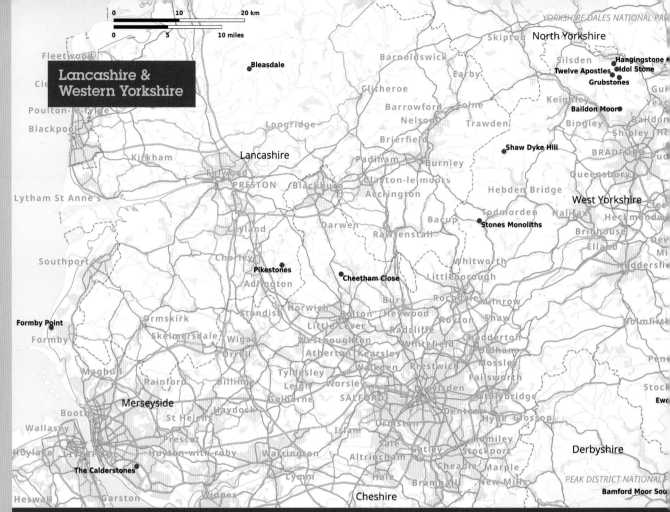

Top 15 Standing Stones in the UK & Ireland (Singles & Pairs)

THE CALDERSTONES
Alt Names: **Caldway Stones, Dogger Stones, Rodger Stones** | **Chambered Tomb** | Nearest Village: **Allerton (Liverpool)**
Map: **SJ 4040 8761** | Sheets: **E275 L108** | Lat: **53.38195N** | Long: **2.89746W**

Six beautifully decorated stones remain of the chambered tomb that once stood at Allerton. At the time of writing, they can still be visited in Calderstones Park, but the plan is to resite them in purpose-built housing at Calderstones Mansion House, and before then the stones will spend some months in conservation. They are decorated with various motifs, including cup-and-ring marks, cup-marks, spirals, arcs, concentric circles, possibly a bronze halberd and dagger, and – highly unusually for a megalithic tomb – footprints. Detailed photographs of the Calderstones were taken in 2007 by Adam Stanford and George Nash, and can be viewed online at the Megalithic Portal.

FORMBY POINT
Ancient Trackway | Nearest Town: **Formby**
Map: **SD 2750 0800** | Sheets: **E285 L108** | Lat: **53.56358N** | Long: **3.09607W**

At Formby Point, you can follow the footprints of ancient people (as well as those of aurochs, wolf, deer and various birds) that were baked into the silt 3,400–5,100 years ago. Erosion is continually exposing and destroying the marks, and they don't last for long; download a guide to finding them from the National Trust website (linked from the site page on the Megalithic Portal). The Trust also organizes guided walks to see the latest examples.

Photo © Barry Teague

PIKESTONES
Chambered Cairn | Nearest Town: **Chorley**
Map: **SD 6269 1719** | Sheets: **E287 L109** | Lat: **53.64987N** | Long: **2.56592W**

Photo © John Miller

With sweeping views over the Lancashire coast, this badly damaged chambered tomb high on Anglezarke Moor is worth visiting despite the vandalism that has taken place over the years, including overscribing the rock art, and the carving (and then attempted removal) of a spiral on one of the stones.

157

"Park at Jepson's Gate and follow the informal path to the left (not the bridleway straight ahead) up over boggy ground to the Pikestones." *Vicky Tuckman*

CHEETHAM CLOSE Alt Names: **Chapeltown, Turton Heights**
Stone Circle | Nearest Village: **Chapeltown (Greater Manchester)**
Map: **SD 7163 1586** | Sheets: **E287 L109** | Lat: **53.63848N** | Long: **2.43055W**

Photo © John Miller

A ruinous stone circle, once about 18.5 × 12.5m (60 × 40ft) in diameter, with six stones remaining, all broken or fallen and none over 1m (3ft 3in) tall. This is a popular site, as it's easily accessible and the area's only circle, with great views to the north, east and southeast. There's a ring cairn to the south of the circle, and other cairns can be found in the surrounding area. An outlier of the circle, reused as a boundary stone, is known as the Mire Stone. It has recently been suggested that the circle had a portal entrance to the southwest.

BLEASDALE ★
Timber Circle | Nearest Village: **Chipping**
Map: **SD 5772 4600** | Sheets: **OL41 L102** | Lat: **53.90845N** Long: **2.64511W**

A unique site in a tranquil woodland setting on private land (seek permission). Here, an outer palisade of oak posts encircled a 1.2m (4ft) wide ditch surrounding a burial mound, in which urns and the cremated remains of two people were found. A causewayed entrance to the west was flanked by posts, and 11 large oak posts ringed the grave. It is suggested the outer palisade may have decayed and disappeared before the inner monument was built.

Photo © Miles Newman

After excavation in the late 19th century the post-holes were reset with wooden posts which were in turn replaced with concrete in the 1930s. The urns can be seen in the Harris Museum in Preston.

EWDEN BECK Alt Name: **Broomhead I**
Stone Circle | Nearest Town: **Stocksbridge**
Map: **SK 2381 9664** | Sheets: **OL1 L110** | Lat: **53.4656N** | Long: **1.64296W**

On a terrace above Ewden Beck, this embanked stone circle in south Yorkshire encloses a Bronze Age cremation cemetery. It can be hard to find as only five stones are upright of a possible eight or nine, and none is taller than 0.75m (2½ft). There may have been 14 or 15 stones originally.

STONES MONOLITHS
Standing Stones | Nearest Town: **Todmorden**
Map: **SD 9250 2370** | Sheets: **OL21 L103** | Lat: **53.70966N** | Long: **2.1151W**

Photo © Richard L. Dixon

Although not Scheduled Ancient Monuments, and of doubtful antiquity, these three stones are still worth the visit. The 3.6m (12ft) stone set in a millstone-like base seems to have appeared some time after 1912, its holes suggesting it has spent time as a gatepost. In the field to the west is another stone, of a similar height. The smaller, third stone, 1.3m (4½ft), is in a field further up Stones Lane. Until the 1950s there were two stones in this field; the missing one may be part of the trough built around the spring.

SHAW DYKE HILL
Standing Stone | Nearest Town: **Hebden Bridge**
Map: **SD 9622 3388** | Sheets: **OL21 L103** | Lat: **53.8012N** | Long: **2.05887W**

A leaning standing stone, 1.6m (5ft 2in) tall, with views across the reservoir. According to Dr David Shepherd (see page 160), who has researched the possible astronomical and landscape alignments of megaliths in the South Pennines, this stone may have been a major lunar standstill marker.

Nearby | At SD 9902 3573, 3.2km (2 miles) ENE of Shaw Dyke Hill, just off the Brontë Footpath on Haworth Moor, is the **Cuckoo Stone**, an interestingly grooved standing stone that's wider than it's tall. A second, smaller stone has been recently erected (or re-erected) close by.

BAILDON MOOR (DOBRUDDEN STONE) Alt Name: **Low Plain**
Rock Art | Nearest Village: **Baildon**
Map: **SE 1371 4009** | Sheets: **E288 L104** | Lat: **53.85685N** | Long: **1.79304W**

Baildon Moor is home to more than 40 rock art sites, including cups and rings in a range of sizes. The Dobrudden Stone stands at SE 1371 4009 by the northeast wall at Dobrudden Caravan Park, having been moved from its original location in the 1950s. See the Megalithic Portal for the full site listings and map references for Baildon Moor.

Nearby | At SE 1304 3908, in Baildon, the **Soldier's Trench** is a much-altered site, which some believe may have been a stone circle later incorporated into an Iron Age settlement. A cup-marked rock is in the bank. The area is known for various UFO sightings!

> "Viewshed from here to Ferrybridge and the wolds. Imagine how the fires at these sites would have been visible on a clear night." Dr Olaf

Propped Stones

David Shepherd, an independent prehistorian working in the north of England

The term "propped stone" refers to large boulders that have been elevated, with one or more smaller rocks found placed underneath. They may appear to be natural features – glacial erratics, outcomes of landslip, and so on – but in places where there is no natural process that can account for the feature.

Golden Stones is located at SD 9292 2654, above Todmorden in the South Pennines, and remains almost in situ. It is a joint-defined section of a finger of Lower Kinderscout grit that has been pried up, with a prop inserted on the extreme edge of the underlying layer.

Another example, the Keld Bank feature, can be found on the west flank of Ingleborough (SD 7476 7725). The boulder appears to have come from the top layer of a post-glacial collapse on a scar 30m (98ft) away. It was halted by the even more precarious-seeming prop.

These two examples illustrate that the propping stones were apparently placed as precariously as possible, as though elevating a boulder had to be "performed" – demonstrating an unusual degree of organized strength, skill and risk-taking.

It may be that the communal performance of construction was the main point, with the completed feature serving to memorialize the period of special activity. There are many other aspects of interpretation – viewsheds, orientation, size, selective use of rock types, differentiation from natural examples.

My own fieldwork in the South Pennines and the Yorkshire Dales has so far led to the recording of nine propped stones on upland around the headwaters of the Lune, Ribble and Mersey, all rivers draining to the Irish Sea. Fieldwork continues in Ireland, Cumbria, the Dales, the South Pennines and the Dark Peak. Increasingly it seems that propped stones are just one easily recognizable facet of a suite of subtle, nuanced interventions in the natural order of things – landscape features as they were before prehistoric people encountered and interpreted them. There is no dating evidence. All the examples lie in areas showing activity from the Mesolithic to the Bronze Age. Thus "proto-dolmens" or "relics of the dolmen tradition" are currently both possibilities. The trick will be to deduce what prehistoric peoples' interpretations and motivations might have been.

Shepherd, D. 2013. "Propped Stones: The Modification of Natural Features and the Construction of Place." *Time and Mind*, Vol 6 Issue 3 November 2013, 263–86. Bloomsbury.

Photo © David Shepherd

Golden Stones, Todmorden

GRUBSTONES   Alt Name: **Hawksworth Moor**
Stone Circle | Nearest Town: **Otley**
Map: **SE 1365 4472** | Sheets: **E297 L104** | Lat: **53.89847N** | Long: **1.79375W**

Thought to be either an embanked stone circle or a ring cairn, with the remaining edge-set stones part of a circular bank. The site, on Burley Moor close to the junction of two trails, was damaged in the 19th century by the building of shooting butts, and in the late 20th century by the construction of a rectangular mound rumoured to be intended as an orgone accumulator! (The existence of orgone, a healing esoteric energy, was proposed by William Reich in the 1930s.)

TWELVE APOSTLES

Stone Circle | Nearest Town: **Ilkley**
Map: **SE 1261 4506** | Sheets: **E297 L104** | Lat: **53.901555N** | Long: **1.80957W**

Photo © Gavin J. Dronfield

The Twelve Apostles are conveniently close to a main footpath on Ilkley Moor, but this hasn't necessarily done them any favours. By the 1970s all the stones had fallen; they were put back up again in an unauthorized re-erection. Some have since fallen and been re-erected again, and many are now loose. The current 16m (52ft) circle has 12 stones but it's thought there were once 20 stones, plus a central pillar, and a raised embankment.

> "The stone circle is messed up but this is a great location."
> Dr Olaf

The circle has wonderful panoramic views and is sited close to where two important tracks across the moor cross, one of which at least is considered to be prehistoric. Various astronomical alignments have been suggested, for example to the midsummer sunrise, which is celebrated here each year.

IDOL STONE   Alt Name: **Hedges (157)**
Rock Art | Nearest Town: **Ilkley** | Map: **SE 1326 4595**
Sheets: **E297 L104** | Lat: **53.90953N** | Long: **1.79963W**

A cup-marked rock, on the main path running between Haystack rock and Green Crag on Ilkley Moor. This is a highly unusual symmetrical arrangement of cups in lines, surrounded by grooves; it was described in the 19th century by J. Romilly Allen as "the most beautiful specimen of prehistoric sculpture".

Photo © Richard Stroud

HANGINGSTONE QUARRY
Alt Name: **Hangingstones Rombalds Moor 126**

Rock Art | Nearest Town: **Ilkley**

Map: **SE 1281 4675** | Sheets: **E297 L104** | Lat: **53.91673N** | Long: **1.80645W**

At this disused quarry above Ilkley there are two panels of rock art with a large number of cup-and-rings and grooves (and some modern carvings). Some of the carvings are more eroded, having been exposed for longer, whereas others were covered by turf until the 19th century.

Nearby | At SE 0955 4696, on the Dales High Way at Woodhouse Crag, is the **Swastika Stone**, covered with cup-marks, including 10 arranged in a swastika-like design with five curved arms. Ilkley Moor is home to hundreds more rock art panels, which can be found via the Megalithic Portal website and app. Other recommended sites are: **Piper's Crag** (SE 0850 4709), **Badger Stone** (SE 1107 4605) and **Barmishaw Stone** (SE 1119 4642). Middleton Moor, about 8km (5 miles) north of Ilkley town, also has lots of rock art. **Middleton Moor 09 to 19** at SE 1098 5128, is a group of around 10 carvings close to each other. On open access land, managed for grouse, but close to a well-worn track.

> "At the foot of the outcrop is a recess known as the 'Fairies Parlour' or 'Fairies Kirk'. In legend, the Saxons attempted to build a church nearby, only to find each morning that the building stones had been moved away further down the hill. After a few days of this, they gave up and built the church down in the valley."
> Andy Hemingway

DEVIL'S ARROWS
Alt Names: **Three Grey Hounds, Three Sisters, The Devil's Bolts** ★

Stone Row | Nearest Town: **Boroughbridge**

Map: **SE 3907 6659** | Sheets: **L99 E299** | Lat: **54.09373N** | Long: **1.40412W**

Three massive stones remain in this dramatic stone row 174m (570ft) long, the stones ranging between 5.5m (18ft) and 6.8m (22ft 3in), with a further 1.5m (5ft) of each stone hidden below ground. The gritstone has weathered into grooves at the top of the stones, giving them a characterful appearance. It is thought the central stone was one of a pair, and there may have been a total of five stones here originally, with one stone broken up to build a bridge *c.* 1600. The very close proximity of the A1(M) indicates the importance of this glacial ridge as an ancient north–south transport link.

Photo © Richard L. Dixon

> "Legend has it these stones were bolts thrown by an irate Devil, aiming for the Christian settlement at Aldborough!" David Raven

THORNBOROUGH

Earthwork Complex | Nearest Village: **Thornborough**

Map: **SE 2851 7945** | Sheets: **E298 L99** | Lat: **54.21N** | Long: **1.56436W**

There are six huge henges sited within 12km (7½ miles) of each other along the River Ure, all with the same design. Three of them cluster together in a single ceremonial complex at Thornborough, part of an archaeological landscape of international importance that includes, as well as the rare triple-henge formation, a cursus, a barrow with three concentric ditches, enclosures, various rows of single or double pits and many later Bronze Age barrows. The triple-ditched barrow and the cursus predate the henges, indicating that the complex developed and increased in importance over time. Fieldwork has produced a large number of flint artefacts from the Mesolithic onward. Although the site has been badly disturbed by quarrying, and the henges have also

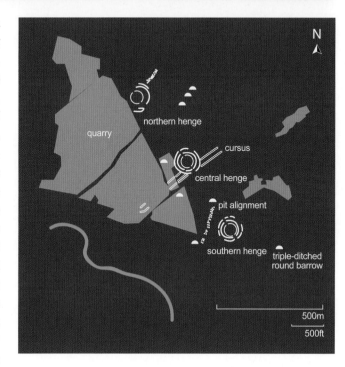

suffered damage from ploughing, these are still spectacular landscape features. The series of henge complexes of which Thornborough is part runs from Catterick to Ferrybridge on the Humber and on to the Trent and the long ridge to Maxey and Etton; it is thought that Thornborough may have played a role akin to that of an important shrine on a pilgrimage route.

TRIPLE HENGES

It has been suggested that the positioning of the three Thornborough henges represents the stars of Orion's Belt; various other archaeoastronomical alignments have been put forward, including that the southern openings in all three henges framed the rising of Sirius (see page 165). The massive henges, ranging in size from 238–244m (780–800ft), are aligned roughly northwest–southeast, each with a bank and an inner and an outer ditch and two entrances. Gypsum deposits have been found, suggesting that the earthworks were deliberately whitened. The henges survive today as earthworks and cropmarks. The northernmost henge is in the best condition, but the central henge is the most dramatic and easiest to walk around.

TRIPLE-DITCHED ROUND BARROW

The oldest structure at Thornborough is probably the triple-ditched round barrow, which has been dated to 3790–3650BC. This would make the feature older than the three henges – the date is very

early for a barrow. The fact that no Bronze Age burials seem to have been added may indicate that the triple-ditched barrow was considered too important to tamper with. Further barrows were built around the henges during the Bronze Age.

CURSUS

Visible as a cropmark and aligned northeast–southwest, the cursus is about 1.6km (1 mile) long and predates the henges, running partly beneath the central henge and across the henge axis.

AVENUE

A 350m (1,148ft) double pit avenue, associated with a barrow, runs NNE–SSW from between the central and southern henges toward the River Ure.

Thornborough Archaeoastronomy

Andy Burnham, founder and Editor of the Megalithic Portal

Anyone standing within the henges at Thornborough would have had their view of the surrounding landscape obscured by the great henge banks. It seems natural, therefore, that the focus would shift to the sky. To investigate possible astronomical links, archaeologist and Thornborough specialist Jan Harding and his team chose what they considered to be the six most likely viewpoints for making astronomical observations within the complex: the entrances of each of the three henges, which create a natural frame looking along the cursus, and along the timber avenue, in each direction; and along the axis of the two large pits or post-holes that align on the triple-ditched barrow to the southeast.

Using the astronomy app SkyMap Pro, the team created images of the night sky from these viewpoints for dates every 500 years from 3500 to 1500BC. They designed a 3D model of the Thornborough complex, and "projected" the images of the sky on to a geo-dome over this simulated landscape. The rising or setting of a total of 40 stars was found to be visible from the chosen viewpoints between 3500 and 1500BC, and the winter solstice sunrise could also be seen. Using the model, the archaeologists were able to position themselves at the selected viewpoints to consider the sky through the reconstructed monuments, taking into account the horizons and woodland cover at the time. In this way, they narrowed down the various star events to determine which were likely to have been most significant.

It was apparent that the southern entrances of all three henges framed the winter solstices at around 3000BC. Also, the eastern end of the cursus was aligned on the risings of stars Mirfax and Pollux between 3500 and 3000BC, and the western end framed the settings of seven stars, including the three of Orion's Belt.

Given the width of the henges' entrances, there were 12 stars rising and 10 setting at the entrance "windows" between 3000 and 2000BC. One of these was Sirius, within the southern entrance for each of the three henges at 3000BC. The archaeologists considered it most significant that the rise of Orion's Belt aligned with the two large pits or post-holes, but only in the first half of the third millennium BC, when it is likely the earlier cursus had been replaced by the new henge complex.

Orion's Belt rises in the direction of the Yorkshire Wolds, where many stone axes have been found, and where many of the worshippers probably lived. It first becomes visible at harvest time, and is seen throughout the winter until spring. This all suggests Orion's Belt as the most significant alignment – in what Harding calls "the close relationship between skyscape and life cycles, a connection anchored by the monuments themselves".

It seems that the glistening gypsum that coated the henge banks, perhaps representing and reflecting the moon, was prepared in nearby pits. This process may also have contributed to the symbolic power of this important location.

For more information see: Harding, J., Johnston, B. and Goodrick, G. 2006. "Neolithic Cosmology and the Monument Complex of Thornborough, North Yorkshire". *Archaeoastronomy* 20

Neolithic Sites in the Landscape

Cathryn Iliffe, researcher into archaeopsychology (mental tools and ancient constructions)

A series of massive henges, cursuses and monoliths can be found in Yorkshire and Northumberland. The earthworks and stones sit in valleys, overlooked by rock art on higher ground. It is likely that sites were located to be intervisible at long distances.

There are six large henges in the Ure valley, flanked to the west by the hills of the Dales and the North York Moors to the east – the triple henges at Thornborough (see page 163), plus Hutton Moor, Nunwick and Cana Barn. Two more can be found at Newton Kyme and Ferrybridge. All about 270m (885ft) diameter, the henges were surfaced with gleaming white gypsum. Other henges, timber circles, mounds and the massive standing stones of the Devil's Arrows, mark all the river crossings of the Humber tributaries, from Catterick to the Don.

The Rudston Monolith (see page 169) stands at a sharp bend in the Gypsey Race, where the stream transforms into an all-year river. There are four cursuses splaying out from the monolith, running roughly north–south, east–west, and out to the SSW. Several henges mark the course of the Gypsey Race westward. The Devil's Arrows, the round barrow at Duggleby (see page 168) and Rudston are all on the same latitude, suggesting long-distance cardinal landscape mapping.

In Northumberland, the Maelmin henges, cursuses and timber circles (see page 194) lie in a landscape very similar to the Ure valley monuments. The Doddington rock art (see page 195) echoes that on the hills of Ilkley and Silsden further south, the North York Moors and Lordenshaws to the north.

The construction of these sites, which would have required great investment in terms of time and effort, gives an insight into the expansive mindset of the builders and their desire to manipulate the landscape.

Eastern Yorkshire

WEST AGRA

Rock Art | Nearest Village: **Colsterdale**
Map: **SE 1424 8175** | Sheets: **E302 L99** | Lat: **54.23126N** | Long: **1.78305W**

Although known unofficially for years, the rock art here was not formally recorded until 2003. There are cup-marks visible on about 10 rocks. Look out for the two more unusual carvings as well, including one resembling a stylized human figure. On private land, as is the Agra Moor stone (below).

Nearby | At SE 1350 8244, about 1km (0.6 miles) WNW of West Agra rock art and up on the moors above Brown Beck Crags, is the 1.3m (4½ft) **Agra Moor** (or Brown Beck) standing stone. Spectacular views overlooking the confluence of Birk Gill and Brown Beck.

> "Stunning motifs, which can be hidden by trees and bracken."
> Anne Tate

YOCKENTHWAITE

Ring Cairn | Nearest Town: **Grassington**
Map: **SD 8997 7937** | Sheets: **OL30 L98** | Lat: **54.20996N** | Long: **2.15528W**

Photo © Richard L. Dixon

This site has been described as a stone circle but the 20 limestone kerb stones look to be all that's left of a ring cairn about 7 × 6.5m (23 × 21ft) in diameter. Four further stones form an outer kerb to the northwest. The tallest stone is 1.2m (4ft), with most about 0.4m (1ft 3in). A possible outlier stands 6.5m (21ft) to the southeast, and there are a couple of similar boulders to the west that may or may not be associated with the remains of the circle.

CASTLE DYKES

Henge | Nearest Village: **Thoralby**
Map: **SD 9823 8729** | Sheets: **OL30 L98** | Lat: **54.28123N** | Long: **2.02867W**

A well-preserved henge, with three entrances – only the eastern, causewayed entrance is thought to be original. It's 75m (246ft) in diameter at the widest point, and about 2m (6½ft) from the top of the bank to the base of the 10.5m (34ft 5in) wide ditch. There's a large stone on the inside slope of the bank to the southeast and there are reports of other stones having once stood at the site, now long gone. After Town Head Farm, follow the Flout Moor Lane track for about 1.6km (1 mile) and the henge is about 100m (328ft) off to the left (south) through a gate.

ACKLAM WOLD

Barrow Cemetery | Nearest Village: **Acklam**
Map: **SE 8027 6169** | Sheets: **E300 L100** | Lat: **54.04496N** | Long: **0.7756W**

Partly excavated in 1849, this is a large barrow cemetery with 17 round barrows, some altered or levelled by farming activities but others visible as mounds. Grave goods found here included a Beaker pot, jet and amber buttons and rings, and bronze daggers. Linear earthworks are thought to be Iron Age, and further finds, including an ornament for a horse's head, and gold necklaces, may be Iron or Bronze Age. One of the burials included what is thought to be a "strike-a-light" kit: a strike-stone of iron pyrites or marcasite and a flint striker. Archaeologists Anne Teather and Andrew Chamberlain have identified 52 probable examples of strike-a-lights in prehistoric burials across mainland Britain.

DUGGLEBY HOWE

Round Barrow | Nearest Village: **Duggleby**
Map: **SE 8804 6688** | Sheets: **E300 L101** | Lat: **54.0903N** | Long: **0.65547W**

A rare Neolithic round barrow, 6m (20ft) high and 38m (124ft 8in) in diameter so very visible in the landscape. Aerial photography revealed a large encircling causewayed ditch 370m (1214ft) in diameter, open to the south. The barrow stands at the source of the winterbourne river Gypsey Race. The site was developed over more than a millennium, with the original grave pit dating to 3600–3500BC, the first mound of turf and topsoil capped by a layer of chalk grit below a layer of clay dating to 2900–2800BC, and the final chalk-dug ditch and mound dating to 2500–2400BC.

The Gypsey Race

Chris Collyer, author of www.stone-circles.org.uk

The Gypsey Race is a winterbourne or intermittent stream that flows through the Great Wold Valley. Flowing both above and below ground, suddenly changing direction as well as disappearing in some years, the stream has been a source of wonder for hundreds of years. The number of monuments that follow its course is evidence for its significance to the prehistoric population of the Wolds. These include a now-destroyed henge close to Burton Fleming, two large round barrows and the Rudston Monolith. The latter stands close to a bend in the Gypsey Race, and there are also four cursus monuments that seem to be focused on, or around, this kink in the stream. Evidence of occupation continues in later prehistory with the Bronze Age Argham Dyke earthwork and the massive Dane's Dyke.

The Mesolithic hunting camp and ritual site of Star Carr lies some way north of the Gypsey Race, south of Scarborough. It once stood on the shores of the now-vanished Lake Pickering. It's clear that the presence of water was important to the people of this region.

RUDSTON MONOLITH

Standing Stone | Nearest Village: **Rudston**
Map: **TA 0980 6774** | Sheets: **E301 L101** | Lat: **54.09385N** | Long: **0.32246W**

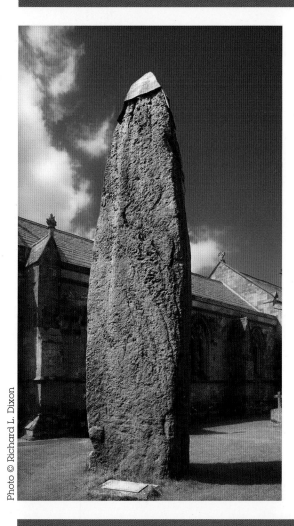

Photo © Richard L. Dixon

Legend tells how the Devil threw this massive stone at All Saints Church and missed, leaving it sticking out of the churchyard. Famously the tallest standing stone in Britain, it is just under 8m (26ft) in height and 5m (16ft) in circumference. Antiquarian investigation in the 18th century indicated the stone extends underground for a further 8m (26ft), but this has been disputed. A jaunty lead cap, deplored by many, protects the broken top. The stone is thought to have been brought here from Cayton Bay or Cornelian Bay, some 16km (9 miles) to the north.

> **"There is a smaller gritstone in the nearby cemetery, along with a slab cist grave."**
> Pat O'Halloran

Markings on its surface have been interpreted as cup-and-rings, and more contentiously as a star map. Nearby are four cursuses, romantically named A, B, C and D. Each is many hundreds of metres long, but hard to spot in the modern landscape other than as cropmarks. The stone may have been erected at the termination of Cursus B. It seems this area was very significant to our Neolithic ancestors, although the almost complete lack of finds means understanding remains elusive.

WILLY HOWE

Round Barrow | Nearest Village: **Wold Newton**
Map: **TA 0616 7235** | Sheets: **E301 L101** | Lat: **54.13603N** | Long: **0.37663W**

Just south of the Gypsey Race, this huge barrow, the second largest in East Yorkshire, is 7.5m (25ft) high and 36.5m (119ft) across. The 20m (66ft) wide ditch surrounding the barrow is visible as a surface depression.

Nearby | Just south of Wold Newton village and the Burton Fleming road is the **Wold Newton** barrow (TA 0452 7287), one of the four largest in Yorkshire, but extensively damaged by ploughing. What you see today is a partial reconstruction after the 1894 excavation.

NAB RIDGE   Alt Name: **Bride Stones**
Round Barrow | Nearest Town: **Helmsley**
Map: **SE 5756 9790** | Sheets: **OL26 L100** | Lat: **54.37337N** | Long: **1.11638W**

Photo © John D. Hunter

An interesting example of how sites can be misinterpreted, this round barrow has been variously identified as a stone circle and a decayed henge monument. The remaining stones appear to have formed part of a kerb, standing in a circular 12m (39ft) bank. The tallest stone is about 0.9m (3ft) high. Marked as "Bride Stones" on the OS map, it's one of several sites with this name.

"Reached after a long climb up the rigg – the view is worth it!" Pat O'Halloran

HIGH AND LOW BRIDESTONES

Stone Circles & Stone Row | Nearest Village: **Grosmont**
Map: **NZ 8500 0463** | Sheets: **OL27 L94** | Lat: **54.42999N** | Long: **0.69124W**

HIGH BRIDESTONES

Just one stone (about 2m/7ft tall) remains upright at the High Bridestones, which may be the remains of two four-poster stone circles. Described by Aubrey Burl as a "megalithic disaster", the site has a striking moorland setting, described as bleak by some. In 1817, Reverend George Young recorded that six stones were standing, while 11 had been upright just a few years before.

Photo © Jim Champion

LOW BRIDESTONES
At NZ 8454 0486, about 500m (1,640ft) WNW of the High Bridestones, is the short Low Bridestones row. These small stones can be hard to find when the grass is long. There are more stones around 100m (328ft) south of this location, of uncertain date, which may be later prehistoric field walls.

DRUIDS' TEMPLE
Alt Names: **Birkrigg Common, Sunbrick**

Stone Circle | Nearest Village: **Sunbrick**

Map: **SD 2923 7396** | Sheets: **OL6 L96** | Lat: **54.15655N** | Long: **3.08519W**

Photo © Richard L. Dixon

A double stone circle in a peaceful setting on Birkrigg Common in Cumbria with views over Morecambe Bay. The 9m (30ft) inner ring has 10 surviving stones and the 26m (85ft) outer ring has 15. Excavation revealed five cremations under a cobbled pavement within the inner ring, one in an inverted, patterned urn.

Nearby | At SD 2627 7442, 3km (just under 2 miles) west of the Druids' Temple, is **Great Urswick** burial chamber. It can be hard to distinguish from the surrounding natural boulders.

LACRA

Megalithic Complex | Nearest Village: **Kirksanton**

Map: **SD 1498 8133** | Sheets: **OL6 L96** | Lat: **54.22057N** | Long: **3.30538W**

At Lacra Bank, on a natural terrace on the fell to the northeast of Kirksanton, there are four stone circles as well as one or two stone rows. The natural boulders here make it a little tricky to identify these monuments at first, but it becomes easier as you walk around and get used to the features while you enjoy the fabulous views over the sea (you can see the Isle of Man on a clear day).

LACRA A (NORTHWEST CIRCLE)
At SD 1498 8133, this is the first circle reached after turning right along the track at the ruined farmhouse. It's not easy to make out. Five stones remain of a 15.7m (52ft) ring, with two more "possibles" pushed aside, perhaps, by a farm track that clips the edge of the circle to the north.

LACRA B (SOUTH CIRCLE)
This 14.6m (48ft) circle is the best preserved of Lacra's monuments. It can be found at SD 1492 8098, close to the edge of the terrace, 352m (1,155ft) SSW of Lacra A. There were probably 11 stones here originally, but only six remain. An inner ring enclosed a central mound 9.7m (32ft) across with a burial, probably a secondary rather than primary one.

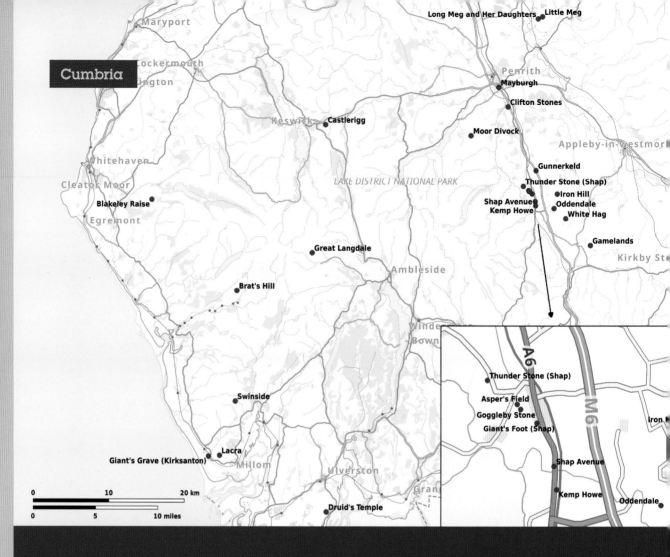

Cumbria

Long Meg and Her Daughters • Little Meg
Maryport
Lockermouth
ington
Penrith
Mayburgh
Clifton Stones
Keswick • Castlerigg
Moor Divock
Appleby-in-westmor
Whitehaven
Cleator Moor
LAKE DISTRICT NATIONAL PARK
Gunnerkeld
Thunder Stone (Shap)
Blakeley Raise
Iron Hill
Shap Avenue
Oddendale
Egremont
Kemp Howe
White Hag
Great Langdale
Gamelands
Ambleside
Kirkby St
Brat's Hill
Winde
Bown
Thunder Stone (Shap)
Asper's Field
Swinside
Goggleby Stone
Giant's Foot (Shap)
Iron
Lacra
Giant's Grave (Kirksanton)
Millom
Shap Avenue
Ulverston
Gran
Kemp Howe
Oddendale

0   10   20 km
0   5   10 miles

Druid's Temple

Top 10 Sites in the UK for Getting Away from It All

LACRA C (SOUTHEAST CIRCLE)

At SD 1501 8097, the three fallen stones of Lacra C, 91m (298ft) east of Lacra B, are identified as the remains of a 21m (70ft) circle by some and as a stone row by others.

LACRA D (NORTHEAST CIRCLE)

At SD 1509 8121, 161m (528ft) ESE of Lacra A, the Lacra D circle is around 18× 15.5m (60 × 51ft) in diameter, with a large flat central stone, 1.8 × 2.4m (6 × 8ft). The six or seven visible stones in the ring have all fallen and some barely poke out of the ground. In 1947 an urn was dug up by the northernmost stone; it is now on display at the Dock Museum in Barrow-in-Furness (where they have a great collection of Langdale axes). It's possible that there was an outer ring of stones, but if so only four remain to the southeast.

AVENUES I AND II

Running ENE from Lacra D is a row of 10 or 11 stones, which extends for around 46m (151ft). Some pairing of stones

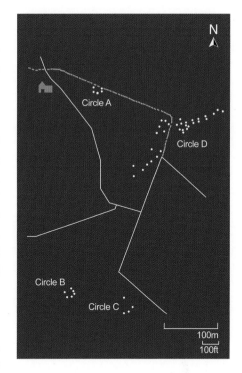

is evident. Some 35m (114ft) southwest of Lacra D, there is also said to be a row running WSW, identified in the 1947 excavation as an 80m (262ft) avenue, although these may just be naturally distributed boulders.

GIANT'S GRAVE (KIRKSANTON)   Alt Names: **Kirksanton, Portals of Eden**
Standing Stones | Nearest Village: **Kirksanton**
Map: **SD 1361 8110** | Sheets: **OL6 L96** | Lat: **54.21834N** | Long: **3.32629W**

Photo © Jim Appleton

Black Combe dominates the landscape beyond this splendid pair of standing stones, 3m and 2.4m (10ft and 8ft) tall respectively, considered to be the remains of a cairn circle. There's a cup-mark on each stone. It's thought there was a lake immediately to the north of the stones at the time they were erected. Records from the 18th century describe the stones standing on a barrow (of which there is now no evidence) and there are also reports of other stones standing with them.

173

SWINSIDE Alt Name: **Sunkenkirk**

Stone Circle | Nearest Town: **Broughton-in-Furness**
Map: **SD 1716 8817** | Sheets: **OL6 L96** | Lat: **54.28242N** | Long: **3.2739W**

Photo © Eric Grindle

This wonderful and well-preserved circle of porphyritic slate is in a beautiful setting high on remote Swinside Fell, with only the nearby farm and the distant road offering any sign of modernity. In fine weather, mist, snow or rain, it's always atmospheric and well worth the walk (some of which is fairly steep). The 27m (88ft) circle has 55 closely set stones (32 still standing), which rise to 2.3m (7½ft). An apparent entrance at the southeast is marked by a wide gap and two stones outside the ring, as at Long Meg and Her Daughters (see page 183). Aubrey Burl points out that from the centre of the circle, there is an alignment across the line of these two portal stones to the midwinter sunrise. A local legend tells that attempts to build a church on the site were foiled by the Devil, who destroyed every night what had been built during the day – hence the name Sunkenkirk. As at many sites, the stones are said to be impossible to count.

BRAT'S HILL Alt Names: **Eskdale, Burnmoor**

Stone Circle | Nearest Town: **Ravenglass**
Map: **NY 1737 0234** | Sheets: **OL6 L90** | Lat: **54.40977N** | Long: **3.27461W**

Up on boggy Burnmoor there are up to five stone circles (the position of two of them is debatable) as well as a cairnfield with, according to some estimates, over 400 cairns. The views are incredible, encompassing Harter Fell, Bowfell and the Scafell range, and down to the sea. Brat's Hill, overlooked by a striking natural rock outcrop, is the largest circle, about 30m (98ft), with *c.* 40 boulder-like stones. It contains five cairns, two of which were opened in the 19th century, revealing fragments of antlers and burnt bones. A pleasant way to get here is via the narrow-gauge Ravenglass and Eskdale Railway, getting off at Dalegarth for Boot station. Then it is an approximately 4km (2½ mile) walk.

Nearby | At NY 1730 0241, about 100m (328) WNW of Brat's Hill, is the 16m (55ft) **White Moss NE** stone circle, with around 11 stones and a central cairn, while **White Moss SW** (a similar size, with 12 to 14 stones and a central cairn, in less good condition) is at NY 1725 0239, a further 55m (180ft) WSW. **Low Longrigg SW** circle is said to be 306m (1,004ft) NNW of White Moss NE, with **Low Longrigg NE** 100m (328) further NNW, but the Low Longrigg circles are hard to find in boggy ground and long grass, and their position has been marked in different places on OS maps of different eras!

BLAKELEY RAISE   Alt Name: **Kinniside**
Stone Circle | Nearest Village: **Ennerdale Bridge**
Map: **NY 0601 1403** | Sheets: **OL4 L89** | Lat: **54.51282N** | Long: **3.45329W**

A really lovely restored 11-stone circle with fabulous views. It's believed the stones from the original circle were taken in the 18th century by a local farmer to use as gateposts; the site was then restored, possibly inauthentically, in 1925 (although the stones used are said to be placed in the original holes). Whether it is a modern fake or not, the circle is charming and sits conveniently beside the road.

GREAT LANGDALE
Ancient Quarry | Nearest Village: **Great Langdale**
Map: **NY 2740 0720** | Sheets: **OL6 L90** | Lat: **54.45497N** | Long: **3.1213W**

Photo © Mike Simon

Roughouts, rejects and worked debris from Neolithic axe industry have been found littering the scree slopes of Pike o' Stickle, fallen from quarries and an axe-factory cave high on the southern face of the fell. The beautiful axes of volcanic tuff greenstone (a narrow vein comes to the surface in Great Langdale) have been found all over Britain and Ireland; at least 15 in the Thames, for example, while in 2000 a greenstone axe, probably from Langdale, was uncovered in Doolin, County Clare. A steep path runs up to Pike o' Stickle; accessing the cave itself would require a dangerous scramble down unstable scree. The site's inaccessibility raises the question why this rock in particular was seen as so important. Other sources of similar rock would have been easier to access, but were clearly less enticing. Perhaps the difficulty of acquiring it was significant. If you're lucky enough to spot one of the prehistoric roughouts, you should leave it in place as this is a site protected by law. Lots of examples of Langdale axes can be seen in Kendal Museum.

Stone Axes

Leslie Phillips, long-standing member of the Megalithic Portal

The earliest stone tools used by the genus *Homo* were flaked to have a single edge. More complex tools, notably the bifacial flaked hand axe, followed. By the Neolithic (c. 4000–2200BC in Britain), the stone axe was characteristically a polished stone implement with a broad cutting edge. Size varied, and larger axes could be hafted. Axes were not only utilitarian but also played significant social and ceremonial roles: they were hoarded, discarded, accompanied burials and were ceremonially or ritually buried on their own.

British and Irish axes are categorized in groups based on source. There are around 30 groupings, of which arguably the most significant is Group VI, from the Great Langdale/Scafell Pike region (volcanic tuff). Axes from this area of the Lake District have been found throughout Britain, and in Ireland and the Isle of Man, accounting for approximately 25 per cent of analysed axe finds in those regions.

Other groups significant for their quantity or distribution include Group I/Ia (uralitized gabbro, epidiorite, or greenstone) originating from Cornwall, near Penzance. Their distribution is primarily in the south, east and Midlands, with some in Wales and Yorkshire. Group VII (augite granophyre) axes, from the Penmaenmawr area of North Wales, were distributed mostly in Wales and the Midlands, with concentrations in the Peak District and at Flamborough Head. Finds from Group XIII are not common, but they are of interest because,

like the Stonehenge bluestones, they come from the Preseli Hills. Distribution is usually centred around the sources, however the Langdale axes (Group VI) appear to have been distributed from Humberside, while Group I may have had its main distribution area in the southeast.

The distribution of finds shows that axes were widely traded, with some theories suggesting they were exchanged for perishable items or livestock, but it is impossible to know whether they were traded directly and specifically, or whether distribution took place more slowly, via gift exchange. Causewayed enclosures may have played a part in this process, as gathering places and trading centres.

For thousands of years Alpine jade axes ("jade" here refers to jadeite, jadetite and nephrite), originating from two areas in the Italian Alps, circulated widely throughout western Europe. The richest concentration of these is found in the Gulf of Morbihan in Brittany, and it is thought the large jade axes found in Britain and Ireland (approximately 130 examples) came from here. These are very highly polished, and so thin they would not be functional. It seems that jade axes were highly valued, functioning as prestige objects or used for ceremonial purposes. A prominent example is Britain's oldest jade axe, dating to 3200BC and found buried at the Sweet Track timber causeway in the Somerset Levels. Other notable sites that have produced axe finds include Carn Brea in Cornwall, Maiden Castle in Dorset and Cairn Holy 1 in Scotland.

CASTLERIGG Alt Name: **The Carles**

Stone Circle | Nearest Town: **Keswick**
Map: **NY 2913 2363** | Sheets: **OL4 L90** | Lat: **54.60284N** | Long: **3.09858W**

Photo © David Young

This is Cumbria's best-known stone circle, recorded by John Aubrey and William Stukeley and celebrated from the time of the Romantics (Keats, Coleridge and Ann Radcliffe all visited here) for its spectacular setting as much as for the magnificent stones themselves. Its accessiblity and popularity mean you're unlikely to get the site to yourself, but this is perhaps Britain's most dramatically sited circle, on a plateau surrounded by a perfect ring of mountains. To the south lie High Rigg and Helvellyn, to the north Skiddaw and Blencathra, to the west the Derwent Fells, and to the east, through a gap, the North Pennines can be seen. It's breathtaking. The circle itself is equally impressive, with 33 large stones still standing of the 38 that remain (there were originally 42). Ten more form a rectangular enclosure extending from the ring into the circle, a highly unusual feature that can only be compared to the Cockpit on Moor Divock (see page 181). This is one of the earliest circles in the UK, dating to the Neolithic rather than the Bronze Age. The stones are glacial erratics, generally about 1m (3ft 3in) tall, with those surrounding the "entrance" gap on the northern side rising to over 2m (6½ft). There are also two cairns inside the circle, as well as a low mound just inside the entrance. A stone 90m (295ft) southwest of the circle, by the wall, was moved to its present position in 1913 and may or may not be related to the circle. In the 1720s Stukeley mentioned a second circle to the west of Castlerigg (the area centred on NY 293 236), although nothing seems to remain of this today.

GAMELANDS Alt Name: **Orton**
Stone Circle | Nearest Village: **Orton**
Map: **NY 6401 0816** | Sheets: **OL19 L91** | Lat: **54.46752N** | Long: **2.55678W**

Photo © Richard Stroud

An irregular 30m (98ft) circle of 43 pink granite boulders (except one of limestone), all of which have fallen or were perhaps deliberately set as recumbents. The stones, none longer than 0.9m (3ft), are set into a slight bank. Knott Scar dominates the northern horizon. A possible carving has been noted on top of a stone in the circle's northwest quadrant, and there may be an entrance to the south.

WHITE HAG
Stone Circle | Nearest Village: **Crosby Ravensworth**
Map: **NY 6074 1161** | Sheets: **OL19 L91** | Lat: **54.49828N** | Long: **2.60769W**

A small circle, about 6 × 5m (20 × 16ft), on open moorland, with sweeping views in all directions. There are 11 boulders in the circle, and an outlier stands 6.5m (21ft) to the southeast. There's a group of four smaller stones to the west.

Photo © Charles Paxton

> **"The outliers suggest this could be the surviving inner circle of a concentric circle similar to nearby Oddendale."** John Miller

ODDENDALE
Stone Rows | Nearest Town: **Shap**
Map: **NY 5920 1291** | Sheets: **OL5 L91** | Lat: **54.50984N** | Long: **2.63165W**

This excellent double circle is made of pink Shap granite boulders, 34 in the 26.3m (86ft) outer ring and 23 in the inner, which forms the kerb of a small cairn. A group of outliers is located north of the outer circle.

> **"Two outlying red granite rocks look remarkably similar in shape to the Thunder Stone at Castlehowe Scar quarry."** Anne Tate

IRON HILL
Stone Circle or Barrow | Nearest Village: **Hardendale**
Map: **NY 5963 1476** | Sheets: **OL5 L91** | Lat: **54.52704N** | Long: **2.62527W**

Photo © Anne Tate

Along with Iron Hill South (see below), Iron Hill North is classified by Historic England (Pastscape) as a bowl barrow – this one being 9m (30ft) in diameter. A field wall has been built over the mound, restricting access to part of it. One of the 11 kerb stones is limestone while the rest are pink granite, and they're all about 0.3m (1ft) tall. Apparently seven further stones were removed in the 1980s.

Iron Hill South, also known as Harberwain and variously identified as a stone circle, cairn circle or bowl barrow, is at NY 5964 1477, just 50m (164ft) south of Iron Hill North. The 6m (20ft) diameter mound is lower than at Iron Hill North, and seven pink granite boulders of the kerb remain. Two similar stones lie to the southeast. Boulders on top of the mound may be the remains of a cist. Antiquarian excavation revealed part of a deer antler, animal bones and a male skeleton.

SHAP

Multiple Stone Rows | Nearest Village: **Shap**
Map: **NY 5670 1380** | Sheets: **OL5 L90** | Lat: **54.51763N** | Long: **2.67039W**

There are a number of sites in and around Shap village. The best way to see these stones, which are in fields and field walls on most sides of the village, is to use the Megalithic Portal app, or else the map produced by the Shap Local History Society. They have identified 11 stone circles, seven burial mounds and a prehistoric settlement in the area, as well as the stones of a possible avenue.

SHAP AVENUE
The stones seem to form an arc that curves northwest from Kemp Howe stone circle (see below), running for c. 2.5km (1½ miles) through the village and across the fields. It's easy to navigate from one stone to the next. The stones are mostly pink Shap granite, and some – the Thunder Stone and Goggleby Stone in particular – are probably glacial erratics. English Heritage records 14 stones, but there may be more. Many suspiciously large stones are embedded in walls or stand in gardens and fields. It's rumoured that stones from the avenue were used in the building of nearby Shap Abbey.

KEMP HOWE
If you are speeding north through Shap on the West Coast Main Line, look out for this sadly abused circle to the left of the railway (at NY 5676 1327). It's also right by the A6. Five or six large individual pink granite stones of this stone row remain in situ. There's some debate as to whether the other stones still exist beneath the tracks or were removed before the embankment was built. This circle is thought

to have been the focus of Shap Avenue, along with a second circle at Carl Loft (now destroyed), on private land behind the Greyhound Hotel at the south end of the village.

GIANT'S FOOT (SHAP)

At NY 5630 1478, on the west side of Shap village, is this very large, flat-topped stone, one of the named Shap Avenue stones (also known as Barnkeld or the Drummer).

GOGGLEBY STONE

At NY 5592 1509, 500m (1,640ft) WNW of the Giant's Foot, is this very large and impressive standing stone (pictured, right), visible from miles around. Once you know it's there, you can see it from all kinds of places around the village.

Photo © Anne Tate

ASPER'S FIELD STONE

In the field next to the Goggleby Stone is another stone in Shap Avenue (at NY 5584 1521, on private land). It has a cup-and-ring mark on the top.

THUNDER STONE (SHAP)

In a field south of the minor road running eastward from Shap to Crosby Ravensworth is the fabulous, very large glacial erratic (at NY 5515 1575) that's usually counted as the first (or last) major stone in Shap Avenue. It's on private land, so ask at the farm or view it from the road.

CASTLEHOWE SCAR

At NY 5875 1547, 3.6km (2¼ miles) east of Thunder Stone (Shap), is Castlehowe Scar, a neat 5m (16ft) circle nestling close to a dry-stone wall in a field. There are 10 pink granite stones and one of blue granite in this. At NY 5818 1561, 590m (1,938ft) west of the stone circle, is another Thunder Stone!

GUNNERKELD

Stone Circle | Nearest Village: **Shap**
Map: **NY 5682 1775** | Sheets: **OL5 L90** | Lat: **54.55314N** | Long: **2.66911W**

Photo © Christopher Bickerton

This rather ruinous concentric circle is right next to the M6 motorway and indeed visible from the southbound carriageway. Three stones remain upright in the 30 × 24m (98 × 78ft) outer circle of 19 large granite stones, two of these uprights forming the entrance on the north side. The inner circle, forming the kerb of a cairn, is around 18 × 16m (59ft × 52ft), with 31 stones. On private land, so seek permission at the farm.

MOOR DIVOCK

Megalithic Complex | Nearest Village: **Askham**
Map: **NY 4828 2224** | Sheets: **OL5 L90** | Lat: **54.59268N** | Long: **2.80193W**

Moor Divock is a remarkable prehistoric landscape, littered with cairns, stone circles, standing stones and other monuments. This is a great place to wander round and see what you can spot.

Photo © Christopher Bickerton

THE COCKPIT

At a junction of several tracks (at NY 4828 2224), the Cockpit stands on the edge of a natural terrace with wonderful views over Ullswater and to the Derwent Fells. This is a large kerb cairn or a stone circle, oval in shape and measuring 27.4 × 31.6m (90 × 104ft), set into a low stone bank. There were two concentric settings of stones, but the outer ring is hard to make out. The tallest stone still standing measures about 0.9m (3ft) and some of the fallen stones extend to 1.8m (6ft). The 5m (16ft) square setting on the eastern side of the circle is a rare formation, possibly original to the circle, which has been compared to the rectangular feature at Castlerigg (see page 177).

COP STONE

At NY 4959 2160, 1.5km (just under 1 mile) ESE of the Cockpit, the impressive Cop Stone is right on the track that leads up across Divock Moor. It's a large, unworked stone (1.7 × 1.2m/5ft 6in × 4ft) forming part of the southwestern boundary of a ring cairn 17m (57ft) in diameter. The cairn's bank can be identified, as well as four more stones protruding by around 0.3m (1ft) from the bank. Records from the 19th century show the bank was continuous at that time, with over 10 recumbent stones in place.

MOOR DIVOCK 4

At NY 4940 2197, next to the track and 415m (1,362ft) northwest of the Cop Stone, is Moor Divock 4, a 10m (33ft) ring cairn, with a mound of turf-covered stones surrounded by a ring of 10 uprights (a further four stones are just southeast of the cairn). An urn, along with a cremation, was found here in the 19th century. From here, the Cop Stone is visible, framed between two standing stones.

MOOR DIVOCK 3

At NY 4931 2219, around 230m (750ft) northwest from Moor Divock 4, a little way east of the track, is a 17 × 15m (56 × 49ft) cairn circle with three large upright stones, plus some on the ground. The stones are around 1.5m (5ft) high. An urn and cremation were found here, too.

WHITE RAISE CAIRN

Around 500m (1,640ft) WNW of Moor Divock 3, further along the track and close to the junction with the path leading west to the Cockpit, this large oval cairn (at NY 4889 2242) is close to the path on its eastern side but can still be tricky to find, requiring a plunge through the bracken! It's about 22m (72ft) long and the central cist is exposed, along with the displaced capstone.

MAYBURGH

Henge or Banked Enclosure | Nearest Village: **Eamont Bridge**
Map: **NY 5192 2843** | Sheets: **OL5 L90** | Lat: **54.64865N** | Long: **2.74667W**

Not even the immediate proximity of the M6 can ruin the atmosphere in this massive banked enclosure. The huge bank, made of river-weathered stones, is still 7.3m (24ft) high in places and 45m (147ft) wide, and surrounds a 90m (295ft) enclosure. There is an entrance to the east. One standing stone remains in the centre; originally there were four, with four more at the entrance (these were destroyed in 1720). William Stukeley suggested there may have been two concentric stone circles within the henge, but there is no evidence for this. The height of the bank gives a very particular sense of being enclosed within the site. A great place to break a journey on the M6.

Nearby | At NY 5232 2837, just over 400m (1,312ft) east of Mayburgh, is **King Arthur's Round Table**. The Victorians may have attempted to turn this henge into pleasure gardens, and the road cuts into it, but still it survives, around 90m (295ft) in diameter. With a bank and an internal ditch, it fits the henge definition more neatly than Mayburgh. Two stones once stood outside the northern entrance (now beneath the road), and there was also another henge, known as the Little Round Table, some 200m (656ft) to the southeast. This is now covered by modern development and barely visible (a shallow ditch can be seen at NY 5238 2817).

At NY 5097 2875, about 1km (0.6 miles) west of Mayburgh, is the 1.8m (6ft) **Skirsgill** standing stone, now hidden among bushes outside a gym in a car park in an industrial estate.

CLIFTON STONES

Standing Stones | Nearest Village: **Clifton**
Map: **NY 5313 2593** | Sheets: **OL5 L90** | Lat: **54.62631N** | Long: **2.72747W**

Photo © Nicola Didsbury

Two Bronze Age standing stones, which lean, with pleasing symmetry, in opposite directions. A third was uncovered during excavation in 1977, along with a small cairn over the remains of several cremations. A lane leads to the field, but they are on private land.

> "In the corner of the field lies a very large misshapen stone. Could it be 'The Hag', as mentioned on the OS map?" Nicola Didsbury

LONG MEG AND HER DAUGHTERS

Stone Circle | Nearest Village: **Little Salkeld**

Map: **NY 5711 3721** | Sheets: **OL5 L91** | Lat: **54.72803N** | Long: **2.66749W**

Photo © Shaun (Stonesy) Bunting

The third-largest stone circle in England, after Avebury and Stanton Drew, Long Meg and Her Daughters is a flattened oval measuring 110 × 93m (360 × 305ft). There are 69 stones remaining, of which 27 still stand, and the circle has two "entrances", to the northwest and southwest. A large enclosure to the north meets the flattened northern segment of the circle. The story goes that the outlier and circle are 13th-century witch Meg Meldon and her coven, turned to stone by wizard Michael Scot. These stones are said to be uncountable; if you manage to count them twice and get the same result, Scot's spell will be broken, or you can hear Long Meg whisper. There's a story that an attempt to blow up the circle in the 18th century was foiled by a violent storm that frightened off the would-be destroyers. Radiocarbon dating following a community excavation in 2015 found a date of 3340–3100BC for hazel-wood charcoal from what looks to be a stone hole just north of the stone circle, suggesting more stones were once present. This date is one of the earliest for a stone circle in Britain.

LONG MEG

At NY 5706 3716, some 22m (72ft) southwest of the southwestern circle entrance, stands Long Meg herself – all 9 tonnes (10 tons) and 3.8m (12ft 5in) of her. She's an impressive red sandstone pillar with rock art, including grooves, spirals and rings, carved into one side. Aubrey Burl points out that this stone, when viewed from the centre, stands in line with two portal stones at the southwest entrance and with the midwinter sunset. If this stone is ever broken, the legend goes, it will run with blood.

LITTLE MEG   Alt Name: **Maughanby**

Kerb Cairn | Nearest Village: **Little Salkeld**

Map: **NY 5770 3748** | Sheets: **OL5 L91** | Lat: **54.73050N** | Long: **2.65853W**

"One or two of the larger stones might be in their original positions, but most have been moved to plough the land. Still worth a visit, with a welcoming ambience." Nicola Didsbury

Little Meg's 11 stones, most fallen, encircle a central cairn that once covered a cist containing an urn with a cremation. There are spirals and cup-and-ring marks on two of the stones (another decorated stone is at the Tullie House Museum in Carlisle). On private land but visible from the field gate.

Jack Morris-Eyton's Shadow Theory

David Smyth, who spent two years researching Jack's work

Before his death in 2011, Jack Morris-Eyton, retired farmer and regular contributor to the Megalithic Portal, spent 18 years developing a theory about the interaction of light and shadows at stone circles and other monuments. With particular reference to Swinside, Castlerigg, Long Meg and Her Daughters, and Stonehenge, he devised a system to demonstrate how these monuments were used as "prediction calendars".

His research began when he noticed the shadows cast by some stones seemed to have a purpose in an overall design. Small boulders on exposed ridges cast long shadows to the valley below, intersecting with horizontal ground shadows. It also appeared that shadows crossed target stones at certain times of the day or year, and stones often seemed to have views to features on the horizon, such as notches, hills or barrows, at precise sun or moon rising or setting points. For example, at Long Meg, the shadow from Long Meg herself falls right across the circle to Stone 1 at midwinter sunset. At the equinoxes and crossquarter days, the shadow reaches other stones in the circle.

Jack used a computer programme to tell him the azimuth and elevation of a celestial event on the horizon. The azimuth is the angle between a celestial body and north, measured clockwise around the observer's horizon. The elevation is the vertical angular distance between a celestial body and the observer's horizon. Together they define the position of a celestial body in the sky, viewed from a particular place, at a particular time. If, for instance, it was a lunar event, he would take bearings from the stones he identified as "moon stones" and note which other stones in the circle, or what feature on the horizon, were associated with it. This process was repeated for solstices and equinoxes. He discovered there were key positions at some sites – either pointer stones or pairs of stones, from which the whole year's calendar could be seen. He also found stones marking what he called "invisible" events – points where the sun or moon rose or set that were hidden behind intervening hills.

For more information, see:
www.megalithic.co.uk/downloads/JackME_Final.pdf

BARNINGHAM MOOR

Rock Art | Nearest Village: **Barningham**
Map: **NZ 0547 0881** | Sheets: **OL30 L92** | Lat: **54.4746N** | Long: **1.91714W**

BARNINGHAM MOOR 20

The Barningham Moor rock art (see map, page 166) is on open-access land, but managed for grouse so March to August (nesting season) should be avoided. Of the many rock art stones in the area, the most complex and striking is Barningham Moor 20 (at NZ 0547 0881, pictured opposite). The carvings include one cup with four rings, six cups in a line and serpentine grooves connecting cups. Packing stones indicate this stone may have originally been upright.

BARNINGHAM MOOR 100

At NZ 0596 0840, some 634m (2,080ft) ESE of Barningham Moor 20, is Barningham Moor 100, a squarish boulder with cup-marks, including some with grooves and penannulars. The more finely carved motifs are much more weathered than the crudely carved motifs; this may result from turf protection or having been carved at different times.

Photo © Cezary Namirski

OTHER BARNINGHAM MOOR SITES

As the number of Barningham Moor 100 suggests, there's a lot of rock art in this area. Other recommended sites nearby are: Barningham Moor 101 (NZ 0596 0838), Barningham Moor 127 (NZ 0488 0823), Barningham Moor 13 (NZ 0499 0885), Barningham Moor 23 (NZ 0528 0917), Barningham Moor 24 (NZ 0444 0830), Barningham Moor 52 (NZ 0563 0831), Barningham Moor 58 (NZ 0523 0767), and Barningham Moor 6 (NZ 0456 0856). See the Megalithic Portal for further information.

SIMONBURN Alt Names: **Davy's Lee, King's Crag, Haughton Common**
Stone Circle | Nearest Village: **Simonburn**
Map: **NY 8021 7120** | Sheets: **OL43 L87** | Lat: **55.03493N** | Long: **2.3111W**

On moorland pasture, this attractive 9m (30ft) circle has 11 visible stones, the tallest of which, an L-shaped "chair", reaches 1m (3ft 3in). Several have cup-marks. Close by are cairns, rock art stones, settlements, enclosures, ancient boundaries and banks, and cist burials – a real treat. The best access (although very boggy in parts) is from the B6318 (Military Road), across the vallum of Hadrian's Wall and past Sewingshields Farm. If you want a dry route, stick to the farm track until you reach the wood just south of Folly Lake, then turn left.

Nearby | At NY 8054 7134, around 350m (1,150ft) east of Simonburn, is the possibly Bronze Age **Davy's Lee** enclosure, a reasonably well-defined curvilinear bank and what may be a burial cairn. Just beyond the southeastern edge of the enclosure is Davy's Lee rock art boulder (at NY 8067 7132), sitting in isolation on a gentle slope. Natural fissures delineate several parts, within which are 12 cup-marks of varying size and shape, some of which may be natural. The enclosure is on private land, although it butts up to the surrounding access land.

At NY 7971 7042, around 1km (0.6 miles) southwest of Simonburn, are the two recently discovered **Queen's Crags** cup-marked boulders, within 60m (196ft) of each other. The smaller has five cup-marks, and the larger has cup-marks and slots from quarrying.

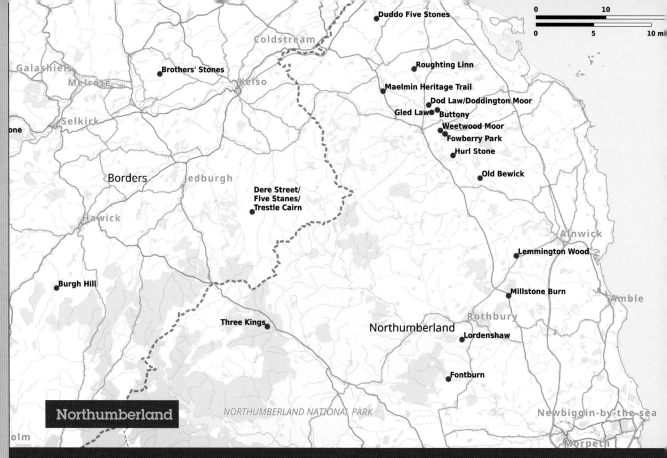

Duddo Five Stones
Coldstream
Galashiels
Brothers' Stones
Melrose Kelso
Roughting Linn
Maelmin Heritage Trail
Dod Law/Doddington Moor
Gled Law Buttony
Selkirk
Weetwood Moor
Fowberry Park
Hurl Stone
Borders Jedburgh
Old Bewick
Hawick
Alnwick
Dere Street/
Five Stanes/
Trestle Cairn
Lemmington Wood
Burgh Hill
Millstone Burn
Amble
Three Kings
Rothbury
Northumberland
Lordenshaw
Fontburn
Northumberland
NORTHUMBERLAND NATIONAL PARK
Newbiggin-by-the-sea
Morpeth

FONTBURN Alt Names: **Fontburn Dod, Fontburn Reservoir**

Stone Circle | Nearest Town: **Morpeth**

Map: **NZ 0325 9364** | Sheets: **OL42 L81** | Lat: **55.237N** | Long: **1.95037W**

A cute little four-poster on private land just to the north of the western end of Fontburn Reservoir and around 600m (1,968ft) SSW of Newbiggin Farm. The stones are small (up to 1m/3ft 3in) and two of them have cup-marks. Online archaeology data service England's Rock Art says: "Ironstone banding and surface cover on two sides is interesting and may have influenced selection for use within a monument." This site is just off a permissive footpath that runs around Fontburn Reservoir. Look out for red squirrels in the area.

Nearby | At NZ 0328 933, 270m (885ft) south of the four-poster, **Fontburn B** is a massive glacial boulder to be found next to a small burn that runs into the western end of Fontburn Reservoir. Its flattish top is decorated with more than 50 cups, cup-and-rings

Photo © Cezary Namirski

"Fontburn four-poster is almost the twin of Hafodygors Wen, over in North Wales." Paul Blades

and cup-and-grooves. Motifs on the side may have been lost to quarrying. This impressive boulder can be reached by following the walk along the south side of Fontburn Reservoir then taking the gate on to access land and following the fence line.

THREE KINGS

Stone Circle | Nearest Village: **Byrness**
Map: **NT 7743 0092** | Sheets: **OL16 L80** | Lat: **55.30185N** | Long: **2.35704W**

Photo © Christopher Bickerton

A charming little four-poster circle with one fallen stone, set in a clearing in Kielder Forest. The stones measure around 1.4m (4½ft) in height, and there's a cist in the middle, which held a cremation burial.

Nearby | At NT 8132 0117, 4km (2½ miles) east of the Three Kings, **Bellshiel Law** is a chambered long cairn located in a military training area on the Otterburn Ranges (search online for access times). The 109m (357ft) cairn more or less doubles in width from 8.8m (29ft) at the west to 15m (49ft) at the east end. It's mostly bare stone with some turf to the north. The enclosure to the south is a later feature, built using stone from the cairn. There are six cairns about 150m (490ft) to the southeast, which are hard to find when the grass is long.

> "The name Three Kings is from a local legend that this was the grave of three kings of Denmark who were killed in battle." Ewen Rennie

LORDENSHAW

Rock Art | Nearest Town: **Rothbury**
Map: **NZ 0522 9915** | Sheets: **OL42 L81** | Lat: **55.28644N** | Long: **1.91931W**

WEST LORDENSHAW MAIN ROCK

Also known as West Lordenshaw 2c, this is a huge piece of rock at NZ 0522 9915 that really stands out on the moorland. This superb example of prehistoric art has 100 motifs surviving on its surfaces, despite having been quarried. It forms the start of a walking trail that takes in an Iron Age hill fort and other rock art sites. Use the Rock Art on Mobile Phones resource (rockartmob.ncl.ac.uk) for directions and information.

Photo © Cezary Namirski

Prehistoric Rock Art in Britain and Ireland

Cezary Namirski has a PhD in archaeology from Durham University

The first publications about British petroglyphs date back to the 19th century, but it's only since the 1960s, with the work of Stan Beckensall in England and Donald Morris in Scotland, that they've been studied in any real depth. Morris and Beckensall's monumental efforts to record the sites, as well as the contributions of K.J.S. Boughey and E.A. Vickerman on West Yorkshire, remain the basis of our knowledge about the distribution of British rock art. New panels are regularly discovered, even in areas that have been previously surveyed. Many decorated rock surfaces lie concealed by the turf, which in some cases has contributed to the survival of actual toolmarks.

British and Irish rock art shares many characteristics with that of Spain and Portugal, as part of the wider horizon of Neolithic and early Bronze Age petroglyphs in Atlantic Europe. However, generally in Britain and Ireland the designs are limited to abstract motifs, with cup-marks and cup-and-ring marks (with up to nine or 10 rings) constituting the vast majority of examples, often accompanied by channels or grooves, sometimes by spirals, and very rarely sub-rectangular designs. The oldest recorded archaeological context for a cup-marked stone comes from the early Neolithic long barrow at Dalladies (Aberdeenshire), while one of the latest is the early Bronze Age cairn at Chatton Sandyford (Northumberland), indicating that the cup-and-ring mark tradition lasted about two millennia. It is distinct from the megalithic art tradition known from the passage tombs of Ireland and Wales.

The main concentrations of rock art can be found in the northeast of England (north and west Yorkshire and Northumberland), western Scotland (Argyll and Galloway), and some areas of Ireland (County Donegal and south Leinster). Despite an overall homogeneity in style, regional patterns can be observed – for example, the rosette motifs at sites around Wooler in Northumberland (the Ringses, Buttony and Hare Law Crags). Most motifs are located on outcrops and boulders in the landscape, but they can also be found on monuments (Matfen in Northumberland and Long Meg in Cumbria), cairns and cist burials (the cist cover from Witton Gilbert in County Durham). Clive Waddington (1998) interprets this as evidence for chronological changes in distribution and use – according to his model the motifs were first carved on outcrops and boulders in the landscape in the Neolithic, and gradually moved to monuments and burials.

Excavations around some of the major rock art panels have proved that they were not created in isolation. For example, adjacent to the cup-and-ring marked Tiger Rock (at Kilmartin Glen in Argyll), remains of a late Neolithic post or stake circle, as well as a clay platform of similar date were discovered (Jones et al. 2011); and at Hunterheugh in Northumberland, a cairn that covered some of the motifs was excavated.

Find out more at England's Rock Art:
archaeologydataservice.ac.uk/era/

EAST LORDENSHAW CHANNEL ROCK

At NZ 0569 9939, northeast of the hill fort, is East Lordenshaw Channel Rock East, also known as Lordenshaw 4b. This large rock has cup-marks, bowls and the longest carved channel in Northumberland (perhaps even in the UK).

> "On the slope edge among other outcrops, Channel Rock is difficult to spot at first, but the minute you see the cup-marks, it really stands out." Anne Tate

LORDENSHAW HORSESHOE ROCK

At NZ 0510 9922, 143m (469ft) WNW of the Main Rock, this rock originally formed the base of a Bronze Age cairn; now all that remains is this highly decorated rock, which takes its name from the rare horseshoe-shaped grooves containing cups. It sits on a 40 degree slope and has 360 degree views.

OTHER LORDENSHAW SITES

There are over 120 panels at Lordenshaw (although some, mainly in West Lordenshaw, are on private land). Other recommended sites in the area are: West Lordenshaw 2d (NZ 0536 9929), East Lordenshaw 3q (NZ 0566 9935), East Lordenshaw 4e (NZ 0567 9940), East Lordenshaw 4f (east) (NZ 0567 9940) and East Lordenshaw 4g (NZ 0560 9939). See the Megalithic Portal for further information.

MILLSTONE BURN

Rock Art | Nearest Village: **Edlingham**
Map: **NU 1184 0524** | Sheets: **E332 L81** | Lat: **55.34104N** | Long: **1.81492W**

MILLSTONE BURN 2H

There's a fantastic range of rock art at Millstone Burn, with 2h (on open-access land, at NU 1184 0524) the best and most complex example; it has three large motifs, two made up of cup-and-two-rings and descending grooves, creating stemmed or flower-like images. As with other moorland rock art sites, the Millstone Burn carvings are most easily found in late autumn, winter and early spring, before the bracken gets too deep. Some carvings may become covered in turf.

Photo © Cezary Namirski

MILLSTONE BURN 1A

At NU 1189 0520, 63m (206ft) ESE of Millstone Burn 2h, on open-access land just east of the A697. An outcrop or earthfast boulder set into the hillside, partially covered in moss and turf, this stone has a large, deep cup with three rings and a groove, and a smaller cup-mark with no rings.

MILLSTONE BURN 1B

At NU 1188 0510, 100m (328ft) SSE of Millstone Burn 2h, is this carved stone, sited east of the A697 and on private land right by the roadside fence, through which it can be viewed. It features a rare oculus carving with two cup-marks (like a figure of eight or a pair of eyes), which may be mossed over.

OTHER MILLSTONE BURN SITES

Other recommended rock art sites in the area are: Millstone Burn 1c (NU 1187 0508), Millstone Burn 1g (NU 1190 0514), Millstone Burn 2g (NU 1186 0522), Millstone Burn 3a (NU 1164 0523), Millstone Burn 3e(i) (NU 1172 0528), Millstone Burn 4a (NU 1151 0516), Millstone Burn 4b (NU 1152 0517), Millstone Burn 5a (NU 1142 0517), Millstone Burn 6b (NU 1129 0519), Millstone Burn 6c(ii) (NU 1134 0522), and Millstone Burn 6d (NU 1136 0521). See the Megalithic Portal for further information.

LEMMINGTON WOOD

Rock Art | Nearest Village: **Edlingham**
Map: **NU 1293 1078** | Sheets: **E332 L81** | Lat: **55.39080N** | Long: **1.79742W**

This rock outcrop features not just cup-and-ring marks, but also the only runic inscription in the Northumberland landscape – it's believed to mean "relics" or "leave behind".

Nearby | At NU 1279 0962, 1.2km (¾ mile) south of Lemmington Wood, is **Corby Crags** rock shelter, a partly quarried outcrop with ledges and seating inside. A tool-cut groove inside the cave led to a triangular stone that covered a cremation burial within an early Bronze Age food vessel. There are rock art panels near the shelter.

> "GPS may be needed to locate the rock, as it is in a dip and often hidden by bushes. The site is in a private wood, but there are paths through it, used by dog walkers." Anne Tate

OLD BEWICK

Rock Art | Nearest Village: **Old Bewick**
Map: **NU 0782 2157** | Sheets: **E332 L75** | Lat: **55.48793N** | Long: **1.87772W**

There are numerous rock art stones, in addition to those described here, to discover in this location, as well as an Iron Age hill fort with its huge earth ramparts and great views.

OLD BEWICK 1A

On this large rock outcrop at NU 0783 2158, overlooking Corby Crags hill fort, Hepburn Ridge and the cairns at Blawearie, is a complex panel covered on the top and two sides by many individual and interlinking rock art motifs, some of which are unique to this stone (including a figure of eight). Natural features have also been worked into the design. Some motifs may have been lost to quarrying.

OLD BEWICK 2

At NU 0776 2155, 70m (230ft) WSW of Old Bewick 1a, and over the fence from its companion, this is a slightly smaller outcrop with cup-and-ring marks, including an interesting cup with duct-and-ring motif countersunk within a bowl. Again, some motifs may have been destroyed by quarrying.

OLD BEWICK 3A

At NU 0772 2158, 56m (184ft) WNW of Old Bewick 2, this boulder is partly embedded in the ruins of an old stone wall. It is decorated with cups, rings and other finely carved motifs, including an unusual (quite worn) foot-shaped groove or reniform (a rectangle with rounded, narrow ends like a kidney).

HURL STONE

Standing Stone | Nearest Village: **Newtown**
Map: **NU 0395 2471** | Sheets: **E340 L75** | Lat: **55.51613N** | Long: **1.939W**

Photo © Anne Tate

So named because the Devil hurled a stone at St Cuthbert on Ros Castle Hill and – as usual – missed, this thin, 3m (10ft) stone may be a relocated prehistoric standing stone or, alternatively, a headless Anglian cross-shaft. After being struck by lightning in the mid-19th century, it was mounted on a concrete plinth. Local tradition says there's a tunnel beneath it, linking two caves. The story goes that explorers who dared enter the tunnel, on reaching the part directly under the stone, found their lights extinguished and heard fairy voices singing a rhyme, causing them to flee in terror. Seek permission from the owners of Lilburn Tower to see it close up, or view it from the road.

Nearby | At NU 0432 2421, 621m (2,037ft) southeast of the Hurl Stone and fenced in on private land at the base of Ewe Hill, is **Newtown Mill**, a well-worn 1.2m (4ft) tall standing stone. The vertical fluting on its top (caused by weathering) says it is far older than the the Devil's Causeway Roman road by which it stands. Two cup-marks linked by a groove have been reported on its south face and a single cup on the north, but these may just be natural.

FOWBERRY PARK

Rock Art | Nearest Village: **Wooler**
Map: **NU 0287 2765** | Sheets: **E340 L75** | Lat: **55.54317N** | Long: **1.95697W**

Photo © Anne Tate

Fowberry Park consists of eight panels on a sloping, quarried outcrop. The most striking is Fowberry Park b (at NU 0287 2765): two parallel rows of 48 small cup-marks, average diameter 2cm (less than 1in). Stan Beckensall, the expert on Northumbrian rock art, says, "there is nothing like this anywhere else."

WEETWOOD MOOR

Rock Art | Nearest Town: **Wooler**
Map: **NU 0222 2821** | Sheets: **E340 L75** | Lat: **55.547456N** | Long: **1.966278W**

There used to be a pleasant walk linking rock art sites on Weetwood Moor, but it is now on private property and the trail is overgrown. Seek permission before visiting.

Photo © Drew Parsons

BICYCLE ROCK

Also known as Weetwood Moor 3a, this is the old walk's first site, at NU 0222 2821. It is carved with six distinctive, large penannulars (incomplete circles), some linked by grooves.

GORSEBUSH ROCK

Also known as Weetwood Moor 5a, this site at NU 0215 2821 is 73m (240ft) WNW of Bicycle Rock. There are four sets of penannular rings and various cup-marks.

PLANTATION ROCK

At NU 0197 2831, 193m (633ft) WNW of Gorsebush Rock, this is the last site on the trail, also known as Weetwood Moor 6a. It has two large motifs of cups-and-rings, and two smaller ones. Other recommended sites in the area are: Weetwood Moor 1a (NU 0233 2822), Weetwood Moor 2c (NU 0226 2821) and Weetwood Moor 7 (NU 0227 2815). See the Megalithic Portal for further information.

BUTTONY

Rock Art | Nearest Town: **Wooler**
Map: **NU 0174 3104** | Sheets: **E340 L75** | Lat: **55.57302N** | Long: **1.97404W**

BUTTONY 4

At NU 0174 3104, this is a really impressive pair of conjoined cup-and-ring motifs. One is a cup with seven complete rings, the other has eight. This rock also has six cups arranged in domino fashion. The Buttony sites are in an atmospheric forest setting on private land, so seek permission before visiting.

BUTTONY 1C

At NU 0173 3103, just 10m (33ft) WSW of Buttony 4, is Buttony 1c, with four concentric ring motifs, linked by serpentine grooves, forming a frieze extending 2m (6½ft) over the side of the rock. These motifs lie close to the ground and may be buried under pine needles and tree roots.

BUTTONY 3

At NU 0174 3104, 12m (39ft) ENE of Buttony 1c, Buttony 3 has some complex motifs including a rare rosette of four cups within seven broken rings. Another cup is surrounded by five complete rings.

BUTTONY 5

At NU 0173 3106, 24m (79ft) NNE of Buttony 1c, this carving features a rare rosette motif with eight cups, and the beginnings of another. There are also two keyhole motifs, worn but still visible, and now protected by pine needles and earth.

Nearby | Around 600m (1,968ft) ENE of the Buttony sites, **West Horton** has another great collection of inscribed rocks (on private land, so seek permission). The sloping bedrock outcrop known as West Horton 1a (at NU 0214 3149) contains cups, grooves and arcs, including a pattern of three cups that echoes the oculus of the motif beside it. Three other motifs form an umbrella effect. Other recommended sites in the area include: West Horton 1b (NU 0215 3156), West Horton 1f (NU 0231 3136), West Horton 2a (NU 0215 3155) and West Horton 2b (NU 0215 3155).

GLED LAW
Rock Art | Nearest Village: **Doddington**
Map: **NU 0092 3070** | Sheets: **E340 L75** | Lat: **55.56995N** | Long: **1.98695W**

GLED LAW 2A

Gled Law is a continuation of the Dod Law scarp, with views across the Till valley and much rock art. On private land at NU 0092 3070, Gled Law 2a has two splendid sets of cup-and-rings, one over 1m (3ft 3in) and sharing the largest number of concentric rings (eight) in Northumberland with Buttony 4; the arc of a ninth ring is visible, along with grooves radiating from the centre. The weathered adjoining motif has six radiating grooves.

Photo © Cezary Namirski

GLED LAW 1

At NU 0106 3066, 144m (473ft) east from Gled Law 2a, this smaller panel features two cups, both with unaligned penannulars (incomplete circles). The eastern motif is in better condition. Note that the site is likely to be covered in turf in summer. Other recommended sites in the area include: Gled Law 2c (NU 0090 5303), Gled Law 2d (NU 0090 3071), Gled Law 2e (NU 0089 3071), Gled Law 2f (NU 0089 3071) and Gled Law 3 (NU 0121 3087). See the Megalithic Portal for further information.

DOD LAW

Rock Art | Nearest Village: **Doddington**
Map: **NU 0050 3172** | Sheets: **E340 L75** | Lat: **55.57913N** | Long: **1.9937W**

East of Dod Law West hill fort is Dod Law Main Rock, an impressive, exposed slab of rock with some unique motifs and, as a bonus, great views across to the Cheviots. The flat surface of this stone has been split into "zones" by curvilinear grooves; the "double boxes" or rectangular grooves enclosing some of the cup-marks are really unusual, and worth the walk!

MAELMIN HERITAGE TRAIL Alt Name: **Milfield Henge**
Reconstructed Henge & Timber Circle | Nearest Village: **Milfield**
Map: **NT 9400 3363** | Sheets: **E339 L75** | Lat: **55.59626N** | Long: **2.09677W**

Near the modern village of Milfield, in the Till valley, was the important Anglo-Saxon royal township of Maelmin. The Till valley is a landscape rich in archaeological heritage, containing a complex of eight henges, some 4,000 years old (possibly forming a processional way), together with other Neolithic and early Bronze Age stone circles, standing stones and burial cairns. Maelmin Heritage has reconstructed one of the wooden henges, which was originally located in a nearby field and found to contain Anglo-Saxon burials. The henge and a reconstructed early medieval house are linked by a 600m (1,968ft) walking trail.

Photo © Iain Murray

ROUGHTING LINN ⭐
Rock Art | Nearest Village: **Ford**
Map: **NT 9839 3673** | Sheets: **E339 L75** | Lat: **55.62416N** | Long: **2.02714W**

> "At the time of our visit, the paths were sufficiently well maintained for wheelchair access." Anne Tate

Described as "one of the most important pieces of rock art in the world" by Stan Beckensall, Roughting Linn is the largest and probably best-known set of prehistoric carvings in the north of England. As it is a Historic England site, it is signposted from the road. The art is carved into a huge dome of sandstone, about 18m (59ft) long, with designs across three sections. The motifs are mostly cup-and-rings, some of which are very deeply cut. In close proximity to the rock art panel is a well-preserved Iron Age promontory fort with up to five impressive ramparts; although covered in trees, its banks and ditches are well defined. A wonderful and impressive site.

Nearby | 1.6km (1 mile) or so WNW of Roughting Linn is another large dome of rock around which are further carved outcrops. At **Broomridge 2** (at NT 9704 3705) there is a set of cups and cup-and-rings, one with seven rings, the rings being made up by angular lines joined together. At its east end, there are also some circular markings made during the excavation of millstones.

At NT 9771 3702, 669m (just under ½ mile) east of Broomridge 2, is **Goatscrag rock shelter**, with rare deer carvings. Experts are unable to agree as to whether they are prehistoric or not. These rock overhangs were used for shelter and as burial places – if the carvings are contemporary with the burials, they are unique in Britain.

DODDINGTON MOOR

Stone Circle | Nearest Village: **Doddington**

Map: **NU 0131 3172** | Sheets: **E340 L75** | Lat: **55.579132N** | Long: **1.980781W**

Up on Doddington Moor (just 800m/½ mile east of Dod Law), only one stone remains upright of this five-stone circle; the other stones are fallen. The footpaths appear to have changed, so GPS will be helpful.

Nearby | At **Hare Law Crags**, north of Doddington Moor, there are seven rock art boulders in the same vicinity. Hare Law Crags 1.3 (at NU 0137 3543) includes two unusual variations on the cup-and-ring theme: a large rosette motif and an oculus (two cups surrounded by two concentric circles). On private land.

Photo © Cezary Namirski

DUDDO FIVE STONES   Alt Name: **Singing Stones**

Stone Circle | Nearest Village: **Duddo**

Map: **NU 9306 4301** | Sheets: **E339 L75** | Lat: **55.68672N** | Long: **2.1121W**

Photo © Dave Head

Stan Beckensall describes Duddo as "one of the most attractive monuments in Britain". This circle of five beautifully grooved, large sandstone stones has a lovely hilltop setting. One of the stones was re-erected in the 1920s, and the others have all probably been moved or re-erected at some point (there were originally six of them). There are various legends associated with Duddo, one being that the stones were erected as recently as 1558 to commemorate the victory of the Earl of Northumberland at Grindon over a party of marrauding Scots. Another story relates how these are all that remains of five men turned to stone for digging up turnips on the Sabbath. The indignity of being petrified caused the men's leader to collapse in shock; this is the stone that was put up again in the 1920s. On private land, with access at the landowner's discretion.

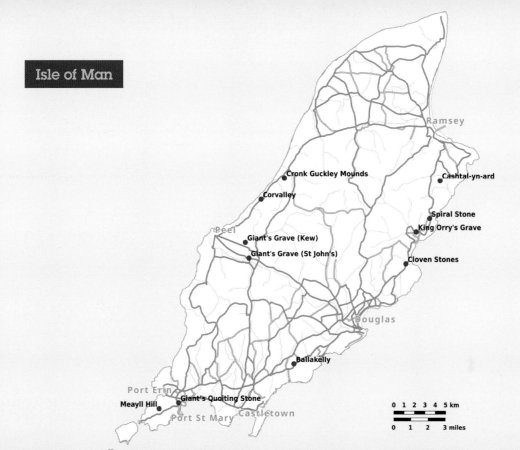

Isle of Man

Cronk Guckley Mounds
Corvalley
Giant's Grave (Kew)
Giant's Grave (St John's)
Peel
Ramsey
Cashtal-yn-ard
Spiral Stone
King Orry's Grave
Cloven Stones
Douglas
Ballakelly
Port Erin
Meayll Hill
Giant's Quoiting Stone
Port St Mary
Castletown

0 1 2 3 4 5 km
0 1 2 3 miles

BALLAKELLY

Chambered Tomb | Nearest Village: **Santon**
Map: **SC 3214 7199** | Sheet: **L95** | Lat: **54.11630N** | Long: **4.56966W**

Set in what is known as the Giant's Field, this site is confused by a jumble of granite boulders, some of which resulted from field clearance in the 19th century. The tomb itself has a rectangular chamber or cist, aligned WNW–ESE and surrounded by a kerb. The stones to the southwest are presumed to be capstones. One of the kerb stones, to the west, has a number of cup-marks.

CLOVEN STONES

Chambered Tomb | Nearest Village: **Baldrine**
Map: **SC 4292 8141** | Sheet: **L95** | Lat: **54.20430N** | Long: **4.40981W**

Clearly visible from the road, this is a remarkable survival in the front garden of a bungalow. The barrow has a chamber with one or two compartments, with two tall 1.8m and 2.1m (6ft and 7ft) portal stones to the NNE. The name "Cloven" refers particularly to the eastern stone, which is split down the middle – probably due to frost action. On the southeast the revetting or kerb can be seen. It's considered to be quite a late example of this type of passage grave.

MEAYLL HILL

Chambered Cairn | Nearest Village: **Cregneash**
Map: **SC 1895 6778** | Sheet: **L95** | Lat: **54.074035N** | Long: **4.76869W**

Photo © Jos Sanders

Just below the brow of the hill and with stunning views over the south of the island and out to sea, this unique monument has six pairs of roofless, T-shaped burial chambers arranged in a circle enclosing a space about 13m (44ft) across. Each pair was originally accessed by a passage from the circle's exterior. The interior contained a central cist or chamber, found under rubble. The stones are not large (the biggest is 1m/3ft 3in tall), but this is a well-preserved, fascinating site. Pottery, white quartz pebbles and cremations were found during excavations in 1893 and 1911. It's suggested it began life as a central round cairn or embanked circle, with the chambers added later, the whole finally being covered by a kerbed cairn. Legend relates that the place is haunted by a troop of ghost riders.

Nearby | At SC 2088 6833, 2km (1¼ miles) ENE of Meayll Hill, is the **Giant's Quoiting Stone**.

GIANT'S GRAVE (KEW) Alt Name: **The Kew**

Chambered Tomb | Nearest Village: **Poortown**
Map: **SC 2743 8340** | Sheet: **L95** | Lat: **54.21720N** | Long: **4.64827W**

The remains of a passage tomb, on private land but visible (indistinctly) from the track. There is some evidence of a mound, and the two rows of stones that form the long rectangular chamber stretch east–west for about 8m (26ft).

Nearby | At SC 2775 8193, 1.6km (1 mile) SSE of this Giant's Grave is another one, in **St John's**. A chamber or cist is built into the wall, right by the road, just along from Tynwald Hill.

CRONK GUCKLEY MOUNDS
Round Mounds | Nearest Village: **Kirk Michael**
Map: **SC 3123 8945** | Sheet: **L95** | Lat: **54.27276N** | Long: **4.59337W**

The Round Mounds project has been investigating some of the 160 round mounds on the island, including the three at Cronk Guckley, where a cist burial, complete with collared urn (indicating an early Bronze Age origin for the site), was discovered during excavations in summer 2017. The excavation also confirmed that the mound is human-made, with layers of earth and turf. Rubbly material found around the mound looks to be evidence of a ring cairn, with the larger blocks of bedrock quarried elsewhere and deliberately placed around the edge of the mound as kerbing. The three mounds have been damaged by ploughing but are visible on a ridge with great views of the sea. They're all around 15m (49ft) in diameter and between 0.5m (1½ft) and 1m (3ft 3in) in height. On private land, so seek permission.

Nearby | At SC 2893 8747, 3.2km (2 miles) WSW of Cronk Guckley, is **Corvalley** cairn (also known as the Devil's Elbow), a badly damaged, large cairn or round barrow, measuring about 29 × 23m (95 × 75ft) and reaching about 1.9m (6ft 2in) in height. There is at least one enclosed chamber or cist, which is roofed and partially walled with slabs of quartz. On private land, so seek permission.

KING ORRY'S GRAVE
Chambered Tomb | Nearest Village: **Minorca**
Map: **SC 4389 8439** | Sheet: **L95** | Lat: **54.231352N** | Long: **4.396505W**

Photo © Jos Sanders

The King Orry with whom this site is linked in legend was Godred, the 11th-century Norse-Gaelic ruler of Dublin and the Isles, who took control of the Isle of Man in 1079. Lots of sites on the island are traditionally associated with him. Here, there are two chambered tombs of the horned or Clyde cairn type, separated by houses and a road – or possibly one very long tomb. Both tombs are aligned northwest–southeast.

The eastern tomb, which stands beside the road, is similar in structure and layout to Cashtal-yn-ard (see opposite). Two chambers, linked by low septal stones, and part of a third chamber, remain, and there is also a horned forecourt, surrounded by a revetted kerb that once held back the cairn. Six upright stones remain in the forecourt and the tomb. Sherds of a plain bowl were found in the first chamber, along with traces of a burial. In the garden across the road (follow the signs) are two further chambers, and a 2.7m (8ft 10in) portal stone. Stumps of other stones suggest a shallow forecourt.

Nearby | At SC 4520 8567, 1.9km (just over 1 mile) ENE of King Orry's Grave, is the **Spiral Stone** at Ballaragh, an earthfast boulder set in the bank of the lane leading to the village. It has three or four spirals and some possible cup-marks toward the lower left of the stone, which can be hard to see. It is the only known example of rock art on the island.

CASHTAL-YN-ARD

Chambered Tomb | Nearest Village: **Glen Mona**
Map: **SC 4622 8923** | Sheets: **L95** | Lat: **54.27552N** | Long: **4.36327W**

⭐

> "**Evening sunlight conditions are required to see traces of five cup-marks. They can be found on the inside of the smaller, left-hand stone that forms part of the entrance to the chambers from the forecourt.**" Adam Stanford

"The castle of the heights", Cashtal-yn-ard is set on high ground with fine views overlooking Maughold and the sea across to Cumbria. This large tomb extends for around 40m (131ft) and has a west-facing square or U-shaped forecourt. A number of stones remain in the façade, the largest of which is 2.3m (7½ft) high. There are five chambers, originally covered by a cairn of loose rock (about 1.2m/4ft high when first recorded) held in place by a kerb, with dry-stone walling in some places. An area of burnt shale and charcoal fragments was found about 3.3m (11ft) behind the final chamber, overlaid with cairn material. The walling, most of the cairn and some of the uprights were removed in the mid-19th century for housebuilding.

Photo © Kammer

199

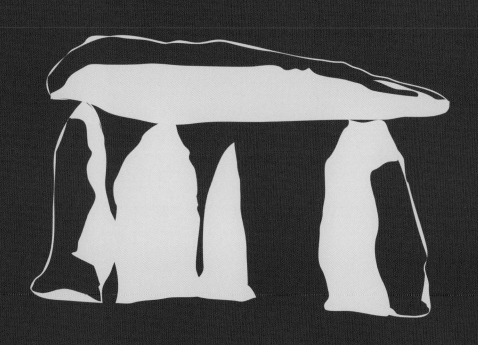

WALES

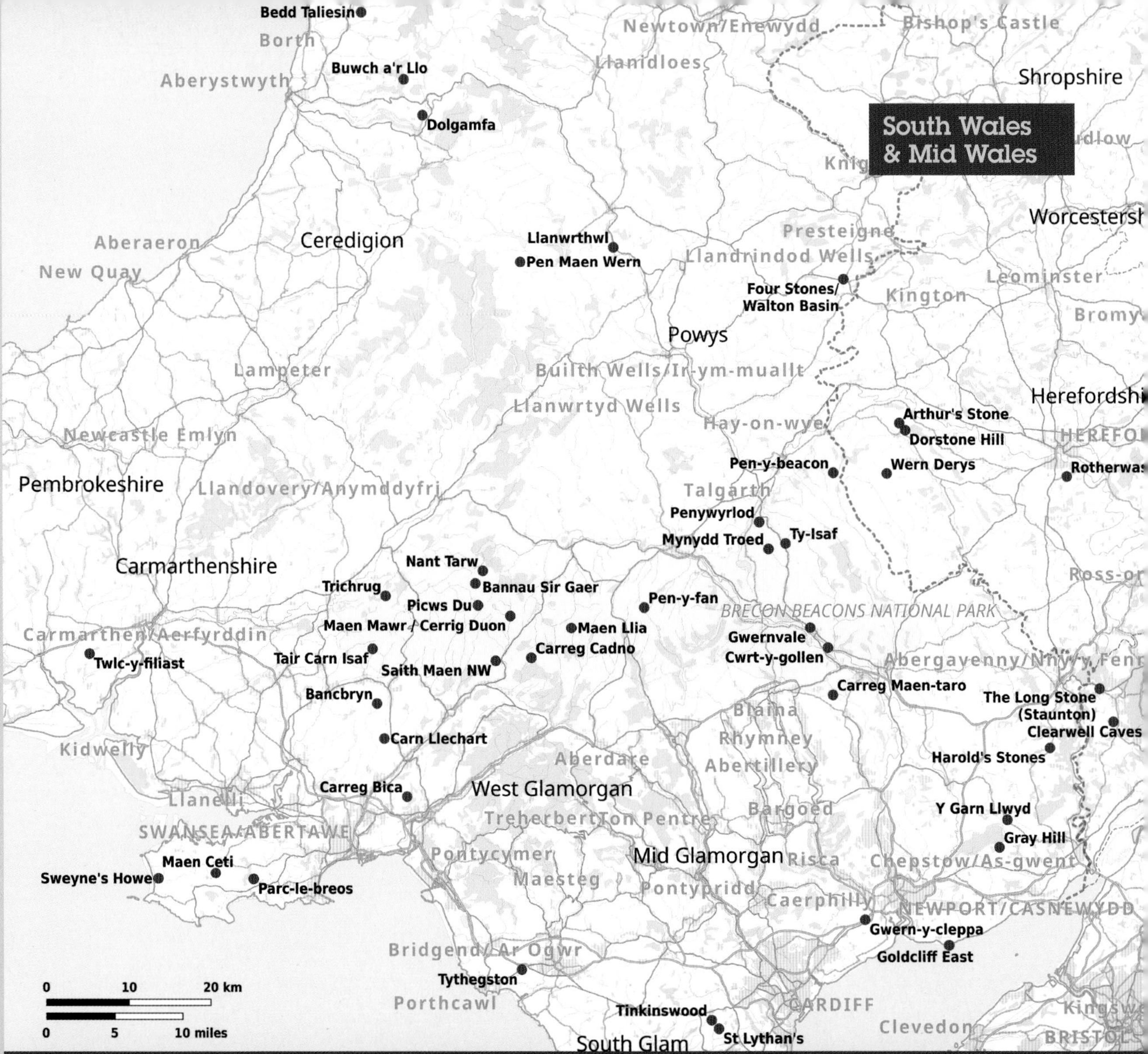
South Wales
& Mid Wales
Bedd Taliesin
Borth
Buwch a'r Llo
Aberystwyth
Dolgamfa
Newtown/Enewydd
Llanidloes
Bishop's Castle
Shropshire
Ludlow
Knig
Worcestersh
Aberaeron
New Quay
Ceredigion
Llanwrthwl
Pen Maen Wern
Presteigne
Llandrindod Wells
Four Stones/
Walton Basin
Leominster
Kington
Bromy
Powys
Lampeter
Builth Wells/Ir-ym-muallt
Llanwrtyd Wells
Herefordshi
Newcastle Emlyn
Hay-on-wye
Arthur's Stone
Dorstone Hill
HEREFO
Pembrokeshire
Llandovery/Anymddyfri
Pen-y-beacon
Wern Derys
Rotherwas
Talgarth
Penywyrlod
Ty-Isaf
Mynydd Troed
Carmarthenshire
Nant Tarw
Bannau Sir Gaer
Trichrug
Picws Du
Maen Mawr / Cerrig Duon
Pen-y-fan
BRECON BEACONS NATIONAL PARK
Ross-o
Maen Llia
Carmarthen/Aerfyrddin
Gwernvale
Carreg Cadno
Cwrt-y-gollen
Twlc-y-filiast
Tair Carn Isaf
Saith Maen NW
Abergavenny/Y Fenni
Carreg Maen-taro
The Long Stone
(Staunton)
Bancbryn
Blaina
Clearwell Caves
Rhymney
Carn Llechart
Kidwelly
Aberdare
Abertillery
Harold's Stones
Llanelli
Carreg Bica
West Glamorgan
Bargoed
Y Garn Llwyd
SWANSEA/ABERTAWE
Treherbert
Ton Pentre
Gray Hill
Pontycymer
Mid Glamorgan
Risca
Chepstow/As-gwent
Maen Ceti
Sweyne's Howe
Maesteg
Parc-le-breos
Pontypridd
Caerphilly
NEWPORT/CASNEWYDD
Gwern-y-cleppa
Bridgend/Ar Ogwr
Goldcliff East
Tythegston
0 10 20 km
0 5 10 miles
Porthcawl
Tinkinswood
CARDIFF
Clevedon
Kingsw
BRISTOL
St Lythan's
South Glam

Top 15 Burial Chambers in England & Wales

1. **Pentre Ifan (Pembrokeshire)** p.220
2. **Lanyon Quoit (Cornwall)** p.42
3. **Bryn Celli Ddu (Anglesey)** p.244
4. **Trethevy Quoit (Cornwall)** p.53
5. **West Kennet (Wiltshire)** p.109
6. **Chûn Quoit (Cornwall)** p.39
7. **Carreg Samson (Pembrokeshire)** p.217
8. **Devil's Den (Wiltshire)** p.113
9. **Trefignath (Anglesey)** p.248
10. **Wayland's Smithy (Oxfordshire)** p.113
11. **Carwynnen Quoit (Cornwall)** p.42
12. **Spinsters' Rock (Devon)** p.72
13. **St Lythan's (Glamorgan)** p.207
14. **Lligwy (Anglesey)** p.249
15. **Mulfra Quoit (Cornwall)** p.41

HAROLD'S STONES

Stone Row | Nearest Village: **Trellech**

Map: **SO 4993 0514** | Sheets: **OL14 L162** | Lat: **51.74271N** | Long: **2.72658W**

Photo © Christopher Bickerton

The village (its name meaning "three stones") is named after this trio of tall stones (all of the local brown "puddingstone"), which lean at a variety of dramatic angles and may once have formed part of a larger monument. The central stone has smoothed surfaces and two large cup-marks. Legends abound here. The stones are said to commemorate a battle won by King Harold – and it is noteworthy that the 1689 sundial in the local church is inscribed with an image of the stones and the words "HIC FUIT VICTOR HARALDAS". Different tales also relate how the giant Jack O' Kent played quoits with the Devil here. In one, Jack, having tossed the three stones to Trellech, then threw a fourth stone that fell short and had to be moved to allow for ploughing. It's been suggested this represents a folk memory of a fourth standing stone.

CARREG MAEN-TARO

Standing Stone | Nearest Town: **Brynmawr**

Map: **SO 2383 1134** | Sheets: **OL13 L161** | Lat: **51.7955N** | Long: **3.10589W**

A fine standing stone, 1.7m (5½ft) tall, which is traditionally believed to commemorate the site of a battle fought between two kings. Historically, it has been used as a boundary stone, which is why it's inscribed "M" on the side that faces Monmouthshire, and "B" on the side that faces Brecknockshire, the old county name (now Powys).

Photo © Cerrig

TRANSLATING WELSH PLACE NAMES

Simon Charlesworth and Stephen Rule

This glossary is to help decipher the meaning of Welsh site names. Note that some letters have mutated over time or for grammatical reasons ("c" to "g" is particularly common). The word menhir, denoting a standing stone, comes from *maen* ("stone") and *hir* ("long").

Welsh	Variants, eg mutations (m) plurals (pl) Anglicizations (Eng)	English	Other uses and notes
bach	fach (m)	small, little	dear (loved)
ban	fan (m), bannau (pl)	peak	
banc	fanc (m)	bank	
bardd	fardd (m), beirdd (pl)	poet, bard	
bedd	fedd (m), beddau (pl)	grave	normally followed by a name
bryn	fryn/mryn (m), bryniau (pl)	hill	
buwch		cow	
bwlch		gap	
bychan	fychan	little, small	
capel	gapel (m), chapel (m), capeli (pl)	chapel	
carn(edd)	garn (m), carneddau (pl)	tumulus	especially cairns
carreg/ cerrig	garreg (m)	stone	
castell		castle	
cawr/ cawres	gawr/gawres (m)	giant/ giantess	
cefn		back	ridge
cegid	cegiden	hemlock	
celli	gelli (m)	grove(s)	
clawdd	cloddiau	hedge	
coch	goch (m)	red	
coed	goed (m)	tree	woodland
coitan	goitan (m), coiten (alt)	quoit	

cors	gors (m)	bog	
craig	graig (m), creigiau (pl)	rock	outcrop
crib	grib (m)	comb	crest
crug	grug (m), chrug (m)	cairn	
cwm	gwm (m), cymau (pl)	valley, glen	
cwrt		court	
du	ddu (m), duon (pl)	black, blackened	
eglwys		church	
filiast	viliast (Eng), miliast (alt)	greyhound (bitch)	
garw	arw (m)	rough	
gollen		hazel	
gorsedd	orsedd (m), (r) ossett (Eng)	throne	bardic meeting point
gwal		lair	
gwaun	waun (m)	moorland	
gwen	wen (m), gwyn	white	also: pure, bare, fresh, new, clean
gwern	wern (m)	alder	
gwrach	wrach (m)	witch	often seen in the mist
gwr	gwyr (m)	husband	
hen		old	
isaf		lower	
llan	lan (m)	church, clearing (of land)	normally followed by a personal name
lle		place	
llech	lech (m), llechi (pl)	slate	can simply be "stone" – as in cromlech (= crooked stone)
llety		lodging house	
llwyd	lwyd (m)	grey	
llyn	lyn (m)	lake	
llys	lys (m)	court	
maen	meini (pl)	stone	
mawr	fawr (m), mawrion (pl)	big	
meirw		(the) dead	
moel	foel (m)	bald	rounded hilltop

morfa		fen	
mynydd	fynydd (m), mynyddoedd (pl)	mountain	
nant	nentydd (pl)	stream	
neuadd		hall	
newydd		new	
pen	ben (m), pennau (pl)	head	also: top (of), peak, end
plas	blas (m)	mansion, palace	
pont	bont (m)	bridge	
pump		five	
pwll	bwll (m)	pool	
rhiw		hill	
rhos		moor	
saeson/ sais		English (man)	from "Saxon"
saith		seven	
tafarn		tavern	

taro		to hit	
tarw	darw (m), teirw (pl)	bull	
tre(f)	dre(f) (m), trefi (pl)	town	
tri/tair		three	
troed	droed (m), traed (pl)	foot	used for foot of hill
twlc		pigsty	
twˆr		heap, tower	
tŷ	dŷ (m), tai (pl)	house	sometimes seen without circumflex
uchaf		upper	also: highest, super
wyth		eight	
y/yr		the	
ystum		curve	

Y GARN LLWYD

Chambered Tomb | Nearest Village: **Gaerllwyd**
Map: **ST 4476 9674** | Sheets: **OL14 L171** | Lat: **51.6667N** | Long: **2.80011W**

A tomb with a dramatically collapsed capstone, partially supported by five upright stones, and with other recumbent stones giving the site a charming higgledy-piggledy appearance. The cairn is mostly missing. The tomb is behind the hedge, near a crossroads on the Chepstow–Usk road.

GRAY HILL

Stone Circle and Row | Nearest Village: **Parc Seymour**
Map: **ST 4380 9353** | Sheets: **OL14 L171** | Lat: **51.63775N** | Long: **2.81347W**

On Gray Hill, with fine views over the Severn estuary, are multiple prehistoric remains, including a small stone circle or possible kerb cairn. It's about 10m (33ft) across, with 13 low stones remaining. Stones inside the circle may be the remains of a setting or chamber. There are a couple of outliers; the one to the northwest, some 55m (180ft) WNW from the circle, is 2.3m (7½ft) tall. It may be part of a stone row, as several other large stones climb from the circle to the hilltop cairn.

Nearby | At ST 4339 9355, 409m (1,342ft) west of the circle, are the remains of a summit cairn. A cairn cemetery is centred around ST 4409 9327, 384m (1,260ft) ESE of the circle. There are apparently nine barrows here, but the vegetation is dense. Good luck!

GOLDCLIFF EAST
Prehistoric Footprints | Nearest Village: **Goldcliff**
Map: **ST 3771 8206 (approx)** | Sheets: **E152 L171** | Lat: **51.53402N** | Long: **2.89935W**

The promontory at Goldcliff is well known for the Mesolithic sites found in the intertidal zone. The remains of an oak forest, as well as flint scatters, wood and bone tools, and animal bones have all been found here, indicating seasonal hunter-gatherer activity. Also, and most famously, there are footprints. As the esturine silts erode, the prints of humans, including small children, are periodically exposed, as well as the prints of birds and animals. Most of the site is accessible only during low tide, and the footprints, by their very nature, are ephemeral – exposed, then eroded and lost for ever

Nearby | At **Uskmouth** at approx ST 328 826, *c.* 5km (3 miles) west of Goldcliff East, the footprints of Mesolithic people have been found, as well as evidence of aurochs, wolves, deer and birds. As at Goldcliff East, the prints' whereabouts are impossible to predict, as they come and go with the tides.

GWERN-Y-CLEPPA
Chambered Tomb | Nearest Town: **Newport**
Map: **ST 2764 8505** | Sheets: **E152 L171** | Lat: **51.55966N** | Long: **3.0452W**

A surprising survival just north of the M4 and close to an industrial estate. Once you know where it is you can see it from the motorway. Seven stones remain, including a probable capstone.

Nearby | At ST 2411 8342, 4km (2½ miles) WSW of Gwern-y-cleppa, is the **Druidstone**, also known as Gwal-y-viliast, on private land in the grounds of Druidstone House. This broad, shield-shaped stone is 2.8m (9ft) tall by 2.4m (7ft 10in) wide and 1m (3ft 3in) thick. The owners request visitors phone ahead to arrange access (contact details are supplied on the Megalithic Portal page for this site).

TINKINSWOOD ★
Chambered Long Cairn | Nearest Village: **St Nicholas**
Map: **ST 0922 7331** | Sheets: **E151 L171** | Lat: **51.45146N** | Long: **3.30781W**

Tinkinswood is the proud possessor of the largest capstone in mainland Britain, a huge 7.4 × 4.5m (24 × 15ft) slab, weighing 36 tonnes (40 tons). This Cotswold-Severn tomb has an east-facing forecourt leading to the main chamber, and a trapezoidal cairn. There's a cist on the northern side. In 1914, the remains of 50 people were excavated from the main chamber. The area near the tomb known as the Quarry was long thought to be the source of the

Photo © Stephen Rule

capstone, but investigation in 2011, which also identified a nearby Bronze Age barrow, found no evidence that this was the case. Local tradition holds that if you spend the night here on May Day Eve, St John's Eve (23 June) or the night before the winter solstice, you will die, go mad or become a poet. A group of boulders to the south is said to be women punished for dancing on the Sabbath.

ST LYTHAN'S Alt Names: **Gwal-y-filiast, Maes-y-felin**
Former Chambered Long Cairn | Nearest Village: **St Nicholas**
Map: **ST 1009 7230** | Sheets: **E151 L171** | Lat: **51.44252N** | Long: **3.29504W**

Gwal-y-filiast means "kennel of the greyhound bitch" and a number of Welsh chambered tombs have similar names – this one seemingly was used as an animal shelter in the early 19th century. The 0.8m (2ft 7in) thick capstone, 4.2 × 3m (13ft 9in × 10ft), is dramatically balanced on three uprights, but few traces of the cairn or mound of this Cotswold-Severn tomb remain. Excavations in 2011 revealed the collapsed façade at the front, along with the rubble that had been used to seal the chamber. The field

Photo © Paul Blades

in which the monument stands is said to be cursed, and it's also said that on Midsummer Eve the capstone spins round three times, and after that (or before, who knows?) all the stones go down to the river to bathe.

TYTHEGSTON
Chambered Tomb | Nearest Village: **Laleston**
Map: **SS 8646 7925** | Sheets: **E151 L170** | Lat: **51.50074N** | Long: **3.63714W**

The capstone, although partially buried in the remains of the cairn, is very impressive, at around 4 × 1.8m (13 × 6ft). There's not a lot else to see, though.

Nearby | At SS 9269 8193, 6.8km (4¼ miles) east of Tythegston chambered tomb, is **Coity** chambered cairn. It's badly damaged, the large, pitted capstone now partially supported by collapsed uprights.

CARREG BICA Alt Names: **Maen Bradwen, Hoat Stone**
Standing Stone | Nearest Village: **Birchgrove (nr Neath)**
Map: **SS 7248 9946** | Sheets: **E165 L170** | Lat: **51.67939N** | Long: **3.84567W**

"A cup-marked stone is a few hundred yards to the north. I can find no mention of it on Coflein or the other monument databases, so it may even be a new discovery!" Paul Blades

A fantastic slab of local sandstone and one of the tallest standing stones in Wales at 4.3m (14ft) high. It is mentioned as a Gower boundary marker in a 13th-century charter of King John. It is said to bathe in the River Neath on Easter Morning.

PARC-LE-BREOS Alt Name: **Parc Cwm**

Chambered Long Cairn | Nearest Village: **Parkmill** | Map: **SS 5373 8984**
Sheets: **E164 L159** | Lat: **51.58837N** | Long: **4.11277W**

A fine example of a Cotswold-Severn transepted chambered tomb, excavated in 1869 and 1960–61, after which it was restored. The name comes from the medieval deer park in which it is situated. The 22m (72ft) cairn is aligned north–south, and the forecourt, with its neat dry-stone walling, leads to a passage built of limestone slabs interspersed with more dry-stone walling. The passage has two pairs of chambers. It's estimated the remains of around 40 people were interred here, and it seems likely that the bodies, or some of them, may have lain elsewhere before being placed in the tomb. Animal bones were also found, including some more recent ones but also others dating to the Ice Age, which were perhaps collected accidentally or deliberately from Cat Hole Cave (see below).

Nearby | Caves near Parc-le-breos include **Cat Hole Cave**, 184m (604ft) NNE at SS 5377 9002, where evidence of human occupation spanning at least 30,000 years has been found. It's best known for its Palaeolithic finds, including the discovery in 2010 of an engraving, possibly of a reindeer, from 12,500–14,500 years ago. Creswell Crags (see page 145) is the only other British site where art from this period has been found. Recent vandalism means the cave is no longer accessible to the public. It is thought the cave may have been used to expose bodies before they were interred at Parc-le-breos. At SS 5316 8812, 1.8km (just over 1 mile) SSW of Park-le-breos chambered tomb, is **Penmaen Burrows**, also known as Pen-y-crug. This badly damaged chambered tomb, with a displaced capstone, two chambers and a passage, is not easy to find, especially in summer when it's very overgrown.

MAEN CETI Alt Name: **Arthur's Stone**

Chambered Tomb | Nearest Village: **Reynoldston**
Map: **SS 4914 9055** | Sheets: **E164 L159** | Lat: **51.59354N** | Long: **4.17928W**

Near one of the few locations on the Gower where the sea is visible to both the north and the south, Maen Ceti is famous for its enormous capstone, 2.2m (7ft 3in) thick and originally measuring about 4m (13ft) across. Part of it has broken off but it's still very impressive, weighing in at about 23 tonnes (25 tons). The burial chamber is set in the remains of a ring cairn, about 23m (75ft) in diameter. Nine uprights remain in the tomb, dividing it into two chambers. The capstone is a natural boulder that was underpinned so a chamber could be hollowed out below (it is considered unlikely that it was ever covered by the cairn). Legends abound here. The name Arthur's Stone comes from the legend that the king, standing on the opposite shore, found a pebble in his shoe and irritably flung it up on to Cefn Bryn. It's also said that after Henry Tudor's troops landed at Milford Haven, they made a detour to visit the site (presumably

Photo © Martyn Copcutt

to support Henry's claim to be rightful king of England), before going on to defeat Richard III at Bosworth Field. Another story says St David split the capstone with a blow of his sword, "In proof that it was not sacred; and he commanded a well to spring from under it."

Nearby | At SS 4902 9056, 120m (394ft) west of Maen Ceti, **Cefyn Bryn Great Barrow** is the largest of the many round cairns in the area. Close to Maen Ceti, it's easier to find than many of the others and has wonderful views out to sea. At SS 4926 9021, about 360m (1,180ft) SSE, is another cairn, **Cefyn Bryn Cairn 2**. It has variously been interpreted as a settlement or a ring cairn with cists. There are other cairns within 1km (0.6 miles).

SWEYNE'S HOWE NORTH
Chambered Tomb | Nearest Village: **Llangennith**
Map: **SS 4211 8992** | Sheets: **E164 L159** | Lat: **51.58595N** | Long: **4.28027W**

A chambered tomb, part of an oval cairn 18.3 × 13.1m (60 × 43ft) and 0.6m (2ft) high. More clearly visible is the inner cairn of much larger stones, with the badly damaged but still quite imposing chamber at its western end. The capstone leans against two uprights.

Photo © Martyn Copcutt

Nearby | At SS 4210 8981, 169m (554ft) WSW of Sweyne's Howe North (and visible from there), is the badly damaged cairn of **Sweyne's Howe South**. It measures 20.7 × 14.9m (68 × 48ft) across and 0.7m (2ft 3in) high. The large slabs visible to the north might have been part of the forecourt or chamber.

CARN LLECHART

Ring Cairn | Nearest Town: **Pontardawe**
Map: **SN 6973 0627** | Sheets: **E165 L160** | Lat: **51.73994N** | Long: **3.88809W**

Photo © Christopher Bickerton

First noted in William Camden's *Britannia* (1695 edition), this may be a stone circle around a cist burial or the remains of a large ring cairn. Approached from the north, the monument can be seen clearly against the skyline. Around 13.5m (44ft) across, it has 25 slab-like kerb stones, none more than 0.9m (3ft). In the middle there's a cist, 2.1 × 1.2m (6ft 10in × 4ft). The capstone is missing, as is the eastern side slab.

209

Nearby | At SN 6967 0627, 60m (197ft) west of the ring cairn, is a chambered tomb. It's ruinous and rather contentious (suggestions having been made that it's the result of quarrying or natural outcropping). The possible capstone is massive: 5.3 × 2.4m (17ft 4in × 7ft 10in).

Wind farm development up on the moorland led to the discovery of what appears to be an important prehistoric ceremonial landscape, with a stone row as well as more than 50 cairns, some kerbed (see below). The row is aligned southwest–northeast and runs for at least 700m (2,296ft). Although the stones are small, they're close together and the row is easy to follow. Sadly, the new roads for the wind farm cut the site into three, it having been mysteriously missed by the pre-development survey.

Nearby | At SN 6863 1021, 274m (899ft) WSW of the stone row, is a cairn cemetery that includes at least 30 cairns of various sizes, scattered along the summit and southern slope of Bancbryn.

At SN 68951 9839, 390m (1,279ft) SSE of the stone row, there is a ruined platform cairn that measures 11m (36ft) diameter and up to 0.5m (1½ft) in height. The remains of a kerb are visible.

Bancbryn Stone Row

Sandy Gerrard, archaeologist and author of the *English Heritage Book of Dartmoor*

The Bancbryn stone row includes a single 717m (2,352ft) line of at least 173 stones, leading downslope from a small cairn. Remarkably, along its upper length, Hartland Point in Devon and Exmoor can be seen at the limit of visibility.

The row was identified after planning permission had been completed for a wind farm. Following the discovery, two areas were excavated prior to construction. Cadw (the historical environment service of the Welsh government) decided there was not enough evidence to support a prehistoric interpretation, although they were unable to offer any alternative.

The archaeological contractors concluded that the alignment was unlikely to be prehistoric because it is not straight, consists of stones of different sizes, the spacing is irregular and most significantly that long rows consisting of small stones are not found in Wales. All these objections illustrate a total lack of appreciation of the varied form and character of rows. Despite the inaccuracy of the conclusions, they have been widely accepted.

Further excavations in 2017 also failed to provide definitive dating evidence. The stones' stratigraphic position was consistent with a prehistoric date and the lack of any historical evidence, combined with the form and context, provide powerful support for a prehistoric date. One of the interesting things discovered during the excavation is that the area in which the row stands had never been cultivated. We looked for evidence of cultivation and found none, whereas ard marks were found on the other side of the hill.

The precise visual relationships at Bancbryn have formed the catalyst for an examination of other rows. The results thus far firmly support the idea that rows were positioned in the landscape to provide precise and particular views to significant places.

TAIR CARN ISAF

Cairn | Nearest Village: **Brynamman**
Map: **SN 6833 1674** | Sheets: **OL12 L159** | Lat: **51.8337N** | Long: **3.91233W**

A cairn cemetery with four cairns named A–D. All four are badly damaged, with C the best preserved, and B the largest, 20m (66ft) in diameter and 2.2m (7ft 2in) high. The cairn at SN 6806 1683 has clearly been sited to provide a restricted and perhaps special view of one its larger neighbours (a link rediscovered by Simon Charlesworth).

Nearby | At SN 6921 1737, just over 1km (0.6 miles) ENE is **Tair Carn Uchaf**, where three cairns (A, B and C) run east–west on the ridge (*uchaf* means "upper"; *isaf*, "lower"). The first two are prominent viewed from Carn Pen-y-clogau. Cairn B is the most impressive, 22m (72ft) across and 3.2m (10ft 5in) high.

Photo © Simon Charlesworth

PICWS DU

Cairn | Nearest Village: **Llanddeusant**
Map: **SN 8117 2185** | Sheets: **OL12 L160** | Lat: **51.8825N** | Long: **3.72784W**

Photo © Simon Charlesworth

On the ridge of Mynydd Du (Black Mountain), this turf-covered mound, topped by a modern walkers' cairn, is 19.5m (64ft) across and 1m (3ft 3in) high. In the centre, an upright slab is the remains of a possible cist.

Nearby | At SN 8215 2234, higher up the ridge and just over 1km (0.6 miles) ENE of Picws Du, is **Fan Foel** cairn. During excavations, cremated bone, flint tools and an urn were found in the cist, and pollen analysis suggests flowering plants were also placed there. There's no longer a great deal to see, although the cist is visible. The cairn has been damaged by walkers taking stones from it. At SN 8243 2206, a further 398m (1,306ft) ESE along the ridge, is **Twr-y-fan Foel**, a turf-covered cairn about 11m (36ft) across, topped by a walkers' cairn. It's in a wonderful setting on the highest peak of Mynnyd Du, with incredible views.

211

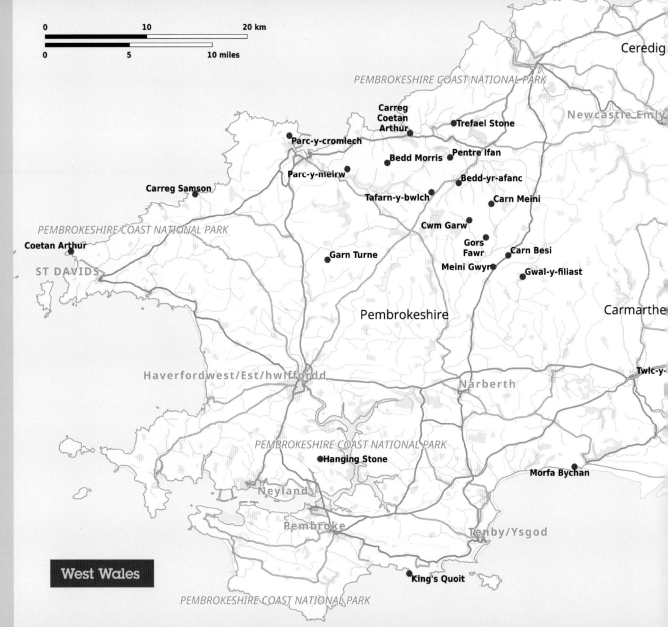

0   10   20 km

0   5   10 miles

Ceredig

PEMBROKESHIRE COAST NATIONAL PARK

Newcastle Emly

Carreg Coetan Arthur

Trefael Stone

Parc-y-cromlech

Bedd Morris

Pentre Ifan

Parc-y-meirw

Bedd-yr-afanc

Carreg Samson

Tafarn-y-bwlch

Carn Meini

PEMBROKESHIRE COAST NATIONAL PARK

Cwm Garw

Coetan Arthur

Gors Fawr

Carn Besi

ST DAVIDS

Garn Turne

Meini Gwyr

Gwal-y-filiast

Pembrokeshire

Carmarthe

Haverfordwest/Est/hwlffordd

Narberth

Twlc-y-

PEMBROKESHIRE COAST NATIONAL PARK

Hanging Stone

Morfa Bychan

Neyland

Pembroke

Tenby/Ysgod

West Wales

King's Quoit

PEMBROKESHIRE COAST NATIONAL PARK

Top 10 Prehistoric Sites in Wales with Breathtaking Views

BANNAU SIR GAER   Alt Name: **Sychnant**
Stone Circle | Nearest Town: **Llangadog**
Map: **SN 8086 2440** | Sheets: **OL12 L160** | Lat: **51.90535N** | Long: **3.73322W**

Up on the open moor in a really beautiful, though isolated, location, this circle can be hard to find. Look for the largest stone, which reaches 0.85m (2ft 9in). There are at least 18 stones here, with a couple completely buried. All the stones are sandstone except one of quartz conglomerate. There are two possible outliers standing to the northwest.

Photo © Simon Charlesworth

TRICHRUG   Alt Name: **Pen-y-biccws**
Cairn | Nearest Village: **Capel Gwynfe**
Map: **SN 6994 2296** | Sheets: **OL12 L160** | Lat: **51.88996N** | Long: **3.89138W**

There are four barrows here, numbered I–IV; only I remains intact, at 20m (66ft) across and 3.3m (10ft 9in) high. Barrow II has a trig point on it. Stone from Barrow III was taken to build a nearby wall. Barrow IV may not be prehistoric at all. A local story about the giant of Trichrug, who was known as a champion pebble-tosser – and who beat neighbouring giants by hurling a huge rock across the sea to Ireland – may be taken to explain all the cairns in the area!

Nearby | At SN 7170 1859, 4.7km (almost 3 miles) southeast of Trichrug, is **Carn Pen-y-clogau**, an impressive cairn 18m (59ft) in diameter and 3.4m (11ft) high. A shelter has been built into the centre. It's only 1.6km (1 mile) from the road but the difficult terrain makes a direct route impossible.

At SN 7275 1890, 4.9km (just over 3 miles) southeast from Trichrug, on the edge of a rocky plateau and with fabulous views, **Carn Pen Rhiw-ddu** is well preserved and measures 11m (36ft) in diameter and 2.2m (7ft 2in) high.

TWLC-Y-FILIAST   Alt Names: **Arthur's Table, Bwrdd Arthur, Ebenezer**
Chambered Tomb | Nearest Village: **Llangynog**
Map: **SN 3381 1618** | Sheets: **E177 L159** | Lat: **51.81946N** | Long: **4.41262W**

A damp and atmospheric tomb in the woods, mossy and full of character, with three uprights and a fallen capstone surviving. Excavation in 1953 found evidence of an 18 × 9m (59 × 30ft) mound, a series of pits and a possible ante-chamber. A pendant and a flint scraper were found just outside the chamber. Twlc-y-filiast is on private land, but can be viewed from a bridge over the stream, which is on a public footpath.

MORFA BYCHAN
Chambered Cairns | Nearest Village: **Pendine**
Map: **SN 2213 0749** | Sheets: **E177 L158** | Lat: **51.73781N** | Long: **4.57745W**

Five cairns, four with chambers, among the jumble of rock and bracken on the ridge. They run north–south, and are impressive even in their ruinous state. Getting up to the tombs involves a very steep climb. Great views.

    Nearby | At SN 2218 0724, 255m (837ft) south of the above site, is **Forest Chamber**, also known as Morfa Bychan beach chamber, a possible burial chamber at the base of the cliff below the Morfa Bychan group. It's on the beach now, but sea levels were lower in the past. Look for the massive stone that may be a capstone, 3 × 2m (9ft 10in × 6½ft) and 0.5m (1½ft) thick.

GWAL-Y-FILIAST   Alt Name: **Bwrdd Arthur**
Chambered Tomb | Nearest Village: **Llanboidy**
Map: **SN 1705 2564** | Sheets: **OL35 L145** | Lat: **51.89919N** | Long: **4.66053W**

Photo © Karen Sawyer

A lovely chambered tomb on a ridge in a very atmospheric wooded setting above the River Taf. Gwal-y-filiast means "the kennel of the greyhound bitch"; Bwrdd Arthur is "Arthur's table". The chunky capstone is supported by four uprights, and points toward the river. A few kerb stones from the mound survive. The walk from the road can be very muddy.

MEINI GWYR   Alt Names: **Buarth Arthur, Glandy Cross**
Henge | Nearest Village: **Eifilwen**
Map: **SN 1417 2658** | Sheets: **OL35 L145** | Lat: **51.90667N** | Long: **4.70285W**

The area around Glandy Cross seems to have been of some significance in prehistoric times. This is an unusual (for Wales) embanked, sub-circular enclosure. There were 19 standing stones here originally, of which two remain upright in the field today, one 1m (3ft 3in) high and the other 1.7m (5½ft). Other stones lying in the circle area and nearby hedges could be associated with the site. The henge, which has an entrance to the northwest, measures 36.6m (120ft) in diameter. Very easily accessible through a gate from the road.

Nearby | At SN 1395 2661, 221m (725ft) west of Meini Gwyr, are the two remaining stones of **Yr Allor** ("The Altar"), both about 1.3m (4ft 3in) tall. There were once three stones here, and it's thought they may have formed a cove. Excavation found evidence of associated quartz cobbles, a pit circle and wooden screening. They are on private land, but viewable through the gate from the road. Look out for a row of three round barrows, cut in half by the building of the road.

CARN BESI   Alt Name: **Dolwilim Dolmen**
Chambered Tomb | Nearest Village: **Eifilwen**
Map: **SN 1563 2768** | Sheets: **OL35 L145** | Lat: **51.91704N** | Long: **4.68224W**

Only the capstone remains of what is thought to have once been a chambered tomb. The location offers sweeping views of the surrounding mountains, and there's also a convenient parking spot close by, next to a reservoir on the A478. However, a barbed wire fence prevents access to the stone.

KING'S QUOIT
Burial Chamber | Nearest Village: **Manorbier**
Map: **SS 0593 9728** | Sheets: **OL36 L158** | Lat: **51.64074N** | Long: **4.8061W**

Photo © Christopher Bickerton

The views across Manorbier Bay from this Pembrokeshire site are wonderful, and the tomb is just a short walk from the beach, along the coastal path. The 4 × 2.5m (13ft × 8ft 2in) capstone is partially earthfast, and also supported by two uprights.

HANGING STONE

Chambered Tomb | Nearest Village: **Llangwm**
Map: **SM 9721 0823** | Sheets: **OL36 L158** | Lat: **51.73599N** | Long: **4. 93831W**

> "One of the best little-known sites in Wales."
> Christopher Bickerton

With its chunky capstone and three uprights this is a very cute burial chamber. There are further stones in the hedge – perhaps a second capstone and more uprights. No traces remain of a cairn or barrow, or of the dry-stone walling noted between the uprights in 1864.

COETAN ARTHUR

Chambered Tomb | Nearest City: **St David's**
Map: **SM 7253 2806** | Sheets: **OL35 L157** | Lat: **51.90451N** | Long: **5.30816W**

In a great location near St David's Head, this burial chamber has a huge collapsed capstone, about 4 × 2.6m (13 × 8½ft), supported on one side by a 1.5m (5ft) upright. There are a couple of fallen uprights and signs of a passage, as well as some evidence of a cairn or barrow. Another tomb of the same name (*coetan* means "quoit") was once found nearby, but destroyed in 1844.

Nearby | At SM 7351 2790, 1km (0.6 miles) east of Coetan Arthur, are the two chambered tombs of **Carn Llidi** on an outcrop of the same name, about 2m (6½ft) apart. The chambers are rock-cut pits, and the capstones are partly supported by uprights. The western capstone is 2.7 × 2 m (8ft 10in × 6½ft); the fallen eastern capstone (not in its original place) is 1.8 × 1.4m (5ft 10in × 4ft 7in). There are beautiful views across the bay.

Photo © Martyn Copcutt

> "Walk north along the coastal trail from Porth Mawr (Whitesands Bay) car park. Around 100m after the track turns west above the third bay (Porth Melgan), look for a narrow, steep trail that heads north up the hill – this will lead you directly to Coetan Arthur."
> Drew Parsons

CARREG SAMSON
Alt Name: **Longhouse Cromlech**

Portal Dolmen | Nearest Village: **Abercastle**

Map: **SM 8484 3351** | Sheets: **OL35 L157** | Lat: **51.95833N** | Long: **5.13291W**

An impressive monument in a spectacular location overlooking Abercastle Bay, Carreg Samson stands at the head of a valley sloping down to the sea and the island of Ynys-y-castell. Seven stones stand, ranging in height from 1.1m (3ft 7in) to 2.2m (7ft 3in), with three supporting the capstone, 4.7 × 2.7m (15ft 5in × 8ft 10in) and 1m (3ft 3in) thick. Excavation in 1968 revealed four more stone-holes, perhaps forming a passage to the northwest. The chamber was found to have been built over a pit (filled in with clay and stones) that could have originally contained the capstone. The name derives from a legend that St Samson of Dol dropped the capstone in place using his little finger.

Photo © Roger K. Read

PARC-Y-CROMLECH

Chambered Tomb | Nearest Town: **Fishguard**

Map: **SM 9422 3907** | Sheets: **OL35 L157** | Lat: **52.01181N** | Long: **4.99994W**

Photo © Roger K. Read

Resembling an Irish wedge tomb, this ruinous burial chamber, 3.9 × 1.8m (12ft 9in × 5ft 11in), is very low to the ground, the capstone resting on three horizontal supporting stones. The tomb is on private land; seek permission at the farm.

Nearby | Centred at SM 9480 3910, 580m (1,902ft) east of Parc-y-cromlech, the three rock-cut Neolithic tombs known as **Garn Wen** are a surprise find behind a terrace of houses in Goodwick. They would have overlooked Fishguard Bay and Dinas Head before the houses were built. Carreg Samson is the largest, with a 4 × 3.2m (13ft × 10ft 5in) capstone. There may be a fourth chamber to the north – nine tombs in total were recorded here in the early 20th century.

GARN TURNE
Chambered Tomb | Nearest Village: **St Dogwells**
Map: **SM 9792 2725** | Sheets: **OL35 L157** | Lat: **51.90703N** | Long: **4.93915W**

Photo © Christopher Bickerton

A badly damaged but still impressive tomb, with an immense capstone, 5 × 3.5m (16 × 11½ft) and 1m (3ft 3in) thick, weighing around 80 tonnes (88 tons). When the capstone collapsed, it knocked over three of its supporting uprights, but several of the chamber's other stones, including one of 2.5m (8ft), still stand, defining the forecourt. A further outlying stone of 2m (6½ft) stands to the southwest. In 2006, a cup-and-ring mark was found on the capstone. Excavations in 2011 and 2012 demonstrated various phases of activity, and identified that an apparently natural outcrop in the forecourt is in fact a quarried stone. It also revealed the original location of the immense capstone: a large pit, found beneath the forecourt, which was then partly backfilled before the construction of the tomb.

PARC-Y-MEIRW Alt Name: **Four Stones**
Stone Row | Nearest Village: **Llanychaer**
Map: **SM 9988 3591** | Sheets: **OL35 L157** | Lat: **52.20294N** | Long: **3.23641W**

Originally at least eight stones stood in this 48.7m (160ft) row aligned northeast–southwest. Four remain standing, with two acting as gateposts and the other two in the hedge beside the road. Two further fallen stones are in the bank. The tallest stone is 2.7m (8ft 10in); the shortest 2m (6½ft).

BEDD MORRIS
Standing Stone | Nearest Town: **Newport**
Map: **SN 0382 3650** | Sheets: **OL35 L145** | Lat: **51.99222N** | Long: **4.85881W**

This 1.8m (6ft) standing stone was toppled by a car in 2011, giving archaeologists the opportunity to confirm its Bronze Age origin (which previously had been in some doubt). It was re-erected in 2012. The stone has been used as a boundary marker, and is also carved with an OS benchmark.

Photo © Roger K. Read

Its name refers to a legend about a highwayman called Morris, who lived in a cave on Carn Ingli. His career came to an abrupt end when he was ambushed by angry locals and hanged at the roadside. His captors are said to have later put up the stone on the spot where he died as a warning to others.

CARREG COETAN ARTHUR
Burial Chamber | Nearest Town: **Newport**
Map: **SN 0603 3935** | Sheets: **OL35 L145** | Lat: **52.01857N** | Long: **4.82824W**

★

A charming dolmen close to the centre of Newport (Pembrokeshire). The capstone is supported by two of the four uprights and tilts at a dramatic angle, perhaps echoing the outline of Carn Ingli to the south. Excavations found cremated bone here, as well as sherds of Beaker ware and grooved ware.

TREFAEL STONE
Rock Art | Nearest Village: **Brynberian**
Map: **SN 1029 4028** | Sheets: **OL35 L145** | Lat: **52.02858N** | Long: **4.76662W**

Photo by Adam Stanford © Aerial-Cam Ltd

At least 70 cup-marks are visible on this lavishly decorated stone, sited alone in a field. Investigation in 2014 confirmed that this tilted slab of Fishguard volcanic tuff, about 2.3 × 2m (7ft 6in × 6½ft), was once the capstone of a burial chamber that had been deliberately reused as a standing stone. The other stones and most of the cairn material have long since been repurposed as field walls. It has been suggested the site may be much older than originally thought – some believe it to have been in use for at least 5,500 years. Beads were found here as well as cremated bones, the remains of a cist, and pottery sherds.

PENTRE IFAN

Portal Dolmen | Nearest Village: **Brynberian**
Map: **SN 0994 3702** | Sheets: **OL35 L145** | Lat: **51.999N** | Long: **4.77004W**

Photo © Íñigo Cía

It's hard to imagine a more dramatic and spectacular monument than Pentre Ifan, star of countless calendars and book covers. The immense 16 tonne (17.5 ton) capstone is tilted on its three supporting uprights, sitting so gracefully it's impossible not to be impressed by the skill of the people who constructed this tomb. And if you've visited any of the other chambered tombs in the area, its size will come as a shock, the supporting uprights reaching about 2.5m (8ft) high. The entrance to the chamber is obstructed by a blocking stone, and there is a semi-circular forecourt at the southern end. Also visible are the remains of a cairn around 30m (98ft) long.

Nearby | At SN 1165 3614, 1.9km (1¼ miles) ESE of Pentre Ifan, **Craig Rhos-y-felin** was suggested, in 2011, as a possible source of the Stonehenge rhyolite bluestones. Evidence from Mike Parker Pearson's excavation here, which was analysed by Rob Ixer and Richard Bevins, does reveal a geochemical match for the rhyolite bluestones, making it a likely quarry site. Geomorphologist Brian John (see page 224), however, suggests that the archaeologists may have misinterpreted natural features and could have mistaken a prehistoric hunters' camp at Rhos-y-felin for a quarry.

A Phenomenological Approach to Dolmens

Vicki Cummings, Reader in Archaeology at the University of Central Lancashire

Dolmens are early Neolithic stone monuments where the main focus appears to have been on the lifting up and display of a large capstone. They were sometimes used for the deposition of the dead, but this does not seem to have been their primary function (see introduction, pages 18–19). Instead, the builders of these sites seem to have wanted to demonstrate their prowess at raising and supporting massive stones. These sites have capstones that are far in excess of the size required simply to create a stone box for burial. The largest dolmen, Browne's Hill in County Carlow in Ireland, has a capstone that weighs over 100 tonnes (110 tons).

A phenomenological approach that considers how people experience things, and how our own experiences of sites may enable us to gain insights into those of the people who built and used them, may help to shed light on the motivations of those who worked with these massive capstones. Most dolmens have their capstone supported by just three uprights. This creates an amazing effect: an enormous stone seemingly almost floating in the sky. Because the stone chosen as the capstone was often a thick and chunky object, the effect of a massive stone lifted up in the air is further enhanced – this was almost certainly deliberate on the part of the builders. Likewise, the stones used to support the capstone are often thin and slender, with just the very smallest part possible touching the underside of the capstone. Again, this was surely deliberate, done to enhance the effect of lifting up a large stone. It is hard to imagine how people with

only Stone Age technology were able to lift up such massive stones. Visitors to these sites today often express amazement, and I think this is exactly what the builders intended. These were people who, after all, had very little experience of built architecture – these dolmens would surely have appeared all the more incredible in prehistory.

It is also worth considering where these sites were located in the landscape. Much has been written on the landscape setting of sites. Dolmens are rather unusual compared to other early Neolithic chambered tombs because they are located in a range of settings. Although this must have been in part down to the availability of suitable stones, we know that the landscape was, in many places, literally covered with glacial erratics deposited by the ice sheets, so the monument builders had plenty of rocks to choose from. In some areas stones close to the summit of hills were picked – this is the case with many of the Cornish dolmens (known as "quoits"). However, while these sites were apparently deliberately skylined, some of the dolmens in southeast Ireland are tucked away at the bottom of stream valleys. These are harder to find, and when you do come across them, it is quite a surprise.

Some sites are also located in relation to other features that may well have been important to people in the Neolithic. Natural features such as rocky outcrops are often visible, as at Pentre Ifan, and it is hard to imagine that people in the Neolithic did not think of these as special, perhaps as the homes of spirits or otherworldly beings.

TAFARN-Y-BWLCH Alt Name: **Waun Mawn**
Standing Stones | Nearest Village: **Brynberian**
Map: **SN 0813 3370** | Sheets: **Ol35 L145** | Lat: **51.96856N** | Long: **4.79451W**

Photo © Lee Walker

Two standing stones, both 1.3m (4ft 3in) high, which lean pleasingly to the north.

At SN 0803 3394, 260m (853ft) northwest of Tafarn-y-bwlch, **Waun Mawn West** is a beautiful 2.3m (7½ft) standing stone in a stunning moorland setting with views over the Preseli hills.

At SN 0835 3405, 413m (1,355ft) northeast of Tafarn-y-bwlch, **Waun Mawn Northeast** has one 1.6m (5ft 3in) standing stone and three fallen ones. Recent excavation and dating by Mike Parker Pearson and team has found an arc of stones, possibly part of a large stone circle that was never completed. They previously suggested that some of the stones were transported to become part of Stonehenge, but this now looks unlikely.

BEDD-YR-AFANC
Passage Grave | Nearest Village: **Brynberian**
Map: **SN 1079 3458** | Sheets: **OL35 L145** | Lat: **51.97738N** | Long: **4.75632W**

With spectacular views over the Preseli Mountains, this is thought to be the only gallery grave in Wales. A long cairn, 15 × 11.5m (49 × 38ft), encloses the two parallel rows of stones that form the chamber. The site can be hard to find as the stones are small, up to 0.4m (1ft 3in) high. Bedd-yr-afanc means "grave of the water monster", referring to a creature said to have once inhabited the nearby River Brynberian. Be aware that the terrain can be very boggy and hard to cross; take care, especially following wet weather.

CWM GARW Alt Names: **The Stones of Arthur's Sons, Cerrig Meibion Arthur,**
Glynsaithmaen N | **Standing Stones** | Nearest Village: **Maenclochog**
Map: **SN 1182 3102** | Sheets: **OL35 L145** | Lat: **51.94576N** | Long: **4.73939W**

"**These stones are said to be a monument to King Arthur's sons, killed by a wild boar.**" "Paulcall"

A fine stone pair, rising to 2.6m (8½ft) and 2.2m (7ft 2in), the narrower stone leaning at quite an angle. You can see them from the road (unless the mist is down).

Nearby | Around SN 115 305, 610m (2,000ft) southwest of Cwm Garw, are the remains of the **Glynsaithmaen**

megalithic complex, where two stone circles linked by an avenue once stood. Surviving stones can be seen near Glynsaithmaen farmhouse, lying in the farmyard, and on both sides of the road running southwest to Gate Farm.

At SN 1282 3154, 1.1km (0.6 mile) ENW of Cwm Garw is **Carn Sian**, identified as a possible cairn, perhaps incorporating a more recent enclosure around a prehistoric site. There's a linear feature right next to it, and

a possible burial chamber 134m (440ft) ESE at SN 1294 3147. All these features were identified by Megalithic Portal members, and they have been included here to show that there are many sites still waiting to be found in the area – and by amateurs!

CARN MEINI
Ancient Quarry | Nearest Village: **Mynachlog-ddu**
Map: **SN 1441 3248** | Sheets: **OL35 L145** | Lat: **51.95976N** | Long: **4.70249W**

Quarrying is said to have begun at Carn Meini during the seventh millennium BC. These outcrops were first suggested as a source of the Stonehenge bluestones in the mid-19th century, and petrological analysis in the 1920s confirmed that spotted dolerite bluestones originated in the Preseli Mountains. Whether the Carn Meini outcrops were the main quarry or just one of a number of sources, and indeed whether the Stonehenge bluestones were quarried here or simply carried to Wiltshire by glaciation, remains controversial (see page 224).

A 2002 survey identified an enclosure on the upper part of the Carn Meini outcrop, which contains dolerite naturally fractured into columns. Partly worked megaliths scattered around may be prehistoric or more modern, as building materials, gateposts and lintels have been quarried here more recently.

At SN 1403 3262 is the rather ruinous Carn Meini chambered tomb, on the central bluestones outcrop at the head of the "river of stones". The uprights have all collapsed, and the 3 × 2.5m (10 × 8ft) capstone lies on a cairn, which is about 15m (49ft) in diameter and 1.5m (5ft) high. A remaining upright in the cairn may be part of the passage. The cairn stones are all very loose, so be careful.

Nearby | At SN 1305 3251, 1km (0.6 miles) west of Carn Meini tomb, this "circle", known as **Bedd Arthur** or Arthur's Grave, is really a horseshoe-shaped setting, some 18 × 7m (59ft × 23ft), the 13 stones (average height 0.8m/2ft 7in) backed by a low bank, and inclined to lean in to the centre. It overlooks the bluestones outcrops of Carn Meini, and the unusual shape has led to speculation that it might have inspired the famous Stonehenge bluestone horseshoe. There has been some suggestion it might be a henge, or related monument. At SN 1283 3328, 1.8km (just over 1 mile) WNW of the Carn Meini outcrop, is **Carngoedog**, which some have identified as the main source of the Stonehenge spotted dolerite bluestones, instead of Carn Meini.

Stonehenge and the Glacial Transport Theory

Brian John, an earth scientist with a special interest in the Ice Age

Despite the commonly held assumption that the Stonehenge bluestones were moved by human agency from Wales to Wiltshire, there are a number of features at the site that point toward the glacial transport theory. First, there are the bluestones themselves. Recent geological studies show that the stones have come from at least 20 different locations in West Wales, making it unlikely that they were deliberately quarried.

It is often claimed that the bluestones are all pillars, selected for setting upright in the ground. But if you look at the fallen stones, the standing stones and the stumps, they come in all shapes, sizes and lithologies. Boulders and slabs are far more common than pillars. The surfaces of the bluestones are heavily abraded – quite unlike the fresh surfaces that would be expected on quarried stone.

The probable Welsh locations from which the bluestones originate are on the rising slope of the Preseli uplands, where there is abundant evidence of intense glacial activity. It is consistent with glaciological theory to propose that these locations were subject to plucking and block entrainment by overriding glacier ice moving from northwest to southeast during the Anglian glaciation.

There are just 43 bluestones at Stonehenge, as against the 82 assumed to have been present originally. It's my view that Stonehenge was never completed. The builders gathered up the stones from the immediate vicinity, and then ranged further afield, using every stone they could find. They eventually gave up on the whole project when the labour costs got too high. So could the ice of the Irish Sea Glacier have reached Stonehenge? Undoubtedly, yes. Computer modelling studies in recent years have shown that a fully developed Irish Sea Glacier could have overwhelmed Lundy and the Isles of Scilly, pressed across the coasts of Cornwall and Devon, and pushed on to Salisbury Plain. Evidence on the ground is more difficult to interpret. Pre-Devensian glacial deposits are known from the Bristol and Bath area, but on Salisbury Plain there are no known glacial deposits. But does that mean there was no glaciation here? Detailed field research is difficult because of the extensive military presence. There are fragments and cobbles all over the place, assumed to have come from destroyed bluestone monoliths. They might just as well have come from glacial deposits, given that any glaciation would have been around 450,000 years ago.

Another line of argument is related to the supposed absence of erratic material in the river terraces of the Salisbury area. Christopher Green claimed he had examined 50,000 pebbles and found only 1 per cent of erratic material – far less than might be expected. However, it appears that he was searching only for quartz pebbles, and that the area examined was of very limited extent. The glaciation of Salisbury Plain was certainly possible from a glaciological standpoint, and there is clear evidence of glaciation well to the east of the Somerset coast. What we still do not know is the precise extent of the ice.

John, B. 2018. *The Stonehenge Bluestones*. Pembrokeshire: Greencroft Books

Healing Stones? The Preseli Bluestones

Julie Kearney, who researches the links between consciousness, creativity and natural energies

In the midst of the giant sarsens at Stonehenge is an inner horseshoe of smaller stones known as the Stonehenge bluestones. These include a variety of rock types; as well as the dolerites from Preseli, and rhyolites from the north Pembrokeshire coast, some, including the Altar Stone, are sandstones from the Senni Beds, many miles from Preseli. While most archaeologists argue that these were quarried and manually transported (not simply moved by glacial action – see opposite), the exact location of the original quarries is still in dispute.

It has been accepted since the 1920s that the spotted dolerite bluestones came from the Preseli Mountains. Timothy Darvill and the late Geoffrey Wainwright proposed evidence for a bluestone quarry site at Carn Meini, citing a match between the shape and size of stones quarried there and those at Stonehenge. Although no convincing geological evidence has been identified to prove that the Carn Meini quarry provided the dolerite bluestone pillars, a chemical match *has* been made between the rhyolite bluestones and the quarry site at Rhos-y-felin (see page 220).

There is little consensus on when the bluestones were quarried, with theories ranging from the early Neolithic to 2300BC. Some evidence suggests that they were originally part of a monument in Wales before being taken down and transported to Wiltshire, but most researchers do now agree that the bluestones were set in place at Stonehenge around 2900BC. How they were moved is still in dispute. But perhaps an even more important question is, why were they moved?

While Mike Parker Pearson argues that the motivation for moving the bluestones such a distance was related to their significance as symbols of ancestral identity, with stones possibly representing deceased ancestors, Darvill and Wainwright suggest another possible reason – that the dolerite stones have a long and respected tradition as healing stones and were moved to build a Neolithic healing monument. Citing Welsh mythology, they connect the bluestones to the holy Welsh healing wells and speculate that a Welsh healing cult migrated eastward, finally establishing a monument at Stonehenge. While the authors agree that Stonehenge was probably multifunctional and also had an astronomical purpose, they believe that the healing properties of the stones would have been the main focus, drawing Neolithic people from all over Europe to visit them.

Additional evidence for the existence of a Stonehenge healing sanctuary is based on the number of Neolithic bodies buried in the vicinity that bear the marks of serious injuries or illness; Geoffrey Wainwright speculated that the Amesbury Archer came all the way from Switzerland to be healed after falling from his horse, but died of a tooth abscess before being buried not far from Stonehenge. The number of bluestone/dolerite chips found in graves and scattered in the area is also notable.

For more information see: Parker Pearson, M. et al. "Craig Rhos-y-felin: A Welsh Bluestone Megalith Quarry for Stonehenge" *Antiquity*. http://eprints.gla.ac.uk/121403/1/121403.pdf

GORS FAWR Alt Name: **Cylch-y-trallwyn**

Stone Circle | Nearest Village: **Crymych** | Map: **SN 1346 2938**
Sheets: **OL35 L145** | Lat: **51.93158N** | Long: **4.71467W**

A lovely if often rather marshy stone circle ("Gors Fawr" means "a large area of boggy ground"), and the only one to survive in the area. In a moorland setting beneath the Preseli Mountains, eight of the 16 stones in the 22.3m (73ft) circle are spotted dolerite bluestones from Carn Meini to the north (see page 223). The tallest stones, in the south, are around 1.4m (4½ft). Antiquarian reports indicate an avenue once led to the two outliers 134m (440ft) to the NNE. These two stones are positioned on a northeast–southwest alignment, pointing toward midsummer sunrise. The circle can get quite overgrown with vegetation in summer, which can make viewing the stones and navigating the boggy terrain more difficult.

Photo © Paul Blades

DOLGAMFA

Kerb Cairn | Nearest Village: **Devil's Bridge**
Map: **SN 7457 7917** | Sheets: **E213 L135** | Lat: **52.39615N** | Long: **3.84482W**

What's left here, in a spectacular Ceredigion moorland setting, is a delightful oval 5 × 4m (16 × 13ft) of 11 uprights – once a cairn kerb. The stones lean out from the centre, where a slight hollow may mark the site of a cist.

> **"Park at Ysbyty Cynfyn, and cross a pretty gorge by a scary bridge – a fairly strenuous walk but worthwhile."** Christopher Bickerton

Photo © Christopher Bickerton

BUWCH A'R LLO
Alt Names: Y Fuwch a'r Llo, The Cow and Calf
Standing Stones | Nearest Village: **Bow Street**
Map: **SN 7229 8335** | Sheets: **E213 L135** | Lat: **52.43316N** | Long: **3.87993W**

Known as the Cow and Calf, this stone pair are chunky boulders 4m (13ft) apart, located beside the track. The Cow is about 2 × 1.25m (6½ft × 4ft), while the squatter Calf is 1.2 × 1.2m (4 × 4ft).

Nearby | At SN 7217 8333, in the plantation and 120m (394ft) west of Buwch a'r Llo, is a third stone, **Maen Tarw**. This was sliced into by forestry machinery at some point in the 20th century. Within 1km (0.6 miles) are further standing stones, rows and cairns. It has been suggested that the stones mark a Bronze Age trackway to the west coast.

BEDD TALIESIN
Round Cairn | Nearest Village: **Tal-y-bont**
Map: **SN 6714 9121** | Sheets: **OL23 L135** | Lat: **52.50255N** | Long: **3.95877W**

Accessibly located beside the road, this kerb cairn contains a 2m (6½ft) long cist with a dislodged capstone. The capstone is inscribed with historical graffiti that can be seen in low light. Legend tells that this is the grave of the bard Taliesin, and also, as at Tinkinswood (see page 206) and Maen-y-bardd (see page 251), that spending the night here will result in going mad or becoming a poet!

CARREG CADNO
Alt Name: Fox Rock
Stone Rows | Nearest Village: **Glyntawe**
Map: **SN 8767 1569** | Sheets: **OL12 L160** | Lat: **51.82849N** | Long: **3.63144W**

Discovered in 2014 by Simon Charlesworth and Dr Peter Hodges and disputed by some, this pair of crude stone rows in Powys, approximately at right angles to each other, share the same stone at the apex of the rows. The NNE row resembles the nearby Saith Maen SE row. It's been suggested that when stones 1–3 of the EW row are viewed from a notch in stone 4, their profile appears to mimic the horizon.

Photo © Simon Charlesworth

Nearby | At approx SN 862 146, 1.8km (just over 1 mile) WSW of Carreg Cadno, is the disputed **Saith Maen SE row**, where the stones appear to have been deliberately placed on the bare rock. The walk there is a very difficult 1.6km (1 mile) across scree slopes, bogs and dense, tussocky grass. At SN 8642 1483, 321m (1,053ft) ENE of the Saith Maen stone row, and on similarly difficult rocky or boggy ground, is **Saith Maen East Cairn**, also known as Sem's Cairn. Another site discovered by Charlesworth and Hodges, this damaged round cairn, just 3.7m (12ft) in diameter and 0.6m (2ft) high, can be difficult to spot at first, but once you know where to look, is visible from over 6.4km (4 miles) away.

MAEN LLIA

Standing Stone | Nearest Village: **Ystradfellte** | Map: **SN 9242 1919**
Sheets: **OL12 L160** | Lat: **51.86085N** | Long: **3.56367W**

⭐

Photo © Cerrig

A truly beautiful and impressive standing stone in a fine, if very remote and desolate, position on the moorland of Fforest Fawr. It's an imposing 3.8m (12ft 4in) tall, 2.8m (9ft 2in) wide and 0.9m (3ft) deep.

Nearby | At SN 9232 1896, 246m (807ft) SSW from Maen Llia, is **Llech Lia** multi-banked henge. It's overgrown and can be difficult to find, although the wimberry bushes that grow all over it are a bonus if you go when the fruit is in season. The henge is roughly circular, about 22m (72ft) in diameter, and with a possible entrance to the east.

> "A common legend attached to standing stones is that at some point during the year, they go to drink at a nearby stream or lake. At midsummer sunset, the shadow of Maen Llia is at its longest, stretching down the hill, through the stream and onto a cairn-topped hillock. The shadow does indeed look like a tongue. Considering the alternative translation for Llia, which is 'to lick or lap', then Maen Llia is literally 'the stone that licks'. A deliberate part of the design, or was it noticed after the stone was raised, and the name came from that?" Cerrig

PEN-Y-FAN

Summit Cairn | Nearest Village: **Libanus**
Map: **SO 0120 2159** | Sheets: **OL12 L160** | Lat: **51.88409N** | Long: **3.43687W**

Photo © Stanata Riha

From the car park on the A470, it's about an hour's trek uphill to the cairn on the summit of Pen-y-fan, at 886m (2,906ft) the highest peak in southern Britain. On a clear day the views over the whole Brecon Beacons range, and as far as the Bristol Channel, are breathtaking. The cairn was rebuilt after excavation in 1991, when a bronze brooch and a spearhead were found inside the chamber.

Nearby | At SO 0075 2133, 519m (1,706ft) WSW of Pen-y-fan's summit (and accessible via footpaths), is the **Corn Ddu** cairn. This is southern Britain's second-highest peak.

MAEN MAWR & CERRIG DUON

Megalithic Complex | Nearest Village: **Abercraf**

Map: **SN 8513 2066** | Sheets: **OL12 L160** | Lat: **51.87264N** | Long: **3.66993W**

> "The stone rows can be nearly impossible to locate when there is any vegetation cover, even if you know where to look!" Simon Charlesworth

On beautiful and remote moorland in the upper reaches of the Tawe valley, this complex of apparently contemporaneous monuments includes the Maen Mawr standing stone – the largest in a short alignment – as well as the Cerrig Duon stone circle and a double stone row. Nearby is another standing stone and (apparently unique in Wales) a quincunx formation. To get to the site from the road, you need to wade across the Tawe, and then head uphill. The ground is often boggy, even on the hill. Look out for Maen Mawr, as the circle is only visible when you are right upon it.

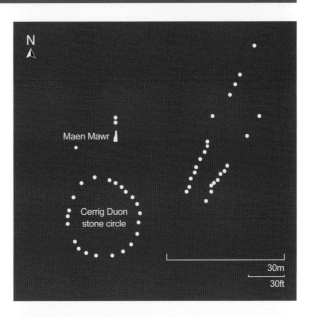

MAEN MAWR

More than 1.8m (6ft) tall, the stone's name means "big stone". It has two much smaller companion stones, and together they possibly form a short stone row.

Photo © Angie Lake

CERRIG DUON

At SN 8511 2061, to the SSW of Maen Mawr, is the Cerrig Duon circle, around 18m (59ft) in diameter, with 20 small stones (none more than 0.6m/2ft in height). One of the stones has fallen. The hole in the circle's southern arc may be a socket for a stone that was still standing in the early 20th century.

DOUBLE STONE ROW

Around 15m (49ft) east of the circle a double stone row begins, running NNE to approximately SN 8520 2060. The western row extends for 42m (137ft), with 17 stones around 0.15m (6in) tall. The eastern row is 25m (82ft) long and has 12 tiny stones. You'll need to get your eye in for these, they really are very small indeed.

Photo © Cerrig

WAUN LEUCI STANDING STONE

At SN 8546 2150, just over 900m (less than ¾ mile) NNE of Maen Mawr, is Waun Leuci, an interesting and colourful lichen-covered stone with a classic playing card shape. Nearby, a little way down the slope, fragments of a fossilized beach can be seen on exposed slabs.

WAUN LEUCI STONE SETTING

At SN 8520 2156, 266m (873ft) west of the Waun Leuci standing stone and 900m (about ½ mile) north of Maen Mawr, is the recently discovered Waun Leuci or Maen Leuci stone setting. The only known quincunx outside the West Country, the setting comprises four stones set in a rough 3m (10ft) square around a central boulder.

Nearby | At SN 8555 2235, 1.7km (just over 1 mile) NNE of Maen Mawr, is **Bwllch Cerrig Duon** barrow, measuring around 24m (78ft) across and 2m (6½ft) high. It's listed as a "possible round barrow" on Coflein, but it's only about 30m (98ft) from the road so worth a look, especially as it is intervisible with so many other sites (including a surprising number of stone circles, passage mounds, cairns and standing stones) through gaps in the hilly horizon.

> **"The Waun Leuci setting is about 30m (98ft) west of the road, on open moorland close to a stream, hiding in tussocky grass. The only clue is the knee-high monolith that dominates the site."** Cerrig

NANT TARW ⭐

Megalithic Complex | Nearest Village: **Trecastle**
Map: **SN 8176 2587** | Sheets: **OL12 L160** | Lat: **51.91883N** | Long: **3.72056W**

Between the River Usk and its tributary Nant Tarw lies a Bronze Age ritual complex with two stone circles and an apparently contemporaneous stone row; its layout has been compared to that of Maen Mawr–Cerrig Duon (see above). As at Maen Mawr, the 3m (10ft) three-stone row at Nant Tarw (SN 8176 2587) has one large stone, now fallen, and two much smaller companions. The fallen stone is 2.7m (9ft) long; the others are 0.4m (1ft 4in) and 0.3m (1ft) respectively.

Photo © Christopher Bickerton

NANT TARW WNW CIRCLE

At SN 8187 2583, some 100m (328ft) ESE of the row is the WNW (or River Usk) stone circle, measuring 19m (62ft) in diameter. There are 15 stones remaining, from 0.15m (6in) to 1m (3ft 3in), with four partly buried. A large recumbent stone lies some 3m (10ft) to the east.

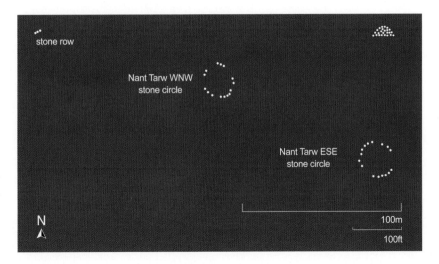

NANT TARW ESE CIRCLE

At SN 8197 2578, some 100m (328ft) ESE of the WNW circle, is the Nant Tarw ESE (or Usk Reservoir) stone circle. An oval of around 22m (72ft), this is the larger of two rings. It has 12 stones, eight of which are fallen and five partly buried. The tallest stone is 1.2m (4ft) while the smallest is just 5cm (2in). The longest of the fallen stones is 1.5m (5ft). Some 30m (98ft) north of here is a further standing stone, on the bank of the Nant Tarw.

GODRE'R GARN LAS

At SN 8198 2587, some 90m (295ft) north of the ESE circle and just above the Nant Tarw river, is the ruined Godre'r Garn Las cairn, which may in fact be the remains of a pair of cairns.

CWRT-Y-GOLLEN Alt Name: **The Growing Stone**
Standing Stone | Nearest Village: **Crickhowell**
Map: **SO 2324 1686** | Sheets: **OL13 L161** | Lat: **51.84504N** | Long: **3.11565W**

Photo © Angie Lake

A fine standing stone, 4.2m (13ft 9in) of red sandstone, set next to a magnificent oak tree just inside the entrance of what was once an army training camp, off the A40. This was the tallest stone in the old county of Brecon.

Nearby | At SO 2396 1783, 1.2km (¾ mile) northeast of Cwrt-y-gollen, is the **Golden Grove Stone**, a blocky 1.2m (4ft) limestone pillar on private land by the Dragon's Head Inn car park. It's also known as the Druid's Altar, which is the name of the steep hill to the west.

GWERNVALE Alt Name: Crickhowell

Chambered Tomb | Nearest Village: **Crickhowell**
Map: **SO 2111 1922** Sheets: **OL13 L161** | Lat: **51.86593N** | Long: **3.1471W**

Photo © Cerrig

Right on the verge of the busy A40, this was once a fine Cotswold-Severn tomb, with a 45m (148ft) long barrow (now marked out by small concrete posts), three side chambers, and a horned forecourt and false portal at the southeast end. The only stone remains visible today are the central chamber, which was lined with large stone slabs, and parts of its long entrance passage leading to the southwest side (and into the road). Excavation in the 1970s demonstrated that the tomb was built on the site of previous settlement.

Nearby | At SO 2218 1846, 1.3km (¾ mile) ESE of Gwernvale, is the **Great Oak Stone**, also known as the Standard Street Stone. Impressively large and slab-like, it's about 2.3m (8ft) high and may have originally been part of a chambered tomb. In more recent times it seems to have served as a boundary marker and was once inscribed with the date 1844.

MYNYDD TROED

Chambered Tomb | Nearest Village: **Llangors**
Map: **SO 1614 2842** | Sheets: **OL13 L161** | Lat: **51.94792N** | Long: **3.22152W**

There's not a great deal to see here, but the site is accessible (just about 100m/328ft from a parking place on the hillside at the top of the minor road between Llangors and the A479) – and the views are amazing. The badly disturbed turfed mound is about 20 × 15m (66 × 49ft) across and up to 1m (3ft 3in) in height. At the northern end, the remains of a chamber can be seen, and other edge-set stones are visible as well.

Nearby | At SO 1603 2774, 689m (less than ½ mile) SSW of Mynydd Troed chambered tomb, is **Cockit Hill**, where a (probable) promontory fort, with a 29m (95ft) long bank and ditch rampart, encloses a spur of Mynydd Llangorse.

Photo © Martyn Copcutt

PENYWYRLOD

Chambered Long Cairn | Nearest Village: **Talgarth**
Map: **SO 1505 3156** | Sheets: **OL13 L161** | Lat: **51.975988N** | Long: **3.238161W**

Penywyrlod was only discovered in 1972 when a farmer began to quarry stone from the mound and uncovered a chamber containing piles of human bone! One of the largest cairns in Wales, this massive structure is 52m (170ft) long and 22.5m (74ft) wide, and still 3m (10ft) tall. It is thought to have a Cotswold-Severn-type layout, with lateral chambers, a forecourt and a dummy portal. Quarrying has revealed some huge stones, one still upright and looking like a portal stone or chamber side stone, with others on the ground that could have been support stones or capstones. On the eastern side, near what would have been the barrow's original edge, are the remains of another chamber or passageway. There are probably several more chambers to be found. Excavations found worked flints and stone, a sheep femur with three holes, and the remains of 11 people, including an intact male skull that showed no obvious cause of death, but an inherited condition that would have caused him to have a broader than usual forehead. The sheep bone with holes could have been a simple flute or whistle, in which case it would be the oldest known musical instrument in Wales.

Bringing the Neolithic Back to Life

Martyn Copcutt, Chair of the Megalithic Portal Society and lifelong stones enthusiast

In 2005, a cast of the male skull from Penywyrlod was forensically reconstructed by Caroline Wilkinson of Dundee University. By painstakingly adding clay layer by layer to represent muscle, skin and hair, she created a realistic likeness of a face that could easily belong to someone living today.

The good condition of the man's teeth allowed analysis of the enamel. Samples from 10 others found in the tomb were also analysed, along with those of nine individuals from nearby Ty Isaf. The strontium-isotope analysis suggested that most of those buried at Penywyrlod did not source their childhood diet locally, but must have grown up at least as far away as the Malvern Hills in Worcestershire, if not further. One only made the journey to the Black Mountains after the formation of their wisdom teeth at around 14 years old. In

fact, it's been suggested that the strontium-isotope ratios of the Penywyrlod individuals are similar to those recorded in northwestern France, potentially supporting the argument that Neolithic culture was brought to Britain by migration from this region. This group lived in the first few centuries of the fourth millennium BC, the time of the very first agriculture in Wales. In contrast, all the individuals from Ty Isaf – who were from the mid- to late fourth millennium, by which time agriculture was established – sourced their diet from the local region of mid-Wales.

For more information see: Neil, S. et al. 2017. "Land Use and Mobility During the Neolithic in Wales Explored Using Isotope Analysis of Tooth Enamel". In *American Journal of Physical Anthropology*. Available online at: dx.doi.org/10.1002/ajpa.23279

233

PEN-Y-BEACON   Alt Name: **Blaenau**
Stone Circle | Nearest Town: **Hay-on-Wye**
Map: **SO 2393 3735** | Sheets: **OL13 L161** | Lat: **52.02932N** | Long: **3.11019W**

Previously identified as a cairn or burial chamber but now believed to be the remains of a 30m (98ft) stone circle. There seems to be an entrance with two radially set portal stones in the southeast. The largest stone, 1.5m (5ft) high and 1.1m (3½ft) wide, leans at a pronounced angle and a possible cup-mark has been identified by the OS benchmark. The other stones, visible near this stone and opposite, are much smaller, barely poking through the turf. The views to Hay Bluff and across the Wye valley are wonderful and a car park makes access easy.

Photo © Martyn Copcutt

PEN MAEN WERN
Standing Stone | Nearest Town: **Rhayader**
Map: **SN 8644 6201** | Sheets: **E200 L147** | Lat: **52.24452N** | Long: **3.23641W**

Photo © Paul Blades

A large stone of white quartz on the summit of Pen Maen Wern. If you're lucky enough to be there when the sun is shining, the stone looks amazing. It's a stocky 1.5m (5ft) tall and 1.4m (4ft 7in) wide.

LLANWRTHWL
Standing Stone | Nearest Town: **Rhayader**
Map: **SN 9757 6372** | Sheets: **E200 L147** | Lat: **52.26207N** | Long: **3.50221W**

An impressive 1.75m (5ft 7in) stone stands close to the south porch of St Gwrthwl's Church, Llanwrthwl. The circular form of part of the churchyard may indicate an ancient enclosure, suggesting, along with the stone, that this may be an example of a Christianized prehistoric site.

Nearby | At SN 9868 6614, 2.7km (1¾ miles) northeast of the standing stone at Llanwrthwl, is **Carn Wen** ring cairn. This badly damaged cairn is 7.9m (26ft) across and 1m (3ft 3in) high, with the remains of a substantial kerb as well as a cist. In 1844, an axe, a bracelet and other remains were found here; at the time a large stone was still standing in the middle of the cairn. Adjoining the cairn to the south is the monument known as the Druid's Circle, a 15m (49ft) banked enclosure, possibly a ring cairn, with a smaller circular structure inside it.

FOUR STONES

Stone Circle | Nearest Village: **Old Radnor**
Map: **SO 2457 6080** | Sheets: **E201 L137** | Lat: **52.240198N** | Long: **3.106079W**

Photo © Andy Spittle

A four-poster stone circle, the stones in a 5.3m (17ft 3in) ring and ranging in height from 1.4m to 1.8m (4ft 6in to 6ft). Legend tells that they mark the burial place of four kings killed in battle hereabouts. When the bells of Old Radnor church ring at night, the stones are said to stir to life and go down to nearby Hindwell Pool to drink.

Nearby | There is not much to see on the ground in the Walton Basin, but the area is home to a number of Neolithic palisades, cursuses and enclosures. At SO 2544 6072, 876m (just over ½ mile) east of Four Stones, is **Hindwell**, the largest palisaded enclosure found in Britain (the second largest in Europe), radiocarbon-dated to 2050BC. Some 1,400 oaks, 6m (20ft) tall, stood in a 2.35km (nearly 1½ mile) long circumference to enclose an area of 34ha (84 acres). At SO 2523 5996 is the 100m (328ft) **Walton Court** ring ditch, identified as a cropmark. There are other large ring ditches in the area, all dating from the middle Neolithic. Two Roman camps overlie part of the site. At SO 2545 5990 is the **Walton palisaded enclosure**, one of the largest examples of its type in Britain, with a curved alignment of pits that can be seen as cropmarks. This alignment is thought to mark the western side of an enclosure measuring about 300m (984ft) across and is possibly associated with a double alignment of pits that appear to form an avenue to the southwest.

EGLWYS GWYDDELOD

Cairn Circle | Nearest Town: **Aberdovey**
Map: **SH 6626 0016** | Sheets: **OL23 L135** | Lat: **52.58312N** | Long: **3.97476W**

A small and little-known cairn circle in a beautiful, south-facing setting on the slopes of Trum Gelli in Gwynedd. Its name means "church of the Irish". The oval ring is 7m (23ft) in diameter with nine stones remaining, the largest 1m (3ft 3in) tall.

Photo © Christopher Bickerton

POWYS | GWYNEDD

235

ANGLESEY/YNYS MON

Mein Hirion

Lligwy

Bedd Branwen

Penrhos Feilw
Presaddfed

Trefignath

Llangefni

Great Orme

Prestatyn
Rhyl

Llandudno

Conwy
Abergele

Gop-y-goleu

Druids' Circle

Llyn-y-wrach

Carnedd-y-saeson

ST ASAPH

Flintshi

Ty-newydd

Din Dryfol

Bryn Celli Ddu

Barclodiad-y-gawres

Bryn-yr-hen-bobl

Bodowyr

Plas Newydd

Bryn Gwyn

Sling

Maen-y-bardd

Hafodygors Wen

Penyc

Denbigh

Mo

Caernarfon

Llanrwst

Conwy

Ruthin/Ruth

Denbigh

Y Garn

Betws-y-coed

Brenig

Bachwen

Capel Garmon

Blaenau Ffestiniog

Pillar o

Ystum Cegid Isaf

Llan Ffestiniog

Owain Glyndwr's House

Maen Twrog

Tyfos

Tyn-y-coed

Cist Cerrig

Bryn Cader Faner

Branas Uchaf

Moel Ty-uchaf

Mynydd Cefn Amlwch

Pwllheli

Gwynedd

Llech Idris

Moel Goedog

Gwern Einion

Dyffryn Ardudwy

SNOWDONIA NATIONAL PARK

Arthog

Powys

Welshpool/

0   10   20 km

0   5   10 miles

North Wales

Eglwys Gwyddelod

Ceredigion

ARTHOG

Stone Setting | Nearest Village: **Arthog**
Map: **SH 6526 1393** | Sheets: **OL23 L124** | Lat: **52.70621N** | Long: **3.99571W**

A rather mysterious stone setting in Gwynedd, which has been interpreted either as a stone circle or the remains of a cairn circle with a stone row. There are six stones grouped together, with a hole for a seventh; a further four stones are located about 2m (6½ft) away and include a striking quartz boulder. The tallest of the 10 surviving stones is 1m (3ft 3in). The remains of a cairn can also be seen to the west. Permission is required to enter the field. This site is at the heart of one of the most complex prehistoric landscapes in North Wales, with many standing stones, cairns, stone rows and hill forts to visit within a few kilometres.

Nearby | At SH 6516 1325, 687m (just under ½ mile) south from Arthog, is **Planwydd Helyg** standing stone, 1.9m (6ft 2in) high and easy to spot from the footpath.

At SH 6617 1384, 912m (just over ½ mile) east of Arthog, is **Carreg-y-big** standing stone, unusually situated below a rocky outcrop and close to the National Trust car park. It's about 1.9m (6ft 2in) high and 1m (3ft 3in) wide and looks entirely different from every angle.

Photo © Peter Boyle

DYFFRYN ARDUDWY ★

Portal Dolmens | Nearest Village: **Dyffryn Ardudwy**
Map: **SH 5886 2284** | Sheets: **OL18 L124** | Lat: **52.78462N** | Long: **4.0942W**

Two portal dolmens stand 8.6m (28ft) apart on the remains of their cairn(s). The smaller one was built first and enclosed in an oval cairn; later this was incorporated into a trapezoidal cairn and a second, larger chamber was added to the northeast, with a v-shaped forecourt. Finds include pottery fragments in a pit in front of the earlier tomb, and a stone pendant from the later tomb. In 2008 possible rock art was discovered: lines and notches pecked on the southern upright of the western chamber. Mysterious lights were reported in the area in 1904–5, which researcher Paul Devereux has attributed to seismic activity linked to the Mochras Fault that runs beneath the site, theorizing that the site was perhaps built to mark such phenomena. Local legend tells that one of the stones is one of three quoits thrown by Arthur from the top of nearby Moelfre, and bears the marks of his fingers.

GWERN EINION

Portal Dolmen | Nearest Village: **Llanfair**
Map: **SH 5873 2861** | Sheets: **OL18 L124** | Lat: **52.83633N** | Long: **4.09907W**

Within view of Moelfre mountain, like a dozen other sites in this part of Wales, this damaged but still dramatic portal tomb standing among ruined farm buildings has had an eventful life, having been robbed of its cairn, used as part of a wall and even as a shed, before being restored. The capstone is 2.4m (7ft 10in) at its highest point, and rests at a severe angle, on two 1.8m (6ft) portal stones and a 1m (3ft 3in) back stone. A standing stone is in the wall of the same field.

237

Photo by Adam Stanford © Aerial-Cam Ltd

Nearby | At SH 5833 2700, 1.7km (just over 1 mile) SSW of Gwern Einion and northwest of the church, are the two **Meini Hirion** standing stones. It's been speculated these are the remains of a stone circle. The stones are 2.3m (7½ft) apart and quite different in appearance; the taller, wedge-shaped stone is 3.25m (10ft 7in), while the other is 1.95m (6ft 4in).

MOEL GOEDOG

Megalithic Complex | Nearest Town: **Harlech**
Map: **SH 5988 3097** | Sheets: **OL18 L124** | Lat: **52.85793N** | Long: **4.08258W**

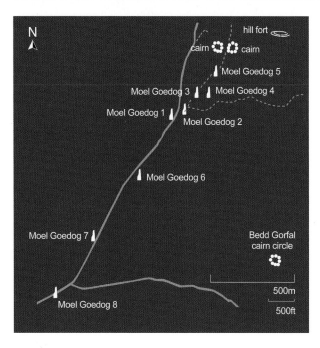

On Moel Goedog, multiple standing stones mark what is thought to be part of the Fonlief Hir ancient trackway, which may have extended from the coast at Meini Hirion, Llanbedr, up to the summit of Moel Goedog. Also here are two ring cairns, a cairn circle and, at the summit, a late Bronze Age hill fort that offers breathtaking views. The ditches and bank are worn, but enough remains to warrant a visit!

STANDING STONES

If approaching Moel Goedog on the road from the southwest, the standing stones are found in the following order:

Moel Goedog 8 (pictured, below) is at SH 5989 3096. This 1.8m (5ft 11in) stone is the first one reached on the road when approaching from the southwest.

Moel Goedog 7 (at SH 6013 3130) is 413m (1,355ft) northeast of Moel Goedog 8. This is the tallest standing stone in the complex, at 2.2m (7ft 3in). Moel Goedog 6 (at SH 6040 3165) is a mere broken stump, 476m (1,562ft) northeast of Moel Goedog 7.

Moel Goedog 1 (at SH 6068 3202) is reached 432m (1,417ft) northeast of Moel Goedog 6, just before the footpath up the hill splits off from the track. It is 1m (3ft 3in) high and leans slightly to the west. Moel Goedog 2 (at SH 6072 3203) is just 41m (135ft) east of Moel Goedog 1. This is a blocky stone 0.9m (3ft) high.

Moel Goedog 3 (at SH 6081 3216) is 156m (512ft) northeast of Moel Goedog 2, while its pair, Moel Goedog 4 (at SH 6089 3216) is 80m (262ft) further east. The last standing stone is Moel Goedog 5 (at SH 6094 3229) 139m (456ft) NNE of Moel Goedog 4.

Photo © Martyn Copcutt

RING CAIRNS

Before you reach the summit with its hill fort, there are two ring cairns. Moel Goedog West (at SH 6105 3244) is 171m (561ft) NNE of Moel Goedog 5. It's about 6.5m (21ft) in diameter with stones (originally 12) up to 1m (3ft 3in) high. Excavation in 1978 uncovered pits containing charcoal and pots with cremations. Moel Goedog East (at SH 6104 3245) is 50m (164ft) east of Moel Goedog West, and thought to be contemporaneous. It has similar dimensions but smaller stones.

You can also take a look at the little-visited Bedd Gorfal cairn circle (at SH 6129 3114), on the slopes of Moel-y-gerddi, 1km (0.6 miles) ESE of Moel Goedog 6.

BRYN CADER FANER
Ring Cairn | Nearest Village: **Talsarnau**
Map: **SH 6479 3529** | Sheets: **OL18 L124** | Lat: **52.89799N** | Long: **4.0115W**

> "An honesty box is by the car park above Eisengrug. The £2 fee goes to charity. The farmer is fed up with the fact that hardly anybody pays it, so please do … £2 is not excessive for one of the most spectacular monuments in Wales!" Eveline van der Steen

A famously spiky ring cairn in a fantastic upland setting – one of the star sites of North Wales. Of the original 30 stones, 15 remain, about 1.8m (6ft) tall, poking up from the cairn at dramatic angles, like jagged teeth or a crown of thorns. On a Bronze Age trackway, positioned for maximum visibility close to the summit of Bryn Cader Faner, it's a truly spectacular monument, despite the damage caused by Victorian treasure hunters (the cist has been destroyed) and being used as target practice in World War II. The long and boggy trek to get here is well worth the effort.

Photo © Jeanette Wright

Nearby | At SH 6409 3584, 888m (just over ½ mile) WNW of Bryn Cader Faner, are the **Y Gyrn** cairns. You can see the concentric rings of stones used to construct the upper (southern) cairn, and it also has a visible collapsed cist. The lower cairn has a kerb with some upright stones. If approaching Bryn Cader Faner from the west instead of the usual southern approach you will walk right in between these two cairns. There are hut circles further along the path. A map is needed.

MAEN TWROG

Standing Stone | Nearest Village: **Maentwrog**
Map: **SH 6640 4060** | Sheets: **OL18 L124** | Lat: **52.9461N** | Long: **3.98977W**

Possibly of prehistoric origin, this 1.1m (3ft 7in) pillar of non-local stone stands outside the church where it was thrown, according to tradition, from a nearby mountain by the giant St Twrog, destroying the pagan shrine that stood where the church is now. It's said the saint's thumb and finger marks can still be seen on the stone. It also appears in the Fourth Branch of the Mabinogi, marking the burial place of Pryderi, king of Dyfed.

LLECH IDRIS

Standing Stone | Nearest Village: **Bronaber**
Map: **SH 7311 3108** | Sheets: **OL18 L124** | Lat: **52.8622N** | Long: **3.88625W**

Photo © Martyn Copcutt

A fine, elegant standing stone, leaning at a pleasing angle and with lots of colourful lichens. It's 3.1m (10ft 2in) tall by 1.5m (5ft) wide and only 0.3m (1ft) deep, with a classic chisel-shaped top. Legend has it that the giant Idris hurled the stone here all the way from the summit of Cadr Idris.

CIST CERRIG

Portal Dolmen | Nearest Village: **Morfa Bychan**
Map: **SH 5433 3841** | Sheets: **E254 L124** | Lat: **52.92328N** | Long: **4.16828W**

Located below Moel-y-gest with its hill fort (a recognizable point across half of western Snowdonia), this is an impressive though extremely ruinous portal tomb, with only three stones remaining. It resembles a giant armchair, or winged figure, depending where you're standing. The surviving stones are the portal uprights and the door slab; the chamber would have been to the west. There are cup-marks pecked into the sloping face of the rock outcrop to the southeast, and also on other rocks nearby. Difficult to get to; a 1:25,000 OS map is needed.

Photo © Christopher Bickerton

240

"From the buildings at Tyddyn-adi, go through the gate above you on the right. Cross the field following the obvious path and bear left at the junction, leaving the right of way. Follow the track until you go through a wall. Bear left toward another wall and you should see the monument on the other side." Roger K. Read

YSTUM CEGID ISAF   Alt Name: **Coetan Arthur**
Chambered Tomb | Nearest Town: **Dolbenmaen**
Map: **SH 4988 4132** | Sheets: **E254 L123** | Lat: **52.9482N** | Long: **4.23577W**

A beautiful site, quiet and out of the way. Huddled beside the field wall, this pleasingly table-like burial chamber has a large capstone, about 4.5 × 3.3m (15 × 11ft), and four remaining uprights. In 1816, Edward Pugh recorded that the farmer had filled in the sides of the monument with stone walling in order to convert it into a sheepfold; he also mentioned the legend that (as at other sites), the capstone

Photo © Christopher Bickerton

had been thrown by Arthur, but due to a slip of the foot, it had fallen wide of its mark. Can be tricky to find if approaching from Rhoslan. Instead, try walking via Ynys Ddu and Ystum Cegid Isaf farms.

Nearby | At SH 4834 4088, 1.6km (1 mile) west of Ystum Cegid Isaf, is **Rhoslan** or Cefn Isaf, a chambered tomb in a field that's often full of buttercups, close to the road. Full of character, it has an immensely thick capstone.

MYNYDD CEFN AMLWCH   Alt Names: **Coetan Arthur, Cefnamwlch**
Chambered Tomb | Nearest Village: **Tudweiliog**
Map: **SH 2297 3454** | Sheets: **E254 L123** | Lat: **52.87917N** | Long: **4.63209W**

A classic chambered tomb with a large capstone, 3 × 1.5m (10 × 5ft), supported by three uprights. Two quartz boulders lie beside it. Despite being rather tightly corralled by a fence to protect it from cattle, the site still has plenty of character and the views are lovely. This is another site associated with the legend of the quoit-throwing King Arthur. Easy to reach via a footpath from the road. There are other cairns nearby.

Nearby | At SH 2371 3283, 1.9km (just over 1 mile) southeast of Mynydd Cefn Amlwch, is the impressive 2.4m (8ft) high **Meyllteyrn** standing stone, covered with lichen and set in the graveyard of a now roofless church. Fantastic views.

At SH 2084 3253, in a field 2.9km (1¾ miles) WSW of Mynydd Cefn Amlwch, is **Llangwnnadl** standing stone, an imposing 3m (10ft) tall.

BACHWEN
Portal Dolmen | Nearest Village: **Clynnog Fawr**
Map: **SH 4077 4948** | Sheets: **E254 L123** | Lat: **53.01902N** | Long: **4.37631W**

241

A perfect dolmen with a fabulous decorated capstone, sited between the sea and the towering mountains, within sight of Tre'r Cieri hill fort – "the town of the giants". It's tightly fenced in but still highly atmospheric. The wedge-shaped capstone, 2.75 × 1.6m (9ft × 5ft 2in), is supported by four uprights, about 1.8m (5ft 10in) tall, and has 110 cup-marks on its upper surface, with eight more on the eastern edge. Many miracles are said to have occurred at the nearby St Beuno's chapel and well.

Nearby | At SH 4299 5107, 2.7km (just under 1¾ mile) ENE of Bachwen, is the **Penarth** chambered tomb, which is in a very ruinous state, the capstone having collapsed on one side. Great views across Caernarfon Bay.

Y GARN

Cairn | Nearest Village: **Beddgelert**
Map: **SH 5513 5262** | Sheets: **OL17 L115** | Lat: **53.05115N** | Long: **4.16276W**

The summit of Y Garn is home to two large cairns, perhaps the finest of the many mountaintop cairns in Snowdonia. These two are the furthest east of the five cairns strung along the Nantle ridge. The views of Snowdonia are wonderful, but reaching the ridge is hard going.

Nearby | At SH 5396 5469, 2.4km (1½ miles) northwest of Y Garn, is the **Mynydd Mawr** summit cairn, offering more wonderful views of Snowdonia. The cairn is 22m (72ft) in diameter and 2.5m (8ft 2in) high, with three more recent dry-stone shelters built into it.

SLING Alt Name: **Yr Hen Allor**

Chambered Tomb | Nearest Town: **Bethesda**
Map: **SH 6055 6695** | Sheets: **OL17 L115** | Lat: **53.18132N** | Long: **4.08819W**

A very ruinous tomb, extremely well-concealed in heavy undergrowth (a nearby telegraph pole may help in navigation). Its other name, Yr Hen Allor, means "old altar".

Nearby | At SH 6348 6811, 3.1km (almost 2 miles) ENE of Sling and up on the summit of Moel Faban, you'll find three cairns in a line along the ridge. A collared urn from the middle Bronze Age was found in one of them during excavation in the 19th century and is now in the British Museum. They're all fairly ruinous, but in good weather the views up to the mountains and down to the straits and Anglesey are brilliant.

CARNEDD-Y-SAESON

Cairn | Nearest Village: **Abergwyngregyn**
Map: **SH 6783 7174** | Sheets: **OL17 L115** | Lat: **53.22619N** | Long: **3.98125W**

In beautiful surroundings, Carnedd-y-saeson ("cairn of the English") has kerbing of two rows of concentric stones, and although damaged is the best example of its kind in North Wales. It's around 14m (46ft) across and 0.3m (1ft) high, with another circle of stones in the interior, about 10.5m (34ft 5in) in diameter, and a large cist, 1.8 × 1.2m (6 × 4ft), the displaced cover of which is clearly visible. It lies in a fascinating prehistoric landscape with a wealth of hut circles, enclosures and stones.

Nearby | At SH 6674 7038, 1.7km (just over 1 mile) southwest of Carnedd-y-saeson, is the **Coed Aber** roundhouse, an Iron Age structure that excavation in 2009 confirmed had incorporated a pre-existing Bronze Age standing stone. The site was later reused as a corn-drying kiln. Can be accessed on a walk suitable for wheelchairs.

BRYN GWYN
Stone Circle | Nearest Village: **Brynsiencyn**
Map: **SH 4623 6693** | Sheets: **E263 L114** | Lat: **53.17716N** | Long: **4.30221W**

Photo © Eric Guile

Two enormous stones, the tallest on Anglesey and indeed in Wales, now rather casually sited in a hedge beside a gate. The taller stone is more pointed and slab-like, 4.2m (13ft 9in) high by 3.2m (10ft 5in) wide and 0.6m (2ft) thick, and once formed the gable end of a cottage. The second stone is blockier, 3.2m (10ft 5in) high, 2.9m (9½ft) wide and 1.5m (5ft) thick. Excavations have found the base of a destroyed stone and holes for others, suggesting that this was once a circle, about 16m (52ft) across and with eight stones, confirming 18th-century reports of further stones here. As to what happened to the other stones, William Hutton wrote at the end of the 18th century that "ignorant country people, supposing money was hid under them, tore them up". From Bryn Gwyn, the midsummer sun is seen to rise over the centre of Castell Bryn Gwyn (see below).

Nearby | At SH 4653 6706, 321m (1,053ft) ENE of the Bryn Gwyn stones, is **Castell Bryn Gwyn**, originally a henge or similar Neolithic enclosure, with a 5.2m (17ft) wide stony bank and a broad, flat-bottomed external ditch. Later it became a hill fort, with impressive earthworks that survive up to 2.6m (8½ft) high.

BODOWYR
Passage Grave | Nearest Village: **Llangaffo**
Map: **SH 4627 6816** | Sheets: **E263 L114** | Lat: **53.18825N** | Long: **4.30228W**

243

A charming tomb with a capstone perched on three uprights. There would originally have been a passage to the east. It's close to the road, which makes it easy to access, and despite being fenced off is full of character.

Photo © Christopher Bickerton

Photo © Gail Johnson

BRYN CELLI DDU   Alt Name: **Black Grove Hill**
Passage Grave | Nearest Village: **Llanfairpwllgwyngyll**
Map: **SH 5075 7017** | Sheets: **E263 L114** | Lat: **53.20758N** | Long: **4.23623W**

Bryn Celli Ddu ("mound in the dark grove") is the most famous passage grave on Anglesey and indeed in Wales. It seems to have been deliberately sited to be prominent on a low sand and gravel knoll in the middle of the Afon Braint river valley. A henge and a circle were built here first, in the Neolithic; the ditch survives. It's believed that the stones were removed (some smashed to pieces) around 1,000 years after the construction of the henge, and a passage grave built in the centre of the henge, the earth from the bank being used for the mound. Two of the stones were used as portal stones for the tomb. A 1.5m (5ft) stone inscribed with a swirling design was buried face-down in a pit; it's now in the National Museum of Wales and a replica stands outside the tomb in what was thought to be its original position in the henge. The passage, aligned to midsummer sunrise, leads to a polygonal chamber; within the chamber is a 2m (6½ft) standing stone that has been shaped into a rounded pillar. The mound covering the tomb is part of the restoration following the 1927–8 excavation; the original was probably much bigger, with a retaining wall of kerb stones. Bryn Celli Ddu is surrounded by a stone circle, and cremated human remains from associated pits have been dated to 3500–3100 and 3310–2900BC, making this one of the earliest stone circles known in Britain.

The Reverend John Skinner, in his *Ten Days Tour Through the Isle of Anglesey* (1804), tells the story of a mysterious figure in white that appeared when the farmer, removing stone for building, first broke through into the chamber. He was frightened off (and who can blame him) but on returning found the figure was merely the pillar in the chamber. He was disappointed to find no treasure. Skinner adds: "The superstition of the common people still suppose this to be the habitation of spirits."

BRYN CELLI DDU CAIRN

At SH 5072 7012, in a field some 58m (190ft) southwest of the passage grave, are the remains of this Bronze Age cairn. Recent excavations and survey led by Ffion Reynolds and Seren Griffiths have found part of a possible cairn cemetery, pits containing pottery and several examples of rock art, all within sight of the main mound.

Colour in the Monuments of Neolithic Europe

Penelope Foreman, a final year PhD researcher at Bournemouth University

Colour is a fundamental human experience – if not a universally constant one. There are individuals who are colour-blind to various degrees, and even some who see extra colours. However, there is something about the perception and categorization of colour that is near uniform across humanity, as evidenced by Brent Berlin and Paul Kay's *Basic Color Terms* and studies into the key mechanisms of colour vision.

I'm interested in trying to discover whether there are any commonalities, significant patterns or demonstrable signs of specific colour selection in Neolithic monuments, both in Wales and England and also in Denmark, Sweden and the Netherlands, that may hint at colour being an important part of Neolithic cosmology – regionally, locally or culturally.

As part of this project I will record the colour of individual stones via both human perception and through the use of a custom-designed digital recording device. The results will be used to generate coloured site plans for visual analysis of patterns, and also recorded in a database to allow for wider and more thorough statistical analysis.

The pilot study designed to test this methodology was conducted at Bryn Celli Ddu. Colour is a definite part of the experience of visiting this site. Entering the passage, you are faced with pale stones standing out of the red earth, dark corners, walls bright with flashes of quartz. The chamber is a space of contrasts. Two stones, almost black, face each other across the chamber, while a bright and quartz-rich stone shines and sparkles with reflected light. Pale grey stones with contrasting textures rise from the deep red soil and stand between these other stones, and a pale pillar stands in silent watchfulness in the chamber corner. The stones display contrasting colours and textures, which would have appeared even more pronounced without the presence of lichen and moss. Though the tomb is surrounded by blue schist outcrops that would have proved a convenient source for monument building stone, instead stones of different colours, textures and shapes were selected and used in its construction.

Full conclusions can in no way be judged from a single site, but the evidence for colour being significant at Bryn Celli Ddu seems to point to a representation of the contrast between light and dark. If colour and light are related in this way, then further examples should be seen across Atlantic Europe – and my research is ongoing. The underlying theme of contrast may also yield potentially meaningful findings should it be found in other sites, with contrasting colours being used in significant areas of monuments to symbolize particular concepts or to designate areas of the site for specific purposes.

Foreman, P. *Colour Out of Space: Colour Usage in the Construction of Monuments of Neolithic Atlantic Europe* (forthcoming)

Details of Penelope's research are linked from the Megalithic Portal page for Bryn Celli Ddu.

At SH 5063 7010, 139m (456ft) WSW of the passage grave, is this broad, almost rectangular stone, 1.8m (6ft 2in) wide and 1.3m (4ft 3in) tall. Rubbed smooth by endless sheep, it shares the same alignment as the passage grave. It's on private land, so seek permission from the farm.

Nearby | At SH 5032 7034, 464m (1,496ft) WNW of the passage grave, is the impressive 3.3m (11ft) **Tyddyn-bach** standing stone, set in a modern clearance cairn.

BRYN-YR-HEN BOBL
Chambered Cairn | Nearest Village: **Llanfairpwllgwyngyll**
Map: **SH 5189 6900** | Sheets: **E263 L114** | Lat: **53.197437N** | Long: **4.218666W**

Within the Plas Newydd estate, the country seat of the Marquesses of Anglesey, is the Bryn-yr-hen Bobl chambered cairn, its name meaning "hill of the old people". Skeletal remains were found here when the tomb was opened in the mid-18th century. The chamber was restored and the mound altered after excavation in 1929–35 (when fragments of Neolithic pottery were found). You'll need permission to see the tomb close up (it is visible from the woods); apply to the estate managers, Jones Peckover, in Anglesey.

Nearby | At SH 5199 6972, 722m (just under ½ mile) north of Bryn-yr-hen Bobl, is the **Plas Newydd** burial chamber, also within the estate. Two chambers with capstones remain – one an enormous slab 11.5 × 9.5m (38 × 31ft) and 3.5m (11½ft) thick. There's no trace of the cairn or mound. Apply to the National Trust for access.

DIN DRYFOL
Chambered Tomb | Nearest Village: **Aberffraw**
Map: **SH 3956 7249** | Sheets: **E263 L114** | Lat: **53.22525N** | Long: **4.4042W**

Photo © Christopher Bickerton

Badly damaged but the stones are huge and the setting is a wonderful and unusual one on a ledge beneath a rocky outcrop. The tomb is oriented northeast–southwest, and originally there was one chamber, which was extended to four in several phases. During excavations in 1969–70 and 1980 traces of the cairn, 47–62m (154–203ft) by 14m (46ft), were found, along with cremated bone and pottery sherds. Interestingly, they also revealed that one of the chambers had a wooden portal "stone", which according to Frances Lynch is "rare but not unknown".

BARCLODIAD-Y-GAWRES

Passage Grave | Nearest Village: **Rhosneigr**
Map: **SH 3290 7074** | Sheets: **E263 L114** | Lat: **53.20738N** | Long: **4.50354W**

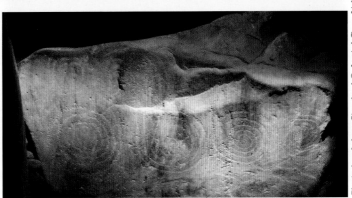

Photo by Adam Stanford © Aerial-Cam Ltd

Barclodiad-y-gawres ("apronful of the giantess") is a reconstructed passage grave with intriguing rock art. The mound was recreated with modern materials after excavation in 1952–3. From the forecourt a passage leads to a large chamber with three side chambers. These were roofed with capstones, one of which survives. The east and west chambers both have decorated end stones, and three further stones in the passage feature pecked designs of spirals, lozenges and zigzags, reminiscent of similar art in Ireland, Brittany and Spain, as well as of the patterned stone found under Bryn Celli Ddu (see page 244). Evidence of a fire was found in the central chamber, apparently put out with what has been described as a "witch's brew" of reptile, fish and amphibian bones (it's also been suggested these were simply the faeces of a resident otter), then a layer of pebbles and limpet shells. An appointment is needed to visit; consult www.cadw.gov.wales for details. Take a torch to view the art.

TY NEWYDD

Chambered Tomb | Nearest Village: **Llanfaelog**
Map: **SH 3443 7387** | Sheets: **E263 L114** | Lat: **53.23597N** | Long: **4.48228W**

Despite the red brick supports, this is a lovely burial chamber, with a huge, cracked capstone, 4 × 1.8m (13ft × 5ft 10in) and 1.2m (4ft) thick. Supporting uprights survive. If the brick supports bother you, it is possible to find an angle where they won't show in a photo. It's thought there was a second chamber at the eastern end. The tomb is surrounded by little concrete posts, indicating the extent of the mound. Excavation in 1936 resulted in Bronze Age finds, demonstrating reuse of this Neolithic site.

Photo © Christopher Bickerton

Photo © Eric Grindle

TREFIGNATH ★

Chambered Tomb | Nearest Town: **Holyhead**
Map: **SH 2585 8056** | Sheets: **E263 L114** | Lat: **53.2933N** | Long: **4.61436W**

Right beside the busy A55, overlooking the aluminium works, but still highly atmospheric. The huge capstone of the collapsed central chamber is broken in two; the eastern chamber, with its 2m (6½ft) portal stones, is more or less intact. The western chamber was the first of the three to be built, dated by stone tools and pottery sherds found here to *c.* 3750BC. The central chamber was added later, with a forecourt at the eastern end, and finally the eastern chamber was built over the forecourt, probably several hundred years later, before the site was covered by a cairn (most of that was removed in 1870).

Nearby | At SH 2539 8095, 600m (1,969ft) WNW, is **Ty Mawr** standing stone, in the middle of a recently developed industrial estate. It's an impressive stone, twisting upward, 2.7m (8ft 10in) high.

PENRHOS FEILW   Alt Name: **Plas Meilw**

Standing Stones | Nearest Town: **Holyhead**
Map: **SH 2270 8094** | Sheets: **E262 L114** | Lat: **53.29566N** | Long: **4.66177W**

A wonderful pair, furry with lichen, easily accessed and with great views over Trearddur Bay and to the distant mountains (despite the houses nearby). They stand 3.3m (11ft) apart, both about 3m (10ft) tall. Local tradition tells of bones, spearheads and arrowheads found in a cist between the two stones, and even that they once stood at the centre of a stone circle, but no investigation has taken place to confirm this.

Nearby | At SH 2276 8165, 717m (½ mile) north, are the remaining three uprights of **Gorsedd Gwlwm** chambered cairn.

Photo © Drew Parsons

PRESADDFED
Chambered Tomb | Nearest Village: **Bodedern**
Map: **SH 3476 8089** | Sheets: **E262 L114** | Lat: **53.29912N** | Long: **4.48099W**

The two chambers of this tomb, 2.2m (7ft) apart, are both ruined but still impressive. The southern chamber is in a better state than the northern one, with a classic dolmen-like appearance and an impressive 4.2 × 3.3m (13ft 9in × 10ft 9in) capstone. Excavations in 2013 found the socket hole of a standing stone within the collapsed chamber, suggesting it stood there before the chamber was built. At some time in the 18th century, a family was living in the southern chamber.

Nearby | At SH 3406 8318, 2.4km (1½ miles) NNW of Presaddfed, is **Tre-gwehelydd** or Maen-y-goredd ("stone of the fish-weir"), a standing stone broken in three, held together with bronze bands. It's 2.6m (8½ft) tall and 1.1m (3½ft) wide, in a fine location with great views. It was said that a second, buried stone lay nearby, although there's no sign of this. At SH 3180 8122, 3km (just under 2 miles) west from Presaddfed, is the 1.4m (4ft 7in) **Shop Farm** standing stone, on private land. Seek permission at the farm.

MEIN HIRION   Alt Names: **Llanfechell 1, Llanfechell Triangle**
Standing Stones | Nearest Village: **Llanfechell**
Map: **SH 3640 9169** | Sheets: **E262 L114** | Lat: **53.3967N** | Long: **4.46199W**

A fine triangular setting in an exposed and windswept spot by the field wall, with great views. The stones are all tall (about 2m/6½ft) and lichen-covered, one with a notably curved profile.

Nearby | At SH 3699 9164, 595m (1,952ft) east of Mein Hirion, is the **Llanfechell 2** standing stone, about 2.1m (7ft) tall and 1.2m (4ft) wide. It leaned at an angle for many years before finally falling in 2009. During re-erection in 2010, a cup-marked rock was found to have been reused as a packing stone in the socket.

LLIGWY
Chambered Tomb | Nearest Village: **Moelfre**
Map: **SH 5013 8604** | Lat: **53.34994N** | Sheets: **E263 L114** | Long: **4.25299W**

A fantastic site, with an enormous capstone (5.2 × 5.9m/17 × 19ft 8in and 1m/3ft 3in thick, weighing 22 tonnes/25 tons) crouching on eight stones like little legs. Built over a natural hollow in the rock, the chamber would have been about 2m (6½ft) high inside. The remains of about 30 people of all ages were found here, along with pot sherds, flints, animal bones and shells. The final burials may have taken place some 1,000 years after the tomb was constructed.

Photo © Jim Appleton

BEDD BRANWEN

Ring Cairn | Nearest Village: **Elim**
Map: **SH 3610 8500** | Sheets: **E262 L114** | Lat: **53.33644N** | Long: **4.46302W**

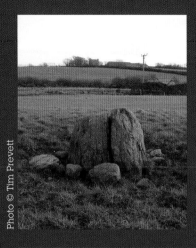

Photo © Tim Prevett

The ruined ring cairn has a kerb and a small standing stone, as well as a cist. About 30m (98ft) across and 1m (3ft 3in) high, its name refers to the legend that this is the burial place of Queen Branwen, from the Second Branch of the Mabinogi. In the 1960s several urns and cremation deposits were found, with jet and amber beads.

Nearby | At SH 3192 8632, 4.4km (2¾ miles) west of Bedd Branwen, is the lichenous **Soar Stone**, also known as Capel Soar, about 3m (10ft) tall. It stands beside a church, just off the road. Within 700m (2,297ft) of this stone, archaeologists investigating a school building site have made the largest-ever Neolithic discovery in Wales, including the ruins of three early Neolithic houses and over 1,500 pottery sherds, lithic artefacts and botanical remains.

GREAT ORME

Ancient Mine | Nearest Town: **Llandudno**
Map: **SH 7708 8310** | Sheets: **OL17 L115** | Lat: **53.33051N** | Long: **3.84543W**

Worked for over 1,000 years, Great Orme in Conwy is the largest Bronze Age copper mine yet discovered in the world. It has been estimated that enough copper was mined here to make more than 10 million bronze axes. There are more than 5km (3 miles) of tunnels, which extend to a depth of 70m (230ft), as well as opencast or surface workings. From March to November (check the website for dates and times), visitors can view a section of the tunnels, and see, in the visitor centre, some of the tools that were discovered there.

Nearby | At SH 7721 8295, 203m (666ft) ESE of Great Orme mine, is **Lletty'r Filiast** ("grave of the greyhound bitch"), a badly damaged but still impressive cairn and chamber overlooking Llandudno Bay. The remains of the cairn are around 10.6m (35ft) wide and 27.4m (90ft) long. The chamber's capstone is broken, with only half still in place. For an unbeatable view of Llandudno, Lletty'r Filiast and the copper mines, try out the cable car (Britain's longest).

LLYN-Y-WRACH

Ring Cairn | Nearest Village: **Capelulo**
Map: **SH 7465 7578** | Sheets: **OL17 L115** | Lat: **53.26415N** | Long: **3.8808W**

A fine ring cairn, about 12m (39ft) in diameter, with a southwest-facing entrance.

"It's in a good position to watch the sun go down over Foel Lus." Christopher Bickerton

DRUIDS' CIRCLE   Alt Name: **Maeni Hirion**

Embanked Stone Circle | Nearest Village: **Penmaenmawr**
Map: **SH 7228 7464** | Sheets: **OL17 L115** | Lat: **53.25299N** | Long: **3.91554W**

A long but straightforward walk up across the moors to the headland brings you to this dramatically sited embanked stone circle. The 35m (114ft) diameter circle has a four-stone portal or entrance, with 10 upright stones in the circle itself, one fallen, and the holes for two more. The bank is about 0.6m (2ft) high, and the tallest stones are about 1.8m (5ft 10in). Excavation in 1958 revealed a central cist and various cremation deposits. The most anthropomorphic stone, known as the Deity Stone, resembles a hooded figure – and apparently it has an aversion to swearing. Legend tells that one notorious blasphemer, who one night came to taunt the stone, was found dead at its base the next morning. So watch your language!

Nearby | At SH 7216 7457, 139m (456ft) WSW of the Druids' Circle, is the romantically named **Monument 280**, which is thought to be the remains of a ring cairn. It's around 16m (52ft) in diameter, with a stony kerbed bank 2–3m (6½ft–10ft) wide. Excavation in 1959 revealed several cremation deposits here.

At SH 7250 7470, 227m (745ft) east of the Druids' Circle, is a further ring cairn (often confused with Monument 280), known as **Circle 278**. An intervening small ridge makes it invisible from the Druids' Circle. It's about 12m (39ft) in diameter with a 2.4m (8ft) bank of rubble enclosing an open space.

MAEN-Y-BARDD   Alt Names: **Cwt-y-bugail, Cwt-y-filiast**

Chambered Tomb | Nearest Village: **Rowen**
Map: **SH 7406 7178** | Sheets: **OL17 L115** | Lat: **53.22808N** | Long: **3.88806W**

A wonderful portal tomb, in a beautifully wild location above the village. The name means "bard (or poet's) stone" (the two alternative names mean "shepherd's hut" and "kennel of the greyhound bitch"). The capstone rests on four uprights, enclosing a 1.2m (4ft) high chamber. One legend tells how a giant threw his spear across the valley at his sheepdog, which was sheltering in the chamber; it fell short and stuck in the ground as the nearby Ffon-y-cawr. This is another site where spending the night in the chamber is risky: you will arise in the morning either a poet or mad.

Photo © Anna Reynolds

Nearby | At SH 7391 7166, 192m (630ft) WSW of Maen-y-bard, is a standing stone called **Ffon-y-cawr** ("giant's staff/stick"), also known as Picell Arthur ("Arthur's spear"). The angle of this 1.8m (5ft 10in) stone is explained by the story that this is the spear the giant threw at his dog.

HAFODYGORS WEN
Ring Cairn | Nearest Village: **Llanwrst**
Map: **SH 7336 6742** | Sheets: **OL17 L11** | Lat: **53.18874N** | Long: **3.89681W**

Generally described as a ring cairn, this interesting site contains four stones set into the circumference of the circle, resembling the four-posters of Scotland and Northumberland.

CAPEL GARMON
Chambered Tomb | Nearest Village: **Capel Garmon**
Map: **SH 8180 5432** | Sheets: **OL18 L116** | Lat: **53.07299N** | Long: **3.76573W**

Photo © Rob Barnett

Despite its location, this tomb is considered a Cotswold-Severn type, due to the trapezoidal cairn, forecourt-with horns and false entrance, and a passage of around 4.5m (15ft) leading to two chambers. One massive capstone remains in place. It was excavated in 1924 and has been heavily restored. A right of way leads to the site. In the 19th century, it was reported that the chamber had been used as a stable, complete with window, door and manger, but that these additions were later removed.

BRENIG
Timber Circle & Cairn Complex | Nearest Village: **Pentre-llyn-cymmer**
Map: **SH 9834 5720** | Sheets: **E264 L116** | Lat: **53.10227N** | Long: **3.51986W**

There's plenty to see around the Llyn Brenig reservoir in Denbighshire, with archaeological trails leading from the main car park. Monuments include various Bronze Age mortuary and ceremonial sites, forming a cairn cemetery and its surrounding environment. It's unusual to find a landscape of this type so thoroughly investigated, in this case prior to the construction of the reservoir in the 1970s. It was intended to enlarge the reservoir but this never happened, leaving more sites visible.

BRENIG 44
One of the most interesting sites is Brenig 44, an unusual ring cairn at SH 9834 5720, shown during excavation to have featured a circle of stakes. The posts visible today are set in the original post-holes.

BRENIG 51
At SH 9898 5656, 903m (just over ½ mile) ESE of Brenig 44, is Brenig 51, a beautifully reconstructed platform cairn with 26 small stones set in a 7m (23ft) wide ring. Excavation had found the cremated

bones of an adult and a child, as well as a bone dagger handle, within this ring. Originally, a wooden post had stood here, but later the space was filled with stones to create a complete platform as seen in the reconstruction.

OTHER SITES

Other recommended sites in the area include: the Brenig 46 cairn at SH 9858 5691; the Brenig 40 round barrow with evidence of possible excarnation platform at SH 9778 5711; the lovely Brenig 8 kerb cairn at SH 9880 5636 and the bouldery round cairn Brenig 47 at SH 9892 5804.

BRANAS UCHAF
Chambered Cairn | Nearest Village: **Cynwyd**
Map: **SJ 0112 3752** | Sheets: **E255 L125** | Lat: **52.92595N** | Long: **3.47232W**

The remains of a chambered tomb with some uprights are still there, but there's no sign of the capstone. The mound, which has been reduced by ploughing, is about 1.8m (5ft 10in) high and 22m (72ft) in diameter.

Photo © Christopher Bickerton

TYFOS
Cairn Circle | Nearest Village: **Llandrillo**
Map: **SJ 0284 3876** | Sheets: **E255 L125** | Lat: **52.93741N** | Long: **3.44712W**

Photo © Christopher Bickerton

This denuded cairn or barrow (or possibly the remains of a stone circle to which a cairn was added) is basically in someone's garden, so do ask for permission; otherwise you can see it from the road. More or less circular, the cairn is about 24m (78ft) across, with an internal ring of kerb stones around 16m (53ft) in diameter, with 13 remaining kerb stones, 0.3–0.6m (1–2ft) tall. Lovely views of the Clwyd range of hills; see if you can pinpoint the site of Moel ty-uchaf (see page 254).

MOEL TY-UCHAF

Cairn Circle | Nearest Village: **Llandrillo**
Map: **SJ 0561 3717** | Sheets: **E255 L125** | Lat: **52.92361N** | Long: **3.40545W**

Photo © David Chaika

A truly lovely cairn circle in a wonderful location, with 41 stones, all about 0.5m (1½ft) tall, in a *c.* 12m (39ft) ring. There is a central cist, an outlier to the NNE and great views (the Tyfos cairn circle is visible from here). Downhill, south of the circle, is a raised, circular platform cairn, around 16m (52ft) in diameter. The area is also known for a strange incident in 1974 (the "Welsh Roswell"), when residents of Llandrillo witnessed strange lights and a huge explosion that have never been fully explained. UFO enthusiasts insisted that the government was covering up the crash landing of an extraterrestrial spacecraft in the Berwyn Mountains.

TYN-Y-COED

Chambered Cairn | Nearest Village: **Rhydyglafes**
Map: **SJ 0477 3960** | Sheets: **E255 L125** | Lat: **52.94533N** | Long: **3.41869W**

This badly damaged tomb, thought to have originally had a circular cairn about 46m (151ft) in diameter, comprises a mutilated cairn some 4m (13ft) high, with a chamber and a very large capstone, about 3m (10ft) long. The capstone is propped up at one end, and the western end is engulfed by the remains of the cairn, which means there's not much chance of accessing the chamber.

Photo © Tim Prevett

OWAIN GLYNDWR'S HOUSE

Rock Art | Nearest Village: **Glyndyfrdwy**
Map: **SJ 1275 4309** | Sheets: **E255 L125** | Lat: **52.97802N** | Long: **3.30087W**

Photo © Christopher Bickerton

A nicely cup-marked stone, situated 250m (820ft) east of a mound associated with the Welsh political hero Owain Glyndwr. The mound is all that remains of a 12th-century castle.

PILLAR OF ELISEG   Alt Name: LLantysilio-yn-lâl

Bronze Age Burial Mound & 9th-century Cross-shaft | Nearest Town: **Llangollen**

Map: **SJ 2026 4452** | Sheets: **E256 L117** | Lat: **52.99205N** | Long: **3.18941W**

The cross-shaft (now lacking its head) was erected in the 9th century by the last king of Powys; it is set on a square base that stands on a prehistoric burial mound. Investigation in 2010–12 demonstrated that the mound is a Bronze Age kerbed cairn with at least three secondary cists, one of which was undisturbed. The cremated remains of multiple individuals were found here.

PENYCLODDIAU

Hill Fort & Cairn | Nearest Village: **Nannerch**

Map: **SJ 1290 6761** | Sheets: **E265 L116** | Lat: **53.1984N** | Long: **3.30529W**

Photo © Christopher Bickerton

A massive hill fort, staggering in its size, and yet only one out of a chain of six running down through North Wales. The hill fort is Iron Age but recent investigations have confirmed the cairn as Bronze Age. The hill fort covers some 21ha (51 acres), mostly enclosed by a single bank or rampart, which in places is formed entirely of stone. To the north, where the lie of the land is less naturally defendable, there are four ramparts. There are multiple hut circles in the interior, but these are hard to see in the undergrowth. The cairn, at the north end of the fort, is 2m (6½ft) in diameter and 0.7m (2ft 3in) high. It was restored in 2010, having been disturbed by the erection of a trig point (since removed) and a walkers' cairn. Excavation revealed a "robbers' trench" where the burial should have been.

Nearby | At SJ 1453 6604, 2.3km (almost 1½ miles) ESE of Penycloddiau, is the smaller **Moel Arthur** hill fort, with some of the largest ramparts in the area. The walkers' cairn in the centre may stand on a Bronze Age barrow, and three Bronze Age copper flat axes were found after a severe storm in 1962.

GOP-Y-GOLEUNI   Alt Name: **The Gop Cairn**

Cairn | Nearest Village: **Trelawnyd**

Map: **SJ 0866 8017** | Sheets: **E265 L116** | Lat: **53.31056N** | Long: **3.37235W**

The largest prehistoric manmade hill in Britain and Ireland after Silbury Hill (see page 108) and Merlin's Mount (see page 112), this mostly turf-covered cairn offers tremendous panoramic views. It's enormous – about 12m (39ft) high and around 90 × 73m (300 × 240ft) in diameter. Excavations in 1886–7 found no passage or chambers, just animal bones. It dates to 4000–3000BC. Immediately below the cairn is a cave, perhaps functioning as a burial chamber, as the remains of 14 people were found here, along with flints and pottery.

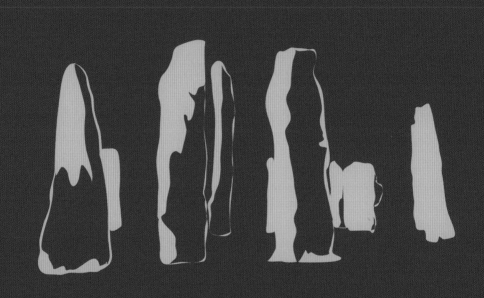

SCOTLAND

Arran & Dumfries and Galloway

ARRAN

North Sannox Farm
Auchencar
Glen Shiel
Auchagallon
Lamlash
Machrie Moor
Monamore
Giants' Graves
Torrylin
Largybeg Point

Campbeltown
Kilwinning
Saltcoats
Irvine
Troon
Prestwick
Ayr
Maybole
Stewarton
Newmilns
Galston   Darvel
Ballochmyle
East Ayrshire
Cumnock
Sanquhar
South Lanarkshire
Biggar
Normangill
Lanark

South Ayrshire

Bargrennan White Cairn
Laggangarn
Boreland
Newton Stewart
Stranraer   Mid Gleniron
Torhousekie
Glenquicken
Bagbie
Cairn Holy
Cauldside Burn
Drumtroddan

GALLOWAY FOREST PARK
New Galloway
Dumfries and Galloway
Castle Douglas
Dalbeattie
Kirkcudbright
High Banks Farm
Twelve Ap
Dumf

0   10   20 km
0   5   10 miles

Top 15 Stone Circles & Rows in Scotland

AUCHENCAR Alt Name: **Druid**
Standing Stone | Nearest Village: **Blackwaterfoot**
Map: **NR 8905 3633** | Sheets: **E361 L69** | Lat: **55.57482N** | Long: **5.34786W**

Photo © David Smyth

A fantastic red sandstone standing stone, furry with lichen, very narrow (about 0.2m/9in thick) and some 5m (16ft) high, tapering to a point. A second stone, broken and fallen, lies to the south, 3.5m (11ft 5in) long and 1.5m (5ft) at the base. The two may have formed part of a setting. Fabulous views over Machrie Bay, and Beinn Bharrain to the north. Aubrey Burl suspected Machrie Moor's large red sandstone pillars may have come from here.

> **"In 2000BC, the star Arcturus would have appeared to skim along the top of Beinn Bharrain (virtually due north)."** David Smyth

AUCHAGALLON
Stone Circle | Nearest Village: **Blackwaterfoot**
Map: **NR 8928 3464** | Sheets: **E361 L69** | Lat: **55.55979N** | Long: **5.3428W**

Set in an archaeologically rich landscape, just over 2km (1¼ miles) from Machrie Moor 10, this unusual monument overlooking Machrie Bay is ringed by a 14.5 × 13m (47ft 6in × 42ft 7in) circle of 15 sandstone blocks that range from 0.5m (1½ft) to 2.3m (7½ft) in height. In 1910 an elderly local, one Mr Sim, was quoted as stating that when he was young, the centre of the circle was flat and free of stones, suggesting the cairn might have been augmented by modern field clearance.

Nearby | At NR 8945 3363, 1 km (0.6 miles) SSE of Auchagallon, is the 1.5m (5ft) **Machriewaterfoot** standing stone. At NR 9084 3511, 1.6km (1 mile) ENE of Auchagallon, is the **Machrie Burn** stone circle, a four-poster of granite pillars each around 0.6m (2ft) high.

Photo © ukvegan

Stone Circles

John Barnatt, recently retired as Survey Archaeologist for the Peak District (National Park)

Some stone circles are impressive communal monuments where many people had a hand in their construction. Others are small affairs built by local farming groups, perhaps comprising only a few extended families. They were built for over 1,000 years, mostly in the later Neolithic and earlier Bronze Age, from around 2500 to 1500BC. The construction phases of individual circles are notoriously hard to date, even after excavation. Material is sometimes recovered from use that spanned hundreds of years, or from after the monument had been transformed into something very different from what was originally intended.

The stone circles we see today are only vestiges of what was once there, some no doubt destroyed before antiquarians were recording ancient sites. We know from archaeological excavations that some stone rings were preceded by others built in timber. In other cases timber rings were never replaced in stone – these were probably common but are often now hard to find. Some sites have central cairns or ring cairns that were fundamental to the design from the outset, while elsewhere small cairns were added later as simple funerary structures. Commonly, circles are only one element within monument complexes with a variety of stone, timber and earthen structures.

In Wessex and southwest England there are large, regularly built circles with carefully spaced stones. These stand in contrast to other rings with irregularly spaced stones that are built to appear roughly circular. Some regions have circles with distinctive architecture, such as the recumbent stone circles of Aberdeenshire with their "altar stones" flanked by tall pillars, and the Clava cairns further north, which feature a stone circle surrounding a chambered cairn or ring cairn. Another particular form is the four-posters of eastern Scotland, with four stones set in a circle or square. On Dartmoor, the distinctive rings at the business end of stone rows stand out from the larger open circles on the moor.

Stone circles were primarily built for the living as gathering places, probably for ceremonies related to the seasons or to the cycle of life, or for communing with the spirits of place. However, it is unlikely that each had one unchanging purpose through time.

MACHRIE MOOR

Megalithic Complex | Nearest Village: **Blackwaterfoot**
Map: **NR 9006 3265** | Sheets: **E361 L69** | Lat: **55.54225N** | Long: **5.32907W**

Machrie Moor is a remarkable place. As well as beautiful views across to Kintyre from some sites, and a wonderful setting amid Arran's hills for the rest, it has such a variety of monuments it's almost like a showroom for stone circles. In addition to the six circles (which had been preceded by timber circles in the same locations) and four chambered cairns (some uncertain), there are field systems, round cairns and hut circles. The larger ancient landscape includes at least a further five stone circles, three stones and one chambered cairn within 5km (3 miles). For example: at NR 9031 3106, 1.6km (1 mile) SSE of Machrie Moor 10, is Tormore 1 chambered cairn; at NR 9244 3225, 2.4km (1½ miles) east of Machrie Moor 10, is Shiskine stone circle; at NR 908 351, 2.6km (just over (1½ miles) NNE of Machrie Moor 10, is Machrie Burn stone circle.

MACHRIE MOOR 10

At NR 9006 3265, this is the first site you reach as you start to traverse the moor. This complex ring cairn has been quite badly robbed for stone and damaged by a track, but is still impressive. Excavation in 1978–9 revealed that it was originally enclosed by a circle of sandstone slabs, of which five remain. Surrounding the circle is a stony bank some 3m (10ft) wide and 0.7m (2ft 3in) high.

MOSS FARM STONE

A fine standing stone at NR 9064 3254, to the left of the main track, the Moss Farm or Machrie Stone is heavily grooved and weathered. It stands close to a modern memorial boulder.

TORMORE 2

As you progress further along the path to the main part of the moor, this chambered cairn is off to the right, at NR 9058 3237. It's badly damaged but the chamber is still visible, measuring around 3 × 0.9m (10 × 3ft) with a fine pair of portal stones to the northeast.

MACHRIE MOOR 5

At NR 9088 3235, overlooking the rest of the moor, is a wonderful pair of concentric circles, made of chunky granite boulders around 0.9m (3ft) to 1.2m (4ft) high. Fingal's Cauldron Seat (Suidhe Coire Fhionn) is the only named monument in the Machrie Moor complex. Look out for the holed stone where, it is said, the giant Fingal tethered his dog, Bran, while he cooked his tea in an enormous cauldron balanced on the circle stones. The inner circle of eight stones is 12m (39ft) in diameter, while the outer circle of 15 stones (including the holed one) is 18m (59ft) across. In 1873 John McArthur recorded the superstition that the holed stone "was believed to contain a fairy or brownie, who could only be propitiated by the pouring of milk through the hole bored in the side of the stone."

MACHRIE MOOR 3

Once there were nine stones in this circle at NR 9101 3245, but only one 4.3m (14ft) giant remains. The broken stumps of several others can be seen, their buried tops and other stones now hidden from view beneath the soil.

MACHRIE MOOR 4

This is a four-poster stone circle at NR 9100 3236, with granite boulders about 0.9m (3ft) high. Aubrey Burl raised the possibility of a fifth stone once existing at the northwest, which would have made this a five-stone circle of the Irish type.

Photo © UKVegan

MACHRIE MOOR 2

At NR 9114 3242 is the most famous of the Machrie Moor circles. Originally there were probably seven or eight tall stones in the 13.7m (45ft) circle, but only three remain intact, great pillars of weathered red sandstone, rising from 3.7m (12ft) to 4.9m (16ft) tall. The stumps of several others can also be seen, as well as two millstones, of a different type of rock, to the southeast, which may have been made from a fallen upright.

MACHRIE MOOR 1

This 11-stone circle, at NR 9120 3240, has alternating sandstone and granite boulders, five of the former and six of the latter. Angela Haggerty found the post-holes of two pre-existing concentric timber circles here, set around a horseshoe of five post-holes, the opening facing northwest. Just outside this opening, post-holes were found of a further, small timber circle that may predate the main timber circles. A further, solitary post-hole was found to the north of the stone circle, between it and Machrie Moor 6.

MACHRIE MOOR 11

This circle, at NR 9122 3242, was more or less completely concealed beneath the peat, before being located by probing and uncovered by Aubrey Burl in 1978–9 (he named it Machrie Moor 11). It's the most easterly circle on the moor, with 10 small stones, all but one of sandstone, in a 13.5 × 12.5m (44 × 41ft) ring. The tallest stone reaches 1.2m (4ft). Between each stone is a pit or post-hole; it is not clear if the timber circle was put up before the stones or if they were contemporaneous.

Photo © Andy Burnham

262

TORRYLIN

Chambered Cairn | Nearest Village: **Lagg**

Map: **NR 9552 2107** | Sheets: **E361 L69** | Lat: **55.44071N** | Long: **5.23420W**

This was probably once a Clyde cairn but stone robbing and the addition of field clearance stones have greatly obscured the original shape of the mound – it's not even possible to say whether there was a forecourt or façade. What can be seen today is a grassy mound with some slabs of the chamber protruding. The side slabs overlap each other where they meet the transverse slabs, a design that was probably intended to help support the roof. An excavation in 1900 found a flint knife, part of a bowl and some human remains here.

Photo © Drew Parsons

"A nice site located a short walk from the village of Lagg, along a well-marked footpath leading toward the coast." Drew Parsons

LARGYBEG POINT   Alt Name: **The Sailor's Grave**

Stone Circle | Nearest Village: **Whiting Bay**

Map: **NS 0536 2334** | Sheets: **E361 L69** | Lat: **55.46505N** | Long: **5.080340W**

Variously described as a stone circle and a stone setting, the two stones on Largybeg Point stand 3m (10ft) apart, apparently aligned with Holy Island in Whiting Bay. One is 1m (3ft 3in) high, the second is about 1.3m (4ft 3in). There's also the possible stump of a third stone, just 0.1m (4in) high, which may be natural. Aubrey Burl suggests these stones may be the remains of a four-poster. A pile of slabs close to the uprights may be the remains of a cist.

Photo © Andy Burnham

GIANTS' GRAVES

Chambered Cairns | Nearest Village: **Whiting Bay**
Map: **NS 0430 2467** | Sheets: **E361 L69** | Lat: **55.4766N** | Long: **5.09806W**

Visiting now it's hard to imagine what this site looked like before the plantation was harvested, and photographs from the early 21st century seem to show somewhere else entirely. The climb up is reasonably hard going but it's worth it for the sweeping views across to Holy Island, and if you go back via the waterfall it makes an excellent circular walk. Both tombs are long cairns of the Clyde cairn type, and quite badly damaged, with the northern, larger tomb in better condition – it's easier to see the horned forecourt leading to the chamber. The fallen capstone features graffiti from the 19th century. Interestingly, the cairns are not aligned in the same direction – the northern tomb has a north–south axis and the southern cairn is at right angles to it. Excavations took place in 1902, when arrowheads, pottery sherds and burnt bone were found, and in 1960. It's believed in some cases the bodies were excarnated (left out to be de-fleshed) before burial.

MONAMORE   Alt Name: **Meallach's Grave**

Chambered Cairn | Nearest Village: **Lamlash**
Map: **NS 0175 2889** | Sheets: **E361 L69** | Lat: **55.51341N** | Long: **5.14139W**

Photo © Jackie Bates

It's a pleasant climb up through the woods to get to this Clyde cairn, high up on the hill with great views of Goat Fell. The tomb has been severely robbed, and the remaining cairn is covered with long grass and bracken. The portal stones are quite impressive, and you can step down into the chamber, which has three compartments and overlapping side panels. The capstones are missing. Excavations in 1961 revealed an impressive forecourt façade, about 8m (26ft) across, consisting of eight uprights set in a shallow curve linked by dry-stone walling. One radiocarbon measurement dated a sample of charcoal fragments to 3160BC. AOC Archaeology have scanned and modelled these cairns; see the Megalithic Portal web page.

LAMLASH   Alt Name: **Blairmore Glen**

Stone Circle | Nearest Village: **Lamlash**
Map: **NS 0188 3342** | Sheets: **E361 L69** | Lat: **55.55410N** | Long: **5.14258W**

You can just about see some of the stones of this four-stone circle from the road, once you know where to look. To access them involves a bit of a fight through the bracken and gorse. The four rounded boulders are large but low, reaching from 0.5m to 1.2m (1ft 8in to 4ft). A central rock-cut cist was opened by James Bryce in 1861 and contained evidence of cremated remains.

GLEN SHIEL
Stone Row | Nearest Town: **Brodick**
Map: **NS 0063 3744** | Sheets: **E361 L69** | Lat: **55.58966N** | Long: **5.16529W**

You can take a rather circuitous walk to find these red sandstone uprights, or pass them on the (one-way) road out from Brodick Castle. The road divides them, with two (3.6m/11ft 9in and 2.3m/7ft 6in tall) in one field and the other (2.5m/8ft 2in tall) across the road. A cist containing a food vessel was found aligned with the stones in 1980.

Nearby | At NS 0100 3661, 970m (over ½ mile) southeast of Glen Shiel, is the **Stronach** standing stone, right by the side of the road out of Brodick.

At NS 0030 3636, 1.2km (¾ mile) SSW of Glen Shiel, is **Stronach Ridge**, where some beautiful rock art is hidden.

Photo © Sandy Gerrard

NORTH SANNOX FARM
Chambered Cairn | Nearest Village: **Sannox**
Map: **NS 0111 4676** | Sheets: **E361 L69** | Lat: **55.67347N** | Long: **5.16442W**

Photo © Andy Burnham

For many years this chambered cairn crouched damply in the forest, green and mossy. The harvesting of the plantation has dramatically changed the setting: now a post-apocalyptic vista of tree stumps has exposed the monument to the sun once more, and revealed the view across to the sea. The badly damaged cairn is around 17 × 14m (56ft × 46ft), having been ploughed over at one end. One chamber is clearly visible. There is a semi-circular platform to the southeast.

Nearby | At NS 0142 4659, 352m (1,155ft) ESE of North Sannox Farm, is a damaged large chambered cairn with one upright remaining. You'll find this one first, as it's close to the car park. The chambered cairn described above is up the hill from this site. Go through the gate in the fence and head to the right up what's left of a twisting, hard-to-see Forestry Commission path.

At NS 0143 4578, in Mid Sannox village and visible from the road, is **Mid Sannox** standing stone, 2.7m (8ft 10in) tall. An 1863 record tells that a double circle of tall standing stones may have existed here until 1836. Just 290m (945ft) ESE of here is another tall stone, **Sannox Bay**, in a private garden.

DRUMTRODDAN

Stone Row | Nearest Village: **Port William**
Map: **NX 3645 4430** | Sheets: **E311 L83** | Lat: **54.76691N** | Long: **4.54375W**

Photo © Martin Dunbar

Originally recorded in the 19th century as a row of four stones, three stones remain today and only one of these is still standing. That one is impressive, however, at over 3m (10ft) tall; the two fallen stones are over 3m (10ft) and 2.7m (9ft) long. Commanding views from here over Dumfries and Galloway, extending across the Machars to the west and as far as the Galloway Hills to the northeast.

Nearby | Around NX 3626 4474, 478m (1,568ft) northwest of the row, are the fine Drumtroddan cup-and-ring carvings. Protected by fencing, these outcrops have at least 84 cup-and-rings. Some cups have up to six rings; others are connected by grooves. Four more groups of motifs are at NX 3628 4472. To the southwest, just inside **Drumtroddan Plantation** at NX 3619 4470, is a panel that includes a cup with four rings.

TORHOUSEKIE Alt Names: **Torhouse Stones, King Gauldus's Tomb**

Stone Circle | Nearest Town: **Wigtown**
Map: **NX 3825 5649** | Sheets: **E311 L83** | Lat: **54.87696N** | Long: **4.52252W**

Photo © Sandy Gerrard

In addition to the beautiful and very accessible stone circle at Torhousekie, which stands beside the B733 in gently rolling farmland, there are also standing stones, a second stone circle, a stone row and cairns, all within a 200m (656ft) radius on the northeast bank of the River Bladnoch.

STONE CIRCLE

There are 19 rounded granite boulders in the circle at NX 3825 5649, graded in height, with the tallest, at 1.4m (4ft 9in), to the ESE. In the centre of the circle are three stones set in a line, which tradition says marks the tomb of King Gauldus. This legendary ruler is thought to be Corbred II, described in George Buchanan's 16th-century *History of Scotland* as the king who fought against the Roman invaders.

STANDING STONES

At NX 3820 5644, 76m (249ft) WSW of the Torhousekie stone circle, are the **Torhousekie West** standing stones with field-clearance rocks (uncertain) between them. Both appear to face the stone circle.

Nearby | Close to the circle and visible from it, on the other side of the road at NX 3838 5651, is the little three-stone row known as **Torhousekie East** or Torhouse East. As it is set on a slightly curving line, it has been suggested these stones may be the remains of a circle. Curiously, when the central stone fell and was re-erected in 1995, archaeological investigation found a possible post-hole, indicating that there may have originally been a timber setting here. At NX 3843 5610, south of the B733 and just off the approach road to Cunninghame Farm, is a standing stone. It's similar in size and shape to the stones of the circle. Cattle are usually kept in this field, which can make it very muddy; the stone can be viewed from the road. To complete this ancient landscape, there are also a number of cairns centred around NX 3817 5665, all just north of the B733 and now very ruined.

MID GLENIRON
Chambered Cairns | Nearest Village: **Glenluce**
Map: **NX 1867 6100** | Sheets: **E310 L82** | Lat: **54.91069N** | Long: **4.83023W**

MID GLENIRON 1

This chambered long (Clyde-type) cairn was constructed in multiple phases. The first, early Neolithic, phase saw the building of a small, oval cairn with a chamber opening from the north. A second cairn was then added in front of the first. A third phase saw the construction of a façade of upright stones; a third chamber was built laterally between the two earlier cairns with its entrance in the west, giving the impression of a long, straight-sided mound with a concave north-facing entrance. In the Bronze Age, nine cremations in funerary urns were placed in the southeastern side of the cairn.

MID GLENIRON 2

At NX 1877 6093, 122m (400ft) ESE of Mid Gleniron 1, is a second multiphase, chambered long cairn: Mid Gleniron 2. Once a free-standing cairn with a small chamber opening towards the east, it was later incorporated into a long cairn with a shallow forecourt at the SSW end. In its final form it measured 14.3m (47ft) in length and up to 12m (39ft) across, but now survives only as a low mound with the remains of a six-stone façade. Neolithic pottery and tools found during the excavation of both cairns can be seen in Dumfries Museum. Another three cairns can be found within a radius of 100m, at NX 1876 6092, NX 1885 6100 and NX 1871 6092.

Nearby | At NX 1984 6441, some 3.6km (2¼ miles) NNE from Gleniron and just off the Southern Upland Way, **Caves of Kilhern** is an example of a Bargrennan-type chambered cairn (see page 268). Although badly damaged, the four chambers are clearly visible and one retains its capstone. It's about 33.5m (110ft) long and up to 1.5m (5ft) tall, and still impressive.

LAGGANGARN
Standing Stones | Nearest Town: **Stranraer**
Map: **NX 2223 7166** | Sheets: **E310 L76** | Lat: **55.00765N** | Long: **4.78137W**

These two prehistoric standing stones are set close together on a low knoll in a forestry clearing on the long-distance, coast-to-coast Southern Upland Way. The sandstone uprights are 1.9m (6ft 2in) and 1.6m (5ft 2in) high respectively, and both stones have been Christianized with 0.6–0.9m (2–3ft) Latin crosses with incised crosslets in the angles on their western faces, in a style associated with the 7th–9th century AD. It's said there were originally 14 stones here, of which seven remained in 1873, the rest apparently reused as gateposts and lintels. A pillar 13.5m (45ft) to the east is said to mark the grave of a farmer who dared to remove some of the stones!

BARGRENNAN WHITE CAIRN Alt Name: **Glentrool**

Chambered Cairn | Nearest Village: **Glentrool**
Map: **NX 3524 7836** | Sheets: **E318 L77** | Lat: **55.07227N** | Long: **4.58199W**

Photo © Debbie Parkes

This chambered round cairn has given its name to the Bargrennan cairn group (as opposed to the more common Clyde-type long cairns), found only in southwest Scotland. About a dozen fit this description, typically with multiple, small, box-like chambers with passages set within round cairns. At present undated, early Bronze Age reuse has been identified at excavated sites. Now set in forestry plantation, the White Cairn is about 13.7m (45ft) across and up to 1.4m (4ft 7in) tall. The chamber and south-facing entrance passage were left open after excavation; a firepit containing cremated bones and oak charcoal were also found. The most recent excavation (2004–5) identified a kerb of stones buried under the collapsed cairn. Check your map reference; there are other White Cairns around here!

BORELAND

Chambered Cairn | Nearest Town: **Newton Stewart**
Map: **NX 4057 6900** | Sheets: **E319 L83** | Lat: **54.98998N** | Long: **4.49342W**

In a clearing in the woods to the north of Newton Stewart, this is a good example of a Clyde-type long cairn. Robbed for road building in the 19th century – it has lost its "horns" and piles of stones prepared for road metal can still be seen next to the cairn today – Boreland is nonetheless an impressive, steep-sided mound of stones some 2m (6½ft) high and 24.5m (80ft) long. It's oriented on a southeast–northwest axis, with the façade at the southeast end. Today, it is topped by a modern marker cairn.

BAGBIE Alt Name: **Kirkmabreck**

Megalithic Complex | Nearest Village: **Carsluith**
Map: **NX 4980 5640** | Sheets: **E311 L83** | Lat: **54.87973N** | Long: **4.34272W**

At Bagbie there is a cairn, a four-poster stone circle and a standing stone, all within around 200m (656ft). The cairn, at NX 4879 5640, is 13.5m (44½ft) across and 1.2m (3ft 11in) high. Two uprights on its eastern side, with a third edge slab to the northeast, are probably the remains of its kerb. The four-poster is at NX 4981 5638, immediately to the northeast, with three small stones still standing. Another standing stone (pictured), 1.6m (5ft 3in) tall, is at NX 4977 5620, 200m (656ft) south of the cairn.

Photo © Ewen Rennie

GLENQUICKEN   Alt Names: **Cambret Moor, Bill Diamond's Bridge**
Stone Circle | Nearest Town: **Creetown**
Map: **NX 5096 5821** | Sheets: **E312 L83** | Lat: **54.896327N** | Long: **4.325583W**

This picturesque stone circle, with dramatic views north toward Cairnsmore and the Minnigaff Hills, was described by Aubrey Burl as "the finest of all centre-stone circles". The 28 low, boulder-like stones are set in a 15.5m (51ft) ring around a central granite pillar, 1.6m (5ft 3in) tall. The tallest stones are in the southeast of the circle, and a gap to the southwest suggests a missing, 29th stone. The central area is cobbled, although overgrown with grass and reeds. In 1850, a second stone circle was recorded 250m (820ft) to the northwest, but no trace of this is now apparent.

CAULDSIDE BURN
Stone Circle and Cairns | Nearest Village: **Anwoth**
Map: **NX 5295 5711** | Sheets: **E312 L83** | Lat: **54.88703N** | Long: **4.29401W**

Photo © Brian Kerr

The 25m (82ft) stone circle has 11 remaining slabs; the largest is only 1.2m (4ft) so they can be hard to find. A slab lying at NX 5298 5723, some 100m (328ft) NNE of the circle, may be an outlier. Under 30m (98ft) NNW of the circle is a well-preserved cairn with a cist at its centre. At NX 5291 5722, 85m (279ft) northwest of the cairn, is a setting of two stones, one upright and the other almost buried in peat. The northernmost cairn, at NX 5290 5725, around 30m (98ft) NNW of the stone setting, is now visible as a hummocky mound, surrounded by a low, stony bank. At its centre is a cist, partially covered by a slab.

Nearby | At NX 5285 5738, 288m (945ft) NNW of the Cauldside Burn circle, is the **Penny Stone**. The impressive rock art here includes a cup-and-ring encircled by a six-circuit spiral 0.6m (2ft) across.

CAIRN HOLY   Alt Names: **Kirkdale, Caldus's Tomb**
Chambered Cairns | Nearest Village: **Carsluith**
Map: **NX 5176 5389** | Sheets: **E312 L83** | Lat: **54.85777N** | Long: **4.31089W**

Famously photogenic, Cairn Holy I and II are a dramatic pair of Clyde-type chambered cairns, set high on the hillside, with great views across Wigtown Bay on a good day.

CAIRN HOLY I

This is the first monument you come to, its curving façade, with eight spectacularly tall, tooth-like stones, approached via a cairn that measures 43 × 10m (141 × 33ft). The large grassy mound is

Photo © Sam Barnes

impressive in itself, but the impact of the portals and horned façade is incredible. The tomb has two chambers, the one at the back sealed off with a large blocking stone, which may have been the original monument, with the second chamber, toweringly portal stones and curving façade added later. A number of important finds here included part of a jadeite axe (now in the Royal Museum of Scotland), as well as Neolithic pottery and a leaf-shaped arrowhead. A large slab in the inner chamber has a multi-ringed cup-mark.

CAIRN HOLY II

Carry on up the track about 150m (492ft) to NX 5182 5405 to see Cairn Holy II, which is less dramatic but only by comparison – at any other site you'd be blown away by the thrusting form of the largest portal stone, and the bed-like capstone now exposed by the erosion of earth covering the cairn. Similar in plan to Cairn Holy I, with a sealed, inner chamber and a second, probably additional chamber, this tomb is in a more dominant position, on a raised knoll. It's also known as Caldus's Tomb, and is another site traditionally believed to be the grave of the mythical Scottish king.

Nearby | At NX 5395 5342, about 2.2km (1¼ miles) east of Cairn Holy, is **High Auchenlarie**, thought to be the remains of a long cairn, the three large standing stones forming part of its façade. More recently it has been suggested that these are simply the remains of two field dykes. However, the arrangement of the stones in an elongated oval around the cairn indicates differently.

HIGH BANKS FARM

Rock Art | Nearest Town: **Kirkcudbright**

Map: **NX 7091 4895** | Sheets: **E312 L84** | Lat: **54.81871N** | Long: **4.01057W**

Photo © Drew Parsons

This 30m (98ft) rock sheet features unusual markings, with some ringed cups set in a mass of single cups that create an appealing "dimpled" effect. Casts of this remarkable rock as well as others nearby are exhibited in the Stewartry Museum in Kircudbright.

Nearby | At NX 6424 4714, 6.9km (4¼ miles) west of High Banks, is **Clauchandolly 1**, a fine rock art panel decorated with three cup-and-ring marks and an oval cartouche-like motif. At NX 6447 4722, 243m (979ft) ENE of Clauchandolly 1, is **Clauchandolly 8**, with three cup-and-ring motifs all in a line. There are several other panels to be explored in the same area west and southwest of the Smithy.

Dowsing at Cairn Holy

Angie Lake

I dowsed Cairn Holy 1 and 2 for ceremonial movement in June 2002. Curious as to how these monuments were originally used, in 1999 I began to ask: "Please show me how the original builders moved during their most important ceremonies at the height of this site's importance." I find dowsing this way can highlight unnoticed parts of a monument that could be important, and the most revered stone or landscape alignment.

My method is to relax, then focus on "being in" those ancient times, while asking to be shown, via the L-shaped copper rods, what I need to learn. Holding the rods in the "search" position (pointing forward, held comfortably at waist level, at right angles to my body), I walk across the forecourt of a tomb, asking for the beginning of a ceremony. The rods move to indicate where this starts. I make an on-site sketch while following all the rods' movements to subsequent positions in the processional route, using different colours to illustrate overlapping routes taken and numbering them in sequence, with different colours used to signify numbers in different dowses (in the diagram, right, my first dowse is numbered in black; the second in red.)

In *Britain 3000 BC*, Rodney Castleden featured a diagram of the building sequence at a Clyde-type chambered cairn, using Cairn Holy 1 as an example: the initial construction of an uncovered cist and façade was followed by the covering of the cairn with a mound of stone. This made me realize why my two dowses there may have had separate, but both important, focal points. As the book was not published until 2003, I could not have been influenced by it. Had I discovered a longer dedication ceremony (red numbers), in which an important person was buried at the tomb's creation? And did the shorter ceremony (black numbers) reflect a final closing ritual, after the tomb had been covered over?

I found the report on the 1949 excavations at Cairn Holy 1 and 2 in 2017. Comparing my dowsing plans with those detailed 1949 forecourt plans, I was intrigued by how close my recorded movements were to the discovered ritual deposits and hearths, also circuiting a spot opposite the tomb's entrance, at the apex of the arc of movement around the forecourt, where archaeologists had recorded a standing stone and a hearth … as if I truly *had* followed the path of that ancient priest.

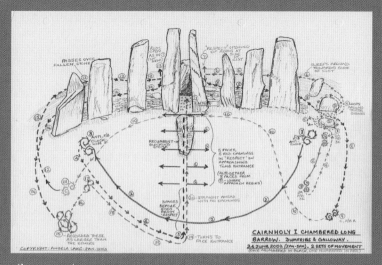

Ceremonies dowsed by Angie Lake at Cairn Holy

TWELVE APOSTLES (NEWBRIDGE)

Stone Circle | Nearest Village: **Newbridge**
Map: **NX 9470 7940** | Sheets: **E321 L84** | Lat: **55.0978N** | Long: **3.6517W**

> "When I first saw this circle in 1992, it was divided in two by a low hedge, the remains of which can still be seen today. Easily accessible, with a gate into the field." Anne Tate

One of Britain's largest stone circles, the Twelve Apostles are set in an important landscape of Neolithic monuments, including two cursuses (visible as cropmarks on aerial photographs), ring ditches, enclosures and mounds. It's an impressively spacious, flattened circle some 80m (262ft) in diameter, its sheer size making it difficult to photograph all at once, with large, solid-looking stones up to 1.9m (6ft) tall. Five stones are still upright of the 11 that remain, a 12th stone having been removed before 1837. All the stones are set with their flat faces in a line with the circumference. Intriguingly, in 1975 it was observed that half of this ring of stones is a true circle with a diameter of 89m (292ft); the other is the arc of a much larger circle, drawn from a point on the circumference of the first. (Note: there is another stone circle of the same name in Yorkshire, see page 161.)

LOUPIN' STANES & GIRDLE STANES

Stone Circles | Nearest Village: **Eskdalemuir**
Map: **NY 2570 9663** | Sheets: **E323 L79** | Lat: **55.25822N** | Long: **3.17057W**

The Loupin' Stanes and the Girdle Stanes are accessed from the same car park. From the Loupin' Stanes you can walk to the Girdle Stanes, either beside the river or across the fields following the route of what may have once been an avenue or stone row – or merely fortunately placed erratics.

LOUPIN' STANES

At NY 2570 9663, this lovely, small circle is nestled on pastureland just to the south of a bend in the White Esk. The 12 low stones form a flattened circle, 11.5 × 10.3m (37ft 8in × 33ft 9in) across. An "entrance" is apparently formed by two taller pillars, 1.6m (5ft 3in) high. The circle's name comes from the local story that "lads, and even a lass" would leap from one pillar to the other (at 2.5m/8ft apart, this seems unlikely!). The low, stony bank on which the stones are set may be field clearance.

Photo © Howard Mattinson

GIRDLE STANES

On the bank of the White Esk at NY 2535 9615, this evocative circle has lost its western stones to the river (several can be seen on the riverbed). Eleven fallen stones and 13 standing stones survive, the tallest about 1.6m (5ft 3in) and the longest fallen stone around 2m (6½ft). The platform on which the stones stand may be a plantation bank or the result of field clearance. A good photograph can be taken from the stile on the walk.

Hidden Evidence: The Lochbrow Project

Kirsty Millican, Historic Environment Scotland

An apparently featureless cow field, Lochbrow is nonetheless one of my favourite archaeological sites in Scotland. Cropmarks, formed by the differential growth of crops over buried archaeology, are best captured from the air, and were first recorded at Lochbrow in 1992, indicating the presence of pits and ditches. These can be interpreted as a timber cursus monument (usually dating to the earlier Neolithic), at least one, if not two, timber circles (dating from the later Neolithic into the Bronze Age) and several round barrows (later prehistoric monuments). This was clearly an important location for a long time.

If you visit the site today (at NY 0951 8935) there is nothing to see. The cursus and timber circles were built of wood, so all that remains are the infilled pits dug to take the upright timbers. The cropmarks give us a rare glimpse into the activities of, and structures built by, our prehistoric ancestors – without aerial photography we would know nothing about this important group of monuments. A lot can be learned about sites like these by considering their place in the landscape. At Lochbrow the cursus in particular seems to mimic the dominant topography. By visiting the site it's been possible to suggest that the topography of this location likely influenced the use and functioning of these monuments, and perhaps the form they took. Ongoing work here involves investigating the possibility of additional sites and features not recorded by the cropmarks. Results so far are promising, and I'm excited by the notion that so much lies buried beneath our feet. With perseverance we may be able to add more to the story of this site.

BALLOCHMYLE ★

Rock Art | Nearest Village: **Mauchline**
Map: **NS 5112 2556** | Sheets: **E327 L70** | Lat: **55.50111N** | Long: **4.35863W**

This large, vertical, red sandstone rockface overlooking a tributary of the River Ayr contains some absolutely amazing and unusual rock art. Carved from the Neolithic to the Bronze Age, the art was only discovered in 1986 during vegetation clearance. There are several hundred cup-and-rings, many with deep cups and multiple rings, unusual square cups, ringed stars and curvilinear grooves. There is also modern graffiti. The site is near a quarry, just over 200m (656ft) south of the A76 and 260m (853ft) northeast of Ballochmyle Viaduct. There is a long stretch of cliff face at this location, and the site is subject to seasonal water flow, so GPS is recommended to find it.

Photo © Brian Kerr

BURGH HILL Alt Name: **Dod Burn**

Stone Circle | Nearest Village: **Skelfhill**

Map: **NT 4701 0624** | Sheets: **E331 L79** | Lat: **55.34731N** | Long: **2.83714W**

In an area full of hill forts and prehistoric settlements, mostly Iron Age, it's nice to find this little egg-shaped circle, 16.5 × 13.4m (54 × 44ft). Thirteen stones remain standing of the 25 on site – none of them very large, ranging from a couple of centimetres to 0.8m (2ft 8in) above ground, and most with

their wider face aligned on the egg-shaped perimeter. One of the prostrate stones is much larger, at 1.5m (5ft) long. Fine views to the Lammermuir Hills some 48km (30 miles) away. A good farm track takes you up almost to this stone setting.

Nearby | At NT 4681 0616, just 215m (705ft) further up the hill from Burgh Hill circle, the well-preserved **Burgh Hill** hill fort has magnificent 360-degree views and two massive ramparts with external ditches. There is evidence of a secondary settlement in the northeastern half of the interior, where hut circles can be seen, along with a standing stone.

If you're heading up to Burgh Hill from Hawick you may pass **Lord's Tree**, a damaged but still impressive cairn about 10m (33ft) across, its circular banks still remaining, at NT 4809 0957. The name was already traditional by the mid-19th century, but there's no tree here now. Within sight, on the opposite side of the road, is **Ca Knowe**, thought to be an ancient burial mound, and traditionally the site of the reading of the burgess roll after the perambulation of the marches.

DERE STREET	Alt Name: **Black Knowe Cairn**
Round Cairn and Standing Stone	Nearest Village: **Hownam**
Map: **NT 7506 1552**	Sheets: **OL16 L80**	Lat: **55.432930N**	Long: **2.395676W**

To make a day of it, start from the well-preserved hill fort Woden's Law (at NT 7677 1254), then walk along Dere Street Roman road to visit Pennymuir Roman camps, Falla Knowe cairn (an insignificant monument to the left of the track at NT 7471 1475, with a fence post in its middle), Dere Street cairn, Black Knowe standing stone, Trestle cairn and the stone circle Five Stanes. For a shorter visit, start from Falla Knowe.

Photo © Anne Tate

DERE STREET CAIRN AND STANDING STONE

At NT 7506 1552, to the left of the Roman road and just over the dry-stone wall, is Dere Street (also known as Black Knowe) cairn, measuring about 9m (29½ft) across and just 0.6m (2ft) high. Five boulders lie on its edge, with four more nearby, presumably removed from the cairn. Across the line of Dere Street, some 70m (230ft) to the east of this cairn, you will see the Black Knowe standing stone, at NT 7513 1554. While this stands only 0.75m (2½ft) high and looks like a natural boulder, it is likely to be a companion to the outlying stones of the cairn. Close by are five broken fragments of the same type of stone as the main stone; it's impossible to tell if they were broken from it.

TRESTLE CAIRN

At NT 7518 1612, Trestle (also known as Dere Street II and Plea Shank) is more a cairn than a stone circle and, while badly damaged in antiquity, is still an impressive site in a lovely ridge location. There are 17 stones (only two still earthfast) within the now demolished cairn, with another 15 broken stones scattered around the site. The two largest stones stand 0.75m (2½ft) tall.

FIVE STANES

Also known as Dere Street III, the Five Stanes circle is at NT 7526 1686, with five stones of which three are still standing. It's a small circle, about 6m (20ft) in diameter, with the biggest stone being 0.85m (2ft 10in). The moorland setting is lovely. Another three stones, some 15.5m (50ft) to the east, may originally have been part of the circle.

THE GLEBE STONE
Standing Stone | Nearest Village: **Yarrow**
Map: **NT 3526 2760** | Sheets: **E337 L73** | Lat: **55.53783N** | Long: **3.02734W**

Photo © Ewen Rennie

Sited in a field just north of Yarrow Water and south of Whitehope Burn, the Glebe Stone is one of three stones close together just west of Yarrow village. It's a chunky stone, about 1.4m (4½ft) tall and up to 1.2m (4ft) wide. There are two possible cup-marks on one side. It was reported that a cairn containing skeletal remains once surrounded the stone, but there is no evidence of this today.

Nearby | At NT 3481 2744, 482m (1,581ft) WSW of the Glebe Stone, is the **Yarrow Stone**; human bones are said to have been found buried underneath in about 1803. The skeletal remains are interesting in light of the 6th-century Latin inscription on one face: "This is the everlasting memorial. In this place lie the most famous princes Nudus and Dumnogenus. In this tomb lie the two sons of Liberalis." Later in the 19th century, it was moved to Bowhill, then subsequently returned, having been marked by the chains used to move it.

At NT 3545 2775, 238m (780ft) ENE of the Glebe Stone, is the 1.6m (5ft 3in) **Warrior's Rest** (Annan Street) stone, in the garden of the cottage named after it and viewable from the gate. Long stone cists found close by indicate that this stone marked the site of an early Christian cemetery. Bronze Age finds indicate that the area had been used for burial over many centuries. In 2003, two previously unremarked cup-marks were found on the eastern side of the stone.

STOBO KIRK
Possible Standing Stone | Nearest Village: **Stobo**
Map: **NT 1826 3765** | Sheets: **E336 L72** | Lat: **55.62557N** | Long: **3.29965W**

One of the oldest churches in the Borders, and the most important church in the Upper Tweed valley in medieval times, this is famously the site where St Kentigern was supposed to have converted Merlin to Christianity. A number of possible standing stones built into the walls of the church include a long, horizontally placed stone in the west wall of the north aisle.

Photo © Nicola Didsbury

SHERIFFMUIR

Standing Stones | Nearest Town: **Peebles**
Map: **NT 2010 4006** | Sheets: **E336 L72** | Lat: **55.64748N** | Long: **3.27115W**

Standing just west of where Lyne Water joins the River Tweed, this is a pair of standing stones, about 2.2m (7ft) apart and aligned north–south. The northern stone is 1.2m (4ft) tall and the southern 1.3m (4ft 3in). Apparently there used to be further stones, about 0.3m (1ft) high, on a curving line running east, but there's no sign of them now.

> "The menhirs are also known as Arthur and Merlin."
> Austen John Reid

BROTHERS' STONES

Standing Stones | Nearest Village: **Smailholm**
Map: **NT 6190 3600** | Sheets: **E339 L74** | Lat: **55.61609N** | Long: **2.60645W**

This pair of standing stones are prominently sited, straddling the summit of Brotherstone Hill, and seem to be aligned with the Cow Stone further down the hill (see below). The southeast stone is 2.5m (8ft); the other, 14m (46ft) away, is just under 2m (6½ft) high.

Nearby | At NT 6216 3620, some 350m (1,148ft) ENE of the Brothers' Stones and clearly visible from there, is the **Cow Stone**, also known as Brotherstone Hill standing stone. It's an irregularly shaped, squarish stone, about 2 × 2m wide (6½ × 6½ft).

At NT 5966 3973, 4.3km (2¾ miles) northwest of the Brothers' Stones, is the 1.6m (5ft) **Purveshaugh** (Earlston) standing stone, sited against a wall a short way off the road. It has its own sign proclaiming it a "standing stone" and is a bit battered and misshapen, with good views of the Eildon Hills beyond.

NINE STONES RIG   Alt Names: **Johnscleugh, Crow Stones**

Stone Circle | Nearest Village: **Cranshaws/Danskine**
Map: **NT 6254 6549** | Sheets: **E345 L67** | Lat: **55.88109N** | Long: **2.60035W**

This jumble of nine boulder-like stones in the Lammermuir Hills of East Lothian once formed a circle about 6.4m (21ft) in diameter. In 1979, a stone was placed in an empty hole (it was possibly the hole's original occupant). Local tradition held that treasure had been hidden in the circle, which might explain the less than pristine state of the place; according to an 1853 record, "various attempts, all unsuccessful, have been made to find it."

Photo © Ewen Rennie

EASTER BROOMHOUSE
Standing Stone | Nearest Town: **Dunbar**
Map: **NT 6801 7662** | Sheets: **E351 L67** | Lat: **55.98144N** | Long: **2.51428W**

Fine sea views across the fields from this 2.7m (9ft) red sandstone stone with three cup-marks on the western side. At its foot you can see deeply carved grooves caused by the cable of a steam plough.

Nearby | At NT 6168 7760, 6.4km (4 miles) west of the Easter Broomhouse stone, is **Kirklandhill** standing stone, a rugged 3.4m (11ft) upright in arable land just to the east of the A199/A198 junction.

CAIY STANE Alt Name: **Camus Stone**
Standing Stone | Nearest City: **Edinburgh (Fairmilehead)**
Map: **NT 2424 6836** | Sheets: **E350 L66** | Lat: **55.90234N** | Long: **3.21319W**

Photo © Diarmid Mogg

This impressive, 2.75m (9ft 3in) red sandstone monolith has six weathered but still visible cup-marks 0.5m (1½ft) from the ground on its eastern side (away from the road). Today it stands captive in a cobbled semi-circle on Caiystane View in south Edinburgh, but the hillside on which it stands was used in the Bronze Age; in 1840, a Mr Stuart recorded that "hundreds of skeletons were at that time found whilst making the roads".

Nearby | At NT 2450 6923, 909m (just over ½ mile) NNE of the Caiy Stane, is the small **Buck Stane**. The **Cat Stane** is at NT 2745 7068, in the suburb of Inch and 4km (just under 2½ miles) ENE of the Caiy Stane. At NT 2828 7050, in Midlothian and 4.6km (2¾ miles) ENE of the Caiy Stane, is the **Ravenswood Avenue** standing stone.

HULY HILL Alt Name **Newbridge**
Standing Stones & Round Cairn | Nearest Village: **Newbridge**
Map: **NT 1234 7261** | Sheets: **E350 L65** | Lat: **55.93851N** | Long: **3.40486W**   Kenneth Brophy

Huly Hill sits west of the junction of the A8 and the M8/M9, under the flightpath of Edinburgh Airport. To the south, a small service area with a petrol station and a McDonald's. To the north, a series of luxury car showrooms. Industrial units abound. It's a Ballardian dystopia, the monument trapped amid the infrastructure of the car. Surprisingly little is known about this setting of three standing stones, with a circular barrow, tumulus or cairn offset. About 30m (98ft) in diameter, it rises to a height of 3m (10ft), having been "tidied up" with a modern wall at some point since it was dug into by Daniel Wilson in 1830. A bronze "spearhead" or dagger was found along with fragments of bone and charcoal. When Fred Coles surveyed the monument in 1899, he was "unable to ascertain the true extent or location of this excavation, or the fate of the contents". It was thought possible that the three remaining standing stones were once part of a circle, but geophysical surveys in the 1970s and 2000s confirm there have only ever been three, and no ditch, either. Two stones are 2m (6½ft) tall and the third 1.3m (4ft 3in). East of the motorway, 320m (1,050ft) away on an industrial estate, at NT 1265 7262, is a fourth stone, 3m (10ft) high, which may, or may not, be connected to the site. There is no interpretation board or sign, and apparently no expectation that anyone will visit, although thousands of drivers and passengers must see this site every day, as do people at an adjacent bus stop, dog walkers, burger-munchers at McDonald's and the pilots of the planes that fly over it. The stones and encircling wall are subject to graffiti, crowded out by the modern world. It takes an effort of will to imagine what this monument might once have been like: a place of death and memory. Now it is a place of lorries, fast food wrappers and paint.

Top 10 Urban Prehistory Sites

Kenneth Brophy, Senior Lecturer in Archaeology, University of Glasgow

1. The Calderstones, Liverpool: The monument was dismantled, moved and re-erected in a confused roadside arrangement in the 19th century, then moved again (twice) in the 1950s into a greenhouse, before going into storage in 2017 ahead of a grand re-erection beside Calderstones Mansion House.

2. Balfarg, Glenrothes, Fife: One of the largest henge monuments in Scotland and now, along with two standing stones and some cut-down telegraph poles, the reconstructed centrepiece of a 1980s housing estate.

3. The Stone of Mannan, Clackmannan: A huge standing stone with a smaller stone fixed on top located beside a tollbooth, moved there in 1833 from a more rural location in Lookabootye Brae; it looks like a huge penis.

4. Ravenswood Avenue standing stone, Edinburgh: A standing stone that as recently as 1903 was surrounded by fields and grazing cattle but is now trapped in a cage on the pavement in a 1930s housing estate.

5. Sandy Road, Perth: This kerbed cairn was excavated in the 1960s, removed ahead of housing development, then reconstructed in its original location in the form of a garden landscaped stone circle in a cul de sac.

6. Huly Hill, Newbridge, Edinburgh: A landscaped barrow with three satellite standing stones situated beside a service station and major motorway intersection, and beneath the flightpath of Edinburgh Airport.

7. King Arthur's Round Table, Penrith: Henge monument near Penrith that was drawn fancifully by Stukeley and then converted into a tea garden by the owner of the neighbouring Crown Inn in the 19th century.

8. The Dagon Stone, Darvel, Ayrshire: A weird stone topped with a stone ball; it has been moved at least three times since prehistory, was once covered in paint by Ludovic Mann and now sits across from a Chinese takeaway.

9. Carreg Coetan Arthur, Pembrokeshire: Portal dolmen situated amid a very middle-class bungaloid area of the village of Newport, overlooked by gardens and constantly monitored by men of a certain age mowing their lawns and washing their 4 × 4s.

10. The Cochno Stone, Clydebank: One of the largest rock art panels in Britain, painted in five colours by Ludovic Mann in 1937, then covered with dozens of scratched names like a huge stone visitor book, it was buried by the authorities in 1965 but never forgotten.

CAIRNPAPPLE HILL

Round Cairn | Nearest Village: **Torphichen**
Map: **NS 9872 7175** | Sheets: **E349 L65** | Lat: **55.92811N** | Long: **3.62251W**

Photo © Anne Tate

Impressive views at Cairnpapple Hill, West Lothian: on a clear day, you can see from Bass Rock in the North Sea to Goatfell (Arran's highest peak) and the mountains of Arran in the Firth of Clyde, south to the Border hills, and northwest beyond Stirling to the Trossachs and Schiehallion. This is one of mainland Scotland's most important archaeological sites, in use as a place of ritual and burial for over 4,000 years. It developed over five different phases, indicating the enduring significance of this place. In the first phase, a simple cremation cemetery had seven small pits in an arc. In the second phase, a henge was built as well as an oval setting of 24 standing stones. In the third phase, *c.* 1800–1700BC, the standing stones were taken down and a cairn was built to cover two central cists. The fourth phase involved enlarging the cairn to twice its original diameter, with the first-phase pits making up its western arc. The fifth and final phase is represented by four extended burials, aligned almost east–west; these have been dated to the Iron Age or first century AD, and are reminiscent of early Christian burials. The two cist burials have been covered by a modern casing, creating the appearance of a huge tumulus. Access to the inside of the chamber is via a steep ladder with handrail.

Nearby | At NS 9684 7250, 2km (1¼ miles) WNW of Cairnpapple Hill, is the enigmatic **Torphichen Stone**, also known as the Sanctuary or Refuge Stone. Standing in the churchyard, this small, squarish stone is believed to be prehistoric, and possibly from Cairnpapple. It has a number of cup-marks on the east face; on the top is an incised cross. Said to have been reused in the 4th century by St Ninian and, by the Irish St Feichin or Fechin during the 6th–7th century, it is thought to have marked a place of sanctuary. Other stones believed to have marked the boundaries of the sanctuary area include the **Gormyre Stone** (at NS 9806 7311) and the **Westfield Farm Refuge Stone** (at NS 9437 7211).

NORMANGILL

Henge | Nearest Village: **Crawford**
Map: **NS 9710 2153** | Sheets: **E329 L72** | Lat: **55.48205N** | Long: **3.62739W**

Despite the road (originally a railway track) running right through it, removing a strip about 11m (36ft) wide, this henge in South Lanarkshire is one of Scotland's best examples of a Class II henge (one with two diametrically opposed entrances). Although you could probably drive through it without noticing, once you know it's there the banks and internal ditch are clear to see. It's about 61 × 55m (200 × 180ft) across and has two unusually wide entrances, each measuring 23m (75ft) across at the gap in the bank, and 17m (55ft) at the gap in the ditch.

The Lives of Stones

Anne Tate, Anglo-Saxon sculptured stone and rock art enthusiast

While the original significance of standing stones may be lost, they are an enduring reminder of long-vanished people and cultures. The Megalithic Portal bears witness to what can happen when time erodes meaning, with horror stories of stones broken up for building material, and stone circles, such as Kemp Howe in Shap, blown up or dragged aside to make way for modern developments; others were destroyed for fear of superstition and magic, cutting the past from the present.

Some stones have had a gentler transition through time, undergoing a process of continuous adaptation and change, in which their purpose was amended and enhanced to give them new life and meaning. Megaliths often dominate their setting, demanding attention, and many ancient sites have been reused because of their special significance – Cairnpapple in West Lothian was a henge in 3000BC, by 2000BC it was a burial complex, and in 1000AD it was used by early Christians – each reuse adding a layer of significance.

As Christianity took hold in Britain during the 3rd and 4th centuries AD, people reused standing stones as memorials, assimilating ancient beliefs to magnify their own. In Powys, Maen Madoc, standing next to the Sarn Helen Roman road, was recarved to mark a Christian burial, and bears a probable 6th-century Latin epitaph to "Dervacus, son of Justus". The Four Pillar Stones near Pontfaen in Pembrokeshire each bear an incised cross of different design; the Laggangarn stones in Dumfries and Galloway are both carved with a Latin cross. In Ireland, the 5m (16ft) prehistoric Doonfeeny Pillar in County Mayo was recut with two Christian crosses. By permanently rededicating a pagan stone to God, it was given a double meaning, perhaps more symbolic than its destruction would have been.

Crosses were added to existing standing stones to signal them as way-markers and as places to give thanks, an example being Bennet's Cross in Devon, a 1.7m (5½ft) tall standing stone that was modified in the 15th century. Many stones were reused as gateposts or rubbing stones. Others have been moved into churchyards or churches, even being incorporated into their fabric. The 12th-century Stobo Kirk, in the Scottish Borders, may have one or more standing stones in its external walls. Similarly, the church of St Mael and St Sulien in Denbighshire not only has a standing stone built into the east wall of the porch but also hosts several ancient crosses, one with a possibly cup-marked base.

As land boundaries became more defined, stones such as Bennet's Cross and Bedd Morris in Cwm Gwaun, Pembrokeshire were co-opted and re-inscribed as parish boundary markers. In more recent times, the Victorians enthusiastically relocated standing stones and burial chambers – the Wallington Hall stone in Northumberland was uprooted from a nearby Bronze Age cairn in the 19th century and used to dress a garden pond.

And so the lives of stones continue, with a number of recently erected stone circles, and modern megaliths occasionally used as grave markers, such as those in Kensal Green Cemetery. Cut from stone to replicate the past, but living far into the future.

Nearby | At NS 9709 2153, some 600m (1,968ft) SSW of Normangill henge, is a ruined cairn on a crest of **Normangill Rig**. A 19th-century record states that most of the stones in the cairn were reused to build field walls in 1855; at the same time, "the bones of a man of large stature" were uncovered. It's still around 26m (85ft) across and 2m (6½ft) tall, with a dry-stone wall forming a large, semi-circular loop around the cairn.

SIGHTHILL PARK Alt Name: **Springburn Stones**
Modern Stone Circle | Nearest City: **Glasgow**
Map: **NS 5969 6642** | Sheets: **E342 L64** | Lat: **55.87045N** | Long: **4.24394W**

Although modern circles are not usually featured in this guide to Neolithic and Bronze Age sites, Sighthill is included here as Scotland's best-known modern stone circle and the first astronomically aligned circle to be built in the UK in over 3,000 years. It was constructed in the late 1970s by amateur astronomer and science writer Duncan Lunan and the Glasgow Parks Astronomy Project, to represent the rising and setting of the sun and moon across Glasgow. Although the project was never fully completed, the stones (from Beltmoss quarry in Kilsyth) all still exist. Sighthill Park is currently undergoing redevelopment and the circle was taken down in April 2016. It is due to be re-erected in the new park, on the original choice of site, which was previously unsuitable due to the tower blocks interfering with the sightlines. Now the blocks have gone, and the circle should be in place by 2019.

THE COCHNO STONE Alt Name: **Whitehill 1**
Rock Art | Nearest City: **Glasgow**
Map: **NS 5045 7388** | Sheets: **E342 L64** | Lat: **55.93464N** | Long: **4.39559W**

Photo © Cezary Namirski

The Cochno Stone (the name coming from the Gaelic for "little cups") is one of the most spectacular and extensive panels of rock art in Britain. It's located in an urban park in Faifley, a housing estate in Clydebank, but you won't be able to see it because, apart from a few brief days in 2015 and 2016, it has been buried beneath a protective 1m (3ft 3in) layer of soil and turf since 1965. The undulating surface of the soft gritstone (sandstone) outcrop, about 15 × 8m (50 × 26ft), is covered in scores of cup-marks, cup-and-ring marks, spirals and other unusual motifs including an incised cross and two four-toe footprints. The 2016 excavation resulted in a very high-resolution scan of the stone, which will be used to create a replica to be displayed on site.

Nearby | Although the Cochno Stone has now been re-covered, there are other cup-and-ring marked rocks within 1km (0.6 miles) to explore: **Auchnacraig 1** at NS 5028 7365; **Auchnacraig 4** at NS 5029 7362; **Whitehill 3** at NS 5115 7386; **Whitehill 4** at NS 5130 7398; and **Whitehill 5** at NS 5138 7403.

GRANNY KEMPOCK Alt Names: **The Kempock Stone, The Lang Stane of Gourock**
Standing Stone | Nearest Town: **Gourock**
Map: **NS 2408 7786** | Sheets: **E341 L63** | Lat: **55.96139N** | Long: **4.81982W**

Nowadays surrounded by buildings and set behind railings, this 1.8m (6ft) tall mica-schist standing stone would once have been in a prominent position on the clifftop overlooking Kempock Point. Its resemblance to a hooded figure is what lies behind the evocative name "Granny Kempock". It's said that those about to embark on a sea voyage would walk round the stone seven times, chanting a verse requesting good fortune and safe passage; and newly-weds would also pass round the stone for good luck and a happy marriage. In 1662, one Mary Lamont, who was later burned as a witch, confessed to planning with others to throw it in the sea.

Photo © Peggy Edwards

RANDOLPHFIELD
Standing Stones | Nearest City: **Stirling**
Map: **NS 7944 9244** | Sheets: **E366 L57** | Lat: **56.10945N** | Long: **3.94019W**

Outside the main police station in Stirling, these two stones are 1.2m (4ft) and 1.1m (3ft 8in) high and about 45m (147ft) apart. Thought to be prehistoric, local tradition has long linked them to a skirmish fought in 1314 on the eve of the Battle of Bannockburn between Sir Thomas Randolph, Earl of Moray, and an English force. At least one of the stones was moved to this site before the police station was built. The larger stone shows signs of having been cut and re-cemented back together. No prehistoric material was found when the site was excavated in 2014.

DOUNE Alt Name: **Glenhead Farm**
Stone Row | Nearest Village: **Doune**
Map: **NN 7549 0046** | Sheets: **E366 L57** | Lat: **56.18042N** | Long: **4.00737W**

Originally thought to be part of a larger monument, this alignment of three prehistoric stones extends for 9m (29½ft). The central stone is 1.2m (4ft) high and has more than 20 cup-marks on both its top and western side (although some are hard to see), and is flanked by two leaning stones that would be about 2m (6½ft) tall if upright. A block at the northern end of the alignment may have split off

Photo © Sandy Gerrard

the northernmost stone. Park at the David Stirling SAS memorial opposite. The row is in an arable field, so access is not available when crops are growing.

SHERIFF MUIR ROW   Alt Names: **Wallace Stone, Lairhill**
Stone Row | Nearest Town: **Dunblane**
Map: **NN 8324 0226** | Sheets: **E366 L57** | Lat: **56.19857N** | Long: **3.88344W**

Photo © Sandy Gerrard

This 68m (223ft) row is aligned southwest–northeast and includes five stones, although it's thought that one stone might be missing from the alignment. The Wallace Stone is 1.8m (6ft) high and the only one still standing; another stone has 19 cup-marks. This was the site of a battle in 1715 and it is also traditionally believed to have been the gathering place for Scottish troops before the Battle of Stirling Bridge (1297).

> **"This alignment once stood beside the major routeway from Stirling toward the north of Scotland. It is probable that this was also a significant prehistoric routeway."** Sandy Gerrard

KINNELL PARK   Alt Name: **Achmore**   ★
Stone Circle | Nearest Village: **Killin**
Map: **NN 5770 3280** | Sheets: **OL48 L51** | Lat: **56.4658N** | Long: **4.31125W**

A delightful circle in parkland southeast of the River Dochart, overlooking the confluence of the Dochart and the Lochay, and the western end of Loch Tay, where steeply sloping woodland forms a sheltered bowl. It's just 10m (33ft) across, with six stones between 1.4m (4ft 7in) and 2m (6½ft) in height. The northernmost stone has three cup-marks on the top. The circle's air of tidy perfection must have been appreciated by the owners of Kinnell House – the Macnabs of Macnab – in the days when an antiquarian feature was a must-have for a country estate.

Photo © Roger K. Read

Nearby | About 5.4km (3.3 miles) WNW of Kinnell, at **Duncroisk**, in Glen Lochay, there's a long, prominent, ridge of quartzite schist rock outcrop centred at NN 5322 3582, with eight groups of cups and rings. The largest rings are 0.25m (9in) in diameter; one rock has 58 cups and another has 60. There are around 200 motifs in total.

More rock art can be found nearby: **Duncroisk 2** at NN 5313 3584; **Corrycharmaig East 4** at NN 5310 3582; **Corrycharmaig East 2** at NN 5294 3588; **Corrycharmaig 3** at NN 5278 3549; **Duncroisk 1** at NN 5311 3640.

TUILYIES Alt Name: **Torryburn**
Stone Setting | Nearest Village: **Tuilyies**
Map: **NT 0291 8658** | Sheets: **E367 L65** | Lat: **56.06217N** | Long: **3.56084W**

An unusual setting of four stones, with a 2.4m (8ft) tall standing stone accompanied by three smaller boulders arranged in a triangle just to its south. The spectacular standing stone has many cup-marks on the eastern face, and deep, weathered grooves cut by the rain.

BALBIRNIE Alt Name: **Druid's Circle**
Cairn Circle | Nearest Town: **Glenrothes**
Map: **NO 2859 0297** | Sheets: **E370 L59** | Lat: **56.21391N** | Long: **3.15298W**

Moved from its original site, 125m (410ft) to the northwest, when the A92 in Fife was widened, and reconstructed to the same layout, this is an interesting, easy-to-visit suburban stone circle. A multiphase site with activity beginning *c.* 3000 BC, the earliest phase was the circle of eight standing stones (of an original 10) associated with mostly female cremation burials. The cist burials within the circle are later (the cup-and-ring-marked cist stone is a replica). Cremated bones, a jet button and beads, a food vessel and a flint knife were found during excavations. The final phase saw the interior of the circle filled with cairn material, which contained sherds of cinerary urns and cremated bone.

BALFARG
Henge | Nearest Town: **Glenrothes**
Map: **NO 2820 0312** | Sheets: **E370 L59** | Lat: **56.21524N** | Long: **3.15929W**

Not far from Balbirnie is the equally suburban Balfarg henge. The site began life *c.* 4000BC when pits were dug to hold sherds of pottery, burnt wood and bone. Later came a 60m (196ft) ditched causewayed enclosure, one of

Photo © Sandy Gerrard

Scotland's largest henge earthworks, with a setting of 16 massive posts up to 4m (13ft) tall. Concentric interior post and stone arrangements are complex, with evidence for multiple timber circles, and it may be that one or more stone circles were then added, of which one stone remains today. The other stone on the site, offset from the circle, is considered to be an entrance marker. The final phase saw a burial in the henge centre, with a beaker and a flint knife, marked today by a flat stone. The site has been sympathetically developed, posts indicating the position of the timber setting.

Nearby | At NO 2848 0314, 282m (925ft) east of Balfarg henge, is the **Balfarg Riding School** mortuary enclosure and henge. Wooden posts show the positions of post-holes. The second of two timber structures on the site was later covered by a mound and a ditch cut around it.

LUNDIN LINKS   Alt Name: **Standing Stones of Lundy**

Stone Circle | Nearest Village: **Lundin**

Map: **NO 4048 0272** | Sheets: **E370 L59** | Lat: **56.21332N** | Long: **2.96121W**

Photo © Jackie Bates

Surely one of the most iconic and spectacular stone settings in Scotland, if not Britain, the towering stones of Lundin Links are probably the remains of a four-poster stone circle with a diameter of 16.5m (54ft). Only three stones remain, standing in manicured isolation on the third fairway of the Ladies' Golf Club. They're visible from the road, but the club is happy to allow access as long as you ask permission, and even have a photocopied information sheet. These red sandstone giants are huge, forming two sides of a rectangle: the NNW stone is 5.2m (17ft) tall, the SSW 4.6m (15ft) and the SSE 4.3m (14ft) tall and 2.1m (7ft) broad. The NNE stone is missing, although it lay by its stump in 1792, broken by treasure hunters. Excavation here in the 18th century found cists, bones (including a skull), and possibly a jet button (now lost).

ABERLEMNO

Standing Stones | Nearest Village: **Aberlemno**

Map: **NO 5228 5592** | Sheets: **E389 L54** | Lat: **56.69201N** | Long: **2.78136W**

> **"From October to Easter the stones are all covered by wooden boxes to protect them from frost, so save your visit till the summer!"** Ewen Rennie

Aberlemno in Angus has four Pictish stones, one in the churchyard and the others beside the B9134, 365m (¼ mile) away to the NNW. There are many Pictish stones listed on the Megalithic Portal website but they are outside the scope of this guide; however, the stone at NO 5228 5592 has six cup-marks on the back, near the bottom, that presumably predate the Pictish carvings (a serpent, a double disc with Z-rod, a mirror and a comb).

Photo © Sandy Gerrard

MEIKLE KENNY   Alt Names: **Baldovie, West Schurroch**
Stone Circle | Nearest Village: **Kirkton of Kingoldrum**
Map: **NO 3176 5415** | Sheets: **E381 L53** | Lat: **56.6741N** | Long: **3.11522W**

Three separate four-poster circles or stone settings, known collectively in the 18th century as the "Druids Alters", lie in an almost straight line near the northeastern edge of West Schurroch Ridge. Meikle Kenny A (at NO 3176 5415) is now a lone standing stone, 1.4m (4ft 7in) tall, its three companions having been removed around 1842. In the woods to the east, the two neighbouring settings

Photo © Golux

are now both reduced to three smallish stones. Meikle Kenny B is at NO 3180 5417, 45m (148ft) to the northeast, and Meikle Kenny C is a further 21m (69ft) in the same direction at NO 3182 5418.

BALGARTHNO   Alt Names: **Farm of Corn, Myrekirk**
Stone Circle | Nearest City: **Dundee**
Map: **NO 3533 3161** | Sheets: **E380 L54** | Lat: **56.47215N** | Long: **3.05134W**

On the outskirts of Dundee in the Charleston housing estate, this 8m (26ft) ring has nine, heavily weathered stones, one of which is standing and 1.5m (5ft) high. Fragments of flint and jet found here are kept at the National Museum of Scotland. The stones are now fenced in to protect them from vandalism.

Nearby | At NO 3458 3102, 952m (over ½ mile) WSW of Balgarthno, the **Devil's Stone** (in Perth and Kinross) is a bulbous standing stone visible from the road through some railings that bridge a gap in a stone wall.

Photo © Robert Law

287

BANDIRRAN   Alt Name: **Woodburn Cottage**
Stone Circles | Nearest Village: **Balbeggie**
Map: **NO 2091 3099** | Sheets: **E380 L53** | Lat: **56.46439N** | Long: **3.28516W**

Set among pine and birch trees close to the wood's western edge, this circle may once have had at least 10 stones. Today, eight are visible, with two of them remaining upright. Nearby, to the east, is another small group of stones, two standing and one fallen. In 1997, a survey by the Perthshire Society of Natural Science suggested that these could form part of a 14.5m (48ft) circle of seven stones.

Nearby | At NO 1520 2626, 7.4km (4½ miles) WSW of Bandirran, is **Murrayshall** standing stone, set in arable land on top of a low ridge. It's a nicely shaped stone, 1.8m (6ft) tall and 1.2m (4ft) wide at its widest point, with a tapering top. In the same field, 30m (98ft) northeast of this stone, the remains of two settlements and a possible roundhouse can be seen as cropmarks in the right conditions.

MONCRIEFFE
Stone Circle | Nearest Village: **Bridge of Earn**
Map: **NO 1360 1933** | Sheets: **E369 L58** | Lat: **56.35838N** | Long: **3.39990W**

In the grounds of Moncrieffe House, where it was re-erected in 1980, this was often listed (controversially) as a recumbent circle, but is now thought to be more typical of Perthshire's small stone circles. This multiphase monument began as a henge with a ring of post-holes, possibly then followed by a kerbed cairn ringed by standing stones, which was then replaced by an eight-stone circle. A stone marked with 15 cups, originally sited in the circle, is now located 9.6m (31½ft) to the west.

FOWLIS WESTER   Alt Name: **Moor of Ardoch**
Megalithic Complex | Nearest Village: **Fowlis Wester**
Map: **NN 9243 2492** | Sheets: **OL47 L52/58** | Lat: **56.4042N** | Long: **3.74471W**

An interesting complex on the moor of Ardoch. The easternmost monument has two circular settings: the kerb of a denuded cairn surrounded by a ruined ring about 4.9 × 5.7m (16ft × 18ft 8in) across. A slab on the SSW side of the kerb has three cup-marks. Northeast of the kerb cairn is a fallen outlier with a cup-mark. A second, prostrate stone lies to the west, close to the western circle, 25m (82ft) from the eastern one. The western circle, also likely to be a cairn, shows signs of having been blasted – the pair of stones at its northern end are split fragments. Four stones of this circle survive, but excavation in 1939 traced the pits of seven other stones.

Photo © Christopher Bickerton

288

Investigating the Forteviot Ceremonial Landscape

Andy Burnham, founder and Editor of the Megalithic Portal

At Forteviot in Perthshire one of the most extensive prehistoric ceremonial landscapes in Britain has been under investigation by the University of Glasgow since 2007. Sites include a palisaded enclosure dating to the later Neolithic (around 2800BC) and measuring around 270m (885ft) in diameter – as big as five football fields. This was marked out with around 150 massive oak posts perhaps 4–6m (13–20ft) high. An avenue just 4m (13ft) wide led in from the north – imagine ceremonially processing this narrow space and the feeling of awe on entering a vast arena.

The Neolithic cremation cemetery here is the largest known in Scotland, which was subsequently surrounded by another timber circle, still over 40m (131ft) across, again marked out with huge oak posts. Later, an earthen henge was built over this circle, with a large ditch up to 2m (6½ft) deep and 7m (23ft) wide. The complex included two other henges, and another circular enclosure (not classed as a henge) immediately to the northwest of the palisaded enclosure was excavated in 2010. This had two concentric ditches that once held timber fences, a fallen standing stone and, at its centre, three adjoining stone coffins (a triple cist) next to a pit containing a complete beaker.

Both large henges showed later activity, including a Bronze Age stone cist (2100–2000BC) sealed with a large capstone with an unusual symbol carved on the underside. This was lifted in 2009, revealing a burial with a rich collection of grave goods, including a bronze dagger, wooden containers and what seems to be a leather bag containing a small knife and a "strike-a-light" kit, presumably for use in the afterlife (see page 168). Large numbers of meadowsweet flowerheads and stalks were found in the cist, left there for the dead, and placing the burial in the late summer. The cist was lined with water-worn pebbles and larger quartz pebbles, followed by a layer of birch bark on which the body (which has been lost) was placed.

In 2012 the excavations extended to nearby Leadketty where another equally huge palisaded enclosure, with a henge and a small four-poster timber structure were found. The four-poster seems to have been surrounded by a timber circle, possibly a high-status house rather than a ceremonial structure. Excavations in 2014–15 at Wellhill, near Dunning, found a further cist burial and early Neolithic pits associated with a possible field ditch and faint linear marks probably made by an ard (handheld plough that does not turn over the soil). Evidence for ploughing and fields in Neolithic Britain is incredibly rare, according to project directors Dr Kenneth Brophy and Dr Dene Wright, both from the University of Glasgow. The finds suggest a farming economy had taken hold here just a few generations after farming began in the region, in 4000BC. Further radiocarbon-dating showed hunter-gatherer activity some two millennia earlier in the form of a very rare example of a Mesolithic pit alignment.

Find out more about the Strathearn Environs and Royal Forteviot (SERF) Project at:
www.gla.ac.uk/schools/humanities/research/archaeologyresearch/projects/serf/

MONZIE
Kerb Cairn | Nearest Village: **Gilmerton**
Map: **NN 8816 2417** | Sheets: **OL47 L52/58** | Lat: **56.39651N** | Long: **3.81349W**

Photo © Christopher Bickerton

In open pasture dominated by the Knock of Crieff, this kerb cairn with nine large, boulder-like stones is defined by a 5.5m (18ft 5in) diameter kerb. A large prostrate outlier, about 2.1 × 1.5m (6ft 10in × 5ft) lies 3m (10ft) to the southwest. Decorated with around 60 cup and cup-and-ring marks (some with up to four rings), it was found during excavations in 1938 to be connected to the circle by a causeway of stone cobbles. By 1966 many of the smaller stones associated with this cairn circle (in legend said to be impossible to count) were no longer evident. The cist within these stones, also now removed, contained burnt bone and quartz fragments; quartz can also be found around the stones.

Nearby | At NN 8798 2431, 227m (745ft) to the WNW of Monzie kerb cairn, is a standing stone called the **Witches' Stone**. It's in a field south of the drive leading up to Monzie Castle.

DALGINROSS   Alt Names: **The Court Knoll, The Roundel, Dunmhoid, Muirend**
Stone Circle | Nearest Village: **Comrie**
Map: **NN 7803 2126** | Sheets: **OL47 L52** | Lat: **56.36791N** | Long: **3.97622W**

A rather charming four-poster in a very damp and mossy clearing beside the road (originally part of a wood), between some houses at the southeastern edge of Dalginross village, next to the cemetery. In 1876, only one stone was still standing, although all were re-erected after a stone cist was found in front of the largest stone. By 1911 two stones had fallen once more and left where they lay. Today, only one remains standing. These stones sit upon a circular platform just above the level of the road, which may be a modern feature. Dunmhoid is said locally to mean "hill of judgement".

CLACH NA TIOMPAN
Stone Circle | Nearest Village: **Gilmerton**
Map: **NN 8296 3286** | Sheets: **E379 L52** | Lat: **56.47327N** | Long: **3.90157W**

Two stones, the tallest 1.3m (4ft 3in) high, survive in this small four-poster circle enclosing a cairn. Excavation discovered the socket holes of the other stones, one lying nearby to the south. To the north, on the other side of the track, is a long cairn once measuring 58 × 11.5m (190 × 38ft), and 1.5m (5ft) high, with four chambers. It was damaged when the road was driven through it in the 19th century.

Nearby | At NN 8259 3299, 391m (¼ mile) west of Clach na Tiompan, is **Glenshervie Burn**, half of another, rather wrecked four-poster stone circle.

ACHARN FALLS Alt Name: **Greenland**

Stone Circle | Nearest Village: **Acharn**
Map: **NN 7679 4249** | Sheets: **E379 L51/52** | Lat: **56.5582N** | Long: **4.00628W**

It's a fair climb up from the village (there and back will take you around an hour and a half) but well worth it for the fabulous views of the mountains and Loch Tay. About 8.8m (29ft) in diameter, the circle is quite ruinous, but the spectacular setting gives all the atmosphere you could want. Seven stones remain of nine, with four still standing; the tallest 1.75m (5ft 8in). A stone wall may contain remains of the others.

Nearby | On the way up, and a good place to take a rest, is the **Acharn Burn** cairn at NN 7607 4294.

Photo © Christopher Bickerton

CROFT MORAIG

Stone Circle | Nearest Village: **Kenmore**
Map: **NN 7977 4727** | Sheets: **E379 L51/52** | Lat: **56.60185N** | Long: **3.95999W**

Croft Moraig is a fascinating and complex site, with a stone circle and an oval-shaped stone setting overlying an earlier timber structure, illustrating the reuse and range of monuments over the Neolithic and early Bronze Age periods. Excavations in 1965 showed it had three phases of construction. In the earliest phase, 14 timber posts estimated to be about 2m high, were set in a penannular (horseshoe) arrangement measuring about 8m × 7m (26 × 23ft), which may have had a central hearth. These posts were later replaced by eight stones in a 7 × 6m (23 × 20ft) oval. An outlying slab, located on the surrounding bank, has 21 cups and two cup-and-rings. The third phase was the addition of an outer circle, 12m (39ft) in diameter, of nine graded stones and two outlying stones (one of which has now fallen), which form an entrance. This outer circle also incorporates three boulders from an earlier phase, making a circle of 12 stones. Two deep burial pits are just outside the circle.

Photo © Hartmut Albert

CARSE FARM
Alt Names: **Dull, Weem**

Stone Circle | Nearest Village: **Kenmore**

Map: **NN 8022 4873** | Sheets: **E379 L52** | Lat: **56.61507N** | Long: **3.95335W**

> "Best to visit when the field has just been harvested and the farmer is in a good mood. I raised a hare as I was crossing to the stones." Hamish

In a field beside the road, just outside the village of Dull, the little Carse Farm 1 four poster forms a rectangle 3.9 × 2.7m (12ft 9in × 8ft 10in). The tallest stone, in the southeast and 1.8m (6ft) high, has three cup-marks, while the northeast stone has 17 cups. Curiously, all the cups are carved on top of the stones rather on their vertical faces. Excavation led to the discovery of a pit full of cremated bone and charcoal, along with a collared urn with geometric decoration.

Nearby | At NN 8028 4846, 270m (885ft) to the SSE of Carse Farm 1, is another circle, **Carse Farm 2**, of which only one stone still stands, with a further two cup-marked stones half-buried.

EAST CULT

Stone Row | Nearest Village: **Caputh**

Map: **NO 0725 4216** | Sheets: **E379 L52** | Lat: **56.5622N** | Long: **3.51075W**

Photo © Sandy Gerrard

On the crest of a ridge, just to the west of East Cult Farm, stands what might be the remains of a stone row accompanied by a profusely cup-marked boulder. Today, a pair of stones stand about 9m (29ft) apart; the western stone is 1.9m (6ft 3in) high and the taller, eastern stone reaches 2.15m (7ft). The cup-marked boulder, which may or may not have stood upright, has 130 cup-marks and a dumbbell (two cups joined by a groove) on its upper face, and three cup-marks on the eastern side.

Nearby | At NO 0449 4106, 3km (1¾ miles) WSW of East Cult, the **Newtyle** (Dunkeld) standing stones are a pair of roughly playing-card or lozenge-shaped stones, close beside the A984 and often partially concealed by the bracken. The taller, westernmost stone is 2.1m (6ft 10in) high, tapering to a point; the other is flat-topped. It has been suggested that the two stones align with midsummer sunset, and also that the very dissimilar shapes of the pair could be interpreted as symbolizing male/female aspects.

LUNDIN FARM

Megalithic Cluster | Nearest Village: **Aberfeldy**

Map: **NN 8807 5057** | Sheets: **OL49 L52** | Lat: **56.63354N** | Long: **3.82637W**

Several sites lie in close proximity at this location. Walking along the track from the A827 main road you will find a single standing stone, known as Tomtayewen, at NN 8783 5059. A pair of small

Photo © Golux

standing stones (the eastern one recently moved by 2.5m/8ft 2in, the western one still in situ) lies by the side of the road at NN 8802 5062, with a cup-marked stone between them. Then, at NN 8807 5057, is the Lundin Farm stone circle, a really delightful four-poster set on a little raised mound above the fields, accessed across a stream by a sturdy wooden bridge. Its stones, which originally surrounded a cairn and now grow around a tree, are 2.2m (7ft 3in), 1.4m (4ft 8in), 1.45m (4ft 10in) and 1.15m (3ft 9in) tall respectively.

A further stone with 43 cup-marks lies 30m (98ft) to the southeast at NN 8807 5054.

CLACHAN AN DIRIDH Alt Name: **Fonab Moor**

Stone Circle | Nearest Town: **Pitlochry**
Map: **NN 9251 5574** | Sheets: **OL49 L52** | Lat: **56.681N** | Long: **3.75612W**

High on the hillside above Pitlochry, the name of this four-poster means "stones of the ascent", which feels extremely apposite after the climb up to get here. Once the site would have had spectacular views down to the Tay and the Grampians, but it's now in the middle of a mature plantation, although still impressive and atmospheric in its forest clearing. Three of the stones are standing, the biggest 1.7m (5½ft) tall

Photo © Golux

and 1.8m (5ft 10in) wide, but just 0.4m (1ft 3in) thick. Fragments of the fourth can be seen scattered on the ground. In 2012, extensive geophysical and laser scanning took place at the site. The results suggest some sub-surface archaeology, but an excavation is yet to be carried out.

Nearby | At NN 9462 5211, 4.2km (2.6 miles) southeast of Clachan an Diridh, **Clach na Croiche**, also known as Balnaguard, standing stone was probably once part of a stone row aligned east–west. It's shapely and imposing, 2.15m (7ft) tall, with eight cup-marks at its base. During ploughing in the 1960s two further stones were found buried, 7.8m (25ft 7in) and 12.5m (41ft) to the east. When the site was excavated in 1971, three further stones in a 9m (30ft) arc were located close to the eastern field boundary, protruding through a layer of large, water-worn stones.

"Local tradition has it that the stones were visited on the first day of May, when a procession was made around them in a deiseil (clockwise) direction." Andy Sweet

CRAIGH NA DUN

Legendary Stone Circle from *Outlander* | Nearest Village: **Kinloch Rannoch**
Map: **NN 7106 5781** | Sheets: **OL49 L52** | Lat: **56.6942N** | Long: **4.1071W**

Photo © Jan Herold

A fictional stone circle that features in the *Outlander* books by Diana Gabaldon and the TV series of the same name. "Craigh na Dun" is one of the most searched-for phrases on the Megalithic Portal so there must be many disappointed the circle doesn't really exist. So here at last is the site of the mythical circle – or at least the filming location from the TV series. There are no stones – these were built for the filming – but it is still a beautiful location overlooking the water. On private land.

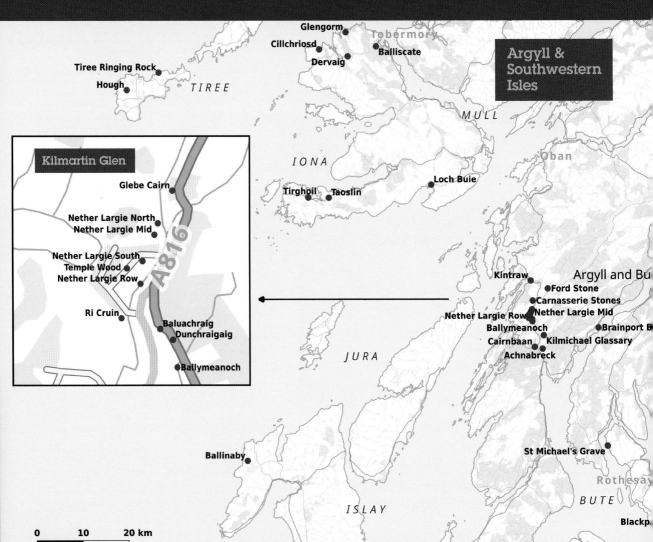

Argyll & Southwestern Isles

Glengorm
Cillchriosd
Tobermory
Dervaig
Balliscate

Tiree Ringing Rock
Hough
TIREE

MULL
Oban

IONA
Tirghoil   Taoslin
Loch Buie

Kilmartin Glen

Glebe Cairn

Nether Largie North
Nether Largie Mid

Nether Largie South
Temple Wood
Nether Largie Row

Ri Cruin

Baluachraig
Dunchraigaig

Ballymeanoch

A816

Kintraw   Argyll and Bu
Ford Stone
Carnasserie Stones
Nether Largie Mid
Nether Largie Row
Ballymeanoch   Brainport B
Cairnbaan   Kilmichael Glassary
Achnabreck

JURA

St Michael's Grave

Rothesay

Ballinaby

BUTE

ISLAY

Blackp

0   10   20 km
0   5   10 miles

Carragh Bhan

North Sannox Farm

ST MICHAEL'S GRAVE
Chambered Cairn | Nearest Village: **Port Bannatyne**
Map: **NR 9947 7031** | Sheets: **E362 L62** | Lat: **55.8841N** | Long: **5.20779W**

On a terrace close to the Kyles of Bute shoreline, this Clyde cairn is in a very ruinous state, severely reduced by robbing and ploughing. Excavation showed the chamber contained two compartments. The interior is full of rubble, and the fallen capstone, 2 × 1.4m (6½ft × 4ft 7in), lies to the south. A rough track at the end of the B875 takes you past this and the nearby sites mentioned below.

Nearby | At NR 9971 7057, 349m (1,145ft) ENE of St Michael's Grave, is **Glenvoidean** chambered cairn, its capstone displaced in recent years. At NS 0063 6932, 1.5km (almost 1 mile) ESE of St Michael's Grave, are the mossy and overgrown remains of **Cairn Ban** chambered cairn.

At NS 0074 6826 (sheet L63), 2.4km (1½ miles) southeast of St Michael's Grave, is **Glecknabae** chambered cairn. This badly disturbed Clyde cairn is now a stony, grass-covered mound, about 18 × 9m (59 × 30ft) and about 1.2m (4ft) high, with the end slabs of the central chamber visible. Excavations in 1903 showed that part of the cairn was built over a shell midden. Two small chambers (the eastern chamber is now destroyed) containing fragments of burnt and unburnt bone, along with pot sherds and flint, were found, and there was also a cist. On the fallen stone east of the cairn there appear to be several cup-marks, but these have not been confirmed.

BLACKPARK Alt Name: **Kingarth**
Stone Circle | Nearest Village: **Kingarth**
Map: **NS 0916 5567** | Sheets: **E362 L63** | Lat: **55.75661N** | Long: **5.04276W**

Three stones still stand of the seven noted in the late 18th century at this circle in Blackpark plantation. The 2.2m (7ft) southern stone was restored after being damaged in 1974. The second stone, 2.8m (9ft) high, has been cracked by weathering. The third stone, also 2.2m (7ft), is supported by an iron bar, and the top of it is almost circular; it's very unusual and striking.

Nearby | At NS 0846 5536, 760m (almost ½ mile) WSW of Blackpark, is the stone row known as **Stravanan Bay** or Largizean Farm. Three large whinstone boulders stand in a field, with fine views across the bay. Aligned northwest–southeast, the three stand 1.5m (5ft) high, 1.7m (5½ft) high and 1.9m (6ft 2in) high.

At NS 0745 6365, 8.2km (just over 5 miles) NNW of Blackpark, is **Craigberoch** standing stone, an angular stone 2.4m (8ft) high and with several cup-marks visible on its southwest face. It's set close to the ruins of Craigbiorach Farm.

Photo © Anne Tate

BRAINPORT BAY
Megalithic Complex | Nearest Village: **Minard**
Map: **NR 9759 9507** | Sheets: **E358 L55** | Lat: **56.10542N** | Long: **5.25635W**

This Argyll site is an interesting and controversial one. There are a number of apparently aligned cup-marked rocks and possible standing stones overlooking Brainport Bay, as well as a group of what have been described as "viewing platforms", built against a rocky outcrop aligned northeast and southwest, with a central cleft on the same alignment – toward midsummer sunrise. In 1994, two standing stones were vandalized – one broken beyond repair.

ACHNABRECK
Rock Art | Nearest Village: **Cairnbaan**
Map: **NR 8555 9067** | Sheets: **E358 L55** | Lat: **56.06067N** | Long: **5.44613W**

Photo © Connor Motley

Concentrated in Kilmartin Glen is an outstanding collection of prehistoric monuments and some of Britain's most impressive rock art. The Achnabreck outcrops are where you'll find the most extensive and complex group of cup-and-ring carvings in Scotland. There are three outcrops in the forestry land, with signposted access. Motifs include cups, cup-and-rings, ringed stars, grooves and spirals; some of the cups surrounded by up to 12 rings. One carving, a cup with seven rings, measures more than 1m (3ft 3in) in diameter – it's the largest in the country. Look for motifs overlying others and the range of different styles, indicating carving over a long period.

Nearby | At NR 8556 9081, 144m (472ft) north of Achnabreck, is **Achnabreck Forest**, also known as Cnoc na Moine, a panel discovered in 2008 after a storm brought down a tree. The **Achnabreck Eastern** panel is at NR 8572 9064, 173m (567ft) east of Achnabreck. Standing stones are at NR 8554 9018, 490m (1,607ft) south of Achnabreck, and at NR 8563 8992, 754m (½ mile) SSE of the main site.

CAIRNBAAN
Rock Art | Nearest Village: **Cairnbaan**
Map: **NR 8388 9106** | Sheets: **E358 L55** | Lat: **56.06338N** | Long: **5.47326W**

There are two groups of rock art at Cairnbaan, just 1.6km (1 mile) from Achnabreck and signposted from the Cairnbaan Hotel. It can be very wet up here, so wear your boots! Cairnbaan 2 (at NR 8388 9106) has some complex and very fine conjoined multiple ringed cups, including a ring linked to a cup by a series of rays. Cairnbaan 1, the second group, is at NR 8399 9103, 114m (374ft) east of Cairnbaan 2, with two panels of decorated outcrops, enclosed by railings. The southern panel is decorated with cup-marks, cups with single and double rings, and a keyhole motif. The carvings of the more weathered northern panel are harder to see.

KILMICHAEL GLASSARY

Rock Art | Nearest Village: **Kilmichael Glassary**
Map: **NR 8580 9350** | Sheets: **E358 L55** | Lat: **56.08612N** | Long: **5.44443W**

Tucked unexpectedly behind modern housing, not far from the road, is the Kilmichael Glassary 1 outcrop, partially protected by an iron fence and covered with over 120 cup-marks and cup-and-rings. These include four cups with unusual keyhole-like rings. Some 60m (197ft) northeast of this stone is the Kilmartin Glassary 2 outcrop, partially buried under tree roots, with numerous single cups as well as three cups with two rings, one cup with four rings and another with five rings. You can explore Hamish Fenton's 3D models of these rock art outcrops by following the links from the Megalithic Portal page for Kilmichael Glassary.

Nearby | At NR 8471 9291, 1.2km (¾ mile) WSW of Kilmichael Glassary, are the three stones of **Dunamuck North**. Only one still stands, the southernmost stone having fallen at some point since 2008. They are very close to the River Add and the walk across the fields from Kilmartin Glassary can be wet. At NR 8483 9248, 447m (1,466ft) SSW of Dunamuck North, are the two further standing stones of **Dunamuck South**. The third set of stones in this group, **Leacaichluaine**, can be found at NR 8483 9232, 160m (525ft) south of Dunamuck South; both these stones are now fallen, but easily spotted.

At NR 8387 9361, 1.9km (just over 1 mile) west of Kilmichael Glassary and close to the river near Dunadd hill fort, is the **Dunadd** standing stone, a squarish, 1.4m (4ft 7in) tall stone, one edge of which seems to have been broken off.

BALLYMEANOCH

Stone Rows & Cairn | Nearest Village: **Kilmartin**
Map: **NR 8337 9642** | Sheets: **E358 L55** | Lat: **56.11123N** | Long: **5.48569W**

A very fine site near Kilmartin, with two more or less parallel rows of standing stones, aligned northwest–southeast, and an attractive kerb cairn. You can see the rows from the road very clearly and access is easy. There are six stones, four in one row and two in the other – these two lean quite dramatically in opposite directions. The tallest stone is 4.1m (13ft 5in) in height. The two middle stones of the four-stone line have multiple cup and cup-and-ring marks (over 70 on stone B). A seventh stone, pierced and cup-marked, has fallen since 1881, and now lies by the kerb cairn at NR 8339 9643, just 30m (98ft) ENE of the stone rows. Although the cairn is damaged, 11 graded stones create an impressive ring of upright slabs.

Photo © Sandy Gerrard

DUNCHRAIGAIG

Cairn | Nearest Village: **Kilmartin**
Map: **NR 8331 9681** | Sheets: **E358 L55** | Lat: **56.11473N** | Long: **5.48706W**

Photo © Sandy Gerrard

A badly robbed but still impressive cairn formed from water-worn stones, now around 30m (98ft) in diameter and 2.5m (8ft) high in the centre, with several cists. Dunchraigaig is not considered part of the Kilmartin linear group of cairns as it is off-line, away to the southeast. Excavated in 1864, one cist, probably the primary burial, contained deposits of burnt bone, perhaps the remains of eight–10 people. A second cist, found in what is now the centre of the cairn (most of its south side having been removed) contained a food vessel and burnt bone. Beneath it, under a paved floor, was a crouched burial, and apparently the lid or roof of this cist had an extended burial on it. The third cist, no longer visible, to the east, also contained a food vessel. Various finds, including a greenstone axe, are sadly lost. On the northern side of the cairn are several earthfast boulders that may be the remains of a cairn.

BALUACHRAIG

Rock Art | Nearest Village: **Kilmartin**
Map: **NR 8312 9696** | Sheets: **E358 L55** | Lat: **56.11601N** | Long: **5.49022W**

A very fine selection of rock art on three outcrops within a protective enclosure, close to the road and therefore easy to find. The largest and most profusely decorated panel has around 15 single-ringed cup-marks, 17 cups with double rings and at least 127 plain cup-marks. The second rock has 10 plain cup-marks; the third, two cups, one with a single ring. From here you can see Dunchraigaig cairn (see above).

Photo © Connor Motley

GLEBE CAIRN

Cairn | Nearest Village: **Kilmartin**
Map: **NR 8330 9894** | Sheets: **E358 L55** | Lat: **56.13379N** | Long: **5.48886W**

From Kilmartin village, an alignment of cairns – a linear cemetery – cuts SSW across the landscape for 5km (3 miles). The northernmost of these, Glebe Cairn, is enormous and very impressive as you walk past, but you can't get inside it. Now 30m (98ft) across and 3m (10ft) high, it was originally at least 4m (13ft) in height. It was excavated in 1864, when a boulder cist containing an inhumation and a tripartite food vessel was found. A second cist to the southwest contained an Irish food vessel and a wonderful necklace made of 28 jet beads. The placement of the cists indicated two separate periods of construction and use. One food vessel is at the National Museum of Scotland, the other in the British Museum; the necklace, sadly, was lost in a fire at Poltalloch House.

Excavations prior to gravel extraction on the plateau nearby, at Upper Largie, resulted in the discovery of two graves. The earlier of these contained three very early Beaker pots, similar to those from the lower Rhine. Other sites identified on the plateau included a Neolithic cursus and a timber circle, 46m (150ft) in diameter.

Nearby | When visiting the rock art, linear cemetery and associated sites at Kilmartin, you'll probably park at the award-winning **Kilmartin House Museum**, which is well worth a visit. It explores the archaeology of the Kilmartin landscape in detail and holds a large collection of prehistoric artefacts, many from the valley itself.

NETHER LARGIE

Cairn | Nearest Village: **Kilmartin**
Map: **NR 8309 9847** | Sheets: **E358 L55** | Lat: **56.12953N** | Long: **5.49194W**

NETHER LARGIE NORTH

Another large cairn in the Kilmartin alignment, Nether Largie North was excavated in 1930, when the whole cairn was taken apart, and has since been entirely reconstructed. The finds included two upright slabs, one of which was carved with two pecked circles (now in the National Museum of Scotland). The cairn now stands almost 2.7m (9ft) high and measures 20m (66ft) in diameter. Visitors can climb down a ladder from the roof hatch into the central chamber to see the large central cist and the underside of the impressive capstone, which is carved with around 40 cup-marks and the outlines of 10 axeheads.

NETHER LARGIE MID

This Bronze Age cairn has been dated to *c*. 2000BC. Before the 1920s, it was around 3m (10ft) tall and 32m (105ft) in diameter. Since then, much of the stone has been robbed for building and road repairs, and it now stands less than 1m (3ft 3in) tall. The two cists this cairn was built to contain are visible: the northernmost is marked by low concrete posts; the other is at the southern edge of the cairn and still has its capstone (although this has been moved so visitors can see inside), together with two of its end slabs. The northwestern slab has at least one cup-mark and the faint pecked motif of a bronze axehead. At the southern edge of the cairn, the remains of the kerb can be seen, and within this is another slab bearing five cup-marks.

Photo © Cezary Namirski

Photo © Heartland Arts

NETHER LARGIE SOUTH

This chambered cairn of the Clyde type is the earliest of the burial sites in Kilmartin's linear cemetery, dating from around 3000BC. The cairn was reconstructed 1,000 years later in the Bronze Age when cists were added to the original structure. Its chamber, now in the centre of the cairn, was divided by stone slabs (in a way that resembles structures on Orkney) to hold selected or curated bones after excarnation, rather than individual burials. In the 19th century, the cairn had reached a diameter of 40m (134ft) but most of it had been removed by 1864, when the tomb was excavated; most of what remains has been heaped up around the chamber. The chamber, entered between the two portal stones, is about 6m (20ft) long and 1.8m (6ft) wide at the north, tapering to 1m (3ft 3in) at the southern end. One cist of the two inserted into the cairn after its construction is still visible.

RI CRUIN

Cairn | Nearest Village: **Kilmartin**
Map: **NR 8255 9712** | Sheets: **E358 L55** | Lat: **56.11714N** | Long: **5.49949W**

Southernmost of the burial sites in the Kilmartin linear cemetery, this reconstructed kerbed round cairn is now about 20m (66ft) in diameter. Originally it had three cists, including one with carved axeheads decorating the inside of the slab at the western end, which can still be seen. When the cairn was excavated in 1870, bone fragments were found in all three cists, all of which had grooved side slabs to make them fit neatly together. A further carved slab, featuring a rake-like motif – or perhaps a halberd or even a boat – was destroyed in the fire at Poltalloch House, but fortunately a cast is kept at the National Museum of Scotland.

TEMPLE WOOD
Alt Name: Moon Wood

Stone Circle | Nearest Village: **Kilmartin**

Map: **NR 8263 9783** | Sheets: **E358 L55** | Lat: **56.12356N** | Long: **5.49874W**

Photo © Cornfield

The two stone circles at this Kilmartin site are among the earliest examples of stone circles in Scotland and maybe in Britain. Temple Wood South is a multiphase monument with a number of unusual elements. This embanked circle has an oval ring of 13 standing stones (there were 22 originally), about 12m (39ft) in diameter, set within a cairn-like covering of water-rolled pebbles. A central cist is, in turn, surrounded by another circle of much smaller stones. Two of the standing stones have rock art; one with very faint concentric circles, the other with a spiral carving that is unusual as one half of the spiral is on one face, the other on the next.

Temple Wood North is some 38m (124ft) from the southern circle. It was only discovered in 1979 and has been reconstructed with concrete markers to illustrate the two main phases of construction. Beginning life as a timber setting, possibly as early as 3500BC, the upright timbers were eventually replaced by an elliptical 10.5m (34ft) setting of five stones with another at its centre. Excavation has revealed that the stone circle was dismantled in prehistoric times, finally being covered with a layer of cobbling. A radiocarbon date of 3000BC was obtained from a charcoal deposit in a stone socket.

NETHER LARGIE ROW

Stone Row | Nearest Village: **Kilmartin**

Map: **NR 8283 9761** | Sheets: **E358 L55** | Lat: **56.12168N** | Long: **5.49535W**

A complex and intriguing stone setting to the west of Kilmartin Burn, close to the Temple Wood circles. A pair of standing stones form the northeast end of the alignment; the western stone of these has three, possibly four, cup-marks. Another pair form the southwest end of the alignment; the eastern stone has five cup-marks. In between the two pairs are two groups of standing stones: one of four and another of five. The northerly group of five stones has a central stone, surrounded originally by four other stones that formed a rectangle around its base; today only three of these "flankers" remain. This central stone has 40 cups and a cup-and-ring motif. The southerly group of four stones are made up of broken upright stones. In 1973, another fallen stone was discovered to the west of the alignment.

Nearby | At NR 8279 9772, 127m (417ft) northwest of the main stone alignment and forming part of it, is **Nether Largie** standing stone. Originally recorded as 1.8m (6ft) high, it now stands 1.5m (5ft) tall on a slight mound, perhaps formed by ploughing around the stone over the years.

CARNASSERIE STONES

Standing Stones | Nearest Village: **Kilmartin**
Map: **NM 8345 0077** | Sheets: **E358 L55** | Lat: **56.15029N** | Long: **5.48798W**

Photo © Cezary Namirski

A splendid pair of 2.6m (8½ft) playing-card stones, the southernmost with a cup mark near its base. Access to these and the Carnasserie rock art is on foot from the Carnasserie Castle car park.

Nearby | At NM 8389 0086 and 9m (30ft) west of the northwestern angle of the castle, is a rock art boulder decorated with deep, large cup-marks. At NM 8222 0267, 2.3km (just under 1½ miles) northwest of the Carnasserie stones, is the magnificent **Ormaig** rock art panel with 200 carvings, many in extremely good condition as they were only uncovered in 1974. There are three main panels including some amazing rosette motifs on the eastern rock. Please treat them with great care.

THE FORD STONE

Standing Stone | Nearest Village: **Ford**
Map: **NM 8668 0332** | Sheets: **E358 L55** | Lat: **56.17459N** | Long: **5.43811W**

Only one stone (3m/10ft high) remains of what was originally a pair, said to mark the site of an ancient grave. The second stone apparently now lies in the garden of Auchinellan House (now a holiday cottage) at NM 8653 0268, some 670m (under ½ mile) to the south.

Nearby | At NM 8689 0356, 320m (1,050ft) northeast of the Ford Stone, at the village crossroads and close to the River Ford, is the **Ford cist**, set into the western side of a natural gravel knoll. While it measures just 0.85 × 0.65m (2ft 9in × 2ft), it has an impressive capstone and both end slabs survive. Have a look for some other stones nearby, all close to the road: at NM 8595 0156, 1.9km (just over 1 mile) SSW of the Ford Stone, is **Creagantairbh Beag** with its broken stump (it was blown down in the 1879 Tay Bridge Gale); at NM 8573 0112, 2.4km (1½ miles) southwest of the Ford Stone, is the **Glennan** stone; at NM 8790 0488, 2km (1¼ miles) northeast of the Ford Stone, is the **Torran Cross** incised stone.

KINTRAW Alt Name: **Danish King's Grave**

Standing Stone | Nearest Village: **Ardfern**
Map: **NM 8305 0497** | Sheets: **E358 L55** | Lat: **56.18778N** | Long: **5.49783W**

This impressively tall stone, marking what is traditionally said to be the grave of a Danish king, stands 4m (13ft) high beside the road and close to four cairns making up a Bronze Age complex. According to a 17th-century drawing by Edward Lhuyd, this is the remaining stone of a four-stone alignment;

Photo © Roger Heath

it was re-erected after falling in 1979. The site looks toward Jura, with very fine views (when it's not raining). Alexander Thom drew attention to an alignment with the saddle of land between Beinn Shiantaidh and Beinn a'Chaolais in Jura and the midwinter sunset. Debate about this continues, although evidence for the alignment includes alternative, higher observation points on the hill. Further stone alignments at this site are said to indicate Dubh Bheinn, where the moon sets at its minor standstill.

CARRAGH BHAN
Standing Stone | Nearest Town: **Port Ellen**
Map: **NR 3283 4781** | Sheets: **E352 L60** | Lat: **55.65013N** | Long: **6.24835W**

A large, square stone on the Isle of Islay, about 2.2m (7ft) tall and leaning slightly, with views north to the Paps of Jura. It's traditionally said to mark the grave of the Manx king Godred Crovan (d. 1095).

Nearby | At NR 3292 4519, 2.6km (just over 1½ miles) south of Carragh Bhan, is **Cragabus** chambered cairn, a very ruinous example of the Clyde group, with no sign of any cairn. Some of the façade survives, and the standing stone to the east is probably a portal stone, suggesting the chamber was originally some 5m (16ft) long, with at least three compartments. Thomas Hastie Bryce's excavation in 1901 produced human bones "in much disorder, though mostly grouped in the corners, and by the sides of the cists." It's very difficult to find a good place to park here, so be careful.

BALLINABY
Stone Row | Nearest Village: **Ballinaby**
Map: **NR 2199 6720** | Sheets: **E353 L60** | Lat: **55.81781N** | Long: **6.43964W**

In the 18th century there were three stones here; now there are only two, one standing, and one broken. The remaining upright is a magnificent slab, almost 5m (16ft) tall, about 1m (3ft 3in) wide and just 0.3m (1ft) thick. About 200m (656ft) to the northeast is another stone, 2m (6½ft) tall, originally much taller and probably deliberately broken.

Nearby | At NR 2483 5761, 10km (6¼ miles) SSE of Ballinaby, is the chambered Clyde cairn **Port Charlotte**, badly damaged by stone robbing and excavation. Excavation in 1976 demonstrated that the façade was

Photo © Sandy Gerrard

303

to the NNE, and the chamber had four compartments. Human bones were found in the second compartment; flint knives, arrowheads and Neolithic pottery sherds were also found at the site.

BALLISCATE — Alt Names: **Tobermory, Sgriob-Ruadh**

Stone Row | Nearest Town: **Tobermory**
Map: **NM 4996 5413** | Sheets: **E374 L47** | Lat: **56.61212N** | Long: **6.07658W**

Photo © Fiona Robertson

Above Tobermory, with fantastic views over the Sound of Mull, is this three-stone basalt row aligned north–south. The northern stone is 1.7m (5½ft) tall, the central stone, which has fallen, is about 2.8m (9ft) long, and the more irregular southern stone is 2.6m (8½ft) tall. Excavation revealed the stump of a fourth stone, aligned to the north of the others.

GLENGORM

Stone Row | Nearest Town: **Tobermory**
Map: **NM 4347 5713** | Sheets: **E374 L47** | Lat: **56.63549N** | Long: **6.18501W**

"A magnificent site. The kerb around the stones may have been added when the stones were re-erected." Nick Brand

Photo © Christopher Bickerton

West of Glengorm Castle, the three standing stones of this row have a dramatic setting on top of a prominent knoll in low-lying land. Two had fallen by the early 1800s, but both had been re-erected by 1942. The enclosure bank surrounding them is not prehistoric. The stones range from 2.05m (6ft 8in) to 2.15m (7ft) in height. The northern stone was re-erected close to its original position; the one to the south has been moved to the northeast in order to take advantage of a cleft in the bedrock. Glengorm is one of the sites that helped Gail Higginbottom develop a landscape model demonstrating the role of astronomical alignments and the horizon in the siting of freestanding stone monuments in Scotland (see page 307).

Nearby | At NM 4134 5524, 2.8km (1¾ miles) WSW of Glengorm, is **Quinish** stone row. Alexander Thom suggested the four stones were aligned toward moonrise at the major southern lunar standstill. Only one stone remains standing.

DERVAIG Alt Names: **Dervaig B, Cnoc Fada**
Stone Row | Nearest Village: **Dervaig**
Map: **NM 4390 5203** | Sheets: **E374 L47** | Lat: **56.59003N** | Long: **6.17297W**

On the hillside above Dervaig, the five-stone row of basalt blocks known as Dervaig Centre now has only two stones standing but is still impressive, all the stones about 2.5m (8ft) tall (or long) and aligned NNW–SSE. The surrounding plantation has now been harvested, dramatically changing the setting from dark and damp to open, with views of the surrounding hills.

Photo © Sandy Gerrard

Nearby | At NM 4393 5189, 143m (469ft) SSE of Dervaig Centre, is **Dervaig D**, a possible stone row (but perhaps just natural boulders) built into a wall.

At NM 4386 5162, 411m (1,348ft) south of Dervaig Centre, **Dervaig SSE**, also known as Dervaig C or Glac Mhor, is another stone row, rather badly treated. Three stones are aligned more or less NNW–SSE: one is a gatepost, one is set in the dyke and one is broken. The tallest reaches 1.7m (5½ft).

NM 4360 5305, about 1km (0.6 miles) NNW of Dervaig Centre, **Maol Mor**, also known as Dervaig A, Kilmore or Frachadil, is also a stone row, some 10m (33ft) long, with four neat stones aligned NNW–SSE, set in a forestry plantation. Three are upright, around 2.2m (7ft) high. The fourth, fallen stone, is 2.5m (8ft) long.

CILLCHRIOSD
Standing Stone | Nearest Village: **Dervaig**
Map: **NM 3772 5350** | Sheets: **E374 L47** | Lat: **56.59981N** | Long: **6.27473W**

Photo © Christopher Bickerton

A 2.6m (8½ft) stone with a level top and vertical sides. Gail Higginbottom (see page 307) proposes that Cillchriosd is aligned to moonrise at the southerly minor standstill. In the opposite direction, the alignment is within a few degrees of the midsummer sunset.

LOCH BUIE

Stone Circle | Nearest Village: **Craignure**
Map: **NM 6177 2510** | Sheets: **E375 L49** | Lat: **56.35806N** | Long: **5.85808W**

Photo © Stephen Sale

Remote Loch Buie has a magical setting, with Ben Buie rising dramatically behind and golden eagles flying overhead, but it is, essentially, in a bog, so come prepared (wellies are essential). Originally a circle of nine granite slabs, the position of one missing stone is now marked by a small boulder. The circle is 12m (39ft) in diameter and the stones, the tallest of which is 2m (6½ft), have been set with their flatter faces turned inward. There are three associated outliers, the tallest is some 40m (131ft) southwest of the circle and 3m (10ft) tall. Stone circles are rare in the west of Scotland, making this a significant site.

Nearby | Hidden among trees at NM 6155 2525, 265m (869ft) WNW of Loch Buie circle, is a ruined kerb cairn. You will probably pass by on your way from the parking spot to the stone circle.

At NM 6163 2542, about 365m (1,197ft) northwest of the circle, the Loch Buie standing stone is about 2m (6½ft) tall.

At NM 5463 3002, 8.6km (5¼ miles) WNW of the circle, are the four **Uluvalt** stones, three of which have fallen (one of these may be a natural erratic).

> "From the parking spot, follow the white marker stones across extremely boggy pastureland. These peter out in front of a clump of trees. Make your way to the fence and follow it along to the left to find the gate to the stones." Fiona Robertson

TAOSLIN

Standing Stone | Nearest Village: **Bunessan**
Map: **NM 3973 2239** | Sheets: **E373 L48** | Lat: **56.32216N** | Long: **6.21113W**

Standing by the Fionnphort road, this stone may be prehistoric or a later way-marker for Iona pilgrims. It's about 2m (6½ft) tall, with a slightly sloping top. David Smyth has examined the role of its shadow, and concluded that at equinox it is notably elongated down its east side. He also highlights possible archaeoastronomical features of the stone, including that, from here, the star Arcturus would have appeared to skim the top of the Burg hill to the north.

Photo © David Smyth

Archaeoastronomy in Western Scotland

Gail Higginbottom, archaeologist and leader of the Western Scotland Megalithic Landscape Project along with astrophysicist Roger Clay and others from the University of Adelaide

Our project uses innovative 2D graphics and 3D rendering techniques to demonstrate that the builders of Bronze Age standing stone monuments chose locations based on particular horizon shapes, considering distance, direction and relative height in relation to a monument's position. It builds on our statistical reassessment of the work of Clive Ruggles, showing that many more sites than previously thought were deliberately oriented to the sun or moon. Significantly, approximately half the sites we looked at have a particular form of horizon shape surrounding them, higher and closer in the north, and further away and lower in the south – we call these "classic sites". The remaining sites, with horizons higher and closer in the south, we label "reverse sites". The relative heights of the horizons affect where the sun and moon are seen to rise and set, and it would seem the megalith builders tried to ensure that these bodies interact with particular peaks or high ground at specific times in their cycles.

This combination of high and low horizons around the monument created great astronomical shows at different times of the year, including the solstices and the minor and major lunar standstills (extreme rising and setting times of the moon, which occur only every 18.6 years). The most spectacular display occurs when these two events coincide.

It's clear there were many essential natural elements to consider and understand when choosing where to build a megalithic monument. The final element was to include one or more alignments between the stones of the same monument, or separate, intervisible monuments, again to indicate one or more of the extreme rising and setting points of the sun and/or moon.

We show that the visible patterns found at Bronze Age sites on the inner isles and mainland of western Scotland were first established in stone at two of the earliest dated "great circles": Callanish on the Isle of Lewis and Stenness in Orkney. To do this, we developed two new methods to formally test the likelihood of a connection between stone circles and astronomy by cross-correlation, comparing the stone directions with the direction of astronomical phenomena crossing the horizon. For the first test, the number of random circles at the same locations which hit the same number of targets as Stenness is 27 and nine for Callanish. The likelihood of the number of astronomical "hits" coming from random chance is 1.25 percent and 1.66 percent respectively. For the second test, looking at the likelihood of the monuments being astronomical, with 47 independent samples for each, the results are 97.87 percent for both sites.

The bane of many an archaeoastronomer has been the large number of potential random errors and "background noise", as well as the inherent number of statistical trials needed – the more stones in a circle, the greater the numbers of trials (testing of each alignment), increasing the likelihood that the pattern observed is due to chance. Our tests have been constructed to overcome these factors, and are, I believe, a breakthrough in the quest to discover when and where complex astronomical and landscape patterns were first associated with standing-stone structures in Scotland, and possibly all of Britain. The statistical results for Stenness and Callanish are compelling.

The visual dominance of the first great circles in the north of Britain seems to have led a cultural transformation that connected standing stones to the local landscape and the motion of the sun and moon across that landscape. Soon after these sites were created, more late Neolithic stone monuments were erected, continuing until the early Bronze Age, mostly in the form of circles in Scotland. By approximately 800BC hundreds of smaller stone circles, single standing stones and settings existed, and these later monuments continued the tradition of connecting with a cosmological landscape ideal that was first set in standing stone more than 2,000 years previously, demonstrating the longevity and relevance of this cosmological system, despite the various radical material and social changes that occurred from the late Neolithic to the late Bronze Age.

Loch Buie and Uluvalt (upper) on Mull are examples of sites with the "classic" landscape around them. These sites are not located next to each other, yet their profiles are very similar (see diagram, below). There are variations in detail but the general factors stay the same. If you go to other locations on the island the mountain chains may not be as extreme in height or you may get one single long, curving range without two distinct peaks. We have statistical evidence showing that the horizon shapes surrounding the sites are significantly different from the general lie of the land; that is, their occurrence is very unlikely to have occurred by chance.

Higginbottom, G. and Mom, V. "Place: The Physical Embodiment of Collective Information" in J.B. Glover, J.M. Moss and D. Rissolo (eds), *Digital Archaeologies, Material Worlds*. Tübingen: University of Tübingen.

The 3D program Horizon, developed by Andrew G.K. Smith, astrophysicist at the University of Adelaide, can be downloaded from: www.agksmith.net/horizon/

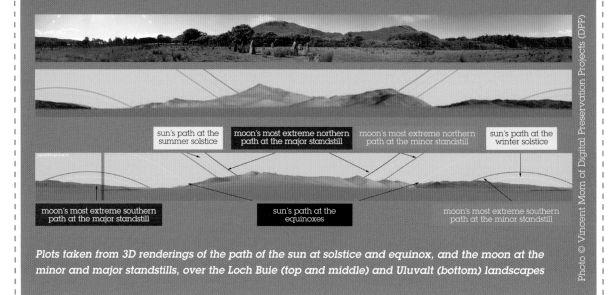

sun's path at the summer solstice

moon's most extreme northern path at the major standstill

moon's most extreme northern path at the minor standstill

sun's path at the winter solstice

moon's most extreme southern path at the major standstill

sun's path at the equinoxes

moon's most extreme southern path at the minor standstill

Plots taken from 3D renderings of the path of the sun at solstice and equinox, and the moon at the minor and major standstills, over the Loch Buie (top and middle) and Uluvalt (bottom) landscapes

TIRGHOIL
Standing Stone | Nearest Village: **Bunessan**
Map: **NM 3532 2242** | Sheets: **E373 L48** | Lat: **56.32N** | Long: **6.28228W**

Photo © Christopher Bickerton

In a field beside the road to Fionnphort, this 2.6m (8½ft) granite pillar is traditionally held to be another marker for the Iona pilgrim route, although it's just as likely to be prehistoric.

Nearby | At NM 3250 2217, 2.8km (1¾ miles) west of Tirghoil, is **Poit na h-I**, a standing stone with a pleasing triangular shape. At NM 3133 2331, 1.6km (1 mile) WNW of Poit na h-I, is the 2.4m (7ft 10in) **Achaban House** standing stone, which may be prehistoric or another later marker of the route to Iona. Ask for permission at the guest house.

TIREE RINGING ROCK
Alt Names: **Balephetrish Gong Stone, Clach a' Choire**
Glacial Erratic with Cup-marks | Nearest Village: **Balephetrish**
Map: **NM 0268 4869** | Sheets: **E372 L46** | Lat: **56.53584N** | Long: **6.83802W**

This large glacial erratic was carried by the ice from Rum to Tiree, and is a much younger type of rock (granodiorite) than anything native to the island. It's covered in more than 50 cup-marks, perhaps relating to the fact that it "rings" if you tap or bang it with a pebble. It's said that if the rock is moved Tiree will sink beneath the waves.

Photo © Andrew Curtis

> **"I was also told if ever Tiree were in trouble, the rock would break open and our ancestors would come out and rescue the island."** Anon

HOUGH
Alt Names: **Tiree 3, Moss B**
Stone Circle | Nearest Village: **Hough**
Map: **NL 9581 4504** | Sheets: **E372 L46** | Lat: **56.49878N** | Long: **6.94503W**

There are two circles up here within about 150m (492ft) of each other, about 1km (0.6 miles) southeast of Hough House. The SSW circle (NL 9581 4504) is the larger, 40m (131ft) in diameter, with 11 fallen stones and the stump of a 12th. There may originally have been more stones, but these are now missing.

Hough NNE circle (NL 9589 4515) – also known as Tiree 3 and Moss A – is 136m (446ft) northeast of Hough SSW. This stone circle has 10 stones, one of which is upright and about 1.8m (6ft) tall. Five others are reduced to stumps and the rest are fallen. A low mound in the centre, about 14m (46ft) in diameter, may be a cairn.

Nearby | At NL 9469 4300, 2.3km (1½ miles) southwest of Hough SSW, is **Middleton** standing stone, 1.6m (5ft 3in) high.

At NL 9731 4259, 2.9km (1¾ miles) southeast of Hough SSW, is the elongated, triangular **Ceasabh** standing stone, 1.9m (6ft 3in) high.

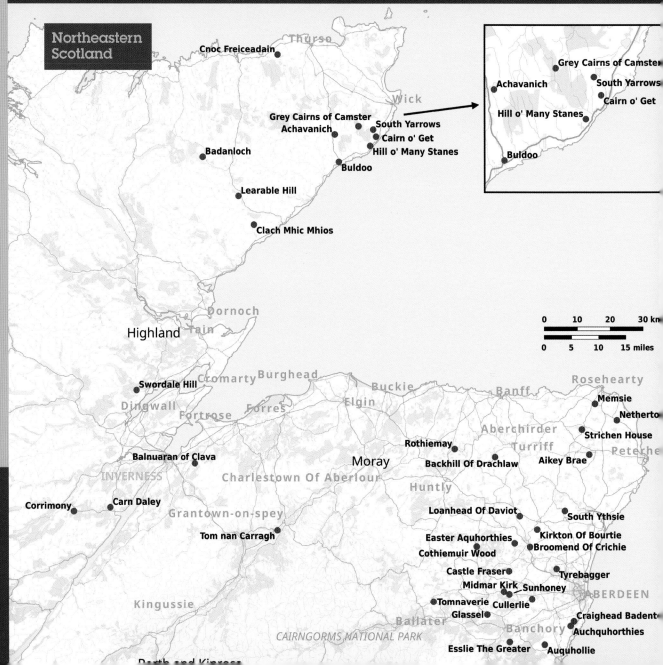

Northeastern Scotland

STONE OF MORPHIE

Standing Stone | Nearest Village: **Hillside**
Map: **NO 7170 6275** | Sheets: **E382 L45** | Lat: **56.75549N** | Long: **2.46443W**

Just off the road, this very impressive 3.4m (11ft) standing stone is said to mark the grave of a son of the Danish general Camus, killed in a battle between the Scots and the Danes. Skeletal remains were indeed found buried underneath it when it was re-erected in the 19th century, having fallen before 1856. It has splendid views of the Angus Hills.

> **"Although the immediate vicinity consists of mundane farm buildings, the stone stands close by some of the best coastal scenery of northeast Scotland."** C. Michael Hogan

ESSLIE THE GREATER Alt Name: **Esslie South**

Stone Circle | Nearest Village: **Strachan**
Map: **NO 7172 9159** | Sheets: **E406 L30** | Lat: **57.01457N** | Long: **2.46732W**

⭐

At Esslie the Greater, a recumbent stone circle, 22.5m (74ft) across, surrounds a ring cairn. The cairn is badly robbed, but you can see the two rings of kerb stones quite clearly. The recumbent, triangular in shape, is about 2.8m (9ft) long. Originally, there were probably eight or nine stones (as well as the recumbent and flankers) in the circle,

Photo © Richard L. Dixon

with five of these now remaining. Two lines of stones run from the ends of the recumbent to the cairn.

Nearby | At NO 7225 9215, some 770m (under ½ mile) ENE from its "Greater" sibling and visible from there, stands **Esslie the Lesser** stone circle. Six stones surround a ring cairn, but the site is often badly overgrown and field clearance confuses matters further.

At NO 7240 9117, just under 1km (0.6 miles) southeast from the Esslies, is **Garrol Wood**, also known as Nine Stanes, a recumbent stone circle with the typical internal ring cairn. This is a wonderfully mossy, lichen-shrouded site, appearing mysterious in its forest setting. Originally eight stones plus the recumbent and flankers, one is now missing and another a mere stump.

Carved Stone Balls

Julie Kearney, who researches the links between consciousness, creativity and natural energies

Found mainly in Aberdeenshire, their distribution coinciding with recumbent stone circle sites, carved stone balls (petrospheres) are thought to have been made from the late Neolithic period, around 5,200 years ago. Made of sandstone, greenstone, quartzite and granite, they generally measure around 7cm (2¾in) across – about the size of a tennis ball – and fit comfortably in the hand. Some are beautifully decorated with ornate carvings of spirals and chevrons, others with concentric triangles, hatches and zigzags, and, of over 425 discovered so far, most are adorned with a precise pattern of carved symmetrical knobs. Dorothy N. Marshall's diagrams of the balls, 387 of which are catalogued in Volume 108 of *Proceedings of the Society of Antiquaries of Scotland* (1976), demonstrate that although a few have small indented cups like golf balls, the majority have anywhere from three to 160 knobs, and most have six. Most balls were discovered during agricultural activity and few have been found in an archaeological context – one exception being a rare find in situ at the Ness of Brodgar in 2013.

Theories about the balls' purpose include use as weights for nets, leatherworking tools, currency, weight measures, thrown weapons, ceremonial speaking stones, oracles, game pieces and ball bearings for monument construction. But the central question remains: what would justify the time and effort spent on the precision and, in some cases, intricacy of the carvings? Another theory speculates that the balls may have been a Neolithic stonemason's "portable résumé". The range in skill shown, from master-craftsman level to basic scratching, may support such a theory, but no balls have been found in graves, indicating they may not have been valued as personal artefacts. Another much-debated theory is that the balls represent very early experimentation with solid geometric figures.

The designs and portability of the balls reminded Australian researcher Lynne Kelly of stone "memory devices" used by some indigenous peoples. Use of these is linked with notable places in the landscape and a tradition of following a journey along structured paths called songlines. They aid in recording knowledge, such as of navigation and astronomy, or of ethical or other guidelines. Kelly believes that the stone balls might be connected to the nearby stone circles as portable memory devices.

The balls can be seen in several museums, including the National Museum of Scotland, the Ashmolean in Oxford, the Hunterian Museum in Glasgow, and the British Museum. A recent report indicates that a six-knobbed stone ball, very similar in appearance to the Scottish stone balls, is on display in the National Archaeology Museum in La Paz, Bolivia – part of an exhibition of finds from Lake Titicaca. New connections? The mystery continues …

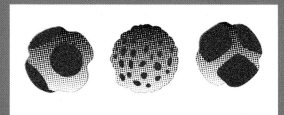

Neolithic carved stone balls

AUQUHOLLIE Alt Name: **Lang Stane**
Standing Stone | Nearest Town: **Stonehaven**
Map: **NO 8233 9080** | Sheets: **E396 L38** | Lat: **57.008N** | Long: **2.29255W**

A good standing stone, 2.35m (8½ft) tall, with fine views. Now in a little fenced enclosure, it is alleged to have once been part of a circle – however there is no evidence for this. An ogham inscription reads "VUO NO N (I) TEDOV". The Pictish carvings that were once visible on the northeast side of the stone can no longer be seen.

AUCHQUHORTHIES
Stone Circle | Nearest Village: **Portlethen**
Map: **NO 9019 9634** | Sheets: **E406 L38** | Lat: **57.058N** | Long: **2.16336W**

A complex site in an open, pastureland setting, with views across to the sea. It has quite a jumbled appearance on first sight, but the recumbent stone circle and ring cairn are both well preserved. It's thought that in its final form the circle was about 18m (59ft) across, and had at least 18 stones, set on the edge of a platform and encircling a cairn. Fourteen stones remain, two are stumps. There is an unusual forecourt feature in front of the recumbent, framed by two stones. The recumbent itself is 2.7m (9ft) long and nearly 1.4m (4ft 7in) tall. The eastern flanker is missing. The rest of the standing stones might seem irregular, but it's believed that there were in fact two circles, with differently sized stones, eight of the larger type and seven or even nine of the smaller. The ring cairn has a more or less continuous kerb, but has been badly robbed.

Nearby | At NO 9036 9608, in a field just over 300m (984ft) southeast of Auchquhorthies, is the 26m (85ft) diameter **Old Bourtreebush** stone circle. Five stones remain (one fallen), with two other possible candidates for inclusion in the circle in the west and east.

At NO 9064 9750, 1.2km (¾ mile) northeast of Auchquhorthies, is the reconstructed stone circle and cairn of **Cairnwell**. It was moved 175m (574ft) northwest of its original position to make way for an industrial site in 1995 and now stands in a landscaped setting beside a road. Excavation showed a complex sequence of activity, from a semi-circle of pits to the monument as it now appears.

Photo © Matthew Chapman

Recumbent Stone Circles

Adam Welfare, an archaeologist with Historic Environment Scotland

Recumbent stone circles are found only in northeast Scotland, although they share several characteristics with many other stone rings scattered throughout Britain and Ireland. Over 70 are known, and their most distinctive feature is a large, horizontal stone positioned in the southern quadrant of the circle. This recumbent stone is the broadest and bulkiest stone and is invariably carefully levelled, although its summit is not necessarily flat. It may have an asymmetric, boat-like profile (as at Aikey Brae and Kirkton of Bourtie) and appear to be raked slightly backward, while its external face is often striking, adding to its impressiveness. Two tall stones fitting tightly against each end of the recumbent are termed "flankers" and together the three form the recumbent setting. The flankers, which usually tower over the recumbent (Cothiemuir Wood, page 319, is a good example) normally form a contrasting pair, with one being slender, while the other is stout. Many have a pronounced curve to their silhouette (as at Midmar Kirk, see page 316) and, together with the recumbent stone they make an important visual statement, often enhanced by a flattening of the ring's curvature in this sector. The remainder of the ring is usually made up of between six and 10 upright stones or orthostats. Their broader faces are generally turned outward, like those of the recumbent and flankers; and they are positioned in pairs either side of the ring's axis, forming a remarkably regular circle behind the recumbent setting – which can appear skewed by comparison. The uprights are also roughly graded in height from the flankers to the shortest stone, which is typically situated somewhere in the ring's northeast quadrant. Their diameter usually measures between 15m and 25m (49–82ft), but larger and smaller examples are found. If there are cup-marks, they almost always occur on the recumbent setting or the adjacent uprights (as at Sunhoney, page 316).

However, a recumbent stone circle is more than a distinctive ring. The stones' footings are generally embedded within a rubble platform encircling a low, flat-topped, polygonal cairn. The platform is usually well founded, but not much larger than the ring, and its outer perimeter is rarely neatly finished. This contrasts with the cairn, which will generally be carefully built, despite being constructed directly on subsoil. Where these are ring cairns, tightly packed kerb stones retain an earth and rubble matrix with a small kerbed court at the centre (as at Auchquhorthies, page 313). The outer kerbs are sometimes turned outward to link with the recumbent or flankers, while kerb stones themselves sometimes crudely mimic the grading of the ring stones. Other cairns appear to lack a central court, while a small group of rings in the extreme northeast are connected with small kerbed stony walls enclosing relatively wide, open courts.

Excavation since the mid-19th century has yielded useful information, but a clear structural sequence was only retrieved from Tomnaverie (see page 317) at the end of the 20th century. A series of dates confirming the origin of these circles in the early Bronze Age was also obtained. The earliest activity was denoted by a small heap of burnt soil, charcoal and pulverized bone: debris from a funeral pyre. This was later enclosed within a low cairn bonded with the platform, at the edge of which the recumbent stone circle was later erected – necessitating the reconfiguration of the cairn behind the recumbent setting so that the kerb linked with the flankers.

The location of the recumbent setting provides the ring with a distinct orientation, although whether the target lies in the sky or the landscape has proved contentious. Until recently, the range of azimuths (an azimuth being the angle between a celestial body and the north, measured clockwise around the observer's horizon) appeared to favour the moon as the focus. This was thought to be supported by the common incidence of cup-marks and milky white quartz in the rings. This mineral, like the orientation and the colours of the stones themselves, was clearly intended to convey meaning, but other aspects of the architecture are also intensely symbolic and every element must contribute to a consistent explanation. The Victorians believed the recumbent setting could be read as a closed doorway, locking ghosts into the circle; but since then it has been slowly comprehended that much of the design appears to have its origin in the architecture of Neolithic chambered tombs. Another level of symbolism construes quartz as referencing the sun, which in radiating warmth and light is synonymous with fire – the means by which the dead who were brought to these places were transmuted into another dimension. Thus, the orientations should be interpreted as generalized solar alignments, which in conjunction with the contrast between the location of the recumbent setting and the smallest upright in the ring, places the emphasis on the winter solstice: the point where the old year dies and the new begins; while the overall symbolism, expressed in the circularity of these monuments, alludes to the cycle of life.

CRAIGHEAD BADENTOY

Stone Circle | Nearest Town: **Portlethen**
Map: **NO 9118 9772** | Sheets: **E406 L38** | Lat: **57.07042N** | Long: **2.14709W**

An unusual site in an industrial setting of huge containers, this reconstructed circle resembles a four-poster, although it seems to have had seven stones originally. All four remaining stones have metal rings attached to their lower faces (once used to tether a flagstaff) and it seems unlikely that any are in their original positions, except possibly the southernmost. The northeastern one has been split using a drill, the marks still clearly visible.

Photo © Sandy Gerrard

CULLERLIE

Stone Circle | Nearest Village: **Echt**
Map: **NJ 7851 0428** | Sheets: **E406 L38** | Lat: **57.12889N** | Long: **2.35659W**

Photo © Martyn Copcutt

Considered by some to be overly manicured, Cullerlie is nevertheless an interesting and unusual site, with a ring of eight large, boulder-like stones that surrounds eight small burial cairns. In the early 19th century there were apparently a number of similar circles to the southwest but no trace of these remains. The site is later than the recumbent circles of the area.

SUNHONEY

Stone Circle | Nearest Village: **Echt**
Map: **NJ 7159 0569** | Sheets: **E406 L38** | Lat: **57.14122N** | Long: **2.47107W**

A lovely if sometimes overgrown recumbent circle, the delightfully named Sunhoney (named after the farm on whose land it stands) is 27m (87ft) in diameter and has 11 red granite or gneiss standing stones along with a large grey granite recumbent, which, although it has slipped (or been moved) and broken, is still impressive at 5.3m (17ft 4in) long. It has more than 30 cup-marks, although some are hard to see. There's a raised platform, 7m (23ft) across and 0.3m (1ft) high, within the circle, probably the remains of a cairn, and cremation deposits were found when the circle was excavated in 1865.

Nearby | At NJ 7260 0712, some 1.7km (just over 1 mile) northeast of Sunhoney, **Barmekin of Echt** is a multi-vallate hill fort with an unusually large number of entrances and five concentric ramparts. It is probably a multiphase monument, as at least one entrance is blocked by a subsequent wall. A 3.3kg (7lb 4oz) Neolithic stone axe made from local chlorite schist was found here in Victorian times and is now in the National Museum of Scotland. It's so big it's thought that it must have been used for cutting down trees.

MIDMAR KIRK

Stone Circle | Nearest Village: **Echt**
Map: **NJ 6994 0649** | Sheets: **E406 L38** | Lat: **57.1483N** | Long: **2.49843W**

Unusually located among gravestones in the churchyard of Midmar Kirk, this recumbent circle of eight stones is 17m (55ft) across. It's thought that there were originally 10 or 11 stones in total. The curved flanking stones, both about 2.5m (8ft) tall, are very striking, resembling horns or teeth. It's a curious place and all the more pleasing for that. The recumbent is massive, 4.5m (14ft) long and up to 1.2m (4ft) wide, and weighing 18 tonnes (20 tons). Five standing stones survive, as well as the two flankers and the recumbent. The remains of a cairn are evident in the southern side of the circle;

Photo © Michael Lindowsky

the cairn could have been cleared away when the graveyard was laid out in 1914.

Nearby | At NJ 6987 0659, just 122m (400ft) or so north of the church, **Midmar Kirk N**, also known as the Balbair Stone, is a fine, slender standing stone in a woodland setting.

GLASSEL
Stone Circle | Nearest Village: **Torphins**
Map: **NO 6490 9969** | Sheets: **E406 L37** | Lat: **57.08686N** | Long: **2.58076W**

> "The forest track to the stones was hard going. Coming back, I followed the river to the road – much easier." Christopher Bickerton

Oddly hard to find if you're not paying attention, Glassel stone circle is in a clearing in woodland, delightful in dappled sunlight. It comprises five standing stones of reddish granite, none of them very tall (1m/3ft 3in is the highest), in a sub-oval setting. The circle is thought to represent a transitional type between recumbent circles and four-posters.

TOMNAVERIE
Stone Circle | Nearest Village: **Tarland**
Map: **NJ 4865 0348** | Sheets: **OL59 L37** | Lat: **57.11937N** | Long: **2.84963W**

Photo © Sandy Gerrard

In a setting that feels rather precarious, almost undercut by a disused quarry, this is a fine recumbent circle. As it is not hemmed in by commercial forestry, the views are wonderful. The 17m (56ft) ring was reconstructed following Richard Bradley's excavations in the late 1990s. There are now 11 stones standing (most of pale red granite), of an original 13, with a 3.2m (10ft 5in) recumbent of grey granite that has two cup-marks. The remains of a central ring cairn can also be seen. The excavation revealed the circle was built on an earlier levelled platform and burial cairn – under the recumbent stone a pit containing charcoal was found, which has been radiocarbon-dated to 2500BC. The apparently organized nature of construction led Bradley to suggest that the entire sequence of building from platform and cairn to final circle was conceived from the outset.

Skyscape Archaeology at Tomnaverie

Liz Henty, Co-editor of the *Journal of Skyscape Archaeology*

Skyscape archaeology is an interdisciplinary way of studying material remains, adopting a phenomenological approach to marry archaeoastronomical research with the known archaeology. This method was applied to recent research into Tomnaverie recumbent stone circle (Henty 2014) to examine the movements of the sun, moon and stars during the year 2580BC, which is the date judged to be the earliest one possible for the construction of the central ring mound (Bradley 2005). When seen from a northeast position outside the circle, below stones 8 and 9, the recumbent arrangement at the southwest appears to form a window to the sky through which an observer can view celestial movements.

In the winter months, between October and February, the setting sun can be observed through this window, with the setting points travelling toward the solstice position and back again. The high full moon would have traversed the recumbent in the winter, but there was apparently no interest in the standstill moon at Tomnaverie. On the night of the winter solstice many bright stars would have set within an hour of each other: the red stars Aldebaran and Betelgeuse to the west of the window, and the bright white Sirius slightly to the south. The stars of Orion's Belt would have appeared to set almost horizontally on top of the recumbent stone. This pastiche of red and white stars corresponds to the red and white (weathered pale grey) stones of the circle. With small variation this cyclical pattern of setting stars would have been visible through the winter months, not just during the year 2580BC but annually, in a spectacular display that was worth staying up for.

In summer the sun sets late in northern Scotland and the sky does not get completely dark, so the long winter nights are more favourable for making celestial observations. Researchers disagree on the nature of the alignments at recumbent stone circles and whether the moon was a specific focus, but considering the repeating solar, lunar and stellar alignments in the winter months it seems likely that circles were built to relate to the winter sky. The sepulchral function of the Tomnaverie circle with its earlier funeral pyres could have been associated with the setting of the sun in the winter, which metaphorically symbolizes death before the spring renewal. It follows that the recumbent arrangement monumentally enshrined the particular configurations of the celestial movements sacred to the builders, creating a holistic cosmology to account for death.

Bradley, R., 2005. *The Moon and the Bonfire: An Investigation of Three Stone Circles in Aberdeenshire*. Edinburgh: Society of Antiquaries of Scotland.

Henty, Liz, 2014. "The Archaeoastronomy of Tomnaverie Recumbent Stone Circle: A Comparison of Methodologies". *Papers from the Institute of Archaeology*, Vol. 24, 2014, pp.45–59.

Find out more about skyscape archaeology at: journals.equinoxpub.com/index.php/JSA

CASTLE FRASER Alt Names: **Balgorkar, West Main**
Stone Circle | Nearest Village: **Kemnay**
Map: **NJ 7150 1253** | Sheets: **E406/421 L38** | Lat: **57.20265N** | Long: **2.47334W**

A fine recumbent stone circle, noted by Aubrey Burl as one of the best examples of its type. It's said there were originally 11 stones here in a 21m (69ft) ring, but one is missing, while others have fallen. One of the stones was knocked over and broken in two in 2002. The recumbent and flankers are really splendid, the 2.25m (7ft 4in) recumbent sitting neatly between flankers that rise to 2.45m (8ft) and 2.7m (8ft 10in) high. The remains of a plough-damaged ring cairn, with a few kerb stones protruding from the mound, can be seen within the circle.

Nearby | At NJ 7174 1252, in the same field as the stone circle, 239m (784ft) to the east, are two standing stones or a stone row. The northeast stone is about 2m (6½ft) in height, the southwest about 1.8m (6ft).

At NJ 7105 1344, just 1km (0.6 miles) northwest of Castle Fraser stone circle, **Woodend of Cluny** or Ton Burn is an extremely impressive 3.3m (11ft) standing stone, covered in lichen and set in a broadleaf plantation.

COTHIEMUIR WOOD Alt Name: **Devil's Hoofmarks**
Stone Circle | Nearest Town: **Alford**
Map: **NJ 6171 1980** | Sheets: **E421 L38** | Lat: **57.26724N** | Long: **2.63649W**

A really lovely location in a woodland clearing. There was some controversy about the area nearby being chosen for a natural burial ground, but it does not impinge on the site. Although the circle is badly damaged it is impressive, with a very large recumbent, 4.3m (14ft) long, and towering 2.7m (9ft) flankers. In 1842 there were still 12 stones but this total is now reduced to eight, with seven still standing. The monument began life as a low cairn, open in the middle, possibly containing a cist. The sockets of two standing stones cut through the cairn, showing that the stone circle was a later addition. The alternative name Devil's Hoofmarks comes from the natural indentations on the recumbent; there are a couple of possible cup-marks as well.

Nearby | At NJ 5965 1939, 2.1km (1¼ miles) west of Cothiemuir Wood, is the wonderful **Old Keig** stone circle. It may be badly damaged, but it still retains much of its power, perhaps due to its enormous recumbent: at 5m (16ft 7in) long, 2m (6½ft) thick and 2.1m (6ft 10in) high, and weighing an estimated 48 tonnes (53 tons), it's the largest and heaviest there is – and it probably travelled 10km (6¼ miles) to get here. The flankers are impressive, too, reaching nearly 3m (9½ft) in height.

> "Still imposing despite most of the east side being destroyed. Like Old Keig, just over 2km (1¼ miles) to the west, this has an excellent recumbent and flankers." Ewen Rennie

This stone has real presence – and fine views. A robbed-out cairn stands within the circle.

At NJ 5527 2794, around 10km (6 miles) northwest of Cothiemuir Wood, is **Ardlair** recumbent stone circle (see photo, page 8), situated in a very impressive location surrounded by hills.

EASTER AQUHORTHIES

Stone Circle | Nearest Town: **Inverurie**
Map: **NJ 7323 2079** | Sheets **E421 L38** | Lat: **57.27695N** | Long: **2.4456W**

An attractive recumbent stone circle, well-kept and neat and, unusually, with all its stones still in place, surrounded by a stone-walled enclosure in a farmland setting. There are 11 stones in the circle plus the recumbent itself, which has three further stones set almost at right angles to it. The standing stones are all red jasper, except the grey granite flanking stones either side of the recumbent. These flankers are the tallest: 2.2–2.4m (7–8ft). The recumbent is 3.8m (12ft 5in) long. The interior may contain a ring cairn and cist, apparently undisturbed.

TYREBAGGER   Alt Name: **Dyce**

Stone Circle | Nearest Village: **Dyce**
Map: **NJ 8595 1322** | Sheets: **E406/421 L38** | Lat: **57.20952N** | Long: **2.23422W**

A wonderful recumbent circle, with a great atmosphere despite the adjacent radio mast and views over Dyce Airport (although a planned bypass will make it noisier in future). Some 18.5m (61ft) in diameter, the circle has stones that are set in a low stony bank that surrounds the remains of a ring cairn. The dark grey granite recumbent is 3.4m (11ft) long, 2.4m (8ft) high, and weighs 21 tonnes (23 tons), while the 10 circle stones, which are from 1.3m (4ft 3in) to 3.2m (10ft 7in) tall, are made of a gritty red granite.

> "To describe Tyrebagger as a beautiful place would be like saying water is wet. I simply don't have the words. I suggest you see for yourself." Sheila Caldwell

Photo © Les Hamilton

BROOMEND OF CRICHIE

Megalithic Complex | Nearest Village: **Port Elphinstone**
Map: **NJ 7791 1968** | Sheets: **E421 L38** | Lat: **57.26723N** | Long: **2.36789W**

Photo © Golux

Close to the main road, an industrial complex and a housing estate, this is a curious site and a melancholy survival of what was an important late Neolithic ceremonial complex. Once there was a six-stone circle inside a small henge, 33.5m (110ft) in diameter, and a 400m (1,312ft) avenue, containing an estimated 72 stones in two rows, that lead south to the river and north to a setting of three concentric circles, 50m (164ft) north of the henge. The stones of the henge circle and avenue were dynamited in the 19th century, leaving just two original stones within the henge, and only three or four stones remaining in the avenue, including one just south of the henge. The three concentric stone circles were also destroyed. The third stone now standing in the henge is a Pictish carved stone that was moved here when the Aberdeen–Inverness railway line was built. It may be a reused prehistoric standing stone, but the fine carvings date to around 600AD.

Nearby | At NJ 7787 1917 and NJ 7783 1922, in woodland some 500m (1,640ft) south of the henge, are the odd stone seats that were constructed from prehistoric cists found when the access road for the now disused papermill was built. The four cists were found at the southern end of the Broomend of Crichie avenue; one was empty, while the others contained Beaker burials.

KIRKTON OF BOURTIE

Stone Circle | Nearest Village: **Oldmeldrum**
Map: **NJ 8009 2488** | Sheets: **E421 L38** | Lat: **57.31404N** | Long: **2.33217W**

Photo © Martyn Copcutt

The recumbent here is absolutely enormous – 5m (16ft) long, 1.9m (6ft 4in) tall and 1.7m (5½ft) wide. Originally there were probably 10 or 11 stones – only four survive. The remaining, eastern flanker is 3m (10ft) tall. Please don't go into the field if there are crops growing; ask for permission at the farm if in doubt.

SOUTH YTHSIE

Stone Circle | Nearest Village: **Tarves**
Map: **NJ 8850 3040** | Sheets: **E421 L30** | Lat: **57.36392N** | Long: **2.19281W**

A really charming circle, set in farmland. It's just 8.2m (27ft) in diameter, with six large, boulder-like stones (the tallest 1.7m/5ft 7in). It may have originally been a four-poster.

> "Very cute little circle, with fine views across the fields."
> Jackie Bates

Photo © Golux

LOANHEAD OF DAVIOT ★

Stone Circle | Nearest Village: **Daviot**
Map: **NJ 7477 2885** | Sheets: **E421 L38** | Lat: **57.34944N** | Long: **2.42089W**

Photo © Richard L. Dixon

This interesting multiphase site has a fine recumbent stone circle, 20.5m (64ft) in diameter, with an interior cist surrounded by a low covering of cairn material and a ring or kerb of smaller stones. The frost-cracked recumbent is large and still has its flankers, and there are eight other stones in the circle, graded in height. The stone east of the eastern flanker has a line of five cup-marks. Nearby is a more recent (*c.* 1500BC) circular cremation cemetery.

Nearby | At NJ 7456 2966, 836m (½ mile) NNW of Loanhead of Daviot, are the remaining stones of the **New Craig** stone circle: a cracked recumbent and its flankers. The stones are impressive (the recumbent is 4m/13ft long) and have been built into a stone wall. A number of other large stones can be seen in the woodland behind.

BACKHILL OF DRACHLAW

Stone Circle | Nearest Town: **Turriff**
Map: **NJ 6729 4633** | Sheets: **E425 L29** | Lat: **57.50597N** | Long: **2.54752W**

Quite an unusual circle for this part of the world, built from six very striking, large pebble-filled conglomerate rocks with no recumbent. The tallest stone is 1.5m (5ft) and the ring is about 8.5m (28ft) across.

> "The stones are unusual in being basaltic with veins of pebbles in them."
> Ewen Rennie

AIKEY BRAE

Stone Circle | Nearest Village: **Mintlaw**
Map: **NJ 9588 4709** | Sheets **E427 L30** | Lat: **57.51397N** | Long: **2.07042W**

Photo © Matthew Davidson

If you walk through the mature plantation to reach this site you'll find it very dark and atmospheric, the trees creaking above you in the wind … stepping out into the sunlight to see the circle is an exciting moment. This is a Buchan-type recumbent stone circle, with a kerbed rubble bank or wall. Excavation in 2001 suggested the circle was imposed on a previous monument, as the holes for the stones cut through the rubble bank. The circle has five erect stones including the impressive and rather whale-like (or phallic, depending on your point of view) recumbent stone and the eastern flanker, and five prostrate stones including the western flanker.

Nearby | At NJ 9610 4974, 2.7km (1½ miles) north of Aikey Brae, **Loudon Wood** can be tricky to find in its plantation setting. It is badly damaged, with just the recumbent and three stones standing, and a few others fallen. The recumbent has been cracked by a recent fire lit beneath it.

STRICHEN HOUSE

Stone Circle | Nearest Village: **Strichen**
Map: **NJ 9367 5449** | Sheets: **E427 L30** | Lat: **57.58041N** | Long: **2.1075W**

Strichen is a site with a fascinating history. In the early 19th century, all the stones of this recumbent circle, except the recumbent and flankers, were taken down by the tenant farmer. The landowner protested, and the circle was reconstructed, incorrectly and in a slightly different place. In 1960, all the stones were removed. The recumbent and flankers were replaced, only to be removed again in 1965 during tree-

Photo © Michael Lindowsky

323

felling operations. Finally, the site was excavated by Aubrey Burl himself in 1979–83, and the circle reconstructed once again, this time in its original position. It's a Buchan-type circle, with the stones set on a low earth bank. There are seven stones in addition to the recumbent and flankers.

NETHERTON

Stone Circle | Nearest Village: **Crimond**
Map: **NK 0433 5722** | Sheets: **E427 L30** | Lat: **57.60496N** | Long: **1.9292W**

This partly restored recumbent stone circle, surrounded by a modern wall and set in a little copse of deciduous woodland, is especially lovely when the bluebells are out. It's about 17m (55ft) across, with eight stones, one of which has fallen. The recumbent is around 2.9m (9½ft) in length.

Nearby | At NK 0276 5716, in a small wooded area 1.6km (1 mile) west of Netherton, **Berrybrae** stone circle has just five remaining stones of an original nine, including the recumbent, 3.3m (10ft 10in) long. The stones are set into an oval bank, 13.7m (45ft) in diameter, which along with the stone circle was the first phase of the monument. A ring cairn in the centre held three cremation burials. The second phase saw the standing stones thrown down, the cairn levelled and an enclosed cremation cemetery created. The bank was reconstructed after Aubrey Burl's 1976 excavation.

MEMSIE

Cairn | Nearest Village: **Memsie**
Map: **NJ 9766 6205** | Sheets: **E427 L30** | Lat: **57.64836N** | Long: **2.04086W**

Once there were three large cairns here – all three around 90m (295ft) in diameter and 12m (39ft) high – as well as lots of small ones, but by 1845 only one remained. It is a well-preserved example and an impressive 24m (78ft) across and about 4.4m (14ft 5in) high. When excavated, a beaker and a broken, leaf-shaped sword were found.

ROTHIEMAY

Stone Circle | Nearest Village: **Milltown of Rothiemay**
Map: **NJ 5508 4872** | Sheets: **E425 L29** | Lat: **57.52639N** | Long: **2.75171W**

Set in a gently sloping field, this recumbent circle in Moray is 28m (92ft) in diameter, and may have had 12 to 14 stones before some of these were removed in the mid-19th century. Only five remain, including the recumbent, which is about 4.3m (14ft) long and up to 1.8m (5ft 10in) in height. It is profusely cup-marked, with at least 19 cup-marks on the top, and 72 on the back, some

Photo © Golux

with rings. The flankers are missing. A geophysical survey suggested there may have been two rings or settings, as at Auchquhorthies (see page 313), or else perhaps a circle with outliers.

Nearby | At NJ 5822 5495, 7km (4½ miles) northeast of Rothiemay is the little **Thorax** stone circle, with all its six stones upright. The stone to the northwest has 22 cup-marks.

TOM NAN CARRAGH

Standing Stones | Nearest Village: **Dulnain Bridge**
Map: **NJ 0111 2464** | Sheets: **OL60/61 L36** | Lat: **57.30161N** | Long: **3.64289W**

The three standing stones here are visible from the A95, on a small hill in the floodplain of the River Spey. About 2.1m (7ft) tall and 100m (328ft) apart, the stones form a dogleg, the lie of the land meaning the end stones are not intervisible. The southerly stone has a partner that lies at its base.

BALNUARAN OF CLAVA   Alt Names: **Mains Of Clava, The Clava Cairns** ★

Clava Cairns | Nearest City: **Inverness**
Map: **NH 7572 4444** | Sheets: **E422 L27** | Lat: **57.47311N** | Long: **4.07398W**

These three large Bronze Age cairns, built around 2000BC, are each surrounded by a circle of standing stones and have given their name to the Clava type of burial cairn. Excavations during the 1990s by Richard Bradley showed the three cairns and surrounding circles at Balnuaran of Clava were all constructed at the same time. Significant amounts of quartz were found, suggesting that the cairns could have glowed white when newly constructed and would have been very striking, at over 3m (10ft) high originally and with a rubble platform extending to the outer standing stones. The kerb of all three cairns is graduated, with the biggest stones to the south or southwest, and causeways link some standing stones with each cairn. It seems likely that each cairn contained a single burial, as at Corrimony (see page 326).

Photo © Jan Holm

BALNUARAN OF CLAVA NE

This chambered ring cairn with a passage and a 16.7m (55ft) diameter kerb is surrounded by a circle of 11 standing stones. Several stones have cup-marks, including two kerb stones, the standing stone northwest of the passage and a horizontal slab in the chamber wall. Originally both this and Balnuaran of Clava SW would have had corbelled roofs with a capstone, covered with cairn material. The monument is aligned with the midwinter solstice; this has been observed by covering the chamber and passage with tarpaulin so the rays of the setting sun can be seen to travel down the passage, dividing the chamber in half and creating an intense beam of light on the back wall.

BALNUARAN OF CLAVA CENTRAL

The central cairn has a central chamber but no passage, and was never roofed. The kerb displays contrasting colours and textures, as well cup-marks, and is 18.3 × 15.9m (60 × 52ft) in diameter. Nine standing stones surround the cairn.

BALNUARAN OF CLAVA SW

Balnuaran of Clava SW has a 16 × 15m (52 × 49ft) kerb and 10 surviving stones in the surrounding circle, through which a road has been built. This monument is almost identical in design and construction to Balnuaran of Clava NE and shares its orientation on the midwinter sun. Viewed from the northeast cairn, the sun would have seemed to set on top of it. Cup-marks can be seen on a foundation stone in the chamber, west of the entrance, and a stone on the south side of the passage.

Nearby | At NH 6878 4508 (sheets: E416, L26), 7km (4½ miles) west of Balnuaran of Clava, **Raigmore**, also known as Stoneyfield, is a reconstructed Clava cairn, moved when its original site was destroyed by road development. It's a multiphase site, once believed to be a stone circle. More recently it was seen as a denuded kerb cairn, but the excavations in 1971–2 showed something more complex, developing from pit-digging and deposition in the early Neolithic, followed by a possibly roofed timber structure with a central hearth, and finally a cairn covering a number of cist burials. It was moved to its present position by volunteers in 1974–5, and has recently been adopted by local people as part of the Adopt a Monument scheme.

CARN DALEY

Clava Cairn | Nearest Village: **Drumnadrochit**
Map: **NH 4945 3146** | Sheets: **E431 L26** | Lat: **57.34867N** | Long: **4.50355W**

A Clava-type burial cairn, 12m (39ft) across, pretty badly damaged. It was excavated in around 1900 but there seem to be no records of this. The kerb is evident on the southern side and the ring of standing stones is mostly missing. Aerial or pole photography is useful here, as the site is much easier to understand from above. See the Megalithic Portal page for a link to a 3D model of this cairn.

CORRIMONY ★

Clava Cairn | Nearest Village: **Cannich**
Map: **NH 3830 3029** | Sheets: **E431 L26** | Lat: **57.33437N** | Long: **4.68793W**

A lovely example of a Clava cairn. Excavation in 1952 led to the discovery of a crouched burial beneath the floor of the chamber; the monument was subsequently restored. It stands on the floodplain of the River Enrick and the kerbed cairn is made of water-worn stones. The chamber is open and the passage is still roofed, so you'll have to crawl in (there's usually a large puddle to add to the fun!). Eleven standing stones surround the cairn, four of which (those nearest the entrance to the passage) have been re-erected

Photo © Christopher Bickerton

– the two to the west are Victorian replacements, made from lintels from the passage. One stone to the northwest has cup-marks on the outer face. The large slab on the top of the cairn, also cup-marked, was probably a capstone.

SWORDALE HILL
Rock Art | Nearest Village: **Evanton**
Map: **NH 5772 6616** | Sheets: **E432 L21** | Lat: **57.66273N** | Long: **4.38657W**

There are at least 28 separate cup-marked rocks here, many discovered since 2011 by Douglas Scott, who also found a henge on the hill's Druim Mor ridge (where there's also a chambered cairn at NH 5788 6614). This is the largest concentration of rock art in the Highlands, a fine display of cup-marks and cup-and-rings. Scott, who suggests a midwinter sunrise alignment for the henge entrance, believes the rock art was ritually created "as a means to contact the spirit ancestors in the underworld as the sun or moon rose out of, or set into, the land of the dead".

CLACH MHIC MHIOS
Standing Stone | Nearest Village: **Lothbeg**
Map: **NC 9404 1508** | Sheets: **E444 L17** | Lat: **58.11199N** | Long: **3.79991W**

Standing among the heather on a hillock in what is surely one of this book's remotest locations (it's not far from the road, but there's not a lot going on up here in Glen Loth), this splendid standing stone is a very impressive 3.3m (11ft) red sandstone monolith, up to 1.4m (4ft 11in) broad. The path – if you can call it a path – from the road can be extremely boggy. In 1911 there were apparently two stones of smaller size nearby, but there's no sign of them now.

LEARABLE HILL
Multiple Stone Rows | Nearest Village: **Helmsdale**
Map: **NC 8925 2355** | Sheets: **E444 L17** | Lat: **58.18683N** | Long: **3.88523W**

Up on Learable Hill, there is a cluster of four groups of stone rows together with a standing stone, stone circle and several cairns. This was clearly a special place in the prehistoric period. The stone rows, in common with others in the region, are composed of small stones, mostly between 0.1m and 0.4m, (3in and 1ft 3in), and many are hidden in the heather. All the rows are of the characteristic Caithness and Sutherland fan-shaped type. The northern group includes at least three lines of stones, while the adjacent one has up to nine individual rows extending for about 54m (177ft). The remaining rows are separated from the northern ones by a large standing stone (at NC 8925 2349) that has been Christianized by a small, incised cross. South of this stone is another group that includes seven lines of edge-set stones. The final group is situated east of the large standing stone and can be particularly difficult to find. Only three stones now survive but it is known to have been more extensive.

The stone circle (at NC 8916 2351) is a short distance to the west of the rows and has at least seven upright, small slabs around an area measuring 20 × 17.5m (65ft 6in × 57½ft). Some of the cairns in the vicinity may be the result of clearance but most are probably associated with the rows and circle.

Nearby | At NC 8757 2830, 5km (just over 3 miles) northwest of Learable Hill, is **Kinbrace Burn** chambered cairn, an Orkney-Cromarty short-horned cairn with a Camster-type chamber. Measuring

17.2 × 16.6m (56ft 5in × 54ft 5in), it's badly robbed and clearly defined only to the north. The near-central chamber is very disturbed and filled with rubble. A heart-shaped serpentine amulet was apparently found here during excavations before 1911, but is now lost. There are more cairns of various types near here, but this one is the closest to the road.

BADANLOCH   Alt Name: Cnoc Molach
Multiple Stone Rows | Nearest Village: **Kinbrace**
Map: **NC 7826 3516** | Sheets: **E448 L17** | Lat: **58.28814N** | Long: **4.07812W**

There are hut circles, a field system and a burnt mound up here on the Cnoc Molach moorland, as well as seven rows of stones, aligned NNE–SSW. Around 28 stones have been identified. The largest stone in the alignment is just 0.7m (2ft 4in) high – most of them are tiny and only visible when the vegetation has died back.

BULDOO   Alt Name: **Latheron Two Stones**
Standing Stones | Nearest Village: **Latheron**
Map: **ND 2000 3369** | Sheets: **E450 L11** | Lat: **58.28452N** | Long: **3.36597W**

Buldoo is a very large standing stone, 3.9m (12ft 8in) tall, with a rather smaller, squatter companion to the southwest.

> "My first thought was that this stone's purpose was as an aid to navigation, like some similarly situated standing stones in the Western Isles!"
> Miles Newman

Photo © Miles Newman

HILL O' MANY STANES   Alt Name: **Mid Clyth**
Multiple Stone Rows | Nearest Village: **Mid Clyth**
Map: **ND 2952 3840** | Sheets: **E450 L11/12** | Lat: **58.32849N** | Long: **3.20504W**

Photo © Adrian Mantle

The best-preserved and most accessible of the multiple-stone-row sites in Scotland, this is an impressive place. The stones may all be less than 1m (3ft 3in) tall, many hidden among the gorse and heather, but there are lots and lots of them – around 200 of the 250 visible in the 19th century, arranged in 22 rows, forming a fan-shaped pattern. If the pattern was ever complete, there would have been over 600 stones originally. Alexander Thom proposed that the stones formed a lunar observatory, and – having made similar observations at other sites – that major and minor lunar standstills can be sighted from here. This is disputed by most current archaeoastronomers and archaeologists – it would seem difficult to use such small stones for sighting.

CAIRN O' GET   Alt Name: **Garrywhin**

Chambered Cairn | Nearest Village: **Ulbster**
Map: **ND 3133 4112** | Sheets: **E450 L11/12** | Lat: **58.35316N** | Long: **3.17502W**

The Cairn o' Get is a Neolithic chambered cairn of the short-horned Orkney-Cromarty type, damaged but still impressive. It seems to have originated as a round chambered cairn and is about 2.2m (7ft 4in) in height, with two horned forecourts, one to the north and one to the south. The passage is 3.3m (10ft 9in) long, open to the sky – as is the chamber itself. Excavations in 1866 found the bones of seven or so people in the antechamber, and a further cremation deposit in the main chamber.

Nearby | At ND 3138 4129, 178m (584ft) NNE of Cairn o' Get, are the **Garrywhin** multiple stone rows. Here, six to eight rows of three to 13 stones radiate from a cairn around 10m (33ft) in diameter, with a cist burial. The stones are small, many hardly showing above the peat. There are further groups of stone rows nearby: at **Broughwin** (ND 3124 4127, ND 3124 4095, ND 3120 4098), **Loch Watenan** (ND 3174 4108), **Groat's Loch** (ND 3102 4065) and **Clash-an-Dam** (ND 3122 4041).

SOUTH YARROWS ⭐

Chambered Cairn | Nearest Village: **Thrumster**
Map: **ND 3048 4320** | Sheets: **E450 L11/12** | Lat: **58.37164N** | Long: **3.19011W**

The South Yarrows long cairn is quite close to the car park and road, but the best way to it is to follow the South Yarrows Archaeological Trail (the link to download a guide is on the Megalithic Portal web pages for these sites). It takes about two hours, has some steep climbs and there are pleasing duckboards across the boggy bits making you feel like you're having a proper adventure. The trail takes in various sites, including, at the start of the trail, a broch on an islet in the loch (a multiphase construction, with the walls remaining to 2.7m/8ft 10in high in places), as well as hut circles, a hill fort and two horned long cairns.

SOUTH LONG CAIRN

At ND 3048 4320, 467m (¼ mile) WSW of the broch, is the southerly long cairn, an Orkney-Cromarty type, built with huge slabs of Caithness flagstone. It retains much of its covering cairn and has a Camster-type chamber with three stalls at the eastern end. A similar, smaller chamber in the middle of the cairn has been destroyed along with half its passage. The cairn is about 78m (255ft) long, varying in height from 1.5m to 3.7m (5ft to 12ft). The profile and the short passage suggest it began life as a chambered round cairn.

Photo © Cezary Namirski

NORTH LONG CAIRN

At ND 3049 4346, 269m (883ft) north of the above long cairn, is another horned long cairn. This is less complete than the south cairn, but some detail of the east-facing chamber can still be seen. Both of these cairns seem to have been reused for centuries; a later cist burial was inserted here, which contained an urn and 70 tiny lignite disc beads from a jet necklace. A carved stone ball (see page 312) with eight knobs was found nearby in the 1930s and is now in the Royal Museum of Scotland.

Nearby | At ND 3129 4403, 1.2km (¾ mile) northeast of South Yarrows, on the eastern shore of the Loch of Yarrows, the **Battle Moss** stone rows include eight more or less parallel rows of 18–21 stone slabs, aligned north–south and stretching about 40m (131ft). None is more than 0.3m (1ft) high – many are much smaller – and about 100 of them remain. Up to 80 of them remain visible above ground or just beneath the surface. Here in 2003 Kenneth Brophy led the first excavation of a Scottish multiple stone row in modern times. No dating evidence was recovered but nothing was found to suggest this is anything other than a Bronze Age monument. Alexander Thom had proposed that this and other sites had lunar alignments, and that the rows here were now irregular because some stones had been moved since erection. However the excavation showed that some stones had been deliberately aligned off-axis, so Battle Moss had not been built as a series of completely parallel lines, thus disproving the alignment theory. In all likelihood, the monument had been constructed over a period of time rather than in one burst of activity. Further research by Alex Carnes has suggested that the stone rows of Caithness and Dartmoor are linked, and that both are gradual developments of the long mound and older long-house traditions of honouring the ancestors.

ACHAVANICH Alt Names: **Loch Stemster, Achkinloch**
Stone Setting | Nearest Village: **Latheron**
Map: **ND 1879 4177** | Sheet **E450 L11/12** | Lat: **58.35687N** | Long: **3.38948W**

Photo © Drew Parsons

330

Achavanich is an unusual horseshoe-shaped setting. The stones have their narrow rather than broad profiles turned toward the centre. There are 34 stones still in position, from an original 54, mostly on the western side. They are set among the heather with a good view of the mountainous Highlands to the southwest; the name means "field of the monks". A cist burial found about 700m (under ½ mile) away was found to contain a Beaker burial that, thanks to recent work led by Maya Hoole, is now recognized as one of the earliest Bronze Age burials in Scotland (2455–2147BC). The young woman, nicknamed Ava, has been facially reconstructed. Analysis of pollen found on pottery buried with her identified many plants and flowers, including meadowsweet and St John's wort, known to have medicinal uses.

GREY CAIRNS OF CAMSTER

Chambered Cairns | Nearest Town: **Wick**
Map: **ND 2601 4420** | Sheets **E450 L11/12** | Lat: **58.37995N** | Long: **3.26689W**

CHAMBERED LONG CAIRN

Surely one of the most impressive, dramatic and well-preserved chambered cairns in Britain, the Orkney-Cromarty-type horned long cairn at ND 2601 4420 is 69.5m (228ft) long, with a forecourt at each end and two separate chambers with their own passages and entrances, each with a sheep-proof gate. They're easily accessible, close to the road and you don't really need a torch as they have roof lights. You will have to crawl, though, so be prepared to get muddy. Excavations in the 1970s demonstrated that the monument began as two round cairns, later joined together with more cairn material. The passages were extended at this time.

CHAMBERED ROUND CAIRN

The round cairn at ND 2608 4403 is a well-preserved Orkney-Cromarty type, some 3.7m (12ft) high and 18m (59ft) across. A passage leads to a central corbelled chamber with dry-stone walling, divided into three by large vertical slabs. Excavation in the 19th century uncovered burnt bones, pottery and flint tools from the chamber, as well as further skeletal remains in the chamber and passage.

Nearby | At ND 2602 4379, about 250m (820ft) south of the Grey Cairns, the **Camster** stone rows are apparently intact, with six rows, up to 26.8m (88ft) in length, running more or less north–south. Many (if not most) of the stones are under peat; in September 2016 only two were clearly visible.

CNOC FREICEADAIN

Chambered Cairns | Nearest Village: **Reay**
Map: **ND 0132 6541** | Sheets: **E450 L11/12** | Lat: **58.56553N** | Long: **3.69805W**

Two Neolithic long-horned chambered cairns occupy the top of the hill, with a view over the decommissioned Dounreay nuclear power station. The cairn at ND 0132 6541 is 67m (219ft) long and aligned northeast–southwest. At ND 0124 6532, just 100m (328ft) from its sibling and set at right angles to it, is the Na Tri Sithean cairn (the name, meaning "the three fairy mounds", originally referred to both tombs). Na Tri Sithean is another long and impressive cairn – at 71m (233ft), it is one of the longest of its type. It has a round mound at either end, probably both containing a chamber.

Photo © Hamish Fenton

It's likely that it began life as two separate round cairns, later joined together.

Nearby | Within 1km (0.6 miles) NNW and WNW of the two cairns are the **Upper Dounreay** stone rows, chambered cairn and standing stone. At ND 0117 6596, 564m (1,850ft) NNW and visible from here, is the stone row at **Creag Bhreac Mhor**.

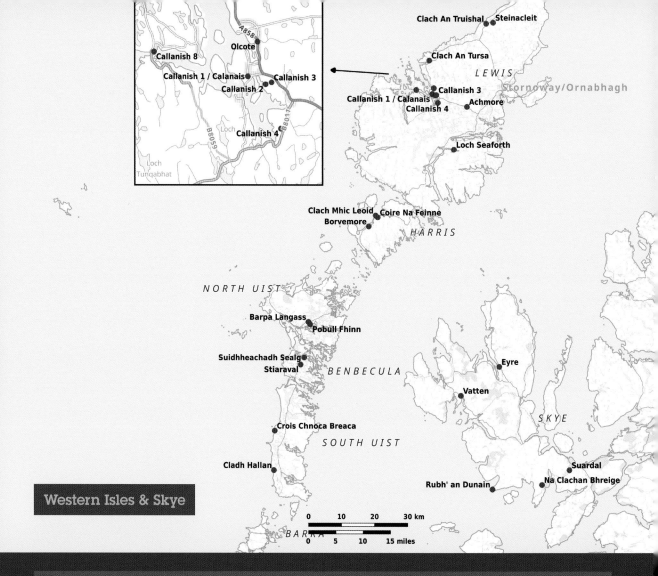

Western Isles & Skye

Callanish 8
Olcote
Callanish 1 / Calanais
Callanish 2
Callanish 3
Callanish 4
Loch Tungabhat
Loch

Clach An Truishal
Steinacleit
Clach An Tursa
LEWIS
Stornoway/Ornabhagh
Callanish 1 / Calanais
Callanish 3
Achmore
Callanish 4
Loch Seaforth

Clach Mhic Leoid
Borvemore
Coire Na Feinne
HARRIS

NORTH UIST

Barpa Langass
Pobull Fhinn

Suidhheachadh Sealg
Stiaraval
BENBECULA

Eyre

Vatten

SKYE

Crois Chnoca Breaca
SOUTH UIST

Cladh Hallan

Suardal
Na Clachan Bhreige

Rubh' an Dunain

BARRA

| 0 | 10 | 20 | 30 km |
| 0 | 5 | 10 | 15 miles |

NA CLACHAN BHREIGE

Stone Circle | Nearest Village: **Elgol**
Map: **NG 5434 1769** | Sheets: **E411 L32** | Lat: **57.18392N** | Long: **6.06695W**

Set amid some truly spectacular scenery on Skye, this is a difficult site to access, surrounded on three sides by water. The route from the Elgol road can be very boggy, with a stream to ford. The name means "false stones". Three stones remain standing, while one has fallen, in a circle originally measuring about 5.4m (18ft) in diameter. The stones are 1.5m (5ft), 2m (6½ft), and 1.8m (6ft) respectively; their prone companion is 3.5m (11½ft) in length. As at many sites, they're said to be men turned to stone, but this time for deserting their wives – a salutary lesson to would-be philanderers.

Photo © Les Hamilton

SUARDAL Alt Name: **An Sithean**
Chambered Cairn | Nearest Village: **Broadford**
Map: **NG 6272 2203** | Sheets: **E411 L32** | Lat: **57.2273N** | Long: **5.93277W**

Photo © Andy Burnham

In a stunning setting, this chambered cairn (probably Hebridean type) is easy to spot, set on a knoll close to the road. It is about 12m (39ft) across and up to 2m (6½ft) high; the larger stones sticking out could be what is left of the chamber. The alternative name means "hill of the fairies", so watch out!

Nearby | At NG 6417 2378, 2.3km (just under 1½ miles) from Suardal, by the roadside in Broadford, a mound covered with flowers and trees has something of an atmosphere of mystery. Known as **Corry**, or Liveras, this badly robbed Hebridean type chambered cairn is about 23 × 16.7m (77 × 55ft), and 4m (13ft) tall. Finds here included an (archer's?) wristguard of grey-green stone (a similar one was found on the beach, perhaps dumped there) and a pottery urn containing a secondary burial. Part of the eastern side of the cairn was destroyed when the road was made, revealing at least one stone cist. The 2.4 × 1.8m (8 × 5ft) capstone is apparently still to the north side of the mound.

RUBH' AN DUNAIN
Chambered Cairn | Nearest Village: **Carbost**
Map: **NG 3934 1636** | Sheets: **E411 L32** | Lat: **57.16381N** | Long: **6.31299W**

Close to the shore of Loch na h-Airde, this would have been an imposing example of a Hebridean-type round cairn built of rectangular slabs of dry-stone wall, surrounded by round boulders from the beach, about 20m (66ft) across and 3m (10ft) tall. The roof is missing, so you can easily

Photo © Les Hamilton

"There is another 'rather doubtful' prehistoric cairn just to the west (at NG 3929 1639), worth having a look for it while you're there. If you find it, send us a photo!"
Andy Burnham

see into the polygonal chamber, and there's a 3m (10ft) passage. During excavation in 1931–2 the remains of six adults were found, along with flint and quartz chips and pottery that offered evidence of the use of the forecourt as a focus for communal gathering. The chamber appears to have been deliberately filled in with earth following the final burial.

VATTEN

Probable Chambered Cairns | Nearest Village: **Dunvegan**
Map: **NG 2984 4399** | Sheets: **E407/410 L23** | Lat: **57.40572N** | Long: **6.49976W**

There are two (probable) Hebridean-type chambered cairns here, sited much like Cnoc Freiceadain (see page 331). Both are pretty ruinous but still impressive on the horizon and worth an explore. The southern cairn is up to 3.3m (11ft) high and 33.5–36.5m (110–120ft) across. Robbing has created a massive central hollow without exposing a central chamber (presumably there is one). The northern cairn is taller, about 5m (16ft) high, and 30m (98ft) across, and in better condition than its sibling.

EYRE Alt Name: **Sornaichean Coir Fhinn**

Stone Row | Nearest Village: **Kensaleyre**
Map: **NG 4143 5251** | Sheets: **E408 L23** | Lat: **57.4888N** | Long: **6.31636W**

Two stones on the shore of Loch Eyre. They're about 4.2m (14ft) apart, the northern stone is 1.5m (5ft) and the southern is 1.7m (5½ft). It's said there was once a third stone, but there's no sign of it now. In folklore, these are the stones that supported Fingal's cooking pot over the fire.

CLADH HALLAN

Prehistoric Settlement | Nearest Village: **Dalabrog**
Map: **NF 7314 2198** | Sheets: **E453 L31** | Lat: **57.17173N** | Long: **7.41035W**

At Cladh Hallan on South Uist the remains of several Bronze Age and Iron Age houses were found in the machair during sand quarrying. Three terraced roundhouses can be visited, thought to be just a fraction of the original settlement, as well as a double roundhouse on the north side of the track. One house showed evidence of continuous habitation and repair over many hundreds of years, which is very unusual. The site is best known for one of the first discoveries of prehistoric mummies ever made in the UK. Two burials showed evidence of mummification, and one body turned out to be a composite – made up of the skeletal remains of three individuals. The head and neck belonged to one man, the jaw to a second and the rest of the body to a third. The head and jaw, like the remains of a woman and infant also found, had been curated for about 300–400 years before burial, but the rest of the body belonged to a man who had died 500 years earlier.

CROIS CHNOCA BREACA

Standing Stone | Nearest Village: **Stoneybridge**
Map: **NF 7340 3366** | Sheets: **E453 L22** | Lat: **57.276401N** | Long: **7.421388W**

This fine pillar of Lewisian gneiss, 2m (6½ft) high, was named for its resemblance to a cross. It is also somewhat reminiscent of a human figure with head and arms, apparently eagerly gazing out to sea. It stands on a mound of packing stones and it is not clear whether it was deliberately installed in its current leaning position.

Nearby | At NF 7703 3211, 3.9km (under 2½ miles) east of Crois Chnoca Breaca, is **An Carra** standing stone, also known as Bheinn a'Charra. It is a fine stone, tapering toward the top, and an impressive 5.2m (17ft) high.

STIARAVAL

Chambered Cairn | Nearest Village: **Gramsdal**
Map: **NF 8121 5260** | Sheets: **E453 L22** | Lat: **57.45131N** | Long: **7.31694W**

This chambered cairn on Benbecula had a southeast entrance, and the passage, of which only the northern side remains, led to a circular chamber. It's difficult to estimate exactly how big the cairn was because much of the stone has been robbed away.

Nearby | At NF 8170 5247, 505m (1,657ft) east of Stiaraval, is the **Airidh na h-aon Oidche** chambered cairn, sited on a hilltop and appearing to form part of the horizon along with two distant hills over on the Isle of Skye 42km (26 miles) away. At NF 8143 5313, 576m

Photo © Hamish Fenton

(1,890ft) NNE of Stiaraval, is the playing-card shaped **Stiarval** standing stone, damaged by frost. At around NF 7360 4952, about 10km (6 miles) southwest of Stiaraval, is **Lionacleit**, where it is possible to see the preserved remains of a prehistoric submerged woodland on the shoreline.

SUIDHHEACHADH SEALG Alt Name: **Gramisdale South**

Stone Circle | Nearest Village: **Gramsdal**
Map: **NF 8249 5521** | Sheets: **E453 L22** | Lat: **57.47555N** | Long: **7.29908W**

A badly damaged circle, originally around 27m (89ft) in diameter. The tallest stone may have had its top broken off – it is now about 1.5m (5ft) high. The five stones of the western arc are less than 1m (3ft 3in) high, some also broken, and there are four or five fallen stones. Within the circle are the low remains of a chambered cairn. There's a standing stone close by to the north, at NF 8250 5528.

Nearby | At NF 8251 5613, 918m (just over ½ mile) north of Suidhheachadh Sealg, is **Gramisdale**, a ruinous stone circle originally c. 26m (85ft) in diameter.

BARPA LANGASS

Chambered Cairn | Nearest Village: **Clachan a Luib**
Map: **NF 8377 6573** | Sheets: **E454 L18** | Lat: **57.57053N** | Long: **7.29154W**

Photo © Hamish Fenton

On North Uist, this is a Hebridean round cairn, which have "funnel" entrances, narrow passages and simple chambers. Early examples, like this one, have a peristalith (circle of stones) around the perimeter. It's about 4m (13ft) high and 24m (80ft) across, with 14 stones of the peristalith visible. The funnel-shaped forecourt is on the eastern side, full of material removed during attempts to find the passage. The oval chamber is 4 × 1.8m (13 × 6ft), roofed with three lintels. There is no access to the interior due to the collapse of part of the entrance passage.

POBULL FHINN   Alt Name: **Ben Langass**

Stone Circle | Nearest Village: **Clachan a Luib**
Map: **NF 8428 6502** | Sheets: **E454 L18** | Lat: **57.56454N** | Long: **7.28207W**

In a breathtaking location just over the hill from Barpa Langass, this circle of about 24 stones, *c.* 18m (59ft) across its longest axis, is built on an artificial platform. The largest stone is about 1.5m (5ft) high.

    Nearby | There are cairns at NF 8323 6297, 2.3km (1½ miles) southwest of Pobull Fhinn and at NF 8334 6290, 2.3km (1½ miles) SSW; at NF 8289 6303 is **Loch a' Phobuill** circle, 2.4km (1½ miles) to the SSW of Pobull Fhinn; a chambered cairn is at NF 8331 6271, 2.5km (1½ miles) SSW of Pobull Fhinn.

Photo © Gareth L. Evans

BORVEMORE

Stone Row | Nearest Village: **Scarista**
Map: **NG 0202 9392** | Sheets: **E455 L18** | Lat: **57.83518N** | Long: **7.02245W**

This fine stone on Harris stands 2m (6½ft) tall, with wonderful views across the sea to Taransay. Two nearby prostrate slabs may have once been upright, part of a stone setting. In the early 20th century there were four fallen stones, and it's said there was a stone circle here but this is unconfirmed.

COIRE NA FEINNE

Chambered Cairn | Nearest Village: **Horgabost**
Map: **NG 0472 9663** | Sheets: **E455 L18** | Lat: **57.8612N** | Long: **6.98054W**

Planted up with flowers, the remains of this chambered cairn sit in the corner of a steeply sloping garden beside the Tarbert to Leverburgh road. The cairn was all gone before the end of the 18th century, but the stones of the chamber and the fallen capstone, 2.2m (7ft) across with two cup-marks on the upper surface, are quite impressive. Human bones were found here in 1859.

CLACH MHIC LEOID   Alt Names: **MacLeod's Stone, Nisabost**

Standing Stone | Nearest Village: **Horgabost**
Map: **NG 0410 9718** | Sheets: **E455 L18** | Lat: **57.86573N** | Long: **6.9916W**

Photo © Elizabeth Yeatts

An impressive stone, possibly once part of a row, in a really spectacular location overlooking the sea. It's 3.3m (10½ft) in height and 1.4m (4ft 6in) wide. Small boulders at the foot of the stone, and two large slabs nearby, are probably the remains of a cairn. The SSW face of the stone has veins of feldspar and quartz. It has been noted that the profile of its top is identical to the most striking part of Taransay behind. Coincidence – or not?

LOCH SEAFORTH   Alt Name: **Sìdeval**

Stone Circle | Nearest Village: **Arivruaich**
Map: **NB 2782 1664** | Sheets: **E457 L13** | Lat: **58.055N** | Long: **6.61548W**

An isolated, ruinous 16.6m (54ft) circle with wonderful views. Seven stones are visible of a probable 10. One stands in the field, one has fallen, there are three in the field wall, one in the north wall of the ruined blackhouse and probably two within the eastern wall and two in the southern wall. About 98m (100ft) south of the circle, below the high-water mark, is a setting of 20 or so stones on the shore.

Nearby | At NB 2724 1455, 2.2km (1¼ miles) SSW of Loch Seaforth, on Lewis, is the 5m (16ft) **Cailleach na Mointeach** kerbed cairn, recently discovered on top of one of the hills that form the "knees" of the female landscape form known as the Cailleach na Mointeach ("old woman of the moors"), also called the Sleeping Beauty (see page 341). This isolated site is a challenge to get to. The nearest road is the reasonable track off the A859 that runs between the end of Loch Seaforth and Loch Skebacleit, and then it is a hike up a steep hill.

ACHMORE

Stone Circle | Nearest Village: **Achmore**
Map: **NB 3174 2926** | Sheets: **E459 L8** | Lat: **58.1704N** | Long: **6.56376W**

Uncovered gradually as peat was cut for fuel, the stones of this circle were first noticed in the 1930s. Investigation in the 1980s by Gerald and Margaret Ponting (now Margaret Curtis) demonstrated that the site was, in fact, a circle, about 41m (135ft) in diameter and with 22 stones, two of which remain upright. From here the hills of the Cailleach na Mointeach or Sleeping Beauty (see page 341) resemble a pregnant woman – this is the only place from where they have this appearance and it seems possible the circle was sited here for this reason. The walk to the site from the parking place is boggy.

CALLANISH   Alt Name: **Calanais**

Stone Circle | Nearest Village: **Callanish**
Map: **NB 2130 3301** | Sheets: **E459 L8** | Lat: **58.19753N** | Long: **6.74513W**

A number of sites come under the general heading of Callanish, although these days the main site is known and signposted by its Gaelic equivalent, Calanais. The Isle of Lewis is a long way from most of Britain, and the journey to get there, whether by air or sea, makes a visit feel like a real accomplishment. On a hillock called Cnoc an Tursa ("hill of sorrow"), the setting of around 40 stones, which incorporates a later chambered cairn with a second cairn nearby, resembles from above a Celtic or wheel cross, with stone rows extending from the circle approximately toward the cardinal points. The double northern row is closed by the arc of the circle. A single stone standing opposite the inmost of the southern alignment suggests that this may also have been a double row originally. Outside the southwest arc of the circle is an outlier, which may be the remains of a second circle.

The stones are of wonderful Lewis gneiss, said to have come from the west side of the ridge Druim nan Eum (NB 228 338), and all are striking no matter what the weather. The tallest, a truly impressive 4.7m (15ft 7in) high, stands in the centre of the circle; the others range down to 1m (3ft 3in). The site was cleared of 1.5m (5ft) of peat in the mid-19th century. The chambered cairn within the circle incorporates the central pillar within the line of its kerb on the west, and two of the circle stones on the east. Some cairn material remains but the double chamber no longer has its capstones. The second cairn, reduced to ground level, impinges on the northeast arc of the circle.

A number of alignments have been proposed for the stone circle; most famous is that it marks the major southern lunar standstill that occurs every 18.6 years, when the moon is seen apparently born from between the thighs of the Sleeping Beauty, skims the horizon and vanishes, only to reappear to shine dramatically into the circle (see box, page 341). A legend tells of a Shining One who passes down the avenue on midsummer morning, heralded by a cuckoo.

The Highlands and Islands Enterprise (HIE) fund is supporting Calanais Visitor Centre to work in collaboration with the University of St Andrews to create 3D scans of the stone circles and map buried features. This amazing site has a car park and a visitor's centre, and the stones are free to enter.

Nearby | Around NB 213 338, 788m (½ mile) north of the stone circle, is **Callanish 16**, a 1m (3ft 3in) high stone between the two most northerly houses of Callanish village, to the east of the road.

Photo © Swen Stroop

What is the Lunar Standstill?

Vicky Tuckman (Morgan), former Editor of the Megalithic Portal

As solstices are for the sun, so lunar standstills are for the moon, but while the solstice takes place twice a year, in June and December, lunar standstills follow an 18.6-year cycle (not the same thing as the 19-year Metonic cycle). They occur when the moon reaches its most extreme point in relation to the horizon; in other words when it is at its highest and lowest point in the sky, and its rising and setting points are at their most northerly and southerly, and the moon appears to stand still before starting to retrace its steps on subsequent nights. At this time, when the moon is closest to the horizon, an optical illusion makes it seem much larger than usual – and the further north you travel, the more impressive this becomes. For a few months either side of the standstill, the effect is almost as impressive.

The moon last reached its furthest southerly point in September 2006. The next major standstill will be in April 2025 – so not too long to wait if you are a follower of deep time.

Both the northern and southern major extremes occur in the same lunar month, but it is the major southernmost rising point that the sites of Callanish seem designed to observe.

CALLANISH 2 Alt Name: **Cnoc Ceann a'Gharraidh**
Stone Circle | Nearest Village: **Callanish**
Map: **NB 2221 3261** | Sheets: **E459 L8** | Lat: **58.19454N** | Long: **6.72913W**

Before the peat was cleared from the site in 1858 only the five stones still standing could be seen. They range in height from 1.9m to 3.2m (6ft 3in to 10½ft). The removal of about 0.9m (3ft) of peat revealed further stones, as well as five holes containing fragments of charcoal, possibly post-holes; these are more or less invisible to the naked eye these days. There's a badly damaged cairn near the centre of the circle. One stone, thought erroneously to have an ogham inscription, was taken to Stornoway where it stood for some 60 years opposite the entrance to Lews Castle until being partially broken up for building material in 1919. This circle is intervisible with several other sites in the landscape; the Pontings have suggested that its major axis alignment represents a symbolic indication of moonrise at the southern major standstill, an alignment that is also found at other sites in the area. In addition, seen from here, Callanish 6 would have appeared silhouetted against the rising moon at the southern minor standstill. When the stones of Callanish 10 were erect, they would have been very conspicuous on the horizon; at the northern major standstill, the moon would have been seen to rise over them and set over Cnoc a' Phrionnsa, a nearby chambered cairn.

CALLANISH 3 Alt Name: **Cnoc Fillibhir Bheag**
Stone Circle | Nearest Village: **Callanish**
Map: **NB 2251 3271** | Sheets: **E459 L8** | Lat: **58.19558N** | Long: **6.72414W**

Probably the most visited of the minor sites, as it's close to the main road. The four stones that stand within the ring are an interesting feature and there has been much discussion about the shape of the site: is it a pair of concentric circles, or perhaps a circle containing a quadrilateral setting? Eight stones stand in the outer ring, ranging in height from 1m (3ft 3in) to 1.7m (5ft 10in), with five fallen.

Nearby | At NB 2268 3207, 659m (less than ½ mile) SSE of Callanish 3, is **Cnoc Fillinhir Mhor** stone row. At NB 2297 3362, 1km (0.6 miles) northeast of Callanish 3 is **Callanish 10** stone circle, excavated in 2003 by Colin Richards and team from the University of Manchester.

Photo © Spumador

The Song of the Low Moon

Grahame Gardner, geomancer specializing in geopathic/technopathic stress remediation

Solar alignments at prehistoric sites are relatively straightforward to demonstrate. The apparent position of sunrises throughout the year has not moved much since Neolithic times, and the sun's cycle is regular and fairly easy to plot. Not so the moon's, however. Because of the wobble in its orbit – like a plate spinning on its rim – the moon can go through the extremes of rising and setting positions in a month that the sun follows over a whole year. Add to this the greater wobble of the 19-year Metonic cycle and other longer-term rhythms, and many archaeologists would argue that lunar alignments are unlikely, as these cycles are just too long-term to have been noticed by ancient people. But just because the cycles would have required observation by more than one generation, doesn't mean that people weren't trying to record them. The night sky must have played a big part in our ancestors' lives, especially in the long, dark winters in the north. The main site at Callanish seems designed for observation of the major southern standstill, as Gerald and Margaret Ponting (now Margaret Curtis) discovered back in the 1980s. When viewed from the end of the Callanish avenue, the low moon skims just above the stones of the east row before setting behind the rocky outcrop of Cnoc-an-Tursa to the south. Then the magic happens … for a brief moment the moon reappears in the centre of the circle, just between the tallest megalith and the cairn, and then vanishes once more. This only happens at the major lunar standstill.

I was at Callanish 2 for the lunar standstill in 2006, gazing southward toward the Sleeping Beauty mountain (the Cailleach na Mointeach, or Old Woman of the Moor), where the lowest full moon since 1987 was expected to rise. As midnight approached I was considering giving up, as it looked like the moonrise would be obscured by clouds, but gave one last glance toward the south, where a faint coppery glow was just suffusing the Sleeping Beauty's thighs. This was it! An ululation of welcome could be heard from the main site of Callanish, and we stood in awed reverence as the beautiful golden disc slid majestically into the sky over the recumbent goddess. I could feel the stones of the circle come alive around us as they drank in the lunar energy. We watched for an hour or two as the moon rolled low over the body and face of the Sleeping Beauty, then as some clouds started to develop, we walked up to the main Callanish stones to join the throng there.

The clouds cleared long enough for a good view of the moon skimming over the stones of the east row as it moved toward setting, but soon it was completely obscured and we could only guess at its position. It looked like that was the end of the show, but right at the crucial minute there was a brief coppery flash in the middle of the circle, like a candle flame guttering – and then it was gone. It felt like the clocks had been reset; the old cycle had ended and a new pattern had emerged to set the tone for the next 19 years.

A longer version is available at:
www.westerngeomancy.org/articles/the-song-of-the-low-moon-2006/

CALLANISH 4 Alt Name: **Ceann Hulavig**

Stone Circle | Nearest Village: **Garynahine**
Map: **NB 2299 3041** | Sheets: **E459 L8** | Lat: **58.17531N** | Long: **6.71339W**

Photo © Sandy Gerrard

Five tall, narrow stones remain here, with their wider faces turned to the interior. The circle is about 10m (33ft) across, and contains the remains of a cairn. The stones are irregularly spaced, suggesting one may be missing. The tallest is 2.7m (9ft) high. Park by the side of the road – it's a short walk through a gate to the boggy site.

Nearby | At NB 2343 2990, about 674m (under ½ mile) ESE of Callanish 4, is **Callanish 5**, or Airigh nam Bidearan, stone row. An "airigh" or shieling was a summer pasture, where families would live in shieling huts tending their cattle. There are five stones forming the row and another outlier to the north – perhaps one day more stones will emerge from the peat. None of the remaining stones is more than 1m (3ft 3in) high. At NB 2465 3034, 1.7km (just over 1 mile) east of Callanish 4, are the remains of **Callanish 6** stone circle.

CALLANISH 8 Alt Names: **Bernera Bridge, Cleitir**

Standing Stones | Nearest Village: **Earshader**
Map: **NB 1642 3424** | Sheets: **E459 L13** | Lat: **58.205409N** | Long: **6.829318W**

> **"The position of the stones at the narrowest point between the islands of Bernera and Lewis is of interest and possibly significant."** Sandy Gerrard

Some 5km (3 miles) west of the main Callanish site, overlooking the bridge that links Lewis to the little island of Bernera, is this very unusual site, unique in Britain. A semi-circle of four standing stones (the tallest is 2.7m/9ft) and a prostrate pillar are sited on a steep slope above a cliff that rises 12.5m (40ft) from the water. There's no suggestion that this was once a whole circle, half of which has fallen – this is how it was built.

OLCOTE Alt Name: **Breasclete Cairn**

Kerbed Cairn | Nearest Village: **Breasclete**
Map: **NB 2179 3473** | Sheets: **E459 L8** | Lat: **58.21324N** | Long: **6.73874W**

This kerbed cairn, only half of which remains, was discovered during improvements to the road through Breasclete. Excavation demonstrated this was a three-phase site, with what have been suggested as ritualistic ard markings found on the original ground surface. A large number of post-holes were also found, probably part of phase two – the construction of the cairn. This is unusual in having two kerbs, the outer one of stones laid flat rather than on end. A cremation urn was found in the central cist, and a path of slabs led to this from the northeast, flanked by posts. The cairn was then covered with some 400 quartz flakes. A poor-quality raw material, quartz is full of symbolism and perhaps linked to funerary rituals. Further excavation found more post-holes, suggesting successive structures. The cairn's original entrance appeared to be aligned on the avenue at Callanish (see page 338). This entrance was later blocked and a second entrance built.

Photo © Sandy Gerrard

Nearby | At NB 2103 3549, 1km (0.6 miles) WNW of Olcote, are the remains of the **Cnoc a Phrinossa** chambered cairn, with great views over the loch. Permission is needed from the landowner to visit.

CLACH AN TURSA Alt Names: **Stone of Sadness, Carloway Row**
Stone Row | Nearest Village: **Carloway**
Map: **NB 2041 4295** | Sheets: **E459 L8** | Lat: **58.28591N** | Long: **6.77214W**

The stone that still stands is 2.4m (8ft) tall and 1m (3ft 3in) across its widest face. Two others lie prostrate and broken – one would have been 4.4m (14ft 8in) and the other 5.2m (17ft) long. On private land – ask permission for a closer view.

CLACH AN TRUISHAL

Standing Stone | Nearest Village: **Ballantrushal**
Map: **NB 3756 5377** | Sheets: **E460 L8** | Lat: **58.3934N** | Long: **6.4929W**

Said to be Scotland's tallest standing stone, this impressive beast reaches 6m (20ft) in height, and is about 1.8m (6ft) wide, with an estimated 2m (6½ft) still underground. It's said the stone was once surrounded by a circle, the stones of which were broken up and used as lintels and in field walls, the last one, apparently, having been taken for a lintel in around 1914. There are plenty of suspiciously suitable stones in the walls nearby, and in 2006 three stone sockets were found, one of which was preceded by a timber post. It appears that a more or less horizontal platform for the circle was created by modifying the natural ground surface.

STEINACLEIT
Possible Chambered Tomb | Nearest Village: **Shader**
Map: **NB 3963 5408** | Sheets: **E460 L8** | Lat: **58.39663N** | Long: **6.45837W**

343

There are great views of moorland and lochs from this enigmatic site, which has in the past been variously identified as a chambered cairn, or, alternatively, as some kind of building. The sign at the site suggests that it is probably best interpreted as a prehistoric settlement with a surrounding stock enclosure.

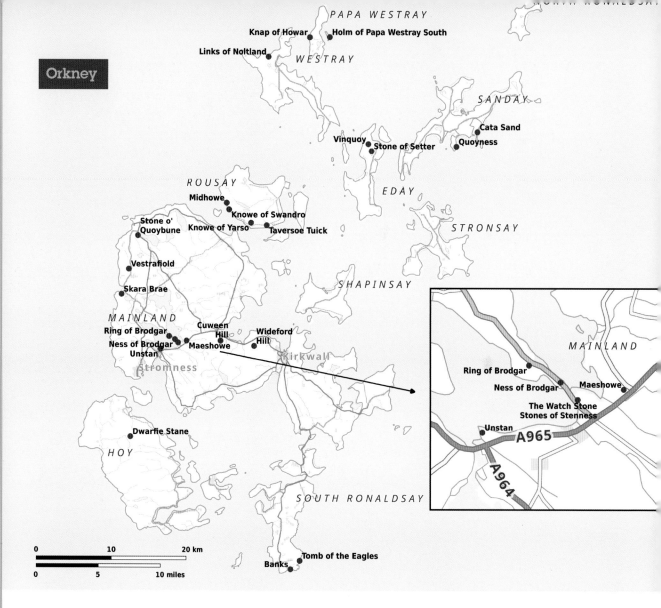

Orkney

PAPA WESTRAY

Knap of Howar
Holm of Papa Westray South

Links of Noltland
WESTRAY

SANDAY

Cata Sand
Vinquoy
Stone of Setter
Quoyness

ROUSAY
Midhowe
EDAY

Knowe of Swandro
Stone o'
Quoybune
Knowe of Yarso
Taversoe Tuick
STRONSAY

Vestrafiold

Skara Brae

MAINLAND
SHAPINSAY

Cuween
Hill
Ring of Brodgar
Wideford
Hill
Ness of Brodgar
Maeshowe
Unstan
Kirkwall
Stromness

Dwarfie Stane

HOY

SOUTH RONALDSAY

Tomb of the Eagles
Banks

0   10   20 km
0   5   10 miles

MAINLAND

Ring of Brodgar
Ness of Brodgar
Maeshowe
The Watch Stone
Stones of Stenness
Unstan
A965
A964

RING OF BRODGAR

Stone Circle | Nearest Village: **Finstown**
Map: **HY 2945 1335** | Sheets: **E463 L6** | Lat: **59.0014N** | Long: **3.22976W**

A narrow strip of land separates the Loch of Stenness from the Loch of Harray. This is the Ness of Brodgar, location of some of the most spectacular prehistoric sites in Britain, wide open to both water and sky. There are stone circles at both ends; the northerly one is the Ring of Brodgar, a Class II henge with a well-preserved ditch hewn out of the solid bedrock by its prehistoric builders. This ditch, 10m (33ft) wide and 0.9–1.8m (3–6ft) deep, was 3m (10ft) deep originally. Within the henge is a stone circle, 103.5m (340ft) in diameter, the stones set just within the scarp of the ditch. There's no bank – and no evidence there ever was one. Just 14 stones remained standing at the Ring of Brodgar in the mid-

19th century, but 13 have since been re-erected, and the sockets of another 13 have been found – it's thought there were probably about 60 stones when the circle was built. Some of the remaining stones are stumps, but the unbroken ones are impressive, between 2m and 4.5m (6½ft and 14ft 9in) in height. In the 12th century AD a man named Bjorn carved his name on one of the northern stones using twig runes.

Photo © Shannon O'Grady

STONES OF STENNESS
Stone Circle | Nearest Village: **Finstown**
Map: **HY 3067 1252** | Sheets: **E463 L6** | Lat: **58.99415N** | Long: **3.20827W**

Photo © John Braid

Four uprights, rising to 6m (20ft) high, remain of a 30m (98ft) circle of 11 or 12 stones, standing on a mound once surrounded by a now-destroyed henge bank and rock-cut ditch 45m (148ft) in diameter, 7m (23ft) wide and 2m (6½ft) deep. Excavation revealed a central setting of stones, with cremated bone, charcoal and grooved ware pottery suggesting, along with radiocarbon-dating, a date of 3000BC. A paved path leads from the entrance to the central hearth, which was once misinterpreted as an altar; a dolmen was constructed over it in 1906, but removed in the 1970s. Today there is a central stone slab with two small upright stones, referred to by some as a cove, the gap between them lining up with Maeshowe (see page 348). There are a number of standing stones nearby; one of these, the Odin Stone, was destroyed in 1814. Prior to that, oaths were taken, love plighted and bargains sealed by grasping hands through a hole in the stone.

Nearby | At HY 3076 1270, just 200m (656ft) northeast of the Stones of Stenness, **Barnhouse** is a settlement of a similar age to Skara Brae (see page 349). Structure 8 appears to have been a ceremonial area, with access through what seems to be a symbolic fireplace. It's believed the buildings were deliberately demolished – what you see now is partly reconstructed on top of the original walls.

NESS OF BRODGAR

Neolithic Settlement | Nearest Village: **Finstown**
Map: **HY 3024 1294** | Sheets: **E463 L6** | Lat: **58.99786N** | Long: **3.21584W**

Photo by Adam Stanford © Aerial-Cam Ltd

Here on the narrow strip of land between the Ring of Brodgar and the Stones of Stenness is where a large notched stone, originally thought to be from a cist, was ploughed up in 2003. This led to the excavations of a large structure, very similar to one at Barnhouse (see page 345). And that was just the beginning. Most recently, archaeologists have found a structure unlike any other at the Ness of Brodgar. "The sheer size and scale of the stones unearthed are unprecedented on this site," said site director Nick Card. "The way the stones are built into the construction is also unique to the Ness. This all suggests that they may have been reused and taken from elsewhere." The dig here is ongoing every July–August but it's covered up out of season, so there's not much to see when the archaeologists aren't working.

THE WATCH STONE

Standing Stone | Nearest Village: **Finstown**
Map: **HY 3055 1264** | Sheets: **E463 L6** | Lat: **58.9952N** | Long: **3.2104W**

Standing 170m (558ft) NNW of the Stones of Stenness, this spectacular standing stone is considered to be associated with the circle. It's 5.6m (18ft 4in) high and 1.5m (5ft) wide. The stump of a second stone, now removed, was found nearby when the road was built. Together, both stones appear to be sentinels marking the approach to the causeway that links the Stones of Stenness site and the Ring of Brodgar as well as the Ness of Brodgar, which is located between them.

UNSTAN   Alt Name: **Knowe of Onston**

Chambered Cairn | Nearest Town: **Stromness**
Map: **HY 2829 1172** | Sheets: **E463 L6** | Lat: **58.98657N** | Long: **3.24942W**

It's well worth the effort of crawling through a very narrow 8m (26ft) entrance passage to the 16 × 6m (52 × 20ft) wide chamber, which is surprisingly bright (there are lights in the concrete roof dome) and spacious, with five stalls on each side. Excavation found flint tools along with crouched burials (typically of later date than Neolithic, so possibly the last to be interred). So many pot sherds were found that the tomb has given its name to this particular type of pottery, Unstan ware, which has a grooved pattern below the rim and a round bottom.

Excavations at the Ness of Brodgar

Andy Burnham, founder and Editor of the Megalithic Portal

The 2017 season was a very successful one at the Ness of Brodgar. Over the eight-week excavation, around 21,500 people visited the site, where an international team were hard at work. The Ness lived up to its reputation of throwing up lots of new questions, but also some magnificent finds, including two items that suggest contact between Orkney and the Stonehenge area. The first was a fragment of pot with decoration reminiscent of pottery from Durrington Walls. The other was a tiny "incense cup" – there are only four other examples of this kind of pot in the UK, all from the Stonehenge area. Usually highly decorated and mostly found in early Bronze Age contexts – often associated with burials – it has been suggested that they were used to carry embers to a funeral pyre or for burning incense during burial ceremonies.

The excavation of a huge midden mound continued during 2017. At first it was thought this was nothing more than a monumental pile of rubbish — conspicuous Stone Age consumption. In 2014, however, the stump of a standing stone turned up at the foot of the mound, and in 2015, sections of walling and uprights were found, followed the next year by massive stone slabs in the remains of a puzzling structure. These structural remnants seemed to represent a chambered cairn, similar to the one excavated at Bookan, at the other end of the Ness, in 2002. As the weeks passed, the sheer scale of the building – known as Structure 27 – became clearer. The building was enormous and the stone slabs so big it was suggested they were re-purposed standing stones. These massive megaliths were used to support uprights that clad the structure's interior wall face. Given its position, Structure 27 is likely to predate many of the other buildings on the Ness. The work in summer 2018 should hopefully have given a better idea of the layout of this building.

Meanwhile, another fragment of pottery added to the evidence that the Neolithic midden was remodelled in the Iron Age, thousands of years after the site was abandoned. Not only was a ditch cut into the mound, but a revetment wall, on the upslope side, was enhanced by a large bank, held at the rear by another revetment wall. "If these structures ran right round the crest of the mound … the visual effect would have been striking in the extreme," said site director Nick Card, of the University of the Highlands and Islands Archaeology Institute.

Over 14 years since the discovery of the Ness complex, the site continues to produce extraordinary artefacts. Nick says, "2017 saw more artwork, stunning stone tools and a beautiful example of an early Bronze Age barbed-and-tanged flint arrowhead, recovered from the exterior of Structure 10." This is the so-called "cathedral" that overlaid the animal bone thought to be a decommissioning feast. Such finds, together with the dating evidence, are key to the idea that the start of the Bronze Age heralded the demise of the Ness, and also confirm that Bronze Age influences made it this far north.

Support the excavations by making a donation or buying a copy of the excellent guidebook at: www.nessofbrodgar.co.uk

MAESHOWE

Chambered Cairn | Nearest Village: **Finstown**
Map: **HY 3182 1277** | Sheets: **E463 L6** | Lat: **58.99658N** | Long: **3.18834W**

Probably the most famous Neolithic chambered cairn or passage grave in the UK, and the largest tomb in Orkney, Maeshowe dates from around 2800BC. Although the corbelled roof was shattered in 1861 by overenthusiastic archaeologists, luckily they didn't do too much structural damage. The design and construction of the tomb is stunning, with beautifully underpinned and dressed slabs giving a smooth appearance, even where they oversail one another as they soar toward the roof. The tomb was built around the non-structural standing stones in the corners of the main chamber. It is thought that the stones that line the entrance passage were also originally standing stones.

The entrance passage, around 10m (33ft) long, leads to the chamber, which is 4.7m (15ft) across and 4.5m (14½ft) high, with the original height possibly as much as 6m (20ft). There are three side cells, and each corner has a buttress to help support the weight of the roof. Just inside the doorway is a triangular niche that holds a huge boulder; this would have been pulled with ropes to close the entrance. As well as the size and magnificent construction, Maeshowe is also famous for its orientation toward winter solstice sunset, when the sun shines down the length of the passage and illuminates the chamber (webcams are usually installed around the time of the winter solstice so you can view this online). It's been speculated that, after thousands of years of disuse, a Viking leader might have been buried here in the 9th or 10th century AD, but there is no evidence for this. The idea came from the radiocarbon-dating of peat used to heighten the bank around the ditch to the 9th century, but this only provides a date for the source of the peat and not the works to the bank. What we do know is that the tomb was broken into by the Norse, who left the largest collection of runic graffiti outside of Scandinavia, as well as carvings of a dragon or lion, an intricately knotted serpent and a seal or walrus. Visits are by guided tour only (booking advised). Parking is at the visitor centre at Stenness, with a bus taking visitors to the site.

Nearby | The **Barnhouse Stone** stands at HY 3127 1217, visible from the main Kirkwall to Stromness road. It's about 3.2m (10½ft) tall and broadens out from the bottom, reaching 1.9m (6ft) wide. It is covered in lichen and appears to be perfectly aligned to the entrance of Maeshowe, 700m (under ½ mile) to the northeast.

CUWEEN HILL   Alt Name: **Tomb of the Beagles**
Chambered Cairn | Nearest Village: **Finstown**
Map: **HY 3642 1277** | Sheets: **E463 L6** | Lat: **58.99729N** | Long: **3.1083W**

Set on a hillside overlooking the Bay of Firth, the chambered cairn at Cuween Hill is still covered by an earthen mound. Attempts to gain access in the 19th century disturbed the corbelled roof, which is now covered by flat stones. However, the corbelling inside is still in good condition. The 5.5m (18ft) entrance passage is very low – it's a long crawl to reach the main chamber. Excavations in 1901 found the remains of at least eight people, along with 24 dog skulls, perhaps representing a totem like the eagles at Isbister (see page 350).

WIDEFORD HILL
Chambered Cairn | Nearest Village: **Hatston**
Map: **HY 4090 1211** | Sheets: **E463 L6** | Lat: **58.992N** | Long: **3.03017W**

A Maeshowe-type chambered cairn, built into the side of Wideford Hill. From the road to Kirkwall it looks like the whole hill is a huge cairn, perhaps representing a deliberate effect by the builders to dominate the local countryside. Entry is via a trapdoor in the roof, with a ladder into the central chamber. There are three side chambers and the original 5m (16ft) long entrance passage, no longer in use. Inside there are rare examples of Neolithic scratch art – a torch is essential.

SKARA BRAE
Neolithic Settlement | Nearest Village: **Sandwick**
Map: **HY 2312 1874** | Sheets: **E463 L6** | Lat: **59.04874N** | Long: **3.34171W**

Orkney certainly does have a multitude of internationally famous sites – and this might be the most famous of all. Skara Brae is a large, well-preserved stone-built Neolithic village, occupied from roughly 3100–2500BC, and just as remarkable as everyone says it is. It was hidden beneath the sand and soil for hundreds of years, until a storm in 1850 partially unearthed it, and it was fully excavated by Gordon

Photo © ABB Photo

Childe between 1928 and 1930. The 10 houses were sunk into the ground and surrounded by their own rubbish, in the form of middens, which acted as insulation. The houses feature a large, square room with a hearth for heating and cooking, ingenious drainage, and the famous stone-built furniture,

349

including beds, cupboards, seats, storage boxes, as well as the "dressers". It is not clear what the use of these so-called dressers actually was; built to the same design and placed in the same position in certain structures directly opposite the entrance, it is now thought that they were more than just furniture and perhaps functioned as altars.

The site was abandoned after about 600 years, although the reason for this change is still uncertain. The weather did get worse around this time, so this may have prompted the abandonment, or it may have been the result of societal changes, from tight-knit to more dispersed groups.

Nearby | There are a number of sites in Sandwick that are traditionally said to have been the sources for the huge stones of Stenness, Maeshowe and Brodgar. **Vestrafiold**, a hill north of the Bay o' Skaill, is the best known. Some quarried stones that never made it off site can still be seen here and recent work has confirmed that megaliths were indeed quarried there. The rock splits easily, making it very appealing to anyone sourcing material for an impressive monument. It's at HY 2410 2200, about 3.4km (just over 2 miles) NNE of Skara Brae.

STANE O' QUOYBUNE   Alt Name: **Wheebin Stone**
Standing Stone | Nearest Village: **Birsay**
Map Ref: **HY 2531 2629** | Sheets: **E463 L6** | Lat: **59.11687N** | Long: **3.30622W**

A fine and impressive stone, almost 3.8m (12ft) high and 1.5m (5ft) wide, on private land but very near the gate, so you can easily see it from the road. This is another of Orkney's standing stones around which a legend regarding a petrified giant has developed. Like the Yetnasteen on the island of Rousay, the Stane o' Quoybune is said to travel to the Boardhouse loch each New Year's morning to drink from the cold waters. Local lore dictates that anyone seeing the stone on its annual trek will not live to see another Hogmanay, so it was not surprising that it was considered unsafe to remain outdoors after midnight and watch for its movements!

TOMB OF THE EAGLES   Alt Name: **Isbister**
Chambered Cairn | Island: **South Ronaldsay**
Map: **ND 4704 8449** | Sheets: **E461 L7** | Lat: **58.7448N** | Long: **2.91675W**

Discovered in 1958 by the late Ronald Simison, the farmer on whose land it stands, the Tomb of the Eagles on South Ronaldsay is a remarkable site. High on the cliffs, with spectacular views of the sea, it's famous for the bones and talons of sea eagles that were found here, which gave it its nickname, and which may represent a tribal/family identity or totem. It's an unusual combination of a Maeshowe type cairn with side cells, and an Orkney-Cromarty type stalled cairn which, although it's been quite badly robbed, is still up to 3m (10ft) high in places. The original roof was removed in antiquity, when the chamber was filled with earth and stones – it now has a concrete roof with skylights. Entry is via the original 3m (10ft) passage – you can either crawl in or use the rather fun little trolley. The tomb was disturbed to the northern and northeastern sides, but the rest was entirely intact, with lots of bones – human, bird and fish. The western side cells mainly held skulls, and recent work on these has found that 16 of the 85 discovered had suffered significant trauma. At least 340 individuals were identified, although some are represented by only a few bones, suggesting excarnation may have taken place at another location before the bones were put in the tomb. There were also many sherds of Unstan ware pottery. Radiocarbon dates suggest the tomb was in use for about 800 years from *c.* 3000BC. There's an interpretation centre in the farmhouse, with various finds from the tomb and an excellent virtual tour.

Nearby | At ND 4646 8411, just 400m (1,312ft) from the Tomb of the Eagles, is the **Isbister burnt mound** (also known as Liddel), surrounding a Bronze Age structure. Although reduced by quarrying (most Orcadian burnt mounds have been lost in this way), it's still almost 2m (6½ft) tall in places, and consists mostly of burnt stones, ash and carbon, added in hundreds of small deposits, basically thrown away after use. (The stones were put in the fire and then added to the water in the trough to heat it.) It seems unlikely that the building ever had a roof, because of the position of the hearth and the size of the trough (1.6 × 1m/5ft 2in × 3ft 3in and 0.6m/2ft deep) – the amount of steam generated would have made it quite unpleasant to work in if it had been an enclosed space.

BANKS   Alt Name: **Tomb of the Otters**
Chambered Cairn | Island: **South Ronaldsay**
Map: **ND 4580 8339** | Sheets: **E461 L7** | Lat: **58.73477N** | Long: **2.93791W**

Hamish Mowatt was landscaping his garden in 2010 when he broke through into an underground chamber. It all got a bit exciting when a camera poked into the hole revealed a human skull … This newly discovered chambered tomb is partly subterranean, with a central chamber and five side cells. Numerous burial deposits and collections of disarticulated bones were found, from at least 15 people, in the one cell that has so far been excavated. Remarkably, DNA testing has revealed that two adults from the tomb had the Hepatitis B virus, which may have caused their deaths.

DWARFIE STANE
Rock-cut Tomb | Island: **Hoy**
Map: **HY 2430 0043** | Sheets: **E462 L7** | Lat: **58.88452N** | Long: **3.31496W**

A unique monument, the Dwarfie Stane on Hoy is not only the only chambered tomb on Hoy, but the only rock-cut (presumably, although this has been disputed) Neolithic tomb in Britain and Ireland. It comprises two cells or chambers cut from a single block of sandstone. The thought that this was done without metal tools is pretty mind-blowing. The squarish stone nearby once blocked the entrance. The Dwarfie Stane has been a popular attraction for visitors to the archipelago for centuries and had a role in Sir Walter Scott's novel *The Pirate* (1822). There's plenty of 18th- and 19th-century graffiti, including some by Major William Mounsey, a former British spy in Afghanistan and Persia (present-day Iran); his name with the date 1850 appears on the south face, above a line of Persian calligraphy which reads "I have sat two nights and so learnt patience" – this apparently refers to his experience of the local midges when he camped here.

MIDHOWE
Chambered Cairn | Island: **Rousay**
Map: **HY 3722 3051** | Sheets: **E464 L5** | Lat: **59.15669N** | Long: **3.09947W**

Built *c.* 3500BC the huge Midhowe chambered cairn on Rousay is Orkney's largest cairn – over 22m (75ft) long. Housed in a protective shed, it is divided by pairs of upright slabs into 12 compartments, several of which contained stone benches. The remains of 25 people were found in the compartments, and Unstan ware pottery was also recovered.

KNOWE OF SWANDRO
Chambered Cairn | Island: **Rousay**
Map: **HY 3753 2966** | Sheets: **E464 L6** | Lat: **59.1491N** | Long: **3.0938W**

At the Knowe of Swandro on Rousay there are Viking, Pictish and Iron Age remains, as well as a recently discovered Neolithic chambered cairn that was thought for many years to be the remains of a broch. Much of the site is under the storm beach and every year there's a risk it will be washed away during the winter. Archaeologists are racing against time to investigate the site.

TAVERSOE TUICK ★
Chambered Cairn | Island: **Rousay**
Map: **HY 4257 2761** | Sheets: **E464 L5** | Lat: **59.13141N** | Long: **3.00517W**

Only two two-storey stalled cairns are known and this is one of them (the other is the less well-preserved Huntersquoy on Eday). The subterranean lower chamber, reached via a 5.8m (19ft) passage, is about 3.7m (12ft) long by 1.5m (5ft) wide and high, and divided into four cells by upright slabs. The upper chamber, covered with a domed roof after excavation in 1937, is divided into two and reached by a 3.4m (11ft) passage. As it's built on a hill, both passages are at ground level. The bones of at least three individuals were found on stone shelves in the upper chamber, and there were three piles of cremated bones in the passage. The lower chamber held further cremated bones, as well as Unstan pottery sherds, a mace head and 35 grey shale disc beads. Both passages had been blocked.

Photo © Drew Parsons

Nearby | At HY 4048 2795, just over 2km (1¼ miles) west of Taversoe Tuick, **Knowe of Yarso** is another Neolithic stalled cairn, where the bones of at least 29 individuals were found – 17 represented only by their skulls – neatly arranged in groups. Scorch marks on the bones and the upper stonework indicate fires were lit within the chamber. The tomb has a modern concrete roof and the chamber is divided into stalls or cells by vertical stone slabs.

LINKS OF NOLTLAND
Neolithic and Bronze Age Settlement | Island: **Westray**
Map: **HY 4280 4930** | Sheet: **E464 L5** | Lat: **59.32619N** | Long: **3.00688W**

This area of sand dunes on the northwest coast of Westray was first recorded in the 19th century but not excavated until the late 1970s. Further investigation is ongoing despite the challenges posed by erosion. Around 30 buildings have been found so far, of both Neolithic and Bronze Age date, including, in 2015, what has been described as the best example of a Bronze Age ritual building discovered in Orkney thus far. In 2009 the site made international headlines with the discovery of the Westray Wife, a *c.* 5,000-year-old sandstone figurine that is one of the oldest representations of a human ever found in Scotland – with what is believed to be Britain's earliest depiction of a human face. The site is open all year round but most of the upstanding structures are covered over for protection outside of the May–September dig season.

Nearby | **Westray Heritage Centre** in Pierowall is where you can see the spiral- and lozenge-carved stone found in the quarry here, known as the Westray Stone. The Westray Wife also lives here, although check she's not being exhibited elsewhere before making a special trip to see her.

KNAP OF HOWAR

Neolithic Settlement | Island: **Papa Westray**
Map: **HY 4830 5180** | Sheets: **E464 L5** | Lat: **59.34934N** | Long: **2.91085W**

This Neolithic farmstead on Papa Westray is at least 1,000 years older than Skara Brae. Knap of Howar means "mound of mounds" and the site was covered by 4m (13ft) of wind-blown sand until it was first excavated in the early 1930s. There are two stone structures here linked by a passage, one a dwelling, the other a barn/workshop. Further excavation in the 1970s produced Unstan ware sherds and radiocarbon dates of 3600–3100BC – at that time, it wasn't on the shore but much further inland, sheltered by a series of dunes. In places the walls retain their full height, with lintels still in place over the doorways, and the house would have had two rooms, divided by stone slabs and wooden posts. Stone shelves and cupboards are built into the walls of one of the rooms of the workshop. The people who lived here bred sheep and cattle, fished, and grew wheat and barley. The houses here are thought to have been part of a larger settlement that awaits further investigation.

HOLM OF PAPA WESTRAY SOUTH
Chambered Cairn | Island: **Holm of Papa (via Papa Westray)**
Map: **HY 5091 5183** | Sheets: **E464 L5** | Lat: **59.34992N** | Long: **2.86496W**

Probably a promontory in the Neolithic, Holm of Papa is a little island off Papa Westray. This large and impressive tomb is a Maeshowe type, but the cairn is long rather than round; the chamber is 20.5m (67ft) long yet narrow, which makes it feel extraordinary. There are 12 side cells, including two doubles, all still intact and with low, lintelled entrances. You enter through a modern roof hatch and down a ladder, instead of crawling through the entrance passage. The tomb contains a number of carved stones; on the lintel over the entrance of the southeast cell are pecked dots and arcs, some making "eyebrow" motifs similar to those found in some Irish chambered tombs. Opposite are circular and zigzag shapes, while south of the entrance, on the southeast wall of the central chamber, there is a double ring and inverted V. Access is by private hire boat, from the Old Pier Papa Westray.

Nearby | At HY 5044 5228, 649m (under ½ mile) WNW, is **Holm of Papa Westray North** chambered cairn. The tomb's main features are still visible even though it has been partly covered over.

STONE OF SETTER
Standing Stone | Island: **Eday**
Map: **HY 5645 3718** | Sheet: **E464/465 L5** | Lat: **59.21899N** | Long: **2.7646W**

On Eday, this is Orkney's tallest solitary standing stone, 4.5m (15ft) high and up to 2.2m (7ft) wide, furry with lichen and riven by weathering. It's very irregular and distinctive in shape. There are three probable small cairns in the vicinity.

Nearby | On the south coast of Eday at Green, the discovery of an unfinished mace head led to a multi-year excavation that identified a Neolithic building with a probable hearth and other internal stonework. More than 100 pottery sherds and 80 Skaill knives – a type of stone tool first found at Skara Brae (see page 349) – were also found. The dig has finished and there is nothing to see on site.

VINQUOY
Chambered Cairn | Island: **Eday**
Map: **HY 5601 3812** | Sheets: **E464/465 L5** | Lat: **59.22711N** | Long: **2.77249W**

There are other chambered cairns on Eday, but this is the only one you can get in (there's a gate to stop the sheep joining you). A restored Maeshowe-type tomb, built from the local red sandstone, it was excavated in 1857 and is about 18m (59ft) in diameter and 2.5m (8ft) tall. The 5m (16ft) entrance passage leads to a polygonal central chamber with four small cells leading off from it. Absolutely fantastic views across much of the archipelago.

CATA SAND Alt Name: **Tresness**
Bronze Age Settlement | Island: **Sanday**
Map: **HY 7044 3967** | Sheets: **E465 L5** | Lat: **59.24256N** | Long: **2.5199W**

Storms in December 2015 revealed a number of potential buildings in the intertidal zone at Tresness on Cata Sand. The site was excavated in 2016–17 (see opposite), revealing an early Neolithic house, the first classic house of this date to be found on Sanday, contemporary with the nearby chambered cairn (HY 7109 3747). Despite the risk from erosion (parts of the site are underwater twice a day), preservation is excellent, as the sandy soil does not destroy bone.

An Early Neolithic House at Cata Sand

Vicki Cummings, Reader in Archaeology at the University of Central Lancashire

Walking to the chambered tomb at Tresness on Sanday in 2015, we came across a series of architectural remains and stone tools on the beach at Cata Sand. As the tools were mainly late Neolithic or early Bronze Age in date, we at first thought we were dealing with occupation remains of the same period, spread widely across the area. However, a geophysical survey showed that occupation remains were restricted to one small area, known as the Grithies Dune. In 2017 we opened a trench over the geophysical anomaly and revealed the remains of an early Neolithic house, defined to the north by a thick wall. Within the house were floor occupation deposits. We also found the remains of at least three hearths, which seem to represent multiple reoccupations of the house, or perhaps the remodelling of the house over time. The northern extent of the house was covered by a thick deposit of midden that may be late Neolithic or even later in date.

Perhaps more surprising was the discovery of two large linear pits cut into the sand. These contained the articulated remains of a number of whales. The eastern pit was excavated and up to 12 whale skeletons were found, although no skulls were recovered. It seems likely that the whales were caught for their blubber during the 19th century: an account of 1875 records that there were multiple decomposing whale carcasses close to Tresness, the smell of which affected the area for miles around. They could, therefore, have been buried to get rid of the bodies and the smell. They were a very peculiar addition to the excavation of a Neolithic structure!

QUOYNESS

Chambered Cairn | Island: **Sanday**
Map: **HY 6766 3779** | Sheets: **E465 L5** | Lat: **59.22547N** | Long: **2.56834W**

The cairn's low passage leads to a central, corbelled chamber, 4 × 2m (13 × 6½ft) and 4m (13ft) high, with six side cells, all with corbelled roofs. Excavations in 1867 revealed skulls and bones from about 15 individuals, placed in the main chamber, side cells and passage. After re-excavation in 1951–2, the cairn was rebuilt to show its stages of construction, rather than its final form.

Nearby | At HY 6764 3753, 260m (853ft) south, is the part-eroded **Augmund Howe** cairn. Surrounding the cairn on its landward side are some hard-to-spot barrows; a further 26 barrows, the **Els Ness** megalithic cemetery, lie 340m (1,115ft) SSW of Quoyness, in the southern part of the peninsula.

Photo © Drew Parsons

Shetland

FETLAR
Hjaltadans

YELL

Pund's Water
Islesburgh
Busta Brae

MAINLAND

Scord of Brouster
Stanydale

FOULA

Lerwick

| 0 | | 10 | | 20 km |
| 0 | 5 | | 10 miles | |

STANYDALE

Possibly Ritual Structure and Stone Circle | Nearest Village: **Walls**
Map: **HU 2853 5024** | Sheets: **E467 L4** | Lat: **60.23547N** | Long: **1.48658W**

This unusual structure stands among Neolithic houses and field systems. It's neither a dwelling nor a tomb, although it does resemble the local heel-shaped cairns. It's horseshoe in shape, with massive, 3.7m (12ft) thick walls enclosing an area 12.2 × 6.1m (40 × 20ft). There are two large post-holes, so it presumably had a timber roof. Evidence suggests at least one of the posts was spruce – and probably arrived as driftwood from north America. Six alcoves are built into the wall, and there were a number of peripheral hearths, which are no longer visible, rather than a central one. The stumps of five or six standing stones, apparently aligned in two sets, stand 12–35m (39–115ft) from the main structure on the north, probably the remains of Bronze Age stone circles or ovals. A number of houses are nearby, all of a similar size. One, at HU 288 503, has a "porch" in front of the entrance, with an enclosure attached.

Nearby | At HU 2560 5165, 3.2km (1½ miles) WNW of Stanydale, is the **Scord of Brouster**. This Neolithic settlement is one of the most complete in Shetland, and also one of the most straightforward to grasp when you're on site, as the houses, clearance cairns and enclosures are easy to identify. Radiocarbon dates put occupation in the late third/early second millennium BC (the ring cairn near the house closest to the road is much more recent – perhaps as many as 1,500 years younger than the settlement). There are at least four houses here, with their associated fields.

Nearby | At HU 2582 5082, 850m (½ mile) SSE of the Scord of Brouster, is **Gallow Hill**, a (possible) chambered cairn, some 25m (82ft) in diameter – unusually big for Shetland. At the centre there is a probable chamber of about 2.5m (8ft) diameter. The setting is beautiful, overlooking the waters of the Voe of Browland.

Photo © Hamish Fenton

ISLESBURGH
Chambered Cairn | Nearest Village: **Brae**
Map: **HU 3345 6845** | Sheets: **E469 L4** | Lat: **60.39857N** | Long: **1.39481W**

Set on Mavis Grind, Islesburgh would have been in a prominent location on a key route for north–south travel and for the portage of boats to and from the Atlantic and the North Sea. This heel-shaped chambered cairn, with two associated enclosures, has a concave façade with a central entrance, from where a narrow passage leads to the small central chamber, now open to the sky.

Nearby | At HU 3488 6739, 1.8km (just over 1 mile) ESE of Islesburgh, in a splendid location overlooking Busta Voe, are the stones of **Busta Brae**. The one still standing is 3.2m (10½ft) and up to 1.8m (6ft) across, a very sturdy and impressive stone thought to weigh about 18 tonnes (20 tons). Local tradition states that the larger stone was thrown here by the Devil from a hill in Northmavine.

PUND'S WATER
Chambered Cairn | Nearest Village: **Brae**
Map: **HU 3265 7117** | Sheets: **E469 L4** | Lat: **60.4237N** | Long: **1.4125W**

With views across Pund's Water, this is a great example of a heel-shaped cairn, its façade measuring at least 15m (50ft), with horns and a central entrance. The passage and chamber are roofless, and the chamber walls are about 1.5m (5ft) high. Some of the roof or cairn material has collapsed into the passage and the chamber. The nearby hill (HU 3265 7117) offers a good aerial view.

HJALTADANS   Alt Name: **Fairy Ring**
Stone Circle or Cairn Circle | Island: **Fetlar**
Map: **HU 6221 9241** | Sheets: **E470 L2/3** | Lat: **60.61014N** | Long: **0.86555W**

This 11.5m (37ft) stone circle or cairn circle has about 22 low stones (as well as some loose slabs) set around an earthen ring about 8m (26ft) across with a 1.5m (5ft) wide southwest entrance. In the centre are two earthfast boulders, which look like cist remains. In legend these are a fiddler and his wife, who legend holds were turned to stone along with a ring of dancing trolls (Hjaltadans means "limping dance"). The site is in a bird-nesting sanctuary so check with the Fetlar Interpretative Centre or the RSPB for the latest access information before visiting.

IRELAND

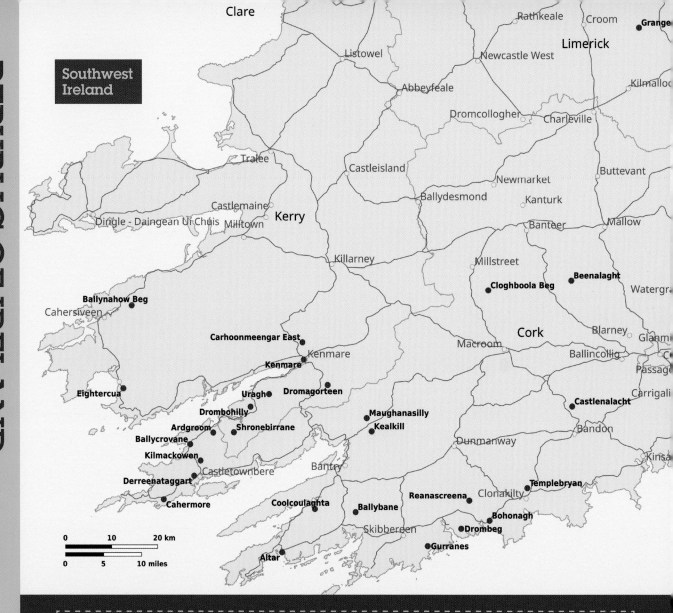

Southwest
Ireland

Clare

Rathkeale · Croom · **Grange**
Listowel · Newcastle West · Limerick
Abbeyfeale · Kilmallo
Dromcollogher · Charleville
Castleisland · Buttevant
Newmarket · Mallow
Ballydesmond · Kanturk
Tralee · Banteer
Castlemaine · Kerry
Dingle - Daingean Uí Chúis · Milltown
Killarney · Millstreet · **Beenalaght** · Watergr
Cloghboola Beg
Ballynahow Beg · Cahersiveen · Cork · Blarney · Glanm
Carhoonmeengar East · Macroom · Ballincollig
Kenmare · Passag
Kenmare · Carrigali
Eightercua · **Uragh** · **Dromagorteen** · **Castlenalacht**
Drombohilly · Bandon
Ardgroom · **Shronebirrane** · **Maughanasilly** · **Kealkill** · Kinsa
Ballycrovane · Dunmanway
Kilmackowen · Castletownbere · Bantry
Derreenataggart · **Coolcoulaghta** · **Reanascreena** · **Templebryan**
Cahermore · Clonakilty
Ballybane · **Bohonagh**
Skibbereen · **Drombeg**
Gurranes
Altar

0   10   20 km
0   5   10 miles

Top 15 Megalithic Sites in Ireland

ALTAR   Alt Name: **Tuama Dingeach na hAltóra**
Wedge Tomb | Townland: **Cove** | Nearest Village: **Skull**
Map: **V 8593 3022** | Sheet: **D88** | Lat: **51.51373N** | Long: **9.64398W**

Photo © Phil Spencer

A reasonably well-preserved wedge tomb in a wonderful setting just 30m (98ft) from the shore. Several of the side stones in the 3.4m (10ft 5in) long structure lean at quite an angle, and there are two roofstones (one 2.7m/8ft 10in long, the second just 0.1m/4in shorter). During excavations in 1989, a pit was found at the east end of the chamber containing fishbones and shells, with a cremation deposit discovered to the west. Access is easy as there is parking in a lay-by next to the site.

COOLCOULAGHTA
Standing Stones | Townland: **Coolcoulaghta** | Nearest Village: **Durrus**
Map: **V 9311 3930** | Sheet: **D88** | Lat: **51.59668N** | Long: **9.54333W**

This pair of nicely shaped stones were removed in 1980 and re-erected in 1983 after complaints from the public. They're both about 1.8m (6ft) tall. Until the early 1970s there was another stone some 60m (200ft) to the SSW, which is said to be buried nearby. The site is signposted, with a parking place that's also convenient for accessing nearby Dunbeacon stone circle.

Nearby | At V 9271 3920, 411m (1,348ft) west of Coolcoulaghta, is **Dunbeacon**, the only stone circle on the Mizen Peninsula. Six of the 11 stones in this damaged but characterful circle are still standing, surrounding a small, leaning central stone.

BALLYBANE   Alt Names: **Rock of the Rings**
Rock Art | Townland: **Ballybane West** | Nearest Village: **Ballydehob**
Map: **W 0184 3867** | Sheet: **D88** | Lat: **51.59197N** | Long: **9.41678W**

Rock art handily located on a small outcrop by the side of the road. Most of the surrounding rock surfaces are pitted and uneven, but those responsible for creating this rock art have taken advantage of a smoother horizontal area, decorating it with a splendid array of loops and rings up to 0.6m (2ft) in diameter, as well as cup-marks and several long, straight grooves.

Nearby | At W 0177 3871, about 70m (230ft) northwest of the roadside panel, is another rock art panel.

Photo © Ken Williams

GURRANES
Alt Names: **Three Ladies, Five Fingers**
Stone Row | Townland: **Gurranes** | Nearest Village: **Castletownshend**
Map: **W 1743 3152** | Sheet: **D89** | Lat: **51.53082N** | Long: **9.19054W**

At Gurranes, three slender, finger-like pillars rise dramatically against the sky, with a fourth stone lying fallen nearby, out of line. There were five stones here originally, but one was removed in the 19th century and now stands in the Somerville Estate at Castletownshend. The stones are impressively tall, the highest reaching 4.3m (14ft).

Photo © Hatsuki Nishio

DROMBEG ★
Stone Circle | Townland: **Drombeg** | Nearest Village: **Glandore**
Map: **W 2467 3516** | Sheet: **D89** | Lat: **51.56455N** | Long: **9.08701W**

With spectacular views down to the sea, Drombeg is probably the best-known stone circle in Ireland, and an excellent example of an axial stone circle. This type of circle, found in counties Cork and Kerry (but having an affinity to the recumbent stone circles of Scotland, see page 314), is characterized by the positioning of a recumbent stone – the axial – usually in the southwest of the circle, directly opposite the two tallest stones, the portals which mark the circle's entrance, with the stones reducing in height from the portal stones to the axial stone. Typically, axial stone circles contain an odd number of stones (from 5 to 19). At Drombeg, there were originally 17 stones in a 9.5m (31ft) ring, of which 15 remain. The stones decrease in height from the 2m/6ft 7in portal stones to the 1m (3ft 3in) recumbent in the southwest. There are three cup-marks on the recumbent, one with a surrounding ring. Pits found within the circle included one containing cremated bone. Some 30m (98ft) to the west are the remains of two hut circles and a fulacht fiadh, where a mound of fire-cracked stone and charcoal-enriched soil, along with a trough, hearth and well, suggest cooking and feasting took place here. The site is easy to find, being well sign-posted and with a car park nearby.

> **"The winter solstice sun sets in the notch in the hills seen through the portals and over the axial stone."**
> Ken Williams

Photo © Jean Renaud

Lithic Symbolism at Drombeg

Terence Meaden, archaeologist and former Professor of Physics at Dalhousie University, Canada

The finest stone circle in southern Ireland, Drombeg is, I propose, replete with lithic symbolism and subtle refinements as to selected shapes and positioning relative to sunrises – not only for the eight traditional agricultural festival days of the year, but for intermediary days, too. All the perimeter stones that remain today are carefully positioned so that at sunrise on 16 optimum dates of the year, shadows are cast either upon the recumbent stone (in the summer half of the year) or upon a grand lozenge stone (in the winter half). One stone bears a carved phallus, while the recumbent has a vulva, both indicative of a fertility religion.

Full details in the open-access *Journal of Lithic Studies*, vol. 4, 5–37, 2017; and in Meaden, T. 2016. *Stonehenge, Avebury and Drombeg Deciphered* Saarbrücken: Lambert Academic.

Photos © Terence Meaden

Carved vulva and phallus at Drombeg

BOHONAGH

Stone Circle | Townland: **Bohonagh** | Nearest Town: **Rosscarbery**
Map: **W 3076 3685** | Sheet: **D89** | Lat: **51.58054N** | Long: **8.99963W**

An impressive axial stone circle with nine of the original 13 stones remaining, including the two portal stones, which reach 2.4m (7ft 10in). Three stones were re-erected after excavation in 1959. The circle is almost 10m (33ft) in diameter, and oriented east–west along the axis from the portal stones to the axial stone. A central pit contained a cremation deposit, and a cup-marked slab was also found. About 16m (52ft) east of the circle is a cup-marked boulder burial. A Bronze Age rectangular wooden house was also excavated at the burial site.

Photo © David Chaika

REANASCREENA

Stone Circle | Townland: **Reanascreena** | Nearest Town: **Rosscarbery**
Map: **W 2640 4106** | Sheet: **D89** | Lat: **51.6178N** | Long: **9.06328W**

Photo © Ken Williams

Surrounded by a low earthen bank with a shallow ditch (usually full of water) and no entrance, Reanascreena ("ring of the shrine") has 12 large, irregularly spaced stones in a 9.1m (30ft) ring, the two portal stones (1.5m/4ft 9in) opposite the axial stone (1.1m/3ft 7in). The circle is aligned east–west. Two pits were found within the circle during excavation in 1961, one with cremated bone fragments. There are several other stone circles within 5km (3 miles) of this site.

"This circle is two or three fields away from the road and difficult to find." Celia Haddon

TEMPLEBRYAN — Alt Name: **Druid's Temple**

Stone Circle | Townland: **Templebryan North** | Nearest Village: **Clonakilty**
Map: **W 3890 4371** | Sheet: **D89** | Lat: **51.64316N** | Long: **8.88335W**

This axial stone circle is on private land, so seek permission, or you can climb the roadside bank to see it without trespassing. Originally an 11-stone circle (nine of which were still standing in the 18th century), now only five remain in the 9.5m (31ft) ring, one of which is fallen. The recumbent is in the SSW.

Nearby | Some 180m (594ft) northwest is a 3m (10ft) ogham stone in an ancient churchyard that is also on private land.

At W 4219 4515, 3.6km (2¼ miles) ENE of Templebryan, is the 2m (6½ft) **Carrig Stone**, said to be the remnant of a pair although a second stone is not in evidence.

At W 4135 3984, some 4.5km (2¾ miles) southeast of Templebryan, the **Ahidelake** standing stone overlooks Inchidoney Bay. Leaning at a very dramatic angle, it is nearly 2m (6½ft) tall (or long).

> "The quartz stone at the centre of the circle is known as Cloich Griene, meaning 'the sunstone'. This is said to be the stone from where nearby Clonakilty got its name." Ebor Benson

CASTLENALACHT

Stone Row | Townland: **Castlenalact** | Nearest Town: **Bandon**
Map: **W 4864 6086** | Sheet: **D86** | Lat: **51.79821N** | Long: **8.74525W**

Photo © John Ibbotson

A splendid stone row, at 13.5m (44ft) the longest in County Cork. The four stones, aligned ENE–WSW, descend in height from 3.4m (11ft) to 1.9m (6ft 2in). The stone lying flat between the two smallest is not part of the original row.

Nearby | At W 4863 6111, 251m (824ft) north of Castlenalacht stone row and visible from it, is a 1.7m (5½ft) tall **standing stone**.

CLOGHBOOLA BEG

Megalithic Complex | Townland: **Cloghboola Beg** | Nearest Town: **Millstreet**
Map: **W 3054 8526** | Sheet: **D79** | Lat: **52.01552N** | Long: **9.01242W**

On a platform of land at the head of the valley in Millstreet Country Park (south of Millstreet), the five-stone circle is just 3m (10ft) in diameter, with an unusual axial stone that's as tall as the portal stones. The complex also includes a well-preserved radial cairn or enclosure (with 19 stones standing), and there are also the possible remains of two stone rows.

> "Comparable to Kealkill but with the rows fallen. This site has the benefit of unrivalled access, including for wheelchair users." FrogCottage42

BEENALAGHT   Alt Names: **An siesar, The Six**

Stone Row | Townland: **Beenalaght** | Nearest Village: **Bweeng**
Map: **W 4852 8731** | Sheet: **D80** | Lat: **52.0359N** | Long: **8.75084W**

Five stones still stand, with one fallen, at this magnificent six-stone row. The stones range in height from 1.8m to 3m (5ft 10in to 9ft 10in).

> "The area is rich in prehistoric remains, especially standing stones." Ken Williams

Photo © Ken Williams

KEALKILL ★

Megalithic Complex | Townland: **Kealkill** | Nearest Village: **Kealkill**
Map: **W 0538 5559** | Sheet: **D85** | Lat: **51.74522N** | Long: **9.37066W**

An interesting and wonderfully located site, with views over Bantry Bay in fine weather. As well as an excellent five-stone axial stone circle, 2.4m (8ft) in diameter (with the recumbent slab in the southwest), there's a pair of standing stones, one very tall and thin and the other shorter and wider, and a cairn. This is one of the few Irish circle sites to have been excavated. Nothing was found except the trenches for a setting of crossed timber "sleepers" that may once have held a stone or wood upright near the centre of the circle. The two large standing stones are about 1.5m (5ft) apart, and the taller of the two was broken at ground level during excavation and re-erected. It would originally have been over 6m (20ft) tall; now it's about 4m (13ft) and the smaller one is 2.4m (8ft) high. South of the standing stones is an 8m (26ft) diameter cairn, incorporating a ring of 18 radially set, sharply pointed stones. Three large, close-set sockets were found in a trench, aligned northeast–southwest, on the northwest perimeter of the cairn.

Nearby | At W 0508 5526, 543m (1,782ft) WSW of Kealkill, is **Breeney More**, where the remains of a stone circle enclosing four boulder burials set in a rectangle can be seen. The stones of Kealkill are visible in the distance.

MAUGHANASILLY   Alt Name: **Ahil More**
Stone Row | Townland: **Maughanasilly** | Nearest Village: **Kealkill**
Map: **W 0432 5841** | Sheet: **D85** | Lat: **51.77042N** | Long: **9.38681W**

A stone row with all five of its block-like stones still standing, in a stunning location on Knockbreteen, overlooking Lough Atooreen. The row, aligned northeast–southwest, is 5.8m (19ft) long. The tallest stone is 1.3m (4ft 3in) high. A piece has broken off one of the stones and lies next to it.

CAHERMORE
Standing Stone | Townland: **Knockroe Middle** | Nearest Village: **Ballydonegan**
Map: **V 5995 4132** | Sheet: **D84** | Lat: **51.60759N** | Long: **10.0223W**

An impressive stone, at least 4m (13ft) tall, very narrow in its north/south profile, with its broader sides facing east/west.

Nearby | At V 5691 4202, just over 3km (almost 2 miles) west of Cahermore, **Killough East** is another classic wedge tomb. Although the tomb is ruinous, what remains is impressive, with a huge capstone or roof slab, 2.7 × 1.7m (8ft 10in × 5½ft). Easily accessed over stiles (there are even signs!).

> "A lovely stone with far-reaching views to the sea. Parking is in a lay-by approximately 250m (820ft) west from the gate to the site."
> David Smyth

DERREENATAGGART
Stone Circle | Townland: **Derreenataggart West** | Nearest Village: **Castletownbere**
Map: **V 6656 4629** | Sheet: **D84** | Lat: **51.65385N** | Long: **9.92894W**

A really charming axial stone circle (pictured on page 368) with lovely views of the mountains and across to the sea. From the portal stones (one 2.4m/7ft 9in, the other broken), the stones decrease in height until the recumbent axial stone is reached, 1.2m (4ft) high and 2.2m (7ft 3in) long. Twelve stones of a probable 15 remain in the 8.5m (28ft) ring, of which three have fallen. Derreenataggart circle is unusual in that its axial stone is in the west, rather than in the southwest.

Nearby | At V 6731 4578, almost 1km (0.6 miles) ESE of Derreenataggart, is **Chaislain Bheara** standing stone, on a rocky outcrop by some recently built houses. It's fenced in, but it's a good tall stone, 3.2m (10ft 5in) high and very narrow.

Photo © Vladimir Nedved

KILMACKOWEN

Standing Stone | Townland: **Kilmackowen** | Nearest Village: **Castletownbere**
Map: **V 6799 4948** | Sheet: **D84** | Lat: **51.68279N** | Long: **9.90943W**

> "When we visited it rained so hard there was no view at all. Still one of my favourites, an absolutely wonderful stone." Jackie Bates

Standing high on Eagle Hill, this magnificent stone can be seen for miles around (given the right weather conditions). It has a classic playing-card shape, measuring 2.9 × 1.7m (9½ × 5½ft), with a thickness of just 0.2m (8in).

Nearby | At V 6805 4936, about 140m (450ft) southeast of the standing stone, is the charming **Kilmackowen wedge tomb**, with a small chamber and cup-marks on one of the side stones.

BALLYCROVANE Alt Name: **Faunkil-and-the-Woods**

Standing Stone | Townland: **Faunkil-and-the-Woods** | Nearest Village: **Eyeries**
Map: **V 6571 5291** | Sheet: **D84** | Lat: **51.713033N** | Long: **9.943685W**

This impressive ogham stone, at 4.7m (15ft 5in) the tallest in Ireland, is likely to have been a prehistoric standing stone. It's set in a splendidly commanding position above Kenmare Bay. The now-weathered ogham inscription has been recorded as MAQI-DECCEDDAS AVI TURANIAS ("of the son of Deich, descendant of Torainn"). Access through the cottage.

ARDGROOM

Stone Circle | Townland: **Ardgroom** | Nearest Village: **Ardgroom**
Map: **V 7087 5534** | Sheet: **D84** | Lat: **51.73609N** | Long: **9.86995W**

Commanding a superb view from its exposed position over Bantry Bay, this fine, although somewhat atypical, axial stone circle has pillar-like stones similar to the slabs of the smaller circle at Drombohilly, 9.6km (6 miles) northeast (see page 370). The tall stones are full of character, rising to around 2m (6½ft).

Photo © Ken Williams

Nine stones remain standing in the ring, with one fallen and another missing (the prostrate stone to the northwest is not thought to be part of the original circle). The axial stone in the SSW is, unusually, not recumbent and has a sharply sloping top. About 6m (20ft) to the east is a further stone with a playing-card silhouette, 2.5m (8ft 2in) high. Signposted from the road, with a small car park at the end of an unpromising track.

Nearby | The following sites are within 1km (0.6 miles) of Ardgroom, but on private land and difficult to get to: the **Ardgroom Outward NE** standing stones are at V 7129 5556, 472m (1,549ft) ENE of Ardgroom; the **Ardgroom** standing stone is at V 7002 5561, 895m (just over ½ mile) west of Ardgroom; the **Ardgroom Outward SW** standing stones are at V 7010 5481, 934m (just over ½ mile) WSW of Ardgroom. The **Ardgroom Outward NE** stone circle is at V 7188 5646, 1.5km (almost 1 mile) northeast of Ardgroom.

At V 7481 5757, 4.5km (2¾ miles) ENE of Ardgroom, is the ruined **Cashelkeelty W** stone circle, with only three stones remaining, as well as **Cashelkeelty E**, the remains of a five-stone circle. Immediately to the south of Cashelkeelty E are three outliers, the surviving stones of a four-stone row.

SHRONEBIRRANE Alt Name: **Drimminboy**
Stone Circle | Townland: **Shronebirrane** | Nearest Village: **Lauragh**
Map: **V 7542 5540** | Sheet: **D84** | Lat: **51.7377N** | Long: **9.80413W**

Shronebirrane stands in a fabulous mountainous setting in the Drimminboy valley, almost painfully wild and beautiful, despite the close proximity of the farmhouse. The circle is about 7m (23ft) in diameter, with eight tall stones (plus one fallen) remaining of a probable 13.

Photo © Vladimir Nedved

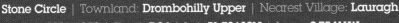

DROMBOHILLY

Stone Circle | Townland: **Drombohilly Upper** | Nearest Village: **Lauragh**
Map: **V 7901 6079** | Sheet: **D84** | Lat: **51.78689N** | Long: **9.75411W**

Photo © Vladimír Nedvěd

Challenging to get to, Drombohilly is fenced off with barbed wire in rough pasture in an ungated forestry enclosure. It's worth the effort, though, as it is a fine circle in a truly spectacular setting, overlooked by Knockatee mountain, with views to the Kenmare estuary. The 8.5m (28ft) circle has nine remaining stones (of 11 originals), unusually pillar-like in shape, with a pair of radially set 2.1m (7ft) portal stones at the NNE. The eastern portal stone leans dramatically. Look out for the rather lovely spiral motif on the central stone, which may have been carved at a later date.

Nearby | At V 7901 6053, 262m (860ft) south of the stone circle and hidden in woodland planting, is **Drombohilly wedge tomb** – easiest to find with sat nav.

> **"One of the most beautiful stone circles on the Beara Peninsula."**
> John Ibbotson

URAGH

Stone Circle | Townland: **Uragh** | Nearest Village: **Tuosist**
Map: **V 8312 6344** | Sheet: **D84** | Lat: **51.81155N** | Long: **9.69551W**

The wonderful five-stone circle of Uragh NE (at V 8312 6344), with its massive accompanying standing stone, is a remarkably beautiful site, set between loughs with hills, forest and waterfalls all around. One of the portal stones has fallen, but that doesn't detract from the impact. The standing stone is a 3m (10ft) giant, set in front of the circle's axial stone.

Nearby | At V 8352 6368, 468m (1535ft) ENE of Uragh NE, lies the ruined **Uragh N** stone circle, with Uragh Wood nature reserve nearby. At V 8251 6303, 726m (almost ½ mile) WSW of Uragh NE, is another

Photo © David Chaika

stone circle, **Uragh SW**. This irregular circle, some 10m (33ft) in diameter, has 10 remaining stones, two of which have fallen, and a central boulder burial. Two of the stones to the south are quartz. It can be hard to find, depending on when the gorse was last cleared.

DROMAGORTEEN Alt Name: **Bonane Heritage Park**
Stone Circle | Townland: **Dromagorteen** | Nearest Village: **Bonane**
Map: **V 9586 6534** | Sheet: **D85** | Lat: **51.83117N** | Long: **9.51137W**

Set within Bonane Heritage Park, this fine axial stone circle, about 10m (33ft) across, has a fantastic and accessible (although steep) setting overlooking the valley. There are 13 stones, six still standing, up to 1.4m (4ft 7in) in height. The axial stone is at the SSW. The circle surrounds a boulder burial. Bonane Heritage Park has a number of other ancient monuments, including another boulder burial and a fulacht fiadh.

> **"Known as the 'Judge and Jury'** as it consists of 13 stones with a central boulder burial. It is the centrepiece of a complex astronomical calendar that includes both solar and lunar cycles."** Tom Bullock

KENMARE
Stone Circle | Townland: **Kenmare** | Nearest Town: **Kenmare**
Map: **V 9068 7071** | Sheet: **D85** | Lat: **51.87842N** | Long: **9.58821W**

Photo © Nastalapat Dilokpad

A nice bit of urban (or suburban) prehistory, Kenmare stone circle is right in the town, in a manicured setting of lawns and leylandii, but it's still an atmospheric place. The largest circle in southwest Ireland, it's 17.4 × 15.8m (57 × 52ft) in diameter and has 15 stones, all smallish, rounded boulders. In the centre is a boulder burial with a massive capstone.

EIGHTERCUA
Stone Row | Townland: **Eightercua** | Nearest Village: **Waterville**
Map: **V 5120 6465** | Sheet: **D84** | Lat: **51.81485N** | Long: **10.15851W**

An impressive four-stone row on the crest of a ridge, the largest reaching 3m (10ft) in height. The row is 9m (30ft) long and aligned east–west. There is some evidence of an adjacent tomb. Ask for permission at the small, white bungalow nearby.

Photo © Vladimir Nedved

371

BALLYNAHOW BEG

Rock Art | Townland: **Ballynahow Beg** | Nearest Village: **Cahersiveen**
Map: **V 5306 8209** | Sheet: **D83** | Lat: **51.97199N** | Long: **10.13904W**

Photo © Ken Williams

The exposed vertical face of this outcrop is decorated with a dramatic array of motifs, including tailed cup-marks and a grid of grooved lines.

> "The boulder is behind a house to the south of a by-road, in the second field (50m/164ft) from the road, to the west of a hedge and bank." Anthony Weir

CARHOONMEENGAR EAST

Rock Art | Townland: **Carhoonmeengar East** | Nearest Village: **Kenmare**
Map: **V 9040 7434** | Sheet: **D78** | Lat: **51.91093N** | Long: **9.59338W**

This fine example of cup-and-ring decoration, on a low sandstone outcrop, was only officially recorded in 2001. Access the site from the quarry track at Lissyclearig.

> "Uniquely in Irish rock art there are six precisely inscribed circles that appear to be preliminary sketches. It is possible that they are not contemporary with the rest of the carving, although the experts consider them to be original." FrogCottage42

Photo © FrogCottage42

GRANGE
Alt Names: **Lough Gur B, Great Stone Circle, Lios na Grainsi**
Stone Circle | Townland: **Grange** | Nearest Village: **Limerick**
Map: **R 6326 4042** | Sheet: **D65** | Lat: **52.51431N** | Long: **8.54182W**

Of all the many prehistoric sites in the wooded hills around Lough Gur, the most well-known is the stone circle at Grange in Limerick. This 23.8m (78ft) embanked circle has an unusual entrance passage, and its stones are placed very close together. The biggest stone is placed in the northeast, perhaps pointing to midsummer sunrise. Research in 2016 indicated that the present appearance of the circle is very much the result of 19th-century intervention, when more than 40 stones were

Photo © Nicki Lievense

added, as well as the interior being levelled and the exterior bank raised. Nonetheless, it is an evocative site.

Nearby | The following sites are within 1km (0.6 miles) of Grange: at R 6331 4032, 106m (348ft) southeast of Grange, is the **Stone of the Tree** standing stone; at R 6328 4054, 120m (394ft) north of Grange, is **Lough Gur C** stone circle; at R 6342 4072, 343m (1,125ft) northeast of Grange, is the **Pillar Stone**; at approximately R 638 411, 866m (just over ½ mile) northeast of Grange, is **Lough Gur E**, which may be the remains of either an avenue or of a court cairn; at R 6419 4066, 955m (over ½ mile) east of Grange, is the **Lough Gur** prehistoric settlement.

At R 6453 4021, some 1.3km (¾ mile) east of Grange, is **Lough Gur** wedge tomb, a large, well-preserved tomb, 9m (29ft) long, which was excavated in 1938. It has a unique double-walled construction. Four large roofstones cover the chamber. A fifth slab, found by the entrance, may have covered the portico. Bones from at least eight people were found in the chamber, along with pottery, and further bones were found in the wall-fillings and outside the gallery.

GAULSTOWN
Portal Tomb | Townland: **Gaulstown** | Nearest Town: **Waterford**
Map: **S 5394 0629** | Sheets: **D75/76** | Lat: **52.20624N** | Long: **7.21164W**

> "Of the many portal tombs in Waterford, this one is my favourite." Ken Williams

In a tranquil tree-lined setting, this is an attractive portal tomb with a chunky capstone, 4.2m (13ft 9in) in length and 1m (3ft 3in) thick. The entrance faces east into the hillside.

KILMOGUE Alt Names: **Leac an Scáil, Harristown Dolmen**
Portal Tomb | Townland: **Kilmogue** | Nearest Town: **Carrick-on-Suir**
Map: **S 5020 2821** | Sheet: **D75** | Lat: **52.403585N** | Long: **7.2617W**

This spectacular dolmen (its name meaning "stone of the warrior/hero") is one of Ireland's largest, with an impressively tilted capstone raised at one end to 4.5m (14ft 8in) by 3.6m (11ft 10in) portal stones. Between the portal stones is a 2.7m (8ft 10in) door stone.

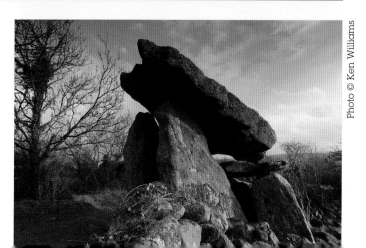

Photo © Ken Williams

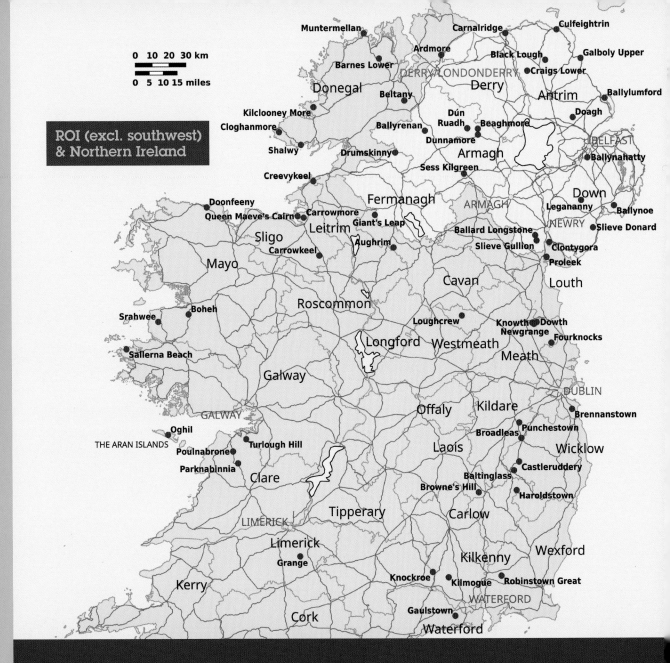

0 10 20 30 km

0 5 10 15 miles

ROI (excl. southwest) & Northern Ireland

Muntermellan
Carnalridge
Culfeightrin
Ardmore
Black Lough
Galboly Upper
Barnes Lower
DERRY/LONDONDERRY
Craigs Lower
Donegal
Derry
Antrim
Ballylumford
Beltany
Dún Ruadh
Doagh
Kilclooney More
Ballyrenan
Beaghmore
Cloghanmore
Dunnamore
BELFAST
Shalwy
Drumskinny
Armagh
Ballynahatty
Creevykeel
Sess Kilgreen
ARMAGH
Down
Doonfeeny
Fermanagh
Legananny
Ballynoe
Queen Maeve's Cairn
Carrowmore
Giant's Leap
Ballard Longstone
Slieve Donard
Leitrim
Sligo
Aughrim
Slieve Gullion
NEWRY
Clontygora
Carrowkeel
Proleek
Mayo
Cavan
Louth
Srahwee
Roscommon
Boheh
Loughcrew
Knowth Dowth
Newgrange
Longford
Westmeath
Fourknocks
Sallerna Beach
Galway
Meath
DUBLIN
Offaly
Kildare
Brennanstown
Oghil
Punchestown
THE ARAN ISLANDS
Turlough Hill
Broadleas
GALWAY
Poulnabrone
Laois
Wicklow
Parknabinnia
Castleruddery
Clare
Baltinglass
Browne's Hill
Haroldstown
Tipperary
Carlow
LIMERICK
Limerick
Kilkenny
Wexford
Grange
Knockroe
Kilmogue
Robinstown Great
Kerry
WATERFORD
Cork
Gaulstown
Waterford

KNOCKROE
Passage Grave | Townland: **Knockroe** | Nearest Village: **Windgap**
Map: **S 4086 3126** | Sheet: **D67** | Lat: **52.43174N** | Long: **7.40000W**

Probably best known for its rock art, this substantial passage tomb has two chambers, east and west, aligned on the rising and setting midwinter sun (in fact, this is said to be the only site in Ireland with these alignments). There are more than 30 inscribed stones at Knockroe, some to be found in both chambers and others in the kerb, mostly to the south of the monument. Cremated human bone was found during excavation, along with pottery, beads, pendants, antler pins and fragments of bone.

ROBINSTOWN GREAT

Stone Circle | Townland: **Robinstown Great** | Nearest Town: **New Ross**
Map: **S 8105 2905** | Sheet: **D76** | Lat: **52.4074N** | Long: **6.80982W**

A curious site, quite confusing to look at and tricky to reach. It's described by some visitors as "elongated", but is considered to be a four-poster, the quadrangle being the circle itself, and the additional stones being outliers. One outlier stands about 4m (13ft) to the southwest, and there is a quartz block between the circle and the outlier. The tallest stone in the circle is 1.6m (5ft 2in).

> "I approached from the west up to between the two farm buildings, then keeping to the left gate. This was a big mistake! Six fields and two steep hedges. Try from the north (a farm track goes that way) or the east, which may be closer to a road." David Smyth

HAROLDSTOWN ★

Portal Tomb | Townland: **Haroldstown** | Nearest Town: **Tullow**
Map: **S 9008 7793** | Sheet: **D61** | Lat: **52.84512N** | Long: **6.66379W**

A beautiful portal tomb, said to have been inhabited during the 19th century. One of the two large roofstones may have cup-marks. The well-preserved chamber has a 1.8m (6ft) door stone set between the portal stones.

Nearby | At S 8414 7134, almost 9km (5½ miles) WSW of Haroldstown, in a field east of the Tullow–Bunclody road, is the imposing **Ardristan** standing stone, some 3m (10ft) tall. Its striking vertical grooves were probably deepened artificially.

Photo © Yggdrasill

BROWNE'S HILL ★ Alt Name: **Brownshill Dolmen, Dolmain Chnoc an Bhrunaigh**

Portal Tomb | Townland: **Kernanstown** | Nearest Town: **Carlow**
Map: **S 7538 7687** | Sheet: **D61** | Lat: **52.837556N** | Long: **6.881136W**

Photo © Frank Luerweg

Although partly collapsed, this is an extremely impressive structure with a truly enormous capstone that may, at an estimated weight of 100–150 tonnes (110–165 tons), be the heaviest in Europe. Three stones (the two portals and the door stone), all around 1.8m (6ft), are still standing, supporting the capstone.

BALTINGLASS

Passage Tombs | Townland: **Pinnacle** | Nearest Village: **Baltinglass**
Map: **S 8855 8925** | Sheet: **D61** | Lat: **52.94706N** | Long: **6.68338W**

Including the remains of three small passage tombs built at different times and partly overlying each other, plus two single-chambered tombs, this site is part of the wider Baltinglass complex of Bronze Age hill forts. A large cairn some 27m (88ft) in diameter, robbed for wall-building, still retains most of its internal features. Recent radiocarbon-dating (published 2017) has revealed the tomb was expanded with more substantial chambers and associated cairns over a 600-year life from approximately 3500–2900BC. In the circular chamber of Tomb III is a large stone basin decorated with a double-armed cross within a cartouche. Some of the roofstones of its narrow passage survive.

CASTLERUDDERY

Stone Circle | Townland: **Castleruddery Lower** | Nearest Village: **Baltinglass**
Map: **S 9159 9421** | Sheet: **D55** | Lat: **52.99111N** | Long: **6.63675W**

Photo © Christopher Bickerton

This embanked 30m (98ft) circle of 29 remaining stones is set within an enclosure that now only exists as a cropmark. Some stones are set upright, others on their long side. Wedge marks in several stones suggest deliberate damage to the circle. Two huge quartz boulders (1.2 × 2.4m/4 × 8ft and 1.8 × 3m/6 × 10ft respectively) appear to form an entrance. To the east of this is a single standing stone.

Nearby | At N 930 032, 9km (5½ miles) NNE, is the 23m (75ft) **Athgreany** stone circle, also known as the Piper Stones and said to be merrymakers turned to stone. The outlier stone is known as the Piper.

BRENNANSTOWN   Alt Names: **Glendruid, Druids' Altar**

Portal Tomb | Townland: **Brennanstown** | Nearest Town: **Dun Laoghaire**
Map: **O 2287 2418** | Sheet: **D50** | Lat: **53.254030N** | Long: **6.159786W**

On private land behind Glendruid House (seek permission to visit), this is a fine portal tomb with a massive, tilted capstone 4.5 × 4.5m (14ft 8in × 14ft 8in) supported on seven much smaller boulders. Two channels have been carved on the top surface of the capstone.

Photo © Vladimir Nedved

BROADLEAS Alt Name: **Piper's Stones**
Stone Circle | Townland: **Broadleas Commons** | Nearest Village: **Blessington**
Map: **N 9292 0761** | Sheet: **D56** | Lat: **53.111243N** | Long: **6.613072W**

There are some 39 stones, often nestling shoulder to shoulder, in this approximately 30m (98ft) diameter circle set among ash, hawthorn and holly trees. One of the stones has a particularly dramatic appearance, apparently split clean in two by the growth of a holly tree.

PUNCHESTOWN Alt Name: **The Long Stone**
Standing Stone | Nearest Townland: **Punchestown** | Nearest Village: **Naas**
Map: **N 9173 1656** | Sheet: **D55** | Lat: **53.19183N** | Long: **6.62838W**

An impressive standing stone that tapers to a sharp point and was found to be 7m (23ft) long when it fell in 1931. Re-erected in 1934, it now stands 6m (20ft) tall. An empty stone cist was discovered beside the original socket, which could not be preserved when the new socket was made.

Nearby | At N 9116 1628, 626m (2,053ft) WSW of the Punchestown standing stone, is the **Craddockstown West** standing stone, in a field opposite the entrance to the racecourse. It's a huge, tapering granite stone, around 4m (13ft) tall, that leans to the west.

PARKNABINNIA ★
Wedge Tombs | Townland: **Parknabinnia** | Nearest Village: **Corofin**
Map: **R 2648 9357** | Sheet: **D51** | Lat: **52.98813N** | Long: **9.09548W**

Around 150 wedge tombs are known in County Clare, with over 70 of them concentrated on the upland limestone region known as the Burren (meaning "stony place"). Several wedge tombs can be found in the Parknabinnia heathland, as well as what appear to be partly worked capstones. Recent excavations in the Parknabinnia court tomb (Cl. 153) found the remains of at least 20 people, who were interred there between *c.* 3690–3375BC and *c.* 2905–2620BC. Interestingly, hares (partly dismembered and whole) appear to have been deliberately deposited in this tomb during the Neolithic.

PARKNABINNIA 3
At R 2648 9357, this is one of the more accessible tombs, close to a minor road leading off the R476. The remains of its cairn survive, the roofstone is over 3m (10ft) long and the sides are formed of single massive slabs. The east (rear) end is closed and the front is partly closed. Recent excavations unearthed the skeletons of a child and an adult.

Photo © Jeff Demetrescu

PARKNABINNIA 2

At R 2606 9331, 493m (1,617ft) WSW of Parknabinnia 3, is the Parknabinnia 2 wedge tomb, partly set into a wall with much of its surrounding cairn still evident. The capstone is cracked but still in place. There may have been a second gallery. Within 200m (656ft) of Parknabinnia 2, there is also a court tomb (at R 2602 9358) and a wedge tomb (at R 2606 9331).

PARKNABINNIA 4

At R 2588 9326, 186m (610ft) west of Parknabinnia 2 is the ruined Parknabinnia 4 wedge tomb, the remains of a chamber set in a substantial mound. There's an upright in front of the tomb that may be the remains of an ante-chamber. Slabs on the west and south of the mound may be the remains of a kerb. Excavations uncovered cremated and unburnt human bone, as well as an unburnt and partially articulated adult outside the NNW end of the chamber.

PARKNABINNIA 1

At R 2574 9341, 205m (673ft) WNW of Parknabinnia 4, is Parknabinnia 1, a large wedge tomb with an unusual position just below the edge of a small escarpment. Within 100m (328ft) of Parknabinnia 1 are three more wedge tombs (at R 2574 9328, R 2575 9335 and R 2572 9338).

CAPSTONE FACTORY

In the same area (approximately R 259 933), in addition to the completed tombs, are unfinished capstones that seem to have been propped up at one end in order to be worked on.

> "Close to Parknabinnia 1 are remains (I found at least five) that look like abandoned workings, where large rough slabs (which abound in the area) were turned into capstones. In short, the area was a capstone factory." Tony "Enkidu41"

POULNABRONE

Portal Tomb | Townland: **Poulnabrone** | Nearest Village: **Ballyvaughan**
Map: **M 2360 0036** | Sheet: **D51** | Lat: **53.04869N** | Long: **9.14003W**

Photo © STLJB

Poulnabrone ("hollow of the millstone") is one of the most photographed sites in Ireland. A dramatic tomb with a slender roofstone balanced on huge slabs, it sits on the Burren's curiously cracked limestone pavement. Surrounded by the remains of a cairn, the tomb is around 1.8m (6ft) tall, the supporting stones standing directly on the pavement. The roofstone (3.7 × 2.85m/12ft × 9ft 4in), which was prised from the surrounding pavement, helps to hold them in place. The eastern portal was replaced after excavation (1986–8) due to a number of cracks in both directions. The mixed bones of at least 35 people were interred here, *c.* 3800–3200BC, dating the tomb to the start of the Irish Neolithic. Other items found here included pottery sherds, a polished stone axe, flint/chert tools, two stone beads and a bone or antler pendant. On the route of many coach tours, you're unlikely to get the site to yourself.

Nearby | At R 2324 9852, 1.9km (just over 1 mile) SSW of Poulnabrone is the large **Poulawack** cairn. Ten graves were found here, holding the remains of 16 people, interred 3000–1900BC.

TURLOUGH HILL
Prehistoric Settlement | Townland: **Oughtmama** | Nearest Village: **Kinvarra**
Map: **M 3141 0732** | Sheet: **D51** | Lat: **53.11232N** | Long: **9.02501W**

The windswept summit of Turlough Hill is the unusual location of a prehistoric settlement. A rampart wall, all the more impressive for being raised on a bank, is still in evidence; to the southwest of this enclosure, hut circles and a very large cairn can be seen. There are around 160 hut circles on Turlough Hill, excavated in 2016. Gaps in the rampart wall suggest that it was not defensive and it has been speculated that the two enclosures here were used for ritual purposes. It's thought that the positioning of Turlough Hill right on the edge of the distinctive Burren landscape may have been significant, and that perhaps this was a seasonal meeting place for people of the Burren and elsewhere. Although precise dating of the whole site is insecure, remains here have been recently dated to the Bronze Age.

OGHIL   Alt Name: **Leaba Dhíarmada agus Gráinne**
Wedge Tomb | Townland: **Oghil** | Island: **Inishmore**
Map: **L 8498 0988** | Sheet: **D51** | Lat: **53.12732N** | Long: **9.71901W**

Photo © Jeff Demetrescu

The Aran Islands are perhaps most famous for their stone forts (*dúns*) and knitwear, but there are a number of wedge tombs as well, and Oghil, on Inishmore, is a good example. The structure is well preserved, with a double wall to the south and a gallery with three roofstones. The site's alternative name means "bed of Díarmuid and Gráinne", referring to the legend of the daughter of the High King of Ireland who eloped with her lover, sleeping on dolmens across Ireland as they fled.

Nearby | At L 8620 0985, 1.2km (¾ mile) east of Oghil, is the **Dún Eochla** wedge tomb, close to the lighthouse and next to the Dún Eochla ring fort (built *c.* 550–800AD).

379

SELLERNA BEACH
Burial Chamber | Townland: **Knockbrack** | Nearest Village: **Cleggan**
Map: **L 5895 5866** | Sheet: **D37** | Lat: **53.55904N** | Long: **10.12937W**

Photo © Gabriela Insuratelu

In a lovely setting overlooking Sellerna Bay, this tomb has a narrow chamber measuring 2.3 × 0.8m (7½ × 2½ft), covered by a roofstone that is propped up by a slab at the western (seaward) end. Three uprights form each of the side walls, and a further upright closes the tomb at its eastern end.

SRAHWEE Alt Name: **Tobernahaltora**
Wedge Tomb | Townland: **Srahwee** | Nearest Village: **Louisburgh**
Map: **L 7953 7446** | Sheet: **D37** | Lat: **53.70609N** | Long: **9.82505W**

> "As the 'Altar Well' (Tobernahaltora), it was formerly venerated as a holy well!" Anthony Weir

A well-preserved tomb, handily close to the road and with lovely views of Lough Nahaltora. A large roofstone, 2.1 × 2.4m (6ft 10in × 7ft 10in) covers most of the chamber. A septal stone divides the portico from the chamber. In wet weather, the chamber tends to flood.

BOHEH Alt Name: **St Patrick's Chair**
Rock Art | Townland: **Knappagh** | Nearest Village: **Westport**
Map: **L 9751 7866** | Sheet: **D38** | Lat: **53.74763N** | Long: **9.55428W**

Behind a house east of Boheh Lough is an isolated rock outcrop that's lavishly decorated with cup-marks and rings. Some 264 motifs have been identified, including the only examples of keyhole patterns in Ireland outside the southwest. Most of the designs are found on the south-facing surfaces – facing away from nearby Croagh Patrick. It may be relevant that, viewed from here, the setting sun appears to roll down the northern shoulder of the mountain on 18 April and 24 August.

DOONFEENY

Standing Stone | Townland: **Doonfeeny Upper** | Nearest Village: **Ballycastle**
Map: **G 0867 3974** | Sheet: **D23** | Lat: **54.29831N** | Long: **9.40359W**

Photo © Phil Spencer

A really splendid standing stone, slender and extremely tall (more than 5m/16ft high). It stands in a graveyard in an ankle-twistingly uneven site next to the road, beside a ruined chapel and with wonderful sea views. This is an excellent example of a Christianized standing stone, with two incised crosses added before the 11th century (they are easiest to see in low sunlight). It also has an impressive crop of lichen.

FOURKNOCKS   Alt Name: **Fourknocks I**

Passage Grave | Townland: **Fourknocks** | Nearest Village: **Naul**
Map: **O 1085 6202** | Sheet: **D43** | Lat: **53.59649N** | Long: **6.32646W**

This tomb may once have been roofed with timber and turf, but now it's covered by a grassed-over concrete dome with apertures that allow light to fall on to the decorated lintels. There are 12 decorated stones in all, one with a human-like figure. The large, pear-shaped chamber is 6.5 × 7.5m (21ft 3in × 24ft 7in), with three recesses opening off it. During the 1950–52 excavations, 65 burials were found here, along with pottery and other items. There are three other mounds in this cemetery group.

> "Entrance by key obtainable from a nearby resident. Details are on the sign by the site."
> Drew Parsons

NEWGRANGE   Alt Names: **Sí an Bhrú, Brú na Bóinne**

Passage Grave | Townland: **Newgrange** | Nearest Village: **Slane**
Map: **O 0074 7272** | Sheet: **D43** | Lat: **53.69463N** | Long: **6.47564W**

Robert Hensey

Newgrange is an internationally important site for a variety of reasons: its scale and sophistication, its megalithic art, and not least its significant archaeological context. Part of the Boyne valley complex, which incorporates the remains of over 40 Neolithic passage tombs as well as numerous other prehistoric sites, this huge passage grave consists of a large, circular mound with an inner stone-built passage and cruciform chamber. It is referred to as Brú na Bóinne in medieval literature, usually translated as "palace" or "mansion on the Boyne", and is associated with a substantial corpus of mythology related to ancient deities such as the Dagda, Oengus and Bóand (the latter a personification of the River Boyne, which surrounds much of the complex). Though Newgrange was lauded in mythological literature, it was not until 1699 that Edward Lhuyd, Keeper of the Ashmolean Museum, first described the architecture, including the "barbarous sculpture" and the "rudely carved" stone at the entrance. In the 1960s the site's excavator, the late Professor Michael O'Kelly, discovered its orientation to sunrise on the winter solstice, and this served to propel the site to further archaeological renown. The solstitial alignment is centred on a feature above the passage known as the roof-box, the origins of which may be the result of an extension to the passage during a late Neolithic phase of enlargement at the monument. Every year (weather permitting) the light enters the chamber, witnessed by a small number of very fortunate members of the public. (Entry by lottery, for which forms are available at the visitor centre.)

Newgrange's cairn is 85m (279ft) in diameter at its widest point and has 97 surrounding kerb stones, predominantly of greywacke (a very hard, dark grey sandstone), many of which are intricately carved. The largest is estimated to weigh 7 tonnes (7.7 tons). This cairn is further surrounded by 12 great stones, approximately one third of the original stones of the Great Stone Circle – an early Bronze Age addition to the site.

The attention the site has received over many centuries, as a result of treasure hunting and so on, is one explanation for the paucity of artefacts recovered from the chamber through excavation, although human bone, beads, pins and stone balls, typical of passage tomb assemblages, have been found.

The conservation and reconstruction of the monument has been criticized, primarily the quartz-covered cairn facing, though it should be noted that revetted constructions are a common element in Neolithic tombs both in Ireland and across Europe. More positively, the overall efforts have allowed access into the monument's chamber, permitted the sizable collection of megalithic art on the kerb

stones to be appreciated, and directly resulted in the discovery of the world-renowned winter solstice alignment. All of this has greatly improved our understanding of the communities that constructed the site as well as our experience of this extraordinary monument.

OTHER STRUCTURES AT NEWGRANGE

To the south and east of the passage tomb, excavation has revealed a circle of post-holes and pits containing animal cremations, which are remnants of a ceremonial site known as Woodhenge. This large wooden enclosure, over 60m (197ft) in diameter, was built in the early Bronze Age, when the tomb was no longer in use. Other significant monuments at Newgrange include the U-shaped cursus to the east of the main mound, which is now barely visible, and the enormous embanked enclosure by the river below.

To visit Newgrange and nearby Knowth (see below), you will need to book a tour at the Brú na Bóinne Visitor Centre at Newgrange. One of Ireland's most popular visitor attractions, Newgrange can get very busy indeed, so it's wise to arrive early or book in advance.

KNOWTH ★

Passage Graves | Townland: **Knowth** | Nearest Village: **Slane**
Map: **N 9969 7342** | Sheet: **D43** | Lat: **53.70112N** | Long: **6.4913W**

Robert Hensey

The main site at Knowth is one of the largest and most decorated passage tombs in Europe, with over 300 carved stones. Between 1962 and 2000, seasonal excavation and restoration led by Professor George Eogan revealed a multi-phase archaeological complex, including 21 smaller tombs and a grooved ware-associated timber circle surrounding the enormous central site.

Knowth 1 contains two passage tombs: an undifferentiated one facing west and a cruciform example facing east, 34m and 40m (112ft and 131ft) in length respectively. Research by Frank Prendergast and Tom Ray has demonstrated conclusively that neither is oriented to the equinoxes, despite a common belief to the contrary.

An interesting recent discovery demonstrates two successive phases of tomb building, evidenced by the apparent "recycling" of at least 24 stones with megalithic art from an older monument, and the extension of both passages, which required an enlargement of the covering mound. A recent dating campaign has confirmed the site's Neolithic credentials, placing its use largely between 3200BC and 2900BC, though significant settlement activity occurred in the 7th and 8th centuries AD

Photo © Frank Bach

383

when the site was transformed into a high-status settlement, followed by further activity during the Anglo-Norman period.

The corbelled roof of the eastern tomb is almost 6m (20ft) high, and the ornate basin found in the chamber, along with the strikingly decorated Maesmawr-type ovoid flint mace head found nearby are two of the most spectacular objects from the site. The latter find, with related artefacts, and the presence of grooved ware pottery, indicate significant and continued connections between Knowth and northern Britain in the third millennium BC. Two small six-knobbed beads, also found in the eastern tomb, appear to be miniature versions of the famous Scottish carved balls (see page 312), suggesting links between Ireland and Orkney around 3000BC.

You can only visit Knowth on a tour booked at the visitor centre at Newgrange.

DOWTH ★

Passage Graves | Townland: **Dowth** | Nearest Town: **Drogheda**
Map: **O 0237 7377** | Sheet: **D43** | Lat: **53.70375N** | Long: **6.45062W**

Robert Hensey

The Dowth complex could be considered the Cinderella of the three Boyne valley "mega-mounds", with intensive geophysical research and other painstaking investigations now revealing the site and its environs to be just as interesting as its more famous neighbours. Though described by various antiquarians, the main site was not formally investigated until 1847, when the Royal Irish Academy led an unsuccessful excavation. About 85m (279ft) in diameter and 15m (49ft) high, it's the least restored and developed of the principal mounds. Dowth Site 1 houses two passage tombs – Dowth North and South – though another potential passage and chamber is hinted at by a straight line carved down the centre of kerb stone 50. The southern tomb shows the well-known passage tomb preference for right-hand sidedness, having a single recess to the right-hand side of the passage, and unusually, an additional annexe. This tomb is accepted by many as having an astronomical orientation on the winter solstice sunset; however, because of its relatively short passage, only 3.3m (11ft) long, sunlight enters its chamber from the beginning of October to late February. There are 115 kerb stones enclosing the monument, with the most notable, perhaps appropriately, dubbed "stone of the suns".

There are two ancillary passage tombs, but evidence of multiple, previously unrecognized, passage tombs nearby has been slowly coming to light.

It is not possible to access the tombs at Dowth, but you can visit the mound to get an idea of how the other tombs looked before modern excavation and restoration.

Nearby | At O 0222 7572, 2km (1¼ miles) north of Dowth, and within sight of the Dowth and Newgrange mounds, is the damaged **Townleyhall** passage grave, with concrete markers showing the position of missing stones.

The Art of the Boyne Valley

Robert Hensey, specialist in Irish Neolithic monuments, art and religion

The number of stones in the Boyne valley with megalithic art, totalling many hundreds, indicates that the region was a major creative hub in the European Neolithic. Art can be found on different media, such as pottery or grave goods, but it is most commonly preserved on the monument's construction features: inside chambers, on the passage uprights and on kerb stones. The classic style of Irish passage tomb art is characterized by circles, cup-marks, spirals, lozenge/triangles, U-motifs, zigzags, serpentiform and radial forms. These core motifs are often combined to make quite complex and beautiful designs.

Picking was the usual technique for creating the art on stone; a fine tool with a hard tip (quartz or flint) and a mallet (probably wooden) were most likely the basic tools used. In recent years, more and more evidence for the application of colour to the construction stones of Neolithic monuments has been found across Europe, and it may be that only a small percentage of the variety of art that once existed has survived.

The combination of unknown motivations for the creation of megalithic art, the varied styles within the tradition, and the possibility that it is entirely abstract do not encourage cohesive interpretation. In the past, accounts of the art in the Boyne valley often mirrored prevailing ideas regarding the monuments on which it was found: that it was linked to sacrifice, for example, or to the burial of elites, or to a goddess of the earth. A long-lived interpretation is the idea that particular motifs are representations of the sun or other heavenly bodies. The discovery and validation of astronomical alignments at several passage tombs has done much to keep this idea in vogue.

One of the limiting factors of previous interpretations of passage tomb art, however, is that too often it has been studied as a phenomenon with a singular meaning and a uniform response, or one that can somehow be separated from other activities associated with the construction and use of the monuments. The penchant for phenomenological interpretation in the 1990s emphasized the art as part of the overall experience of entering and moving within a monument. Other bodily interpretations include how the art may have been used in Neolithic ritual, in particular its relationship to forms seen by individuals in trance states.

More recent work has changed the emphasis to artistic process, memory and performance, away from the viewer and the more usual end-result driven interpretation. These approaches have stimulated new ways of looking at passage tomb art as well as many new questions. What kind of performances surrounded these activities? How was the art used in maintaining or changing conventions – for instance, how did later populations in the Boyne valley relate to older iterations of art? To these questions we have few answers. It seems the art will continue to be a source of intrigue and mystery, and perhaps this was always part of its role.

LOUGHCREW Alt Name: **Sliabh na Caillí**

Passage Graves | Townland: **Corston** | Nearest Town: **Oldcastle**

Map: **N 5860 7758** | Sheet: **D42** | Lat: **53.74469N** | Long: **7.1125W**

> "The site is one of the best in Britain and Ireland, and the views are amazing. On a clear day it feels like you can see every mountain range in Ireland." Paul Blades

Famous for its equinox alignment and rock art, Loughcrew is one of the four most important passage graves, along with Carrowkeel (see page 390), Carrowmore (see page 391) and Newgrange (see page 381). Around 30 graves and mounds remain here. The site extends across two hills: Carnbane East and Carnbane West (*carnbane* means "white cairn"). Carnbane East is also known as Sliabh na Caillí, or the Hag's Mountain, and legend relates that the mounds were dropped from her apron. Some cairns are locked, with signs informing where to get the keys (it is worth accessing them as the locked cairns contain the best rock art). There is a car park between the two hills. This free site is open from the end of May until the end of August (check dates before travelling), with access to Cairn T at both the spring and autumn equinox at dawn.

Photo © Jeff Demetrescu

CAIRN T

On Carnbane East, the well-preserved Cairn T has a kerb of 47 exceptionally large stones, one of which ("the hag's chair") is over 3m (10ft) long and 2m (6½ft) wide and covered with rock art. There is also fine decoration on 19 of the uprights, eight roofstones and two sill stones. It is also surrounded by six satellite tombs that contain a variety of decoration, including solar designs. At equinox, the rising sun illuminates the passage and chamber of Cairn T, including the back stone, intricately decorated with what appear to be sun symbols.

CAIRN U

Often the first structure reached on Carnbane East, Cairn U is a kerbed cairn with a roofless passage grave. Four recesses open off the central chamber and there are 13 beautifully decorated stones.

CAIRN S

Also part of the Carnbane East complex is Cairn S, a kerbed cairn containing a small roofless passage tomb, with a recess opening off the main chamber. Five of the uprights are decorated.

CAIRN L

On private land and currently inaccessible; this is one of the two large cairns on Carnbane West, containing a passage grave with seven side recesses. The tomb contains 18 decorated stones, including a limestone pillar known as the Whispering Stone. This is lit up by the rays of the rising sun at Imbolc and Samhain (Cairn M, east of Cairn L, is also aligned in this direction). In 1999 Irish archaeoastronomer Paul Griffin theorized that some of the carvings were made on 30 November, 3340BC and may be the first record of a solar eclipse. The cairn is surrounded by four smaller tombs, some with decorated stones.

CAIRN D

The largest of the Loughcrew monuments, measuring some 55m (180ft) across, Cairn D is something of a mystery as the mound is apparently empty, containing neither passage nor chamber. Eight smaller mounds surround Cairn D.

PROLEEK Alt Name: **The Giant's Load**
Portal Tomb | Townland: **Proleek** | Nearest Town: **Dundalk**
Map: **J 0826 1103** | Sheet: **D29** | Lat: **54.0372N** | Long: **6.34826W**

Situated in the grounds of Ballymascanlon House Hotel, this is a really impressive portal tomb, with a massive, 3.2 × 3.8m (10ft 5in × 12ft 5in) capstone, balanced rather precariously on two portal stones over 2.1m (6ft 10in) high, and a shorter, 1.8m (5ft 10in) side stone, which is buttressed by a modern support. You may notice the pebbles on top of the capstone – tradition states if you throw one up there and it doesn't roll down again, you'll be married within a year. Or you can make a wish, not necessarily wedding-related.

> **"Local legend says the capstone was put in place by the Scottish giant Parrah MacShagean, who reputedly is buried nearby, hence the name 'the Giant's load'. Another tale says it was brought by a giant from a nearby mountain."** Ray Spencer

Nearby | At J 0834 1100, 80m (262ft) ESE of Proleek dolmen, **Proleek wedge tomb** also deserves a visit. It's 6m (20ft) long and widens to over 1m (3ft 3in) at the western end.

Photo © Jeff Demetrescu

> **"There is a much easier approach from a minor road which runs north from Ballymascanlan to Greenore road near the new bridge. Drive until you come to a bridge across the stream on your left. Take the left fork of the lane and approach Proleek by a pathway at the back of the golf course."** Brian T. McElherron

AUGHRIM
Wedge Tomb | Townland: **Bawnboy** | Nearest Town: **Ballyconnel**
Map: **H 2880 1656** | Sheet: **D26** | Lat: **54.09743N** | Long: **7.56057W**

When the Quinn Group were quarrying on Slieve Rushen, they relocated this fine wedge tomb in the grounds of the Slieve Russell Hotel in Ballyconnel. (When the Quinn Group subsequently collapsed, it was claimed this was "caused by fairies" due to the moving of the tomb!) The ruined gallery, about 6m/20ft long, is set in a low cairn retained by a kerb. During excavation three cist burials were found inside the kerb, and inhumed and cremated bone, along with Beaker and food-vessel pottery, was recovered from below the cairn and inside the gallery.

GIANT'S LEAP   Alt Names: **The Giant's Grave, Burren**
Wedge Tomb | Townland: **Burren** | Nearest Village: **Blacklion**
Map: **H 0787 3523** | Sheet: **D26** | Lat: **54.26589N** | Long: **7.87990W**

The Cavan Burren, like its Clare namesake, is a limestone region and considered one of the finest landscapes of its type in the country. Here, there are prehistoric field systems, glacial erratics and fossils, as well as a fine collection of wedge tombs. Walking trails in the Cavan Burren Park showcase a series of monuments. Giant's Leap wedge tomb, a very well-preserved example adjacent to the Giant's Leap gorge, is over 7m (23ft) long. Three of the five roofstones cover the chamber, and there are possible cup-marks in the one at the front. Two of the supporting stones lean toward each other, forming a triangular entrance. The site is very reminiscent of a French *allée-couverte*. For more information on this and other sites in the park visit: www.cavanburrenpark.ie

Nearby | At H 0743 3526, 438m (1,437ft) west of the Giant's Leap and also in the Cavan Burren Park, is the **Tullygobban** wedge tomb. It's ruinous but still impressive. The name is thought to derive from a tradition of attributing the building of such sites to the Gobán Saor, the master craftsman of Irish folklore. This is the closest site to the visitor centre.

Photo © Gaby Burns

Modified Boulders of the Cavan Burren

Gaby Burns, retired teacher, cartographer, caver and boulder-monument specialist

A limestone plateau, mostly covered in mature coniferous woodland, the Cavan Burren is part of the Marble Arch Caves UNESCO Global Geopark and recognized as a relict landscape, fascinating from geological, botanical and archaeological perspectives. The name Burren comes, appropriately, from the Gaelic *boireann* – stony place. As well as the limestone underfoot, there are hundreds of glacial erratics, abandoned by the withdrawal of the ice sheets. These are generally sandstone, and often the limestone around them has been eroded away, leaving some on naturally formed pedestals. The area is also the nucleus of a whole range of modified boulder monuments, with numerous additional examples to be found in adjacent areas. The sandstone boulders display various modifications – slab removal, creation of overhangs and pits, pedestal enhancements, repositioning and, in more than a third of the examples, propping.

Many of the boulders exhibit Atlantic rock art, but even more significantly a new form of rock sculpting has been identified. All of these new forms of boulder modification can be verified by the presence of "evidence" boulders and a significant number of comparative examples. Many of the most significant monuments display directional ridges and align with others on similar solar alignments. They are fully integrated with prehistoric settlement features – both huts and walls – and although these have not yet been dated, the integrated landscape, including the boulder monuments, is closely associated with the nearby wedge tombs. Over 150 modified boulders have been recorded in the Cavan Burren and immediate surroundings – two thirds of these have some form of rock art or sculpting, and more than half of the monuments have three or more modifications. Such a density and range of boulder monuments has yet to be found anywhere else in Europe.

The full range of modifications, observed on many of the monuments, can be illustrated by describing a few of the main examples. A boulder with verifiable sculpting is PB48 – this is an "evidence" boulder due to the fact that it is a split boulder with two sections still in place. One section has extensive working while the corresponding section remained unworked. The monument has a prominent elongated ridge with channels, peak and notches. These features have also been observed on dozens of other boulders, including evidence boulders. PB48 can also be shown to have had several slabs removed to provide the necessary work surfaces. What is so interesting about this monument is that another one, PB46, has been created with identical features. PB46, unlike PB48, has a prominent prop which has been inserted to present the sculptings on the required level. The elongated ridges of the two rocks have identical elevation and direction – both point to exactly the same point in the sky.

Burns, G., and Nolan, J. 2017. *Burren-Marlbank: A prehistoric monumental landscape*. Free download at cavanburren.ie and the Megalithic Portal page for Giant's Leap.

CARROWKEEL Alt Name: **Carrowkeel-Keshcorran Complex**
Passage Tomb Complex | Townland: **Carrowkeel** | Nearest Village: **Castlebaldwin**
Map: **G 7523 1206** | Sheet: **D25** | Lat: **54.05718N** | Long: **8.37898W**

Photo © Jon Sullivan

Set high above Lough Arrow, Carrowkeel is a truly wonderful place to visit. It's a complex of 15 passage tombs, and one of the four most famous monument complexes in Ireland, along with Newgrange (Brú na Bóinne, page 381), Loughcrew (page 386), and the nearby Carrowmore tombs (see opposite). Seven more can be found to the west in the Keshcorran complex, many on nearby hilltops.

These are probably also passage tombs but many have not been excavated. The Carrowkeel tombs were opened in a rather rushed way by R.A.S. Macalister in 1911, who was convinced they were Bronze Age. Human cremations were found, as well as pottery, beads, pendants and small white stones not unlike children's marbles. Excavations to modern standards have put the dating back to between 3350 and 3100BC – making them older than the pyramids at Giza, but they were still in use in the Early Bronze Age (2000BC). The site is well sign-posted and there is a car park.

CAIRN K

Cairn K is one of the best preserved of the tombs, and also the tallest. The 4.5m (14ft 9in) passage leads to a chamber with two side chambers and an end chamber. The corbelled chamber roof is 3.4m (11ft) high, and covered by a large flat roof slab. In 1911 burnt bone as well as antler and bone pins, stone beads, balls and pendants, and a Bronze Age bowl were found here.

> **"We sat in the dark and listened to the rain dripping through the cairn into the passage. A wonderful moment."** Jackie Bates

CAIRN F

Partly ruined by the collapse of a massive roof slab, Cairn F was described by the 1911 excavators as "one of the most impressive and interesting ancient structures remaining in Ireland". The 1.4m (4ft 7in) entrance is more imposing than any of the other cairn entrances, and the interior has a different layout from any of the other Carrowkeel monuments, with five recesses opening off a 3.6m (12ft) chamber that widens inward from 0.6m (2ft) at the entrance. The construction of the chamber shows a high level of technical skill, with packing stones tilting the slabs (preventing rainwater from entering) and diagonally placed stones used in the corners to narrow the space to be covered by roofstones. A broken standing stone was found between the innermost pair of recesses, with human ashes and a set of water-worn stones nearby.

CAIRN H

This has the best-preserved kerb of any of the tombs, but you can only get a little way into the passage, as the chamber was wrecked during the 1911 excavations, making it inaccessible. The passage and chamber may have had a combined length of about 8.5m (27ft 10in).

CAIRN G

One of the most impressive and thrilling of Carrowkeel's tombs, Cairn G includes a lightbox, a letterbox-like space above the entrance lintel that admits the light of the setting sun around the time of the summer solstice, illuminating the back of the chamber. It's quite a tight fit to squeeze around the entrance slab, but once you're in you can look back out through the lightbox. The low passage is about 2m (6½ft) long, leading to a chamber 2.3m (7½ft) high, with two side chambers and an end chamber. The tall uprights support the lintels and corbelling, and there's a large flat roof slab above the main chamber. Stone pendants, balls and beads, as well as burnt bone, were found here in 1911.

CAIRN E

Sited at the top of a heather-covered ridge, it's a tough scramble to access this unusual hybrid: a court tomb with a long mound, and a passage grave. The mound is 10.7 × 36.6m (35 × 120ft), rising to 2.4m (8ft) in the middle. At its SSE end, there is a large stone, 3.6m (12ft) long and 0.9m (3ft) high, placed in a way that the excavators believed to indicate a large porch, reminiscent of the horned long barrows such as Hetty Pegler's Tump (see page 80). There is a cruciform chamber but no gallery.

CAIRN B

Also up on the ridge, Cairn B contains a pair of spiral carvings on the eastern side of the chamber, identified in 2010.

Nearby | At G 7128 1262, 4km (2½ miles) west of Carrowkeel and sitting atop Keschcorran mountain, is **Kesh** cairn, the best known of the Keshcorran complex. The cairn is unopened, so it's not known if it has a chamber, but this seems likely. On the mountain's western side are 17 caves, associated with many fairy legends.

At G 7725 1626, 4.7km (3 miles) northeast of Carrowkeel, is **Heapstown** cairn, an enormous structure some 61m (200ft) in diameter and rising to 6m (20ft), despite the removal of many of the stones for construction. You can clearly see some 30 of the kerb stones. As with Keshcorran, the site has never been excavated but it is assumed to contain a passage tomb.

CARROWMORE

Passage Graves | Townland: **Carrowmore** | Nearest Town: **Sligo**
Map: **G 6622 3371** | Sheet: **D25** | Lat: **54.25112N** | Long: **8.51904W**

The tombs of Carrowmore are the earliest and least architecturally sophisticated of the Irish passage tombs, with their chambers simply constructed out of large boulders. The people responsible for building them may have moved east, with monuments developing in sophistication as they went, culminating in the impressive cairns of Loughcrew and the Boyne valley. However, the Carrowmore monuments make up for their lack of sophistication by their huge variety and number, with around 30 still remaining out of more than double that number originally.

Photo © Kai Hoffman

The two main areas of the site extend either side of a road, with a car park beside the cottage that serves as a visitor centre. You can follow the recommended visitor route, join a guided tour or simply do your own thing. The majority of monuments are satellites of Tomb 51, also known as Listoghil. The tombs are known by the numbers 1–59, given to them in 1837 by George Petrie in a report for the Ordnance Survey. Site 7 and Site 5 are particularly photogenic, chunky dolmens, and Site 7 is also surrounded by a wonderful circle of 32 boulders. Sites 11, 26 and 57 are good examples of stone circles. Carrowmore is open from Easter to the end of October (check dates before travelling).

CARROWMORE 51 (LISTOGHIL)

Listoghil is the only Carrowmore tomb that was definitely covered by a cairn, although the one you see today was reconstructed after the tomb was excavated. The chamber has a huge roofstone like the lid of a grand piano. It has been suggested that Listoghil is aligned with sunrise on the cross-quarter days of Samhain and Imbolc, which from here is seen to occur in a dip between the hills on the horizon, known as the Saddle. It is not known whether there was a passage when the tomb was first built, or indeed whether it was immediately covered with the cairn.

Nearby | At G 7003 3574, around 4.5km (2¾ miles) ENE of Carrowmore, is **Abbeyquarter** chambered tomb. At this unusual site, remains of a tomb, very similar to some of those at Carrowmore, can be seen on a roundabout in a housing estate, with various additions, including a large crucifix and a statue of the Virgin Mary.

QUEEN MAEVE'S CAIRN

Cairn | Townland: **Knocknarea South** | Nearest Village: **Strandhill**
Map: **G 6260 3458** | Sheet: **D25** | Lat: **54.25875N** | Long: **8.57456W**

Photo © Anthony Hall

A huge cairn on the summit of Knocknarea, from where it dominates the surrounding countryside. Named for the mythical Queen Maeve, it has never been excavated and is assumed to contain a passage grave. Around 5m (16ft) in height and 15m (49ft) in diameter, it has been damaged by people climbing over it. There is a smaller cairn about 30m (98ft) ENE. Bones from a child and an adult, from around 3500BC, were discovered in a cave on Knocknarea.

CREEVYKEEL

Court Tomb | Townland: **Creevykeel** | Nearest Village: **Cliffony**
Map: **G 7192 5455** | Sheet: **D16** | Lat: **54.4387N** | Long: **8.4335W**

A fine example of its type, close to the main Sligo–Bundoran road, Creevykeel has been extensively reconstructed. The wedge-shaped cairn was originally about 60m (197ft) long. The passage opens into a large oval court that leads to a gallery with two chambers. The largest stones are at the entrance, reaching about 1.8m (6ft) high. There are also three additional single-chambered tombs behind the gallery. The tomb was excavated in 1935, and a stone bead, along with cremated bone, pottery, and two clay balls, were found.

Photo © Jeff Demetrescu

SHALWY   Alt Name: **Muinner Carn**

Court Tomb | Townland: **Shalwy** | Nearest Village: **Kilcar**
Map: **G 6481 7531** | Sheet: **D10** | Lat: **54.624758N** | Long: **8.545569W**

A fine, well-preserved court tomb with a very impressive double-lintelled portal, with a gabled top stone giving the site the appearance of a little ruined house. A possible door slab lies in the front chamber, and the large roofstones of the gallery are supported by corbels.

CLOGHANMORE

Court Tomb | Townland: **Malinmore** | Nearest Village: **Glencolmcille**
Map: **G 5189 8260** | Sheet: **D10** | Lat: **54.68918N** | Long: **8.74674W**

Photo © Sergejus Lamanosovas

Aligned east–west, this large tomb, 39m (130ft) long (including the 13.7m/45ft) long oval court), has parallel twin galleries on each side of the entrance. The two western galleries are each divided in two, and one has a large roofstone. Faint carvings on some court stones may be prehistoric. The 46.3m (151ft) cairn reaches 1.5m (5ft) in height to the east. The monument's appearance was altered by restoration (such as the addition of dry-stone walling) at the end of the 19th century.

KILCLOONEY MORE

Portal Tomb | Townland: **Kilclooney More** | Nearest Village: **Ardara**
Map: **G 7221 9672** | Sheet: **D10** | Lat: **54.81755N** | Long: **8.43308W**

Photo © Ken Williams

Two portal tombs at either end of the remains of a long cairn, the fabulous Kilcooney More II, with its enormous roofstone (3.7 × 4.2m/12ft × 13ft 9in), being the larger. You can clearly see the padstone set between the back stone and roofstone, positioned to get the angle of the tilt just right. Kilcooney More I, the small tomb at the other end of the cairn, has partly collapsed.

BELTANY

Stone Circle | Townland: **Tops** | Nearest Village: **Raphoe**
Map: **C 2544 0036** | Sheet: **D6** | Lat: **54.85039N** | Long: **7.60476W**

In a great setting with fine views, this wonderful circle is named for an alignment to the rising sun at May Day, or Beltane. The 45m (147ft) circle is probably the kerb of a very damaged cairn, which stands on a 0.5m (1½ft) artificial platform. Around 60 stones of a possible original 80 remain, many set close together and some leaning dramatically. The tallest (2.7m/8ft 10in) stone in the WSW faces a 1.4m (4½ft) cup-marked triangular slab at the ENE; these two stones create the alignment to May Day sunrise. Some 20m (66ft) to the

Photo © Michelle Holihan

southeast is an outlier, and there are other standing stones to the north and northwest. Large stones in the circle's centre may indicate that a structure, perhaps a passage tomb, once stood there. When first recorded (in 1836) the site was already disturbed, with stones removed for wall-building.

BARNES LOWER

Standing Stones | Townland: **Barnes Lower** | Nearest Village: **Kilmacrenen**
Map: **C 1077 2445** | Sheet: **D2** | Lat: **55.06727N** | Long: **7.83217W**

A pair of stones set quite closely together, each with both faces decorated. The larger stone is a broad slab, 2.2m (7ft 2in) high by 2.4m (7ft 10in) wide, its eastern face covered in cup-marks, some with rings, and shallow grooves. The smaller stone is narrower, and has cup-marks and a cross on its western face, and more cup-marks on the eastern side.

MUNTERMELLAN   Alt Names: **The Dane's Cove, Díarmuid and Gráinne's Bed**

Portal Tomb | Townland: **Muntermellan** | Nearest Town: **Dunfanaghy**
Map: **C 0180 3877** | Sheet: **D2** | Lat: **55.196029N** | Long: **7.972474W**

A stunning setting with views to Errigal and Muckish mountains. The tomb has very large back and side stones, and the thin, leaning portal stones are around 2.5m (8ft 2in) high. The larger of the two roofstones, 3m (10ft) long, has fallen and leans against the western portal stone. Much of the cairn, some 24m (78ft) long, is still in evidence.

ARDMORE   Alt Name: **The Muff Stone**

Standing Stone | Townland: **Ardmore** | Nearest Village: **Muff**
Map: **C 4726 2642** | Sheet: **D7** | Lat: **55.0828N** | Long: **7.26074W**

This fine rectangular block stands on a ridge overlooking Lough Foyle. It's 2.25m (7ft 4in) high, and the southeast face is decorated with around 40 cup-marks, including numerous cup-and-rings. There's one lonely cup-mark on the northeast face.

DRUMSKINNY

Stone Circle | Townland: **Drumskinny** | Nearest Village: **Kesh**
Map: **H 2009 7072** | Sheet: **D12** | Lat: **54.58436N** | Long: **7.69008W**

An accessible and rather charming circle (although perhaps somewhat tamed by its neat grass and gravel surroundings), with 31 stones still standing of an original 39, and one fallen, the tallest reaching 1.8m (6ft). Some of the stones are modern replacements of lost originals. To the northwest is a small kerbed cairn some 4m (13ft) in diameter, and stretching south from this is a 15m (49ft) alignment of small stones.

DÚN RUADH · Alt Name: **The Red Fort**
Ring Cairn | Townland: **Dunroe** | Nearest Village: **Crouck**
Map: **H 6231 8453** | Sheet: **D13** | Lat: **54.70491N** | Long: **7.03424W**

Photo © Ken Williams

Although stones were taken from Dún Ruadh to build the school 450m (1,476ft) to the west, this is still an impressive site. An open cobbled area, defined by 17 stone uprights linked by dry-stone walling, is surrounded by the horseshoe-shaped remains of the cairn, which is itself surrounded by the bank and ditch of a henge. There is an entrance to the southwest, and a number of cists, some excavated in the 1930s, were found in the cairn. Excavation also found a Neolithic settlement beneath the henge and cairn. Open all year, but always ask permission from the owner of the farm located at the end of the lane leading from Crouck old school.

Nearby | At approximately H 6245 8530, around 744 metres (just under ½ mile) NNE of Dún Ruadh, is **Cloghmore** court tomb. At H 6178 8390, 814m (½ mile) WSW of Dún Ruadh, is **Aghascrebagh** ogham stone, with another standing stone around 30m (98ft) further on, at H 6167 8397.

DUNNAMORE · Alt Name: **Díarmuid and Gráinne's Bed**
Wedge Tomb | Townland: **Dunnamore** | Nearest Town: **Cookstown**
Map: **H 6849 8088** | Sheet: **D13** | Lat: **54.67136N** | Long: **6.93914W**

Despite the cart track that runs between the gallery and the kerb stones of the cairn, this is a well-preserved and impressive tomb, 14m (46ft) long, and with good views to the south and west. The portico retains its roofstone, and three large roof slabs remain on the main chamber.

BEAGHMORE
Megalithic Complex | Townland: **Beaghmore** | Nearest Town: **Cookstown**
Map: **H 6844 8425** | Sheet: **D13** | Lat: **50.69002N** | Long: **6.93917W**

In central Tyrone and east Fermanagh there are a number of circles with small stones and companion alignments of larger stones. Here at Beaghmore, on the edge of the Sperrin Mountains, there is a fascinating group of seven irregular circles of closely set stones (six in pairs) and nine or more stone rows or alignments, as well as a number of cairns, all of which was revealed by peat cutting in the 1930s. Some of the stones are just a few centimetres tall, while the tallest rise to 1.8m (6ft). The long rows all run to a cairn. The cairns seem to have preceded the circles. Low stone banks, perhaps derived from Neolithic field clearance, were found beneath some of the site's features. Professor Clive Ruggles suggested a number of astronomical alignments, especially moon-focused ones, at this site.

BEAGHMORE A AND B

Beaghmore A is a 10.7m (35ft) circle with 54 stones. A number of stone rows are between Beaghmore A and Beaghmore B, which is a 12m (39ft) circle with 44 stones. The rows head to a cairn between the circles, where a porcellanite axe was found.

BEAGHMORE C AND D

Beaghmore C is 18m (59ft) in diameter and very misshapen. Impressive stone rows run to a cairn between it and the neighbouring 15m (49ft) Beaghmore D circle.

BEAGHMORE E

Known as the "Dragon's Teeth", Beaghmore E stands alone and is filled with hundreds of small, closely-set upright stones. On the eastern side, it incorporates an earlier cairn, to which a 30m (98ft) row leads. A cist under the cairn was found to contain fungus, moss and twigs, as well as a cremation.

BEAGHMORE F AND G

Beaghmore F and Beaghmore G both have a 9m (30ft) diameter, and a row runs between them to an embanked and ditched cairn. Beaghmore G has a pair of 1.2m (4ft) portal stones.

Nearby | Within 6km (3¾ miles) of this site there are more stone circles, stone rows, and tombs, which are too numerous to mention individually but include **Beleevnabeg** stone circle (at H 6913 8296) and row (at H 6935 8278), and the **Davagh** complex of tombs, stone circles and rows (around H 706 867).

Photo © David Chaika

SESS KILGREEN

Passage Grave | Townland: **Seskilgreen** | Nearest Village: **Ballygawley**
Map: **H 6040 5843** | Sheet: **D19** | Lat: **54.47235N** | Long: **7.07132W**

A badly damaged monument in a very damp site (bring your wellies), but the main draw here is the fine rock art, with lozenges and sets of concentric circles visible on two of the stones. In the next field (at H 6026 5861) is another heavily decorated slab (now eroded), said to be the reused capstone of a chamber. Ask for permission as the approach to the site is through a farm off the main road.

BALLYRENAN   Alt Name: **Cloghogle**

Passage Grave | Townland: **Ballyrenan** | Nearest Village: **Newtownstewart**
Map: **H 3733 8318** | Sheet: **D12** | Lat: **54.69530N** | Long: **7.421811W**

There are two (or you might say three) portal tombs in this often overgrown and atmospheric setting. One is an unusual double tomb, with two capstones, both with possible cup-marks on their upper surfaces. One of the capstones has been lifted higher by a lintel stone balanced on two portals. On the other side of the cairn is another, smaller portal tomb, which has lost its capstone.

Photo © Ken Williams

SLIEVE GULLION   Alt Name: **Cailleach Beara's House**

Passage Grave | Townland: **Slieve Gullion** | Nearest Town: **Newry**
Map: **J 0248 2033** | Sheet: **D18** | Lat: **54.12187N** | Long: **6.43338W**

Photo © Jeff Demetrescu

A stiff climb up Slieve Gullion (or Slieve na Calliagh) takes you to the highest passage grave on the island of Ireland, right at the top of the mountain, with outstanding views. It's a very atmospheric place, the lintelled passage leading to a corbelled octagonal chamber, with an additional chamber or recess set in the wall opposite the entrance. The chamber is illuminated by the midwinter sunset. Cremated bone, a barbed and tanged arrowhead, and flint and chert flakes were found in the passage and chamber. In 2015 volunteers helped repair some of the damage done by weather and hillwalkers, with dislodged stones threatening to block the entrance. Cailleach Beara's House is named for an aspect of the triple moon goddess, who is also referred to as the Hag (or Nun) of Beare, and is the subject of a famous Old Irish poem.

CLONTYGORA   Alt Name: **The King's Ring**
Court Tomb | Townland: **Clontygora** | Nearest Town: **Newry**
Map: **J 0987 1942** | Sheet: **D29** | Lat: **54.11217N** | Long: **6.32081W**

Photo © Vladimir Nedved

A badly damaged but still very dramatic site, in a prominent position. Many of the U-shaped forecourt's uprights remain – these are massive, as are the side stones of the three-chambered gallery. A large roofstone, more than 3m (10ft) long, survives over one of the chambers. Cremated human bone, worked flint and pottery sherds were found during excavation. In view in the next field, about 90m (295ft) to the east, is what may have been a large wedge tomb, with eight stones surviving.

Nearby | At H 9953 2133, 10.5km (6½ miles) west of Clontygora, is **Ballykeel** portal tomb, an excellent example of a "tripod dolmen", with the remnants of its cairn. The portal stones are 2m (6½ft) tall, and the roofstone is almost 3m (10ft) long. At the far end of the cairn is a cist, and two lines of stones are set within the cairn, parallel to the kerbs. A javelin head and a flint flake were found in the cist, and three Ballyalton ware decorated bowls in the chamber.

BALLARD LONGSTONE
Standing Stone | Townland: **Milltown** | Nearest Town: **Newry**
Map: **J 0162 2337** | Sheet: **D29** | Lat: **54.14935N** | Long: **6.44551W**

At just 1.4m (4½ft) high, the Ballard Longstone does not fully live up to its name, but the stone has a lovely pointed outline and the surrounding landscape is beautifully wild and unspoilt in feel.

Photo © James Dempsey

SLIEVE DONARD Alt Names: Ballagh Beg, The Great Cairn, The Greater Cairn

Passage Grave | Townland: **Newcastle** | Nearest Town: **Newcastle**
Map: **J 3580 2769** | Sheet: **D29** | Lat: **54.18023N** | Long: **5.92073W**

Photo © Nicki Lievense

On the summit of Slieve Donard, Northern Ireland's highest mountain, is this large cairn, some 36 × 43m (118 × 141ft) across and 1m (3ft 3in) high. It's all that remains of a ruined passage tomb, the chamber entirely destroyed. Some larger stones, which may have been part of the structure, can also be seen. The views are wonderful, making the trek uphill, which can be hard going, well worth the effort. The central, well-defined cairn is a walkers' cairn. A smaller cairn, known as "the Lesser Cairn" is some 200m (656ft) away to the northeast.

> **"The views from here are spectacular: with the clouds wisping around you, it truly feels like being on top of the world."** Nicki Lievense

BALLYNOE

Stone Circle | Townland: **Ballynoe** | Nearest Town: **Downpatrick**
Map: **J 4813 4038** | Sheet: **D21** | Lat: **54.29073N** | Long: **5.72588W**

This large circle, about 33m (108ft) across, contains more than 50 stones of varying heights up to 1.8m (6ft). Inside the circle is an arc of six standing stones supporting a raised platform; a 1.5m (5ft) high oval mound has also been built in the interior, edged with a kerb of uprights. Partial excavation in 1937 demonstrated that the mound is in fact a cairn, with a cist at either end, containing cremated bones. There are several outliers, including a pair on the western side that could mark an entrance. This seems to be aligned on the setting sun at equinox. At winter solstice the sun, seen from here, seems to slide down between the Mountains of Mourne, which form a fine backdrop to the circle.

Nearby | At J 562 503, 12.8km (8 miles) northeast of Ballynoe, is **Audleystown** court tomb, which is very similar in design to a Scottish Clyde cairn. It was only rediscovered in 1946 by the farmer and excavated to reveal the remains of 34 individuals.

LEGANANNY

Portal Tomb | Townland: **Legananny** | Nearest Village: **Dromara**
Map: **J 2887 4340** | Sheet: **D20** | Lat: **54.32305N** | Long: **6.02016W**

A spectacularly balanced "tripod dolmen" with fabulous views of the Mountains of Mourne. The angled capstone is 0.6m (2ft) thick and over 3m (10ft) long. The supporting stones are 2m (6½ft) and 1.8m (6ft) tall at the southern end, and one of them is missing a very distinctive L-shaped chunk.

Photo © Martin Heaney

BALLYNAHATTY   Alt Name: **The Giant's Ring**

Henge | Townland: **Ballynahatty** | Nearest City: **Belfast**
Map: **J 3272 6770** | Sheet: **D15** | Lat: **54.54024N** | Long: **5.95011W**

Photo © Ken Williams

Just 6.5km (4 miles) south of central Belfast, this is a very impressive site, the circular bank (created from clay, boulders and gravel taken from the interior) reaching some 3.6m (11ft 8in) in height and surrounding an enclosure around 180m (590ft) across. There are five gaps or entrances, at least three of which are probably original. A burial chamber stands within the monument, slightly off centre, comprising five large boulders and a similarly hefty capstone.

BALLYLUMFORD DOLMEN   Alt Name: **The Druid's Altar**

Portal Dolmen | Townland: **Ballylumford** | Nearest Village: **Ballylumford**
Map: **D 4305 0160** | Sheet: **D9** | Lat: **54.84175N** | Long: **5.774W**

A lovely bit of urban prehistory, this splendid burial chamber sits outside a house on the Ballylumford Road, surrounded by ornamental paving and a little chain fence. Despite this somewhat unprepossessing location, the site has a lot of character.

DOAGH

Holed Stone | Townland: **Holestone** | Nearest Village: **Doagh**
Map: **J 2416 9068** | Sheet: **D14** | Lat: **54.748756N** | Long: **6.07247W**

Photo © Nicki Lievense

Set on an outcrop with fine views, this standing stone has a 0.1m (4in) hole around 0.9m (3ft) off the ground (it has been noted that this is about groin level). Historically, couples who wished to wed would hold hands or pass a handkerchief through the hole, and today newlyweds still visit the stone, and flowers are left here.

> **"There is a groove on the top of the stone, at right angles to the direction of the holes. If you look through this groove toward Belfast, it intersects with Ben Madigan (Napoleon's Nose on the Cave Hill)."** Tman

GALBOLY UPPER

Passage Graves | Townland: **Galboly Lower** | Nearest Village: **Waterfoot**
Map: **D 2901 2445** | Sheet: **D9** | Lat: **55.0507N** | Long: **5.98221W**

This area offers beautiful scenery, fine sea views and a number of passage graves to explore. At Galboly Upper, there are three graves, two ruinous but one in good condition. A further, smaller example can be found just over 500m (1,640ft) to the northeast (at approximately D 290 245), close to the road in Galboly Lower.

Photo © Nicki Lievense

CRAIGS LOWER
Passage Grave | Townland: **Craigs Lower** | Nearest Village: **Ballymoney**
Map: **C 9740 1728** | Sheet: **D8** | Lat: **54.993462N** | Long: **6.47904W**

Close to the road, this charming passage grave has great views. The capstone sits on eight, closely set uprights, at a height of 1.7m (5½ft). The mound that covered the tomb was removed during the 19th-century excavation. The capstone was struck by lightning in 1976 and subsequently repaired.

Nearby | At D 0216 1830, 4.9km (3 miles) east of Craigs Lower is **Ballymacaldrack** court tomb, with a kerbed cairn containing an unusual southwest-facing chamber. The forecourt leading to the passage was added some 500 years after the main part of the structure was erected.

BLACK LOUGH
Standing Stones | Townland: **Loughguile** | Nearest Village: **Loughguile**
Map: **D 0810 2347** | Sheet: **D8** | Lat: **55.04684N** | Long: **6.30957W**

Black Lough II is a fine slab of basalt, 3.7m (12ft) high and 1.3m (4ft 3in) wide at the base. Two further stones can be found at D 0842 2328 and at D 0803 2369.

> **"Black Lough I is being used as a gatepost 107m (351ft) southeast of Black Lough II. Black Lough III stands 256m (840ft) northwest of Black Lough II."**
> Dick Glasgow

CULFEIGHTRIN
Standing Stones | Townland: **Ballynaglogh** | Nearest Town: **Ballycastle**
Map: **D 1477 4076** | Sheet: **D5** | Lat: **55.200631N** | Long: **6.198263W**

There are two basalt standing stones in the graveyard of St Patrick's church in the parish of Culfeightrin. The taller, near the door of the church, is almost 3m (10ft); the other 1.6m (5ft 2in). A third stone lies 5.5m (18ft) to the NNW.

Nearby | At D 1473 3481, almost 6km (3¾ miles) south of the Culfeightrin stones, are the **Duncarbit** standing stones. Also known as the Slaught or Eoin-Ruaidh stones, they stand just 2m (6½ft) apart, and it's thought they could be a portal and back stone of a destroyed portal tomb. Legend holds they mark the burial place of John Roe McDonnell, killed during the retreat from the Battle of Glenshesk.

CARNALRIDGE   Alt Names: **The White Wife, Cloghagalla**
Standing Stone | Townland: **Carnalridge** | Nearest Town: **Portrush**
Map: **C 8475 3872** | Sheet: **D4** | Lat: **55.18829N** | Long: **6.67018W**

This whitewashed stone is known as the White Wife, a stone cemented on top providing her head. Despite being only 1.2m (4ft), it's very prominently sited, so visible from some distance.

Further Reading & Resources

Archaeology

Bradley, R. 1998. *The Significance of Monuments.* London: Routledge

Burl, A. 2000. *The Stone Circles of Britain, Ireland, and Brittany.* Yale: Yale University Press

Burl A. 1993. *From Carnac to Callanish: Prehistoric Stone Rows of Britain, Ireland and Brittany.* Yale: Yale University Press

Cummings, V. 2017. *The Neolithic of Britain and Ireland.* London: Routledge

Cunliffe, B. 2013. *Britain Begins.* Oxford: Oxford University Press

Harding, J. 2003. *Henge Monuments of the British Isles: Myth and Archaeology.* Stroud: The History Press

Hovell, G. 2009. *Visiting the Past: A Guide to Finding and Understanding Britain's Archaeology.* Stroud: The History Press – one of the best simple introductions to the subject

Miles, D. 2016. *The Tale of the Axe: How the Neolithic Revolution Transformed Britain.* London: Thames and Hudson

Milligan, M. (photographer) and Burl, A (author) 1999. *Circles of Stone.* London: Harvill Press

Pitts, M. 2000. *Hengeworld.* London: Arrow

Pryor, F. 2003. *Britain BC: Life in Britain and Ireland Before the Romans.* London: HarperCollins

Stonehenge

Parker Pearson, M. 2012. *Stonehenge: Exploring the Greatest Stone Age Mystery.* London: Simon & Schuster

Parker Pearson, M. Pollard, J. Richards, C. 2015. *Stonehenge: Making Sense of a Prehistoric Mystery.* York: CBA

Richards, J. 2017. *Stonehenge: The Story So Far.* London: Historic England

Bowden, M. Soutar, S. Field, D. Barber, M. 2015. *The Stonehenge Landscape: Analysing the Stonehenge World Heritage Site.* London: Historic England

Cleal, R. Montague, R. Walker, K. 1999. *Stonehenge in its Landscape: Twentieth-century Excavations.* London: English Heritage (free download from Archaeology Data Service)

Regional Guides

Barnatt, J. Bevan, B. Edmonds, M. 2017. *An Upland Biography: Landscape and Prehistory on Gardom's Edge,* Derbyshire. Oxford: Windgather Press

Bradley, R. & Nimura, C. (eds.) 2016. *The Use and Reuse of Stone Circles: Fieldwork at Five Scottish Monuments and its Implications.* Oxford: Windgather Press

Cooke, I. 1996 *Journey to the Stones: Mermaid to Merrymaid – Ancient Sites and Pagan Mysteries of Celtic Cornwall.* (out of print)

Darvill, T. 2004. *Long Barrows of the Cotswolds & Surrounding Areas.* Stroud: History Press

Field, D. McOmish, D. 2017. *The Making of Prehistoric Wiltshire.* Stroud: Amberley Publishing

Gerrard, S. 1997. *The English Heritage Book of Dartmoor.* London: Batsford

Gibson, A. 1997, 2005. *Stonehenge and Timber Circles.* Stroud: The History Press

Hedges, J.W. 1987. *Tomb of the Eagles: Window on Stone Age Tribal Britain.* New Amsterdam Books

Leary, J. & Field, D. 2010. *The Story of Silbury Hill.* London: Historic England

McDonald, N. 2012. *Isle of Man, A Megalithic Journey.* Carolina: Lulu.com

Marshall, S. 2016. *Exploring Avebury.* Stroud: History Press

Morgan, V & P, 2001. *Rock Around the Peak: Megalithic Monuments of the Peak District.* Sigma (out of print)

Morgan, V & P, 2004. *Prehistoric Cheshire.* Landmark (out of print)

Pollard, J. & Gillings, M. 2004. *Avebury.* Bristol: Bristol Classical Press

Ponting, G. 2000. *Callanish.* Glastonbury: Wooden Books

Pryor, F. 2010. *Seahenge: A Quest for Life and Death in Bronze Age Britain.* London: HarperCollins

Welfare, A. 2011. *Great Crowns of Stone.* Edinburgh: RCAHMS (now available as an ebook from Apple iTunes, and additional 280-page gazetteer and appendices downloadable from the Megalithic Portal)

Wickham-Jones, C. 2015. *Between the Wind and the Water: World Heritage Orkney.* Oxford: Windgatherer Press

Archaeoastronomy & Other Perspectives

Cope, J. 1998. *The Modern Antiquarian*. London: Thorsons

Devereux, P. Too many books to list – one being 1999. *Places of Power: Measuring the Secret Energy of Ancient Sites*. London: Cassell

Heart of Albion Press www.hoap.co.uk: many interesting books published by Bob Trubshaw – again too many to list

Heath, R. 2007. *Alexander Thom, Cracking the Stone Age Code*. Pembrokeshire: Bluestone Press

Hutton, R. 2015 *Pagan Britain*. Yale: Yale University Press

John, B. 2008. *The Bluestone Enigma: Stonehenge, Preseli and the Ice Age*. Pembrokeshire: Greencroft Books

Meaden, T. 2016. *Stonehenge, Avebury and Drombeg Stone Circles Deciphered*. Saarbrücken: Lambert Academic Publishing (Much of this is available online at oxford.academia.edu/TerenceMeaden)

Morris, J. 2013. *Solving the Neolithic Universe*. North Charleston: CreateSpace

Osman, S. 2010. *Quicksilver, Serpent's Gold*. London: Marion Lloyd Books. Introduce your younger family members to ancient mysteries – I'm told some of the characters and ideas were inspired by the Megalithic Portal!

Ruggles, C. (ed) 1988, 2010. *Records in Stone: Papers in Memory of Alexander Thom*. Cambridge: Cambridge University Press

Ruggles, C. 1999. *Astronomy in Prehistoric Britain and Ireland*. Yale: Yale University Press

Tilley, C. 1994. *A Phenomenology of Landscape: Places, Paths and Monuments*. Oxford: Berg

Wiseman, N. 2015. *Stonehenge and the Neolithic Cosmos*. Self-Published

Groups, Societies & Magazines

British Archaeology Magazine / Council for British Archaeology: www.archaeologyuk.org

Current Archaeology Magazine: www.archaeology.co.uk

The Prehistoric Society: www.prehistoricsociety.org

Lithic Studies Society: www.lithics.org

Megalithomania Conference and YouTube Channel: www.megalithomania.co.uk

Time and Mind – The Journal of Archaeology, Consciousness and Culture: published by Taylor and Francis Online

Northern Earth: www.northernearth.co.uk – pretty much the last small press "Earth Mysteries" magazine standing, along with Meyn Mamvro in Cornwall www.meynmamvro.co.uk

Phone & Tablet Apps

The Pocket Guide to Megaliths: the official Megalithic Portal app for iPhone and Android, www.megalithic.co.uk/app

Ancient Sites "Soundgate" app: explore Cave Acoustics and Stonehenge, Rupert Till / University of Huddersfield

Other Resources

Irish Stones CD-ROM ebook (Anthony Weir)

Standing with Stones video travelogue (Rupert Soskin and Michael Bott)

Stone Circles CD-ROM (Tom Bullock)

The Kilmartin Sessions: The Sounds of Ancient Scotland Audio CD (Kilmartin House Trust)

All of the above are available from www.megalithic.co.uk/shop

Free ebooks & Downloads

Academia.edu is a social networking site where members have uploaded many thousands of their own academic papers that otherwise languish in closed access journals. It is open to all to join.

Archive.org contains a vast archive of defunct web pages, so if you encounter a dead link while browsing, this is the place to try. It also has a comprehensive library of out of copyright books.

BAJR Guides and Resources – many freely downloadable guides and software resources at www.bajr.org/BAJRResources

Burns, G. & Nolan, J. 2017. Burren-Marlbank *A Prehistoric Monumental Landscape Burren, Cavan*: self-published free download from cavanburren.ie and The Megalithic Portal page for Giant's Leap.

Harte, J. *Research in Geomancy 1990–1994*:

Readings in Sacred Space, also *Alternative Approaches to Folklore 1969–1996* download from www.hoap.co.uk/download.htm

Moshenska, G. (ed.) 2017. *Key Concepts in Public Archaeology*. London. UCL Press, Free download

Ruggles, C. & Cotte, M. (Eds) 2010, 2017. *Heritage Sites of Astronomy and Archaeoastronomy in the context of the UNESCO World Heritage Convention: A Thematic Study – Introductions to Archaeoastronomical Sites around the World* ICOMOS / Ocarina Books. Part 1 (2010) download from openarchive.icomos.org Part 2 (2017) download from ocarinabooks.com

Sidestone Press – many freely readable books online, many about continental European sites, but much applies to the UK as well: www.sidestone.com

Spikins, P & Wright, B. 2017. *The Prehistory of Autism*. Rounded Globe. Could the unique insights of people on the autistic spectrum have helped develop technologies and innovations in prehistory? Free download at roundedglobe. com in the History section

Tilley, C. & Cameron-Daum, K. 2017. *An Anthropology of Landscape*. London. UCL Press (free download)

There are many more free downloads and links at the Megalithic Portal, filed under News and Links.

Blogs & Websites

The Megalithic Portal www.megalithic.co.uk

Chris Collyer's www.stone-circles.org.uk

Stone Pages www.stonepages.com

Sandy Gerrard's stonerows.wordpress.com

Dave Parks' www.dartmoorwalks.org.uk

Peter Knight Books/Tours www.stoneseeker.net

Kenneth Brophy's Urban Prehistorian theurbanprehistorian.wordpress.com

Howard MR Williams' Archaeodeath blog howardwilliamsblog.wordpress.com

The Northern Antiquarian megalithix.wordpress.com

Stonehenge All. stonehengealliance.org.uk

Heritage Action heritageaction.wordpress.com

The Modern Antiquarian www.themodernantiquarian.com

Digital Digging edited by Henry Rothwell www.digitaldigging.net

Megalithic Ireland www.megalithicireland.com

Tom FourWinds' tour of Ireland www.megalithomania.com

Anthony Weir's www.irishmegaliths.org.uk

The Folklore of Ireland's Prehistoric Monuments by Howard Goldbaum voicesfromthedawn.com

Online Site Databases

With many thanks to the following for their information and assistance in the compilation of this book:

Canmore www.canmore.org.uk from Historic Environment Scotland www.historicenvironment.scot

Coflein www.coflein.gov.uk from National Monuments Record of Wales www.rcahmw.gov.uk

Pastscape www.pastscape.org.uk from Historic England www.historicengland.org.uk. (The Pastscape site is being phased out and information moved to local HERs.)

Many local Historical Environment Records (HER) in England are searchable at the Heritage Gateway www.heritagegateway.org.uk

English Heritage www.english-heritage.org.uk (including photo and document archive)

The Archaeology Data Service has many "grey literature" reports, monographs, project archives and much more archaeology dataservice.ac.uk

Archaeological Survey Database from the National Monuments Service of Ireland www.archaeology.ie

Northern Ireland Sites and Monuments Record

England's Rock Art archaeologydataservice.ac.uk/era/

CADW (Wales) www.cadw.gov.wales

Geograph resource of geo-referenced photographs for Britain and Ireland www.geograph.org.uk

Flickr Photo Sharing www.flickr.com

Index

Page numbers in **bold** refer to main site entries; page numbers in *italic* refer to captions

Author Acknowledgements

Special thanks to:

Fiona Robertson, Jackie Bates, Francesca Corsini

Martyn Copcutt (TheCaptain), Simon Charles-worth (Sem), Anne Tate (AnneT) and Rune for assistance with planning.

Ruth, Lydia and Rowan

Thanks to the site selectors and checkers:

West of England: Martyn Copcutt with Tim Prevett (TimPrevett)

South of England: Amanda Peters (Coldrum)

Midlands & East of England: Victoria Tuckman (Vicky) with Christine Clarke (Chrispy)

North of England: Anne Tate, Martyn Copcutt, Christine Clarke, Dr Cathryn Iliffe, Richard Stroud (Rich32) and Pat O'Halloran (Kelpie)

Isle of Man: Simon Charlesworth

Wales: Simon Charlesworth, Chris Bickerton (Postman) and Peter Boyle (PAB)

Scotland: Anne Tate, Christine Clarke, Ewen Rennie (Cosmic), Sandy Gerrard (SandyG), Martyn Copcutt, and Connor Motley (Coin)

Ireland: Anthony Weir, Rune, Christine Clarke and Jan Herold (Klingon)

Thanks to Mike Parker Pearson, Vicki Cummings and everyone who kindly contributed an article to this book (see Contents, pp.4–5, for details)

Also thanks to: Mary M (Bat400), Howard MR Williams, Mick Miles, Dave Armstrong, Jim Leary, Sean Page, David Morgan, Martin Lenhart, Rob Ixer, Katy Whitaker, Susan Greaney, Susan Hall and all the people who generously allowed us to quote them and who sent in photographs.

Photo Credits

Every effort has been made to trace the copyright holders and we apologise in advance for any unintentional omissions or errors. We would be pleased to apply any corrections in any future edition of this book. We would like to thank the following photographers (*key*: (t) top; (m) middle; (b) bottom; (l) left; (r) right; (c) centre):

4clydesdale7 p.81b; ABB Photo p.349; Hartmut Albert p.291b; M.J. Allen p.125; Jim Appleton pp.173, 249; Frank Bach p.383; Laurence Baker p.123; Sam Barnes p.270t; Rob Barnett p.252; Jackie Bates pp.264, 286t; Christopher Bickerton pp.66, 82t, 135b, 136b, 180b, 181, 187t, 203t, 209b, 215, 218, 226b, 230b, 235b, 240b, 241, 243b, 246, 247b, 253 (top and bottom), 254b, 255, 288, 290, 291t, 304b, 305b, 309t, 326, 376t; Paul Blades pp.35 (top and bottom), 37t, 39t, 42b, 44, 48t, 52, 59, 99, 207, 226t, 234b, 376t; Mike Bodman pp.108; Peter Boyle p.237t; John Braid, pp.345b, 348; Shaun Bunting p.183; Andy Burnham pp.46t, 122, 262b, 263b, 265b, 333t; Gaby Burns p.388; Richard Cassidy p.91; CazzyJane pp.36 (top and bottom), 39b, 42t, 46b, 47t, 50t, 51t, 63b, 65t, 67, 70 (top and bottom), 71bt; Cerrig pp.203b, 228t, 230t, 232t; David Chaika pp.254t, 364t, 370b, 397; Jim Champion pp.40b, 84, 85, 104, 107t, 113t, 170b; Matthew Chapman p.313; Simon Charlesworth pp.211, (top and bottom), 213, 227; Iñigo Cia p.220; Martyn Copcutt pp.6, 26, 48b, 49, 55, 56b, 57, 58, (top and bottom) 60b, 64 (top and bottom), 65b, 72t, 73 (top and bottom) 74, 75, 76, 77b, 80, 147b, 208, 209t, 216, 232b, 234t, 238, 240t, 316, 321b; Cornfield p.301; Ben Cremin p.107b; Andrew Curtis p. 309b; Nicky Dancer p.79; Matthew Davidson p.323t; Jeff Demetrescu pp.78, 377, 379, 386, 387, 393t, 398b; James Dempsey p.399b; Nicola Didsbury pp.182, 276b; Nastalapat Dilokpad p.371t; Richard L. Dixon pp.117, 135t, 136t, 138b, 143, 145, 159, 162, 167, 169, 171, 311, 322b; Gavin J. Dronfield p.161t; Martin Dunbar p.266t; Peggy Edwards p.283t; Valery Egorov p.127; Gareth L. Evans p.336b; J. J. Evendon p.77t; Steve Fedun pp.141b, 144; Hamish Fenton pp.87, 93b, 115, 116, 141t, 331, 335, 336t, 357; Graeme Field pp.56t, 72b; fostersice p.124; FrogCottage42 p.372b; Sandy Gerrard pp. 60t, 265t, 266b, 283b, 284t, 285, 286b, 292, 297, 298t, 303b, 305t, 315, 317b, 342, 343; Golux pp.8, 287t, 293, (top and bottom) 321t, 322t, 324; Roy Goutté pp.45 (left and right); Eric Grindle pp.174, 248t; Eric Guile p.243t; Anthony Hall p.392b; Les Hamilton pp.320, 332, 333; Richard Hayman p.102; Dave Head p.195b; Martin Heaney, p.401t; Heartland Arts p.300; Roger Heath, p.303t; Jan Herold p.294; Peter Herring p.121; Historic England p.164; Kai Hoffman p.392t; Michelle Holihan p.394b; John F. Holl p.153; Jan Holm p.325;

John D. Hunter, p.170t; Robert Hurworth, p.86; John Ibbotson p.365; Gabriela Insuratela pp.380; Gail Johnson, p.244; Kammer p.199; Roy Kennie pp.140, 142; Brian Kerr pp.269, 273; Angie Lake pp.62, 71t, 229, 231b; Sergejus Lamanosovas p.393b; Robert Law p.287b; Nick Le Boutillier, pp.38, 40, 47b, 53t; Nicki Lievense, pp.373t, 400, 402 (top and bottom); Michael Lindowsky, pp.317t, 323b; Luerweg, Frank p.375b; Adrian Mantle, p.328b; Thomas Marchant, p.50b; Howard Mattinson, p.272; Terence Meaden, p.106 (left and right), 363b; John Miller pp.157b, 158t; Diarmid Mogg p.278; Vincent Mom p.308; Connor Motley pp.296, 298b; Iain Murray p.194; Cezary Namirski pp.120, 185, 186, 187b, 189, 193, 195t, 282, 299, 302, 329; Peter Nash p.131t; Vladimir Nedved pp.368, 369b, 370t, 371b, 376b, 399t; Miles Newman pp.158b, 328t; Hatsuki Nishio, p.362; Shannon O'Grady p.345t; Aled Owen-Thomas p.223; Debbie Parkes p.268t; Drew Parsons pp.192, 248b, 263t, 270b, 330, 352, 355; Charles Paxton p.178b; Jedfish Ping p.93t; PJ Photography p.51b; Tim Prevett pp.133b, 134, 250, 254m; Robin Potticary p.14; Nicola Pulham p.382; pxl.store p.126; Roger K. Read pp.217, (top and bottom), 219t, 284b; Jean Renaud p.363t; Ewen Rennie pp.268b, 276t, 277; Anna Reynolds p.251; Standa Riha p.228b; Fiona Robertson p.304t; Stephen Rule p.206; Stephen Sale p.306t; Alun Salt pp.133t, 138t; Jos Sanders pp.197, 198; Karen Sawyer p.214; David Shepherd p.160; Mike Simon p.175; Steve Simmons p.83, 113b; Skyscan p.150; STLJB p.378; David Smyth pp.259t, 306b; Phil Spencer pp.361t, 381; Andy Spittle p.235t; Spumador p.340; Adam Stanford (Aerial-Cam Ltd.) pp.37b, 82b, 112, 119, 131, 219b, 237b, 247t, 346; Guy Stephenson p.139; Duncan Stirk p.152; Swen Stroop p.339; Richard Stroud pp.161b, 178t; Jon Sullivan p.390; Sam Tait p.147t; Anne Tate pp.179, 180t, 191(top and bottom), 275, 280, 295; Barry Teague p.157t; Travellight p.109; ukvegan pp.259b, 262t; D.L. Upton p.81t; Lee Walker p.222; Guy Wareham p.68; Jim W p.63t; Jim Wearne p.53b; Emmanuel Weber p.118; Scott Whitehouse p.110; Ken Williams pp.19, 361b, 364b, 366, 369t, 372t, 373b, 394t, 396, 398t, 401b; Jeanette Wright 239; Elizabeth Yeatts p.337; Yggdrasill p.375t; David Young p.177

Maps

Maps created with QGIS mapping software. UK map backgrounds Ordnance Survey Open Data, Crown copyright and database right (2018)

Join the Megalithic Portal

The Megalithic Portal has a huge database of ancient sites from the UK and worldwide. You can join the Megalithic Portal Society as a Contributory Member. Benefits of membership include: free code for our iPhone or Android app; full data downloads for GPS or Sat Nav devices; 20% discount off items in our online shop, including winter solstice cards, calendars and diaries.

For a free extra year's membership of the Megalithic Portal Society (two years for the price of one), go to **www.megalithic.co.uk/double**

Megalithic Portal apps for iPhone and Android

The apps offer:

- Detailed maps that use GPS to show your current position, overlaid with site locations.

- Worldwide site database that downloads to your phone for use without a phone signal.

- Tools to estimate stone heights and get weather information and sun/moon times.

- Filter for site type and condition etc (iPhone).

More details at **www.megalithic.co.uk/app** or search for Pocket Guide Megaliths from the Apple or Android app store (small charge).